DOMESDAY BOOK

Index of Persons

History from the Sources

DOMESDAY BOOK

A Survey of the Counties of England

LIBER DE WINTONIA

Compiled by direction of

KING WILLIAM I

Winchester
1086

DOMESDAY BOOK

37
Index of Persons

J. McN. Dodgson & J. J. N. Palmer

PHILLIMORE
Chichester
1992

1992

Published by

PHILLIMORE & CO. LTD.
Shopwyke Hall, Chichester, Sussex

© J. McN. Dodgson & J. J. N. Palmer, 1992

ISBN 0 85033 703 8

Printed and bound in Great Britain by
Bookcraft (Bath) Ltd.

Publisher's Note

Medieval cathedrals often took so long to build that their completion ceremonies looked back not only to the long-departed original architect but to one or two of his successors who also failed to survive until the 'topping out'. Dr. John Morris approached Phillimore, in 1969, with a proposal that the entire text of Domesday Book should be translated afresh into modern English to provide the first ever uniform English version, free from the inconsistencies and transliterations of the mainly Victorian translations that impeded research and comparative study. With the help of such scholars as Herbert Finberg, W. G. Hoskins, Vivian Galbraith and John Dodgson, the work was begun in 1970 but, seven years later, with only half a dozen counties completed, Dr. Morris tragically died at the early age of sixty. Professor Dodgson took over and saw the whole translation – and the rapidly growing apparatus of notes – through to completion, co-ordinating what had now become a team of around forty scholars engaged on the project. The county-by-county edition was finished in time for the Domesday Ninth Centenary celebrations of 1986, and Dodgson turned his attention to the 'cumulative' index and analysis that had been discussed since 1970 but could now begin in earnest with considerable input from Dr. John Palmer of the Hull University Domesday Project. John Dodgson died, sadly, in 1990 with the Persons and Places parts just completed in respect of his personal input. J. D. Foy, working independently, had by then finalised his great subject index in typescript.

The magnitude of their achievement earns increasing recognition with every year that passes and for decades to come historians and students will have cause to recall Morris's inspiration and Dodgson's industry. Like most pioneers they suffered from critics and detractors, ranging from the first question asked by the then chairman of Phillimore, in 1969, 'but surely anyone working on Domesday is able to cope with medieval calligraphy and abbreviated Latin?' to 'why are they wanting to change the translation on which I've based my lectures for the past 30 years?'. But they persisted and, in the end, prevailed. They made our greatest public record reliably and cheaply available for the first time since 1986 and, with their unique three-part Index, provided the first comprehensive apparatus to meet the needs of serious study and historical research. Their publisher is proud to have worked with them and to have seen their scholarly edifice constructed to stand as an enduring monument to their memory.

INDEX of Persons and Personal-Names and Index of Surnames, Titles and Descriptions of Persons mentioned in the Phillimore Translation of DOMESDAY BOOK

These are indexes to the translations made or edited by Dr. John Morris and the editors of the several county volumes 1–34 of the Phillimore edition of Domesday Book.

The nucleus of Index A, the index of persons and personal-names, has been provided by the indexes which originally appeared in the county volumes. Here, however, errors have been corrected, omissions supplied, material from the notes added, and an extensive system of cross-references included. In addition, Index B, the index of surnames etc., adds a further level of cross-reference. So there is here something more than a mere accumulation.

Because of the vicissitudes which befell the preparation of the Phillimore Domesday Book, not the least of them the untimely death of Dr. John Morris its General Editor, there was no opportunity to complete the standardisation of personal-names and descriptions which he appears to have intended in the modern English translation and the annotations. The county volume editors and the Index volume editors have had to do the best they could in difficult circumstances for lack of a fully articulated scheme.

It might seem that Dr. Morris had not made enough allowance for the difficulty of the Domesday Book personal-names. These have been the concern of name studies for three generations represented, principally, by Olof von Feilitzen, *The Pre-Conquest Personal-Names of Domesday Book* (Uppsala, 1937); Thorvald Forssner, *Continental Germanic Personal-Names in England in Old and Middle English Times* (Uppsala, 1916); Gosta Tengvik, *Old English By-Names* (Uppsala, 1938); Gillian Fellows-Jensen, *Scandinavian Personal-Names in Lincolnshire and Yorkshire* (Copenhagen, 1968) and John McN. Dodgson's articles in NOMINA IX (1985) pp. 41–45 and *Domesday Studies*, ed. J. C. Holt (Boydell Press for Royal Historical Society, Woodbridge, 1987), pp. 121–137.

In effect, the personal-names in the Latin text of Domesday Book are in an 'encoded' form. They are disguised by the phonetic modifications made by Norman French clerks in dealing with names which are Anglo-Saxon, French, German, Danish, Norse, Welsh, Breton, Irish and Biblical, some of which were foreign to them; and the names are disguised again by the various scribal conventions of Old English, Norman French and medieval Latin orthography, and the accidents of transcription from one script to another. As a result it is difficult, in many instances, to decode the Domesday Book personal-name form into the Old English or Anglo-Danish or Continental German personal-name it represents.

The county volume editors adopted various conventions in 'translating' the DB personal-names. Some county volumes have followed the particular conventions of modern name-study (Fellows-Jensen's Old Norse, von Feilitzen's West Saxon Old English) and some Dr. Morris's system. The discerning eye may see the result in such entries as those for the synonyms 'Azor' and 'Atsurr' or 'Saxulf' and 'Saksulfr'; and for the several personal-names in '-kell/ -ketel/ -ketill'.

Some other variations of form are due more to the intractable nature of the subject than to inconsistency of method. Four instances follow:

1. When considering how to decode and index the Domesday Book representations of the numerous Old English compound personal-names with *Athel-* as first element, we have to reckon not only with the Old English dialect variants *Aethel-* and *Ethel-* but also with the cognate Old German *Adel-*, *Adal*. Quite a number of men with continental German names came into England at the Norman Conquest. Hence, Domesday Book 'Adelelm' may represent either an Anglo-Saxon name *Athelhelm*, or a German name *Adelhelm*.

2. In late Old English, the personal-name themes *Athel-* (dialect variants *Aethel-*, *Ethel-*), *Alf* (variants *Aelf-*, *Elf-*), *Alh-* (*Aelh-*, *Ealh-*) and *Ald-* (*Eald-*, *Eld-*) are all reduced to a common form written *Ael-*, *Al-*, *El-* and often confused with one another. So, Domesday Book *Alstan* may stand for Old English *Athelstan* or *Alfstan* or *Alhstan*, and Domesday Book *Aldreda* (modern Audrey) for one or another of the Old English feminine personal-names *Athelthryth*, *Alfthryth*, *Alhthryth* or *Aldthryth*.

3. The Domesday Book personal-name *Alger* could represent Old English *Aelfgar*, or *Aethelgar*, or Old Norse *Alfgeirr*. The second elements in these are old English *-gar*, Old Norse *-geirr*, both represented indiscriminately by Domesday Book *-ger* (as is Old German *-ger* as well). So Domesday Book *Alfger* might represent an English name *Alfgar* or a Scandinavian name *Alfgeirr*. In the indexes the Domesday Book form *Alnod* has usually been rendered *Alnoth*, the late Old English form most likely represented by the Domesday spelling. But *Alnoth* itself is not completely decoded; the form could represent a personal-name in its own right, or any of the Old English personal-names *Aethelnoth* or *Aldnoth* or *Alfnoth*.

4. The Old English personal-name theme *-beorht* (variants are *-berht*, *-byrht*, *-bryht*, *-briht* and *-brict*) and the Old German cognate *-berht*, *-bert* could be equally well represented by a Domesday Book spelling *-bert*; the choice is not always obvious.

Dr. Morris's representation of some of the ancient personal-names in this index by partly modernised forms requires a caution. There is inconsistency in the handling of some elements, such as, for instance, Old English and Old German *-wig* (rendered indifferently *-wi*, *-wy*, *-wige* in the translation and indexes; usually *-wi(us)* in the Latin text); Old English *-wine*,

Old German -*win* (rendered -*win*, -*wine* indiscriminately; usually -*win(us)* in the Latin); Old English -*weald*, -*wald*, Old German -*wald* (rendered -*wald*, -*wold*; usually -*uuald(us)* or -*uuold(us)* in the Latin); Old English -*sige* (rendered -*si*; in the Latin -*si(us)*, *sin(us)*); Old English -*maer*, -*mer*, Old German -*mar*, -*mer* (all rendered indifferently -*mar*, -*mer*; in the Latin text -*mer(us)*, -*mar(us)*).

The employment, by a modern editor, of an actual or conjectural modern analogue or descendant of an 11th-century personal-name is not always a fortunate thing. To put Modern English (and Middle English) *Edward* for Old English *Eadweard* would be logical and apt, whereas Modern English (or French) *Albert* for Old English *Aldbeorht* or *Athelbeorht*, although cognate, would be a solecism, for there is no certain continuity of the use of Albert as an English personal-name back to the Norman Conquest. The danger of too free a 'translation' of the DB personal-names is realised under 'Geoffrey'.

The form of the Middle English personal-name *Geoffrey* represents a medieval linguistic confusion, in both French and English, of a variety of originally distinct Old German masculine personal-names such as *Walafrid*, *Godfrid* (modern *Godfrey*), *Gosfrid*, and *Gausfrid*, which developed Old French derivative variants such as *Gal-*, *Gau(f)-*, *God(e)-*, *Gof-*, *Gos-*, *Gaos-* and - *frid*, -*froi*, -*frei*. In Domesday Book most of the instances indexed here as 'Geoffrey' are in fact instances of *Goisfridus*; but *Gaufridus* (= *Galfrid*, *Walafrid*) is the name in the Latin text at BKM 23, 16, CAM 14, 72; 77, LIN 59, 1, NTT 9, 118, GLS G4, HRT 1, 13 and SRY 36, 1; *Gausfridus*, *Gaosfridus*, at NFK 4, 18; 44., 29, 1; 3., 31, 1-5; 8; 17; 31; 44 and SFK 67, 11; *Gosfridus* at SFK 53, 5-6., 61, 1., and 67, 12, 32; *God(e)fridus* at BDF 4, 1, and LIN 8, 39.

Another sort of problem is exemplified by the Domesday Book personal-name *Pirot*. This is not a known personal-name. Until good evidence has been established for such a name in use in 1086, we must reckon with the possibility of a scribal mistake for the personal-name *Picot* (compare BDF 24, 18, with CAM 21, 9).

Index B, the Index of surnames etc. is a supplement to Index A, partly derived from it and partly the result of a new examination of the text. The county volumes were inconsistent in the index-coverage of certain categories of person. For example, references in the translation to 'a man of N', 'N's man', 'Y, N's man', 'Y Man of N', where N is a named lord, are numerous; yet the county volumes index less than a hundred names in this connection. Again, Domesday Book contains many references to thanes, named or not, but the county volume indexes rarely have much to say about 'a/the thane', 'N's thane' or 'thane of N'.

Because of these discrepancies, a simple cumulative index would have been unrepresentative, so new entries were worked up for some categories such as 'Englishman', 'guard', 'lawman', 'thane', and the existing material was revised for others, such as 'earl' and 'count'. Many inconsistencies have been thus resolved.

Index B has also improved the coverage of ecclesiastical persons and institutions. In some county volumes the Church holdings had been indexed under the head-words of the fief- headings, so that, say, the holdings of a major monastery may have been entered under the head-words 'Church' or 'Saint' rather than under the (place-)name of the monastery concerned, or they may have been entered under 'Abbot', or under the personal-name of the individual who held that office. Some consistency has been brought into this material. In dealing with such references as 'N, abbot of Y' and 'Abbot N (of Y)' or 'The abbot of Y', references to church personnel have been organised according to the alphabetical order of the abbot's personal-name or of the (place-)name of the institution. The general aim has been to place all references to its holdings under the name of the institution concerned rather than under whatever head-word happens to appear in the translation text. For example, in Index B, all references connected with Battle Abbey appear under 'Abbot/Abbey: Battle' regardless of whether they occur in some particular allusion to the abbot, the abbey, the church or the patron saint. However, other clergy of convents, colleges and cathedrals have been distinguished from their institutions by separate headings, and cross references have been made to entries in which individuals are personally named. The categories of clergy discriminated are 'Abbess/Abbey of'; 'Abbot/Abbey of'; 'Bishop of'; 'Canons of'; 'Church of'; 'Monks of'; 'Nuns of'.

In Index B, the editors have conflated under the simple noun constructions like 'N, a clerk' and 'N, the clerk'; these are all included under 'clerk: *see* N'. This avoids the awkward question whether such phrases in the Domesday Book Latin text as *N. coquus* and *N. clericus* mean 'N. **as** cook' or 'N. **thes** clerk'; or whether these are descriptions or surnames. The reader should be wary about this. In this index the entry 'Cook: *see* Asketill' would refer to an Index A entry 'Asketill, a cook LIN 22, 26' representing the Latin text *Anschitillus quidam coquus*, whereas 'Cook: *see* Humphrey' would refer to 'Humphrey Cook GLS 71' representing the Latin text *Hunfridus cocus* (which might well have been translated 'Humphrey the cook').

With the considerable efforts they have made to iron out inconsistencies, their interpolations of comment and correction and cross-reference, and their compilation of the Index of Surnames etc., the editors of this volume hope they will enable the reader to compare like with like in Domesday Book over all England despite the discrepancies of form, from one county index to another. They have been faithful to the published work but they have exceeded it wherever necessary or practicable. An index of personal-names is not an index of persons, and vice versa. The identification of any one man named Aelfric with any other named in the long list of instances of that personal-name in Domesday Book, especially those in which there is no distinctive surname, is a matter for the speculation or the deductions of manorial historians, biographers and genealogists. This index volume is not that etymological dictionary of Domesday Book personal-names which the philologists may have been expecting; but this volume has accelerated the preparation of that.

In Index A the material for each Christian name is organised as follows:

a.   The Christian name alone.

b.   Cross-references to the Christian name used as a surname.

c.   The Christian name followed by descriptive matter (presented as a word-by-word alphabetical order). Titles are indexed as though they **followed** the name. Earl Algar would be indexed as though his name were 'Algar Earl'; Abbot Geoffrey of Tavistock as though his name was 'Geoffrey of Tavistock Abbot'.

d.   Cross-references to various forms of the Christian name.

e.   The Christian name followed by "'s' " and descriptive matter.

Some well-known individuals appear in Domesday Book under different names, name-forms or titles. In Index A, such individuals are indexed under the most common form of their name with the variants and alternatives indicated between slashes; Richard son of Count Gilbert/of Clare/of Tonbridge; Abbot Geoffrey/of Tavistock. Cross-references are given under the variant forms. In Index B, the individual name-forms are separately indexed, with the cross-references and the alternatives. This enables the reader to locate, easily, all references to the individual as well as the individual references to particular name-forms.

Persons bearing a by-name or surname or described by an addition to their name (e.g. 'N. a baker'), or described not by their own name but by their relationship to a named person ('N's brother'), will be listed particularly in Index B, the index of Surnames etc.

Material in [ ] is commentary or correction made by the editors of the present volume. Material in ( ) is editorial, either an expansion of abbreviated form, or matter which distinguishes the instance of a name from another, and it may be used to conflate more than one head-form.

In Indexes A and B, the instances of each category are referred to the county volumes of the Phillimore Domesday Book, by volume (county name), chapter number and entry number. The volume references are arranged in the alphabetical order of the county names, using the following two and three-letter abbreviations:-

Bedfordshire	BDF	Middlesex	MDX
Berkshire	BRK	Norfolk	NFK
Buckinghamshire	BKM	Northamptonshire	NTH
Cambridgeshire	CAM	Nottinghamshire	NTT
Cheshire	CHS	Oxfordshire	OXF
(Flintshire	FLN)	Rutland	RUT
(Lancashire	LAN)	Shropshire	SHR
Cornwall	CON	Somerset	SOM
Cumberland: *see* Yorkshire		Staffordshire	STS
Derbyshire	DBY	Suffolk	SFK
Devon	DEV	Surrey	SRY
Dorset	DOR	Sussex	SSX
Essex	ESS	Warwickshire	WAR
Flintshire: *see* Cheshire		Westmorland: *see* Yorkshire	
Gloucestershire	GLS	Wiltshire	WIL
Hampshire	HAM	Worcestershire	WOR
(Isle of Wight	IOW)	Yorkshire	YKS
Herefordshire	HEF	(East Riding	ER)
Hertfordshire	HRT	(West Riding	WR)
Huntingdonshire	HUN	(North Riding	NR)
Kent	KEN	(Lancashire	LAN)
Lancashire: *see* Cheshire and		(Cumberland	CUM)
Yorkshire		(Westmorland	WES)
Leicestershire	LEC		
Lincolnshire	LIN		

J. McN. Dodgson, University College, London.

J. J. N. Palmer, University of Hull.

On the Feast of St Willibrord of Utrecht, 1988.

PART ONE

Personal Names

Personal Names

... of Barthetona	SFK	41,11
... of Houdain	SFK	7,2
A.	ESS	34,15
	NFK	9,10;89. 10,81
Aba/Abba	LIN	68,43
	NFK	1,61. 9,7
	NTH	23,19
	OXF	EN11
Aba/Abba: *see also* Abo		
Ab(b)et(us): *see* Abbot		
Abbot	DEV	3,95
Abel the monk	KEN	*3,5*
Aben: *see* Habeinn		
Abo, Earl Harold's man	HRT	1,10
Abo: *see also* Aba/Abba		
Abraham the priest	GLS	W4
Acard	BKM	17,22
	SSX	11,96
	WOR	23,11-12
Acard of Ivry	BDF	23,17
Acard the priest	SSX	11,81
Acwulf	NFK	7,8
Acwulf, a thane	SFK	12,1. 59,1
Adalhaid (fem.): *see* Adelaide		
Adam	ESS	EKt
	KEN	5,40;74;94;104-107;141-142;154;163; 184. 7,14. 9,51
	NTH	2,11
	OXF	7,12;22;39-40;47;52-53
Adam son of Durand Malzor	ESS	63
Adam son of Hubert	KEN	5,6;24-25;71-77;93;125;130. 13,1
	OXF	7,45
	SRY	5,8;18
Adam (son of Hubert)	HRT	5,2-6;17-19
Adam, son of Robert, son of William	HRT	*8,1*
Adam, the Bishop of Lincoln's man	LIN	7,32;52
Adelaide, wife of Hugh of Grandmesnil	BDF	54
	HRT	43
	LEC	41
	WAR	45
Adelaide (fem.): *see also* Adalhaid, Adelheid, Adeliza		
Adelelm	SFK	35,5;7-8
Adelelm: *see also* Adelhelm, Aethelhelm		
Adelheid (fem.): *see* Adelaide		

Adelhelm	NFK	13,20. 66,28
Adelhelm: *see also* Adelelm, Aethelhelm		
Adelina (fem.) the jester	HAM	1,25
Adeliza (fem.): *see* Adelaide		
Adelo	SFK	*14,36*
	YKS	9W39
Adelulf of Marck	ESS	20,15;27
Adelulf (of Marck)	ESS	20,13;22;24;29;54;57-58;68-69;79
Adelulf: *see also* Adolf/Adulf, Aethelwulf		
Adelund	SFK	14,32;36;58;98
Adelund: *see also* Aethelhun, Alun		
Ademar: *see* Aethelmer		
Adestan	CAM	14,73
Adestan of Weston Colville/Alestan	CAM	AppxD
Adestan: *see also* Aethelstan, Alestan		
Adolf/Adulf	DEV	1,72
	HEF	15,5
	SOM	19,24;76. 21,78
	WAR	17,52
Adolf/Adulf: *see also* Adelulf, Aethelwulf		
Adwin: *see* Eadwine, Edwin		
Aedi	SFK	6,171
Aefic	DBY	6,37-38
	HUN	19,12. 29,3
	WIL	68,32
Aefic, a thane	DBY	6,42
Aegelfride (fem.)	YKS	1N98
Aegelfride (fem.): *see also* Egelfride		
Aeldiet (fem.?)	WOR	19,13
Aeldiet (fem.?): *see* Aldgeat, Aldith, Ealdgyth		
Aeleva (fem.)	DEV	17,19
	NTH	27,1
	SOM	21,57
	WIL	1,20. 13,9
	WOR	23,5
Aeleva the widow	NTH	18,50-51
Aeleva (fem.): *see also* Aelgifu, Aethelgifu		
Aelfeth, a girl (fem.)	BKM	19,3
Aelfeth (fem.) : *see also* Godwin (son of?)	BRK	1,8. 61,2. 65,17
: *see also* Aelfgyth		
Aelfeva (fem.)		
	CON	5,2,6
	DEV	16,40;166. 23,25. 24,2-4. 25,20. 34, 31. 36,7. 37,1. 52,50
	DOR	26,71. 49,2. 57,14
	ESS	90,20. B3a(x2)
	HAM	64,1
	HEF	34,2
	HRT	5,24
	KEN	5,69
	NFK	8,24-25;34-35;87
	OXF	B10. 26,1
	SHR	4,14,3-4;6. 4,21,6;14
	SOM	6,7. EDe1
	SFK	7,36;38-39. 21,50. 84,3
	SSX	9,58. 10,92
	WAR	22,22. 28,13. EN4. EBW5
	WIL	26,22
	WOR	11,2

Aelfeva : *see also* Seric son of
   : *see also* Sired son of

(another) Aelfeva	SHR	4,14,4
Countess Aelfeva/mother of Earl Morcar	DBY	S5
	ESS	B3j
	HRT	5,24
	LEC	12
	NTH	8,13
	NTT	S5
	SFK	1,97-99. 16,10
Aelfeva, Askell's man	BDF	18,5
Aelfeva, Earl Harold's sister	BKM	4,21
Aelfeva the nun	WOR	2,54
Aelfeva Thief	DEV	24,22
Aelfeva, wife of Harold, a thane	BKM	17,22
Aelfeva, wife of Hwaetman	MDX	25,2-3

Aelfeva: *see also* Countess Aelfeva
   : *see also* Aelfgifu, Alfeva
Aelffled (fem.): *see* Aelfled
Aelfgar: *see* Alfgar, Algar

Aelfgeard/Aethelgeard/Algeard	SHR	4,3,13

Aelfgeard: *see* Alfyard, Algeard
Aelfgeat: *see* Alfgeat, Algeat

Aelfgifu (fem.)	LIN	13,44

Aelfgifu (fem.): *see also* Aelfeva, Alfeva

Aelfgyth (fem.)	SFK	54,2

Aelfgyth (fem.): *see also* Aelfeth, Alfgeat a
   woman, Alfith

Aelfhere	YKS	1N34

Aelfhere: *see also* Alfhere
Aelfhild (fem.): *see also* Alfhild

Aelfhild Dese	BRK	31,3
Aelfled (fem.)	BDF	10,1
	DEV	35,25
	ESS	B3a(x2);f
	HEF	10,42;56
	HRT	5,6. 20,6
	SFK	6,38;57;211. 8,31;53;55-56;78-111. 33, 12. 52,1
	SRY	5,13
	WAR	16,14
	YKS	1W53

Aelfled (fem.): *see also* Aelffled, Aethelfled,
   Alflaed, Alfled
Aelfnoth: *see* Alfnoth, Alnoth

Aelfric	BDF	E3
	BRK	1,1;5. 7,14;19. 21,17. 32,1. 36,3. 41,5. 44,5. 51,1. 54,2. 64,2. 65,8
	CAM	*5,11. 26,21*
	CHS	2,21. 8,29;34;39-40
	CON	5,2,5;8;22;24;27-28. 5,3,6;9. 5,11,4-5. 5,17,3. 5,24,18;21-22. 5,25,4
	DBY	3,6. 6,13;16;18;20;22-23;33;44;53;94; 98
	DEV	3,35;38. 15,15;75. 16,91;117. 17,24; 27;57-58;85;87;97;107. 19,21;28. 25,6; 25. 29,1-3. 31,4. 34,27;57. 39,16. 40, 1-2. 42,21. 47,3-4. 52,44-45
	DOR	1,24;28-29. 6,4. 26,38;42;59. 49,16. 55,19;26;*28*. 56,12;51;59;65

ESS   1,15. 4,1;3;14. 18,32. 20,37;44;69. 22,
        24. 28,3. 32,2;25. 33,8;17. 35,13-14.
        36,8. 41,1. 54,2. 57,6. 60,2. 68,7.
        B3a(x11)
GLS   1,5. 32,2. 35,1. 41,3-4. 52,4. 67,4. E3;
        31
HAM   3,8. 21,2. 23,5;38. 35,3;6. 45,7. 48,1.
        57,2. 68,9. 69,11-12. NF3,12. 9,1;6;18;
        24;26-28;33;40-44. IoW7,19;20. 8,
        10-12. 9,16;23
HEF   1,31;36;73. 10,34. 14,11. 15,10
HUN   19,7
KEN   M5;7. 5,16;46;84;110;166
LEC   14,28;30
LIN   2,3;28. 3,8-9. 4,75. 9,1. 12,40;96. 16,
        18. 20,1. 22,20;25. 30,19. 37,1-2;6. 57,
        15;18;29;33. 65,1. CK,36;53
NFK   1,2;77;136;145. 6,6. 8,18. 9,49;114.
        11,1. 21,26. 29,5-7. 35,6. 52,1
NTH   4,29. 18,44;58. 23,18. 43,9
NTT   5,6. 9,52;64. 10,15. 18,4. 29,1. 30,8;
        10;13;27-29;32;34;50;55
OXF   6,11. 27,2-4. 35,3. 58,35-36. EN10
SHR   3b,4. 4,3,1;9. 4,5,1;10-12;15. 4,7,3. 4,
        9,2-3. 4,14,24. 4,15,1. 4,21,2;10;15;17
SOM   1,28. 2,7. 5,18;37;40-41;57;59. 8,19;
        30. *16,2.* 19,17;27;58. 21,35;37;50;65;
        87. *24,10.* 25,1-2;17;25;*43.* 37,4;*11.
        45,4.* 46,18
STS   11,26. 17,5
SFK   1,102. 2,20. 3,66;94;100. 4,13;19;21;
        40. 5,7. 6,40;57;90;110;116;191-192;
        309 -310. 7,40;48-49;66;75;79;104;
        108;118;121;134;137. 8,6;*12*;55;*81.* 9,
        2. 14,41;44;49. 16,15-16;20(x2);35;38;
        41(x2);42. 19,18. 21,23;63. 23,2-3. 25,
        60(x2);64-65. 26,14. 31,20;56. 36,5;
        12-13. 38,11;20. 43,5;7. 51,1. 56,5. 64,
        1. 67,6. 74,13(x4). ENf4
SRY   5,1d;4. 19,29;35
SSX   9,83. 10,28;57. 11,31
WAR   4,4. 16,57;66. 17,3;64. 21,1. 22,8;11.
        40,2. 44,9
WIL   24,6. 25,28. 26,16. 27,3;15;21;25. 29,
        5. 32,15. 37,2. 48,6. 61,1. 67,16-17.
        68,4;6;19
WOR   8,4;9b-9c. 26,3;11;14
YKS   9W26;78

Aelfric: *see also* Brictric father of
      : *see also* Edmer brother of
      : *see also* Edric son of
      : *see also* Ordric brother of
      : *see also* Wihtgar (father of)
      : *see also* Wihtgar son of
Aelfric, a man-at-arms   DOR   3,17
Aelfric, a royal thane   BDF   24,15
                                    BKM   43,5;10
                                    CAM   13,11
                                    SFK   3,88
Aelfric, a thane   DEV   17,13. *25,25*

	DOR	55,44 (cf 55,48 *note*)
	ESS	4,11. 20,6
	SOM	1,1. *5,59. 19,68*. 21,65. 24,10. 37,11
	SFK	4,11. 9,1
Aelfric, Aelfric Small's man	BDF	25,3
another Aelfric	BRK	1,1
Aelfric, Aelmer of Bennington's man	HRT	20,4. 36,17
Aelfric (Aubrey?)	DEV	17,88-89
Aelfric Big	ESS	20,41
Aelfric, Bishop Wulfwy's man	BKM	53,7
Aelfric Black, Archbishop Stigand's man	HRT	2,1-3;5. 37,1
Aelfric, brother of Aethelstan and Alsige	LIN	26,45
Aelfric, brother of Edric, Wihtgar's man	SFK	76,3
Aelfric, brother of Godwin the priest	CAM	*31,1*
Aelfric, brother of Harold and Guthfrithr	LIN	CS,21
Aelfric, brother of Wulfa	SOM	*19,68*
Aelfric, Burgred's man	BDF	3,15;17
	NTH	EB2
Aelfric Bush, Swein's man	HRT	34,6
Aelfric Catchpoll	MDX	3,9
Aelfric Child: *see* Young Aelfric, Aelfric Young		
Aelfric Colling	DEV	*19,40*
Aelfric Doda	DOR	7,1
Aelfric, Earl Waltheof's man	HRT	19,2
Aelfric, Edric's man	SFK	26,13
Aelfric, Eudo son of Hubert's reeve	CAM	AppxL
Aelfric, father of Edric	SHR	3c,8
Aelfric, father of Wihtgar	SFK	25,1;60
Aelfric, Godric the sheriff's man	BKM	44,1
Aelfric Godricson, the sheriff	CAM	B14
Aelfric, Godwin son of Wulfstan's man	HRT	20,9
Aelfric, Harold's man	NFK	4,26
Aelfric, Harold's thane	NFK	51,5
Aelfric Hunter	DOR	*56,6;52;57;60*
	WIL	13,2
Aelfric Kemp	CAM	21,2;3. 25,*1*;2;*3*
	ESS	32,38. 33,16. 39,5;7
	SFK	16,41. 28,7. 38,2. 76,4
Aelfric, King Edward's chamberlain	BKM	34,1
Aelfric Little	HRT	36,4
Aelfric Little, of Hampshire	SOM	*1,27*
Aelfric Mapson	HEF	E6
	WOR	18,6
Aelfric Mouse	CAM	*31,2*
Aelfric of Alderford	ESS	90,49
Aelfric of Flitwick	BDF	25,2
Aelfric of Hemingford & Yelling	HUN	D7 (cf 22,1-2). EHu
Aelfric of Hopewella	SFK	6,110
Aelfric of Horseheath	CAM	AppxF
Aelfric of Melksham	WIL	67,15
Aelfric of Sanford	SFK	26,12b
Aelfric of Snailwell	CAM	AppxA
Aelfric of Stowey	SOM	*6,13*
Aelfric of Thatcham	BRK	1,38
Aelfric of Thriplow	CAM	AppxH
Aelfric of Weinhou/Wenhou	SFK	39,17. 46,3
Aelfric of Wilbraham	CAM	AppxC
Aelfric of Wymondley	HRT	Appx
Aelfric Pig	DEV	*34,10*
Aelfric Pike	DEV	28,13

Aelfric, Queen Edith's man	BKM	43,11
Aelfric Scova	HRT	5,22. Cf 5,10
Aelfric Small, a royal thane	BDF	24,16. 25,3
	HAM	69,53. NF9,20-21;(40)
	WIL	67,18-21
Aelfric son of Bondi, Ulf's man	SFK	7,37
Aelfric son of Brictric	SOM	47,21-22
Aelfric son of Brown	SFK	16,11
Aelfric son of (?Edwin) the smith in	SFK	6,110
Carlewuda: see also Edwin the smith		
Aelfric son of Everwacer, the reeve	SOM	*8,33*
Aelfric son of Goding	BKM	12,32. 57,17
Aelfric son of Mergeat	LIN	T5. CK,27
Aelfric son of Rolf, burgess of Ipswich	SFK	74,8-10
Aelfric son of Wihtgar	SFK	25,1;60
Aelfric son of Wulfgeat	SFK	16,2-3. 68,1
Aelfric Starling	SFK	25,71
Aelfric Stickstag, half man of Edric	SFK	7,77
Aelfric, the Abbot of Chertsey's man	MDX	8,2
Aelfric, the Abbot's reeve	SOM	8,33
Aelfric the beadle	BDF	57,3v
Aelfric the deacon	SFK	38,22
Aelfric the doctor	HAM	NF9,12
Aelfric the priest	CAM	19,1
	ESS	24,3;5. B3a
	HAM	3,5;7
	HRT	37,7
	LEC	8,5
	SOM	*5,64. 16,3*
	SFK	2,17. 3,64;74-78. 16,30. 74,14
Aelfric the priest, a thane	SOM	*5,64*
Aelfric the reeve	SFK	1,17;30 *note*;60 *note*;103
Aelfric, the reeve of the Abbot (of St	SFK	14,152
Edmund's)		
Aelfric the sheriff	HUN	B10. D20
Aelfric the sheriff's son, mother of	HUN	B10
Aelfric the sheriff's wife	HUN	B10
Aelfric Varus	BKM	12,31
Aelfric Wand	ESS	25,24;26
	SFK	1,100-106
Aelfric Whelp	OXF	40,3
Young Aelfric [= Aelfric Child]	CAM	32,3
	ESS	32,6
Aelfric Young [= Aelfric Child]	SOM	*5,25*
Aelfric: see also Alberic, Alfric, Alric, Aubrey		
Aelfric's father	ESS	20,44
	HAM	NF9,41;44
	LIN	CS,21
Aelfric's son	SHR	3c,14
Aelfric's wife	SRY	19,35
Aelfrun (fem.): see Alfrun		
Aelfsige: see Alfsi, Alsi		
Aelfstan: see Alfstan		
Aelfswith (fem): see Alswith		
Aelfthryth (fem.)	ESS	3,1
Aelfw(e)ald: see Alfwold, Alwold		
Aelfw(e)ard: see Alfward, Alfweard, Alward		
Aelfwaru (fem.): see Alware		
Aelfwen (fem.)	BKM	14,18. 35,3

Aelfwen (fem.): *see also* Aelfwynn, Aethelwynn, Alwynn
Aelfwig: *see* Alfwy, Alwy
Aelfwin, brother of Goda, Ulf's man   SFK   7,37
Aelfwin Odson   CAM   AppxJ
Aelfwin of Hinton Hall   CAM   AppxP
Aelfwin: *see* Aelfwine, Alwin(e)
Aelfwine: *see* Aelfwin, Alwin(e)
Aelfwold: *see* Alfwold
Aelfwy: *see* Alfwy, Alwy
Aelfwyn (fem.): *see* Aelfwynn
Aelfwynn (fem.): *see* Aelfwen, Aelfwyn, Alwynn
Aelgifu (fem.): *see* Aeleva, Aethelgifu
Aelid (fem.)   NTH   2,12
Aelid (fem.): *see also* Aethelgyth
Aellic   BKM   5,15
    HUN   13,2. 15,1
    WIL   67,68
Aellic, a royal thane   BKM   5,18
Aelmer   BDF   56,6
    BRK   1,11;20-21. 7,47. 22,11. 34,1. 43,1. 54,2
    BKM   12,4;11;13. 24,2
    CAM   1,16. 14,17;81. 29,12
    CHS   8,15. FD5,3. R1,9
    CON   5,22. 5,1,15. 5,2,13. 5,3,7. 5,5,22. 5,7,3. 5,9,4. 5,24,11;20
    DBY   1,30. 6,30
    DEV   3,47;49;60;85. 15,23. 16,18;50;66;75; 84;94;105-106;119;121;131;136;142; 145;147;149;158;164;170. 17,91;105. 19,15;23;35-36;40;46. 21,11. 28,10. 34,9;11;25;38;40;43. 36,9;19-20; 25-26. 39,14. 42,7;22. 44,1. 50,2. 52, 20-21
    DOR   3,14. 9,1. 26,43;61;66. 30,4. 34,4. 36, 11. 47,5-7. 54,5. 55,7;*18;25*;35. 56,24. 57,7
    ESS   20,59;74. 24,36. 33,22. 34,4;14. 35,3. 48,1-2. B3q
    GLS   1,23;67. 68,8;11. 78,8. E22. WoB5
    HAM   1,W8. 3,1. 23,58. 69,46;54. IoW7,5;11
    HEF   36. 1,24-27. 8,2;6. 9,2;9. 10,34. 14,10, 31,7
    KEN   5,201
    LEC   5,1. 10,8. 19,3;15-17
    LIN   2,1;5;21;23. 3,6. 27,26. 51,1-2. 56,6. 59,11. CS,29
    NTH   2,1;8. 6a,24. 18,21;37
    NTT   9,70. 10,46
    OXF   59,2
    SHR   4,4,9;23. 4,9,2. 4,14,1;8;11;29. 4,19, 13. 4,20,1. 4,27,19-20. 4,28,2. 6,12; 15-16
    SOM   5,68. 8,17;20-21. 19,62. 21,14;52;73; 85;87-88;*92*. 22,1;3. 25,6;9;41;55. 30, 1. 37,1;*8-9*. 46,23
    STS   1,40. 8,13;16. 12,20. 13,3. 17,6

	SFK	1,73-74. 3,95. 6,9;92;209;239. 7,79; 80(x2);83;101;104;121. 8,61. 13,3. 16, 20. 21,90;*100*. 32,23. 38,6. 41,4;6
	SRY	5,15;17. 17,3. 19,18;21;28;34;39; 45-46;48
	SSX	10,49;52;95;97;116. 11,9
	WAR	17,8;15;21-22;57-58;65. 23,1-2;4. 28,2
	WIL	30,1;3;6. 64,1. 67,30
A(elmer)	NFK	10,6-7;9;13
A(e)lmer	NFK	64. 8,14;127. 9,64;150. 10,10-11. 13, 9. 14,25. 19,39
Aelmer, a forester	SOM	*46,3*
Aelmer, a royal thane	BDF	53,6
	BKM	29,3
	CAM	33,1
	ESS	12,1. 34,6
Aelmer, a thane	BKM	14,35
	SOM	*21,73. 37,8*
	SFK	4,42
Aelmer, Aelfric son of Goding's man	BKM	12,32
Aelmer, Aelfric's man	HRT	2,2
Aelmer, Aelfric of Flitwick's man	BDF	25,2
Aelmer, and his brothers	LIN	CK,19
Aelmer, Ansgot's brother	HAM	18,3
Aelmer, Asgar the constable's man	HRT	5,11
Aelmer, Askell's man	BDF	23,42
Aelmer Blackson	CAM	AppxK
Aelmer, Bondi the constable's man	BKM	17,9
Aelmer, Brictric's man	BKM	23,18;22
Aelmer Child: *see* Aelmer Young, Young Aelmer		
Aelmer, Count Alan's man	CAM	*14,82*
Aelmer, Earl Gyrth's man	HRT	24,1
Aelmer, Earl Harold's man	BKM	12,24
Aelmer, Earl Leofwin's man	HRT	34,1
Aelmer, Earl Tosti's man	BDF	49,2-3
Aelmer, Earl Waltheof's man	CAM	13,3;12. 25,8
Aelmer Eastry, a thane	DEV	*15,47*
Aelmer, Edeva's man	CAM	14,49
Aelmer, Edeva the fair's man	CAM	*32,8*
Aelmer Holdfast	ESS	61,2
Aelmer Hunter	SRY	4,2
Aelmer Milk	ESS	B3r
Aelmer (Milk)	ESS	33,23
Aelmer of Bennington, a royal thane	HRT	4,16. 5,13. 20,4-5;8. 34,7. 36,1-3;5; 7-8;10-12;14-18. 37,10. 38,2
Aelmer of Borley	ESS	90,49
Aelmer of Bourn	CAM	*14,23-24;47;49-52*
Aelmer of Cottenham	CAM	AppxO
(Bishop) A(elmer) (of Elmham)	NFK	10,12
Bishop A(e)lmer (of Elmham) Stigand's brother	NFK	1,28 *and note*; 61;68. 8,12. 9,20;30-31; 178. 10,2-13;16-17;19-21;25-26;28; 30-33;35;42-43;45-47;60;63;65-68. 25, 3. 31,5. 65,8
	SFK	2,3-5. 3,96. 6,311. 7,4. 8,42. 18,1;4;6. 19,11;14-16;18;20. 64,3. 75,4
(Bishop) A(e)lmer (of Elmham) Stigand's brother	NFK	10,10-11;23;28;70;72-75;79-81;85-92
	SFK	19,1-3;9;13;17
Bishop Aelmer (of Elmham)'s wife	NFK	10,28
Aelmer of Hoo	BDF	23,48

Aelmer of Weston	HRT	Appx
Aelmer of Wootton	BKM	23,33
Aelmer, reeve of Richard son of Count Gilbert	ESS	90,78
Aelmer, Robert son of Wymarc's man	CAM	25,5
Aelmer Rufus	DEV	*15,33*
Aelmer son of Colswein	CAM	*14,23-24.* AppxJ
Aelmer son of Goding	CAM	*13,12. 25,8*
A(e)lmer son of Godwin	NFK	65,2-6
Aelmer the beadle	DOR	*56,63*
Aelmer, the King's reeve	SFK	8,60
Aelmer the monk	WOR	2,27
Aelmer the priest	BRK	B7
	CAM	*26,29. 31,1*
	DEV	25,19
	SFK	1,56
another Aelmer the priest	BRK	B7
Aelmer, Wulfmer's man	BDF	55,4
Aelmer, Wulfward White's man	MDX	15,2
Young Aelmer [= Aelmer Child]	CAM	AppxL
Aelmer Young [= Aelmer Child]	HEF	10,63
Aelmer: *see also* A(elmer), A(e)lmer, Aethelmer, Almer		
Aelmer's father	BDF	56,6
A(e)lmer's son	NFK	4,8
Aelmer's wife	SFK	6,209
Aelmund: *see* Aethelmund		
Aelred	KEN	5,121;170
	WAR	16,59
Aelred of Yalding	KEN	D25
Aelred: *see also* Aethelred		
Aelric: *see* Aethelric, Alric		
Aelsi Bereson	CAM	*31,2*
Aelsi: *see also* Aethelsige, Alsi		
Aelstan: *see* Aestan, Aethelstan		
Aelward	NFK	30,4
Aelward of Felbrigg	NFK	9,158
Aelward: *see also* Aethelward, Alweard		
Aelwaru (fem.): *see* Alware		
Aeschere	ESS	B3a
	SFK	1,123f
Aescman	SFK	58,1
Aescred: *see* Ashred		
Aescwulf	CHS	1,3. 8,7
Aescwulf: *see also* Asulfr, Aswulf, Essulf		
Aestan	YKS	10W6
Aestan: *see also* Aelstan, Aethelstan, Estan		
Aethelbald	ESS	B3a
Aethelbald: *see also* Ailbold, Albold		
Aethelbeorht: *see* Aethelbrict		
Aethelbrict	ESS	B3a
Aethelbrict: *see also* Aethelbeorht, Aethelbyrht, Albriht		
Aethelbyrht: *see* Aethelbrict		
Aethelfled (fem.)	DOR	37,11
Aethelfled (fem.): *see also* Aelfled, Alflaed, Alfled		
Aethelfrith	DOR	9,1. 47,3-4;9
	SOM	22,24;26
Aethelfrith: *see also* Alfrith		
Aethelgar: *see* Algar		
Aethelgeard/Algeard/Aelfgeard	SHR	4,3,13

Aethelgeat: *see* Algeat
Aethelgifu (fem.): *see* Aeleva, Aelgifu
Aethelgyth (fem.)   ESS   20,46. 33,6-7;19-20
                                           LIN   57,43
                                           NFK   21,3(?);20. 31,20-25;34-35;37. 42,1
                                           SFK   33,1;13. ENf5
Aethelgyth (fem.): *see also* Wada son of
              : *see also* Aelid, Ailid
Aethelhard [?Aitard], a man-at-arms   CHS   9,17
Aethelhard   CHS   R3,1
                                           DOR   49,7
                                           SSX   11,8
Aethelhard the monk   DEV   *34,53*
Aethelhelm   BRK   22,12
                                           ESS   35,7;12
                                           HEF   23,5-6
                                           KEN   9,11
                                           LEC   36,2
                                           LIN   26,22
                                           WIL   24,18;26
                                           YKS   14E17
Aethelhelm, Kolsveinn's man   LIN   22,26
Aethelhelm: *see also* Adelelm, Adelhelm
Aethelhild (fem.): *see* Ailhilla
Aethelhun: *see* Adelund, Alun
Aethelmer   DEV   15,31
Aethelmer: *see also* Aelmer
Aethelmund   CHS   R1,14
Aethelmund: *see also* Aelmund, Almund
Aethelnoth: *see* Alnoth
Aethelred   KEN   5,51. 11,1
Aethelred Bot   KEN   9,17;49
King Aethelred   GLS   12,1
(King) Aethelred, King Edward's father   SHR   4,1,12
Aethelred: *see also* Aelred
Aethelric   DEV   16,132
                                           DOR   3,15-16. 30,1
                                           LIN   12,69
                                           SFK   1,18. 6,112. 14,38. 16,18;26;31. 26,17;
                                                  18;20. 67,10
                                           WOR   26,3
Aethelric, brother of Bishop Brictric   HEF   1,45
                                           WOR   E5
Aethelric of Burgh   SFK   8,6;9. 32,23;28. 67,23 (cf 26,16)
Aethelric, wife of   SFK   14,38
Aethelric: *see also* Aelric, Agelric, Alric, ?Atilic
Aethelrun (fem.)   DOR   56,23
                                           SOM   *6,14*
Aethelsi   SFK   1,19
Aethelsi: *see also* Aethelsige
Aethelsige   NFK   9,86
Aethelsige: *see also* Aelsi, Aethelsi, Alfsi, Alsi,
   Alsige, Eisi
Aethelstan   ESS   18,43
                                           LIN   C24. 4,9. 12,20;76. 26,45. 30,33. 48,1;
                                                  11. 57,10;13-14;19;22;27-28;30;36-37;
                                                  44;48;50;54-56
                                           SFK   1,19;55. 4,18. 16,7;26. 74,13
                                           YKS   14E19 *and note.* 21W2. CE49
Aethelstan, a thane   SFK   4,1

Aethelstan, brother of Alsige and Aelfric	LIN	26,45
Aethelstan of Frampton, Guy's man	LIN	CK,66
Bishop Aethelstan (of Hereford)	HEF	13,1
Aethelstan son of Godram	LIN	T5. CK,66
Aethelstan: *see also* Adestan, Aelstan, Aestan, Alstan, Athelstan, Estan		
Aethelswith (fem.): *see* Alswith		
Aethelward	DOR	36,2. 55,14
	SFK	7,5
	WOR	8,10a-10b. 23,6
Aethelward, Earl Algar's thane	WOR	15,2
Aethelward son of Bell	SFK	25,20
Aethelward, the King's reeve	SFK	7,18;36
Aethelward: *see also* Aelward, A(i)lward, Alward, Alweard		
Aethelwaru (fem.): *see* Alware		
Aethelwig: *see* Aethelwy, A(i)lwy, Alwig, Alwy		
Aethelwin	SFK	8,65
Aethelwin: *see also* Aethelwine, A(i)lwin, A(i)lwy, Alwin, Alwine		
Aethelwine: *see* Aethelwin		
Aethelwold	DEV	*16,174*
	KEN	M17. *2,16.* 5,67;84-85;167;198
	NFK	23,11
	NTT	9,41
	SOM	21,49;83
	SFK	6,123
	SRY	5,28
Aethelwold of Eltham	KEN	D25
Aethelwold the chamberlain	KEN	5,66;*99-100;134*
Aethelwold the priest	SFK	3,31
Aethelwold: *see also* Alwold		
Aethelwulf	CAM	26,23;43
	KEN	6,1
	YKS	13E14
Aethelwulf the chamberlain	BDF	40,3
Aethelwulf, William of Percy's man	LIN	22,32
Aethelwulf: *see also* Adolf/Adulf, Aiulf, Alwulf		
Aethelwy	SFK	6,46
Aethelwy: *see also* Stanhard son of		
Aethelwy/A(i)lwin/A(i)lwy of Thetford	NFK	1,239 *and note.* 9,14;25;29;60;100; 104-105. 65,10
	SFK	7,1 *and note*
Aethelwy (etc, of Thetford)	NFK	9,72-73;75;81;89-93. 66,84
Aethelwy: *see also* A(i)lwy		
Aethelwynn (fem.): *see* Aelfwen, Aelfwynn, Alwen, Alwynn		
Agelric	SOM	47,20
Agelric: *see also* Aethelric		
Agemund	HAM	3,9. 23,10. 45,2. 69,22;26;37. NF9,9; 28
	NTH	19,1. 55,5
	NTT	6,12
	SSX	9,41;55;76. 10,89
	WIL	37,11
another Agemund	HAM	69,22
Agemund: *see also* Agmundr, Amund		
Agenet	SFK	14,13
Agenwulf	WIL	19,4
Agenwulf's father	WIL	19,4

Agmundr	LIN	3,33. 28,3;14-17;25;29;32;36;42. 33,1. 67,26. 68,45. CS,3. CW,3;13
	YKS	10W8
Agmundr: see also Godric son of		
Agmundr, brother of Sigketill	LIN	28,11
Agmundr son of Valhrafn, a lawman	LIN	C3
Agmundr the priest	LIN	68,47
Agmundr: see also Agemund, Amund		
Agnes (fem.)	ESS	47,2
Agnes, daughter of Alfred of Marlborough and wife of Thurstan of Wigmore	HEF	19,10
Ailbern	SFK	16,18. 25,68;85
Ailbold the priest	SFK	14,13 note; 39
Ailbold: see also Aethelbald, Albold		
Aildag	NFK	61,2
Ailhilla [= ? Aethelhild (fem.)]	SOM	21,60
Ailid (fem.): see Aelid, Aethelgyth		
Ailward: see Aethelward, Alward		
A(i)lwin	NFK	1,28;41;78. 9,145;183. 19,31. 30,3. 43, 1;4. 66,67
A(i)lwin Child: see Young A(i)lwin		
Young A(i)lwin [= A(i)lwin Child]	NFK	8,133
A(i)lwin: see also Aethelwine, Aethelwy, A(i)lwy, Alwin, Alwy		
A(i)lwy	NFK	9,5;12;16;19-20;23;62;70;100;101;108; 157;228. 10,30. 66,78
A(i)lwy of Colchester, a reeve	NFK	17,22
A(i)lwy: see also Aethelwine, Aethelwy, A(i)lwin, Alwy		
Ainuar	SFK	25,89
Ainulf	ESS	B3a
Ainulf: see also Einulf		
Aisil	SHR	4,12,1. 4,27,30
Aitard	NFK	9,26;94;140;160;165-166;198. 66,80
	SFK	7,4
Aitard [?error for Aethelhard]	CHS	9,17
Aitard of Vaux	NFK	1,120-122
Aitard, R. Bigot's man	NFK	1,106;111
Aitard the priest	NTT	B13
Aiulf	CON	1,18. 4,14. 5,7,12
	DEV	41. 17,18. 35,7. 39,8
	DOR	12,16. 56,40
	SOM	21,58
	WIL	24,39. 67,59
	WOR	1,2. 2,4. 8,24
Aiulf: see also Edmund son of		
Aiulf the chamberlain/the sheriff	BRK	57
	DOR	49
	HAM	S3
	WIL	55
Aiulf (the chamberlain/sheriff)	DOR	1,8;15. 19,11
Aiulf the chamberlain: see also Humphrey brother of		
Aiulf: see also Aethelwulf, Eyiolfr		
Aiulf's son	WIL	67,59
Akeli	CAM	37,1
Aki	BRK	44,4. 62,1
	ESS	24,45. 53,1
	HRT	B10
	LIN	38,1;13. CS,34

	NTH	33,1. 55,4
	STS	1,35. 11,8. EW2
	SFK	6,57;85. 66,1-4;13-14;16
	WAR	12,9
	WIL	24,21. 60,1. 66,7
	WOR	26,6
Aki, a royal Guard	MDX	17,1
Aki, a royal thane	BDF	23,15;38
	CAM	17,4
	HRT	20,13. 22,1
Aki, Earl Harold's man/the Dane	CAM	17,5-6
Aki, Earl Harold's thane	HRT	37,22
Aki son of Siward, brother of Vigleikr: *see*	LIN	T5
Vigleikr		
Aki's two sons-in-law	WIL	60,1
Akile Suffering	SFK	7,37
Alan	BKM	12,9;12
	HUN	20,9
	NTH	18,26-30. 56,47-48
	SFK	37,5
	SSX	10,1;49;79;116
Alan: *see also* Richard son of		
Count Alan (of Brittany)	CAM	14. B1-2;12. 29,10. 35,1. ESf. AppxF
	DBY	7,13
	DOR	25
	ESS	21. 1,13
	HAM	18
	HRT	16. B2. 37,19
	LIN	12. 1,33. 67,18. CS,4;18. CN,7;18; 21-22;25-26. CK,38;65-69;71
	NFK	4. 1,11;57;197;215. 9;49. 10,19. 12, 35. 32,1. 66,63
	NTH	20
	NTT	2
	SFK	3. 1,122f. 4,13. 13,3. 26,12a;12d;15. *46,10.* 76,17. EC2. ENf2;4. Also folio 291a
	YKS	6. SN,CtA. C24;28;30;32-33. CW42. SN, Y4-7. SW,An3;18. SN,B6;10; 16-18;27. SE, Wa7-8. SE,P4-6
Count A(lan, of Brittany)	NFK	10,59
Alan of Burwell	CAM	*14,69.* AppxA
Alan the clerk	KEN	M13
Alan the steward	HUN	20,6
Alberic: *see* Aubrey		
Albert	BRK	56
	BKM	35,1
	CAM	32,36. AppxM
	CON	5,3,16-17
	ESS	11,7
	LIN	S13
	NFK	26,2-5
	RUT	ELc3
	SHR	4,3,5;54-56;65. 4,26,2
	SFK	8,13;56-58. 14,11
	SSX	12,25
	WIL	26,9. 27,11
	WOR	8,14
Albert: *see also* Burnt Albert		
Albert, Drogo of Beuvrière's man	YKS	14E45

Albert Grelley	CHS	R4,2
Albert of Lorraine/the clerk/chaplain	BDF	49
	BRK	1,1
	HEF	18
	KEN	13
	LIN	ER,1
	MDX	7,1
	RUT	7. R21
	SRY	34
	WAR	1,8
Albert of Sandon(?)	HRT	Appx
Albert, Roger of Poitou's man	LIN	16,14
Albert, the Abbot of Ely's man	CAM	32,39
Albert, the Abbot of Ely's steward	CAM	32,37
Albert the chaplain/clerk: *see* Albert of Lorraine		
Albold	MDX	10,2
Albold the cleric	SFK	14,13;39 *note*
Albold Cook	HAM	1,8
Albold: *see also* Aethelbald, Ailbold		
Albrict	SOM	43,1
Albrict: *see also* Aethelbrict		
Alchen	SHR	4,21,10
Alchen: *see also* Alcher(?), Alcwine(?) Alfkil(?)		
Alchere	DBY	6,28;30;32;50
	DEV	39,2. 40,3. 47,7
	ESS	27,11
	SHR	4,3,4;60;65;71. 4,27,35
	STS	10,8
	SSX	11,41
Alchere: *see also* Alchen(?), Ealhhere		
Alcolm	YKS	30W19-21
Alcude	LIN	22,3
Alcwine (?): *see* Alchen		
Aldbert	DOR	26,64
Aldbert: *see also* Ealdbeorht		
Aldchurl	DEV	3,41;62. 15,59;71. 16,72. 20,2
Aldchurl: *see also* Ealdceorl		
Alded, wife of Oswald	HAM	2,4
Alded (fem.): *see also* Aldgyth, Ealdgyth		
Aldelin, William of Warenne's man	LIN	15,1
Aldeva (fem.)	BRK	65,13
	BKM	12,4
Aldeva, a thane	SOM	*28,1*
Aldeva (fem.): *see also* Aldgifu, Ealdgifu, Edeva/Aldeva		
Aldgeat (fem.?)	WOR	19,13
Aldgeat (fem.?): *see also* Aeldiet, Aldith		
Aldgifu (fem.): *see* Aeleva, Aethelgifu, Aldeva, Ealdgifu		
Aldgyth (fem.)	SFK	67,15. 74,6
	YKS	5E27 *and note.* CE6
Aldgyth (fem.): *see also* Aeldiet, Alded, Aldgeat, Aldith, Ealdgyth		
Aldhild (fem.)	DEV	19,44
Aldhild (fem.): *see also* Ealdhild		
Aldith (fem.)	BRK	65,21
	DBY	6,51
	NFK	60
	SHR	4,3,49;54. 4,10,4. 4,25,3
	SOM	5,42

Aldwulf	NFK	20,26
	SFK	7,80;82;107-109
	YKS	C11. 25W19
Aldwulf, a thane	DEV	17,13
Aldwulf: *see also* Alwulf		
Aldwy the priest	NFK	9,82
Aleifr	LIN	13,33
Aleran the Frenchman/Aleran	CAM	AppxC
Alestan/Adestan of Weston Colville	CAM	AppxD
Alestan/Adestan: *see also* Aethelstan		
Alfeah	HAM	2,5. 3,1
Alfeah: *see also* Alfheah		
Alfeva (fem.)	ESS	37,5
Alfeva (fem.): *see also* Aelfeva, Aelfgifu		
Alfflaed (fem.): *see* Alflaed		
Alfgar	ESS	B3a
Alfgar the priest	ESS	B3a
Alfgeard: *see* Alfyard		
Alfgeat	BRK	1,40
	CON	5,8,2
	DBY	6,58
	DEV	*42,7*
	HAM	23,58
	HEF	13,1
	HUN	19,27. D11
	KEN	*5,38*
	SOM	5,47;53. *19,14.* 25,31
	STS	1,38;39. 8,7
	SFK	1,102. 6,216. 16,35. 25,73. 29,6. 54,3
	SSX	9,131. 13,52
	WAR	16,41
	WIL	5,2. 67,32
	WOR	26,9
Alfgeat, a thane	SOM	*5,47*
Alfgeat, a woman [= ?Aelfgyth (fem.)]	SOM	*25,8*
Alfgeat, Alstan of Boscombe's man	HRT	28,3
another Alfgeat	BRK	1,40
Alfgeat, Earl Algar's man	CAM	14,47
Alfgeat Ghost	CAM	*14,47*
Alfgeat of Aylesbury	BKM	12,16
Alfgeat Puttock	SOM	*5,4*
Alfgeat, Queen Edith's man	BKM	14,40
Alfgeat son of Wulfgeat, a monk	WOR	26,16
Alfgeat the priest	CAM	5,40
	SOM	16,5
Alfgeat: *see also* Algeat		
Alfgeirr: *see* Alfger		
Alfger	SFK	1,111
Alfger: *see also* Alfgeirr, Algar		
Alfgrimr	YKS	C10
Alfheah	CON	5,7,2. 5,24,16
	DBY	6,34. 7,4
	ESS	37,17
	NFK	4,2;17;29. 9,233
	NTT	10,34;51. 28,1
	SHR	4,25,2
	SFK	14,43
	SRY	19,2
	SSX	10,80. 12,34
Alfheah, a thane	DBY	6,42

Alfheah, half man of Manulf	SFK	4,15
Alfheah the priest	ESS	B3a
Alfheah: *see also* Alfeah		
Alfhelm	ESS	39,9
	HAM	69,48
	OXF	12,1
	STS	2,8
	SSX	9,2
	WOR	23,6
Alfhere	DEV	35,15
	GLS	32,11. 52,7
	HAM	3,1
	KEN	2,25;32
	NFK	1,77;135. 27,1. 49,3. 54,1
	SOM	3,1
	SRY	21,5
	SSX	9,92;120. 10,17;53;99
Alfhere: *see also* Godwin son of		
Alfhere, Harold's thane	NFK	26,5
Alfhere: *see also* Aelfhere		
Alfhild (fem.)	DEV	52,51
	GLS	74,1
	HEF	23,3
	SOM	*37,8*
	WIL	67,87
Alfhild, a thane	SOM	37,8
Alfhild, mother of the Abbot of Glastonbury	SOM	*8,24*
Alfhild (fem.): *see also* Aelfhild		
Alfhild's husband	WIL	67,87
Alfith the Englishwoman (fem.)	ESS	24,35
Alfith (fem.): *see also* Aelfgyth		
Alfkell	WOR	26,7
Alfkell: *see also* Alfketill, Alfkil		
Alfketill	YKS	6N26. 9W25. 14E26
Alfkil: *see also* Alchen, Alfkell		
Alflaed (fem.)	NFK	1,150. 8,29
Alflaed (fem.): *see also* Ael(f)-, Aethel-, Al(f)-, -fl(a)ed		
Alfled (fem.), Archbishop Stigand's man	CAM	*26,21*
Alfled (fem.): *see also* Alflaed, Elfled		
Alfnoth	SFK	49,1
Alfnoth: *see also* Alnoth		
Alfred	BRK	7,43. 22,3. 33,8. 65,18
	BKM	12,26;30
	CAM	26,20;22. *31,2.* 32,12
	CON	5,11
	DEV	*1,25.* 3,19. 15,9;31;59-60. 16,141. 17, 15-16
	DOR	26,13;18;48. 28,1. 40,4
	ESS	24,26;54. 37,5. 90,69
	GLS	EvO9
	HAM	23,7. NF3,2
	HUN	19,18
	KEN	M8. 5,11;174;208
	LEC	29,6
	LIN	S11. CS,9-10;16-17. CN,4-5;12. EN,2
	MDX	7,4
	NFK	59. 1,111;120-121. 2,8. 9,29. 66,82
	NTH	18,67-75. 35,23. 47,1. 55,3;6. EH6
	NTT	1,66. 14,3

	OXF	6,10. 7,13. 35,26;31
	SOM	1,28. *2,8*. *3,1*. 5,38. 17,5-6. 19,*14*; 40-42;47;49;51;53;61;69;79. 47,18
	STS	12,28
	SFK	32,4. 36,8
	SRY	8,10. 31,1
	SSX	8,1. 10,1-2;87. 12,55
	WAR	39,2-3
	WOR	2,18
	YKS	1N19. 1E59. 1W30. 5W38. 9W40. 29W21
Alfred: *see also* Robert son of		
Alfred, a man-at-arms	KEN	5,128
	SSX	9,1
	WOR	1,1c
Alfred, Asgar's man	HRT	33,10
Alfred, Asgar the constable's man	HRT	4,13. 20,10
Alfred Big	KEN	*2,16*. 5,124
Alfred, Durand Malet's man	LIN	44,2
Alfred, Guy of Craon's man	LIN	57,1;5-7
Alfred, Hardwin of Scales' man	CAM	*13,2*
Alfred, Kolsveinn's man	LIN	26,17
Alfred, nephew of Thoraldr	LIN	C23
Alfred, nephew of Wigot	OXF	43
Alfred, Odo the crossbowman's man	LIN	48,2
Alfred of Lincoln	BDF	31. 32,7
	LIN	27. CS,8;25. CK,2;68
	NTH	ELc3
	RUT	2a. R7;9. ELc6-7;18
Alfred of Marlborough	HAM	36
	HEF	19. 1,8;56-57
	SOM	34. 17,1-2
	SRY	33
	WIL	26. M11
	WOR	8,26a
Alfred (of Marlborough)	HEF	2,2
Alfred of Marlborough: *see also* Agnes daughter of		
Alfred of Marlborough: *see also* Osbern uncle of		
Alfred of Marlborough's daughter	HEF	19,6;10
Alfred of 'Spain'	DEV	38
	DOR	45. *8,2*
	GLS	W19
	HEF	20
	SOM	35. 1,1;6. *2,8*. *8,5*
	WIL	54. *1,1*
Alfred of 'Spain': *see also* Walter brother of		
Alfred of Thame	BKM	51,3
Alfred of Wick	SOM	*47,18 and note*
Alfred of Wing	BKM	12,12
Alfred, Osbern of Arques' man	LIN	41,1
Alfred, reeve of Richard son of Count Gilbert	ESS	90,74
Alfred the Breton	DEV	39. *15,60 and note*. 16,94. *35,4*
Alfred the butler/a man-at-arms	DEV	*15,16-19;32-33;55*
	DOR	*15,1. E1*
	SOM	*19,39;80;86*
Alfred (the butler/a man-at-arms)	DOR	26,42;62
Alfred the clerk	OXF	29,17
Alfred, the Count of Mortain's man	NTT	4,5;7
Alfred the Englishman	NFK	9,78

Alfred the marshal	CON	5,1,3
Alfred the priest	HAM	64
	NFK	2,12
Alfred the sheriff	DOR	49,15
Alfred the steward/a man-at-arms	KEN	5,128
	SOM	*5,46*
Alfred's father	KEN	M8
Alfric: *see* Aelfric, Alric		
Alfrith	GLS	19,2
Alfrith: *see also* Edwin Alfrith		
: *see also* Aethelfrith		
Alfrun (fem.)	DEV	24,6-8;15
	DOR	28,6
Alfrun (fem.): *see also* Aelfrun		
Alfsi	BRK	1,34;40
	BKM	56
	CAM	14,73. *17,2.* 22,1. 26,18. *31,1*
	CHS	5,7;9
	CON	5,21. *4,22.* 5,5,19. 5,24,12
	DBY	6,11;61
	ESS	18,30. 20,78. 27,3. 34,3. B3a(x3)
	HAM	6,4;16. 11,1. 23,67. 43,4. 67,1. IoW2, 1. 9,8
	HEF	9,8
	HUN	19,6
	KEN	5,178. 9,10
	LEC	17,14
	NFK	*1,94. 15,25*
	NTH	56,40
	NTT	2,7. 9,2;43;77;90;95. 14,5. 30,29
	OXF	58,28-29
	SOM	5,36. 6,12. 24,15-17;20;37. 37,7. 46,15
	STS	11,39. EW4
	SFK	6,191. EC2
	WAR	12,11. 16,41-42;59. 44,10
	WIL	36,1. 57,1. E5
	WOR	16,1
Alfsi: *see also* Leofwin brother of		
Alfsi, a thane	BKM	14,45
Alfsi, Alli's man	BDF	47,1
Alfsi Beard	CAM	*31,2*
Alfsi Bowl	ESS	37,4
Alfsi Bowl: *see also* Bolla		
Alfsi, brother of Alli	BDF	47,1
Alfsi Child: *see* Young Alfsi		
Alfsi, Edeva's man	CAM	14,68
	HRT	16,11
Alfsi Illing	DBY	S5
	NTT	S5
Alfsi Loholt	CON	*5,24,17*
Alfsi of Bromham/Queen Edith's man	BDF	2,1. 23,28-29
Alfsi of Faringdon	BRK	65,7-8. Cf 1,34
	GLS	1,66. 11,14. 78,1
	OXF	1,9
Alfsi (of Faringdon)	BRK	1,34
	GLS	78,12
Alfsi of Faringdon's son	BRK	B1

Alfward: *see also* Godwin brother of
Alfward, a royal thane   GLS   6,5
Alfward, a thane   BKM   14,20
                                                          DOR   *36,2* (cf 55,48)
                                                          NTT   9,69
                                                          SOM   1,21. *5,65. 8,4. 21,6;54. 27,3. 35,12*
                                                          WIL   3,1
(a third) Alfward   HEF   1,10b
Alfward, Aelmer of Bennington's man   HRT   38,2
Alfward, ?Algar's brother   ESS   34,22
Alfward, Alric son of Goding's man   BDF   24,6
Alfward, Alstan of Boscombe's man   HRT   28,5
another Alfward   GLS   39,5
                                                          WOR   8,16
(another) Alfward   HEF   1,10b
Alfward, Archbishop Stigand's man   HRT   4,4;17
Alfward Bellrope   BDF   25,1
Alfward, Bishop Wulfwy's man   BDF   24,23
Alfward Child: *see* Young Alfward
Alfward Colling   WIL   67,14
Alfward Colling: *see also* Alward Colling
Alfward Croc   SOM   *6,1*
Alfward Dore   ESS   62,1
Alfward, Earl Algar's man   HRT   4,10. 37,2;20
Alfward, Earl Harold's man   HRT   17,2;4;8-9
Alfward, Earl Harold's thane   HRT   17,3
Alfward, Earl Oda's thane   HEF   23,6
Alfward Froward   HRT   Appx
Alfward Glebard   SOM   *24,25*
Alfward, Goding's man   BKM   17,20
Alfward Hunter   SOM   *19,51*
Alfward, King Edward's man   CAM   *32,8*
Alfward of Mardley   HRT   42,13. Appx
Alfward of Munden   HRT   Appx
Alfward, Robert son of Wymarc's man   CAM   32,24
Alfward son of Reinbald   GLS   78,11
Alfward the cleric   SSX   3,3
Alfward the goldsmith   BRK   65,5
Alfward the goldsmith's father   BRK   65,5
Alfward the priest   BRK   7,8
                                                          WIL   1,23e. 19,2
Alfward, Tovi's man   BKM   43,2
Young Alfward [= Alfward Child], a royal thane   BKM   4,28. 14,21
Alfward: *see also* Aelfw(e)ard, Alward
Alfward's brothers   SOM   47,14
Alfward's father   SOM   47,14
Alfwin, Alfwine: *see* Aelfwine, Alwin(e)
Alfwold   BDF   3,17. 53,1
                                                          BRK   B7
                                                          CAM   23,1
                                                          CHS   12,4
                                                          CON   5,6,6-7. 5,24,24
                                                          DBY   6,39. 12,5
                                                          ESS   B3a(x2)
                                                          GLS   39,12. 53,1. 67,5. 78,10
                                                          HAM   NF8,1. 9,43
                                                          HEF   21,1
                                                          HUN   6,6
                                                          KEN   5,30
                                                          LEC   14,31-32. 29,19-20

	NFK	8,117. 9,150
	NTH	EB2
	NTT	9,17;66
	SOM	5,16;41;43;66. 8,17. 19,15. 24,33. 25, 36;38;52. 28,2. 36,1-2;5;10-11;13-14
	STS	17,18
	SFK	*16,6*
	SSX	9,130. 10,58
	WAR	16,17. 17,67. EBW4
	WIL	38,1. 67,97. 68,9
	WOR	15,13. 23,2. 26,2;10. 27,1
Alfwold, a thane	DEV	*35,9*
	HAM	1,W1
Alfwold, and his brothers	HUN	19,15;17. D21
Alfwold, Bishop Wulfwy's man	BDF	34,2
Alfwold, Earl Edwin's thane	WOR	1,1c
Abbot Alfwold (of Holme)	NFK	8,128. 10,87
Bishop Alfwold (of Sherborne)	DOR	2,6. 27,9-10
	SOM	EDo1
Alfwold of Stevington, a royal thane	BDF	2,8. 15,1-2;4-7
Alfwold the bald	SOM	*36,7*
Alfwold the chamberlain	BRK	1,43. 65,15
Alfwold: *see also* Aelfwold, Alwold		
Alfwold's sister	WIL	38,1
Alfwy	BRK	65,3
	CAM	26,23
	CON	4,13. 5,11,3
	GLS	5,2. 19,2. 32,1. 69,2. 70,2. E31-32
	HAM	28,9. 43,4. 53,1. 69,4;10;24;46
	HEF	10,61
	NTT	9,5;12;22;70
	OXF	B10. 6,16. 55,2. 58,32;37. 59,21 *note*
	SOM	19,74;80. 21,6;9;12-13. 22,4. 24,36. 35,1-5;10;12;15;17-23. 36,5. *37,11*. 46, 13
	SSX	13,54
	WAR	3,4. 22,13. 27,4. 28,5
	WIL	24,9. 41,3;7. 45,3. 54,1. 65,1. 67,23; 88. 68,29
	WOR	8,9b;9e-9f;10a;10c;22. 17,1. 18,3-4
Alfwy: *see also* Saewulf father of		
Alfwy, a thane	SHR	4,16,2
	SOM	*37,11*
(another) Alfwy	WOR	8,22
Alfwy Black	GLS	E31
	WOR	8,9b
Alfwy, brother of Brictric	WIL	67,10
Alfwy Chafersbeard	BRK	65,22
Alfwy, Earl Harold's man	GLS	5,1
Alfwy Hiles: *see* Harold, his man		
Alfwy Hunter	ESS	90,70
Abbot Alfwy/Aethelwig (of Evesham)	WOR	11,2. 26,15-16
Alfwy/?Alwin son of Banna	SOM	*1,27. 6,9. 8,5. 35,13-14;16;24*
Alfwy/?Alwin (son of Banna)	DOR	45,1
Alfwy son of Saewulf	HAM	69,17
Alfwy son of Thurber	HAM	69,16;29-31
	WIL	67,26
Alfwy, the King's reeve	SOM	*35,1*
Alfwy the sheriff	OXF	58,27
Alfwy: *see also* Aelfwig, Aelfwy, Alwin, Alwy		

Alfwy's wife	WIL	24,9
Alfyard: *see* Aelfgeard		
Alfyard's sons	BRK	7,24
Algar	BRK	B4. 21,2
	CON	5,15. 4,7. 5,1,4. 5,2,15. 5,11,6
	DBY	6,43. 17,12
	DEV	3,22;26;37;62;73-74;82-84. 15,79. 16,
		33;63. 17,25;34;36;39;41-42;51. 19,
		16-17. 20,9. 23,4;10. 25,5;24. 52,41-42
	DOR	3,10. 26,67. 55,3. E3
	ESS	18,25. 23,33;37. 30,20. 32,12. 34,17.
		37,17. 43,6. 56,1. 90,62
	GLS	6,2;7. E9
	HAM	23,52. 40,1. NF6,1. 9,45. IoW7,6
	HEF	1,70. 10,45
	LEC	40,41
	LIN	4,36;67. 26,27. 57,23-24;46-47. 68,20.
		CK,60
	NFK	1,173;182;229. 4,50. 6,5. 9,6;63. 10,
		32. 35,9. 41,1. 44,1. 66,41
	NTH	4,1;26-27. 26,10-11. 41,4. 54,1
	NTT	9,24. 30,19;23;26
	OXF	7,1. 54,1
	SHR	4,7,5. 4,11,1. 4,14,14. 4,16,1. 4,18,1.
		4,25,6. 4,27,4. 6,32
	SOM	5,20;26-27;47. 8,*11*;13. 19,5;28;31;45.
		20,3. 21,4;74;22,14. 24,6. 25,1;4;
		10-11;*43*. 27,2
	STS	ED6
	SFK	6,106;197. 7,18;118;124. 8,*59*;62. 12,
		5. 16,36. 19,12. 21,55-56. 27,10. 28,3.
		64,3. 66,13
	SSX	9,104. 10,79
	WAR	17,64
	WIL	3,5. 25,2. 41,9. 48,10. 53,1. 66,5. 67,
		31;52;56
	WOR	8,20
Algar: *see also* Brictric son of		
: *see also* Godwin son of		
Algar, a free man of Harold	NFK	1,169-171
Algar, a royal thane	SFK	7,71
Algar, a thane	DEV	*17,94*
	DOR	55,46 (cf 55,48 *note*)
	SOM	*5,47*
Algar, ?Alfward's brother	ESS	34,22
Algar, Archbishop Stigand's man	CAM	26,23
Algar Cappe	CAM	*5,37*
Algar Cappe: *see also* Cabe		
Algar ?Colling	SHR	4,7,5
Algar, Count Alan's man	LIN	CK,66
Earl Algar	BDF	23,20
	BKM	39,1. 52,1-2
	CAM	1,10;15;18;22. 10,1. 13,1-2;4-7;*8-9*.
		14,27;47;71. 16,1. 18,2. 21,5. 26,5-6;
		14-18;20;22-26;31-32;36-37;42. 27,1.
		31,1;7. 32,4;8;*20*;21;23. 35,1-2. 38,1;
		3-4. 39,2. 41,4
	DBY	1,16;20;37
	ESS	15,1-2. 22,9. 41,2. 72,2. 81,1. 82,1. 90,
		65

Almer: *see also* A(e)lmer
Almund   STS   8,4;11;14-15;23
                                   WAR   12,4;7. 17,9
                                   YKS   29W39-40. 30W10

Almund: *see also* Alward son of
(another) Almund   SHR   4,20,3
Almund/Aethelmund/Ealhmund   SHR   4,3,45;47-48;63;67. 4,8,1;16. 4,20,3;
                                           11;17. 4,21,8-9;18. 4,27,17;21

Almund: *see also* Aethelmund, Alhmund,
  Ealhmund
Almund's son   SHR   4,27,18-21
Alnoth   CHS   23,2
                                   CON   5,17. 5,19. 5,3,2;26. 5,5,4. 5,12,1. 5,
                                           26,3-4
                                   DBY   7,13. 14,11
                                   DEV   14,1;3-4. 16,25;39;47;73;95;155. 24,9.
                                           25,16-17. 34,20-21. 39,12-13. 52,36
                                   DOR   47,1. 55,10. 57,12;19
                                   ESS   B3a
                                   GLS   41,5. EvM112
                                   HAM   1,W18. 2,10. 3,6. 23,23. 27,2. 43,6.
                                           NF3,8. 9,7. IoW7,7. 8,3. 9,21
                                   HEF   10,19;52;75
                                   HRT   5,4;7
                                   KEN   5,95. 9,25-26
                                   LEC   17,21. 43,8
                                   LIN   C14. 3,21;25. 4,8. 8,13;17;19;31;39.
                                           12,80. 16,22. 26,10;21;23. 28,7. 44,1.
                                           49,5. 63,12. 68,1. CW,1
                                   MDX   7,7
                                   NFK   1,105-112. 8,47
                                   NTT   5,11. 9,79
                                   OXF   7,3. 24,2
                                   SOM   5,8;*61;66*. 8,9;*22. 18,2*. 19,19;54. 25,
                                           49. 36,7. 45,4;12
                                   SFK   6,32(x2);100;196. 16,30
                                   SSX   9,6;24. 10,16;39;58;68;96. 11,44;82.
                                           12,8;11
                                   WAR   17,9;68
                                   WIL   5,1. 26,18;21. 27,7. 28,6. 66,8
                                   WOR   15,1

Alnoth: *see also* Harding son of
Alnoth, a royal thane   BKM   4,38
Alnoth, a thane   SOM   *5,61*
Alnoth, Archbishop Stigand's man   HRT   5,17;26
Alnoth, Archbishop Stigand's thane HRT   38,2
Alnoth, brother of Asketill, Fenkell and   LIN   CS,38. CN,30
  Sighvatr/Godwine
Alnoth Child: *see* Young Alnoth
Alnoth Grutt, Archbishop Stigand's man   HRT   5,3;14
Alnoth, Harold's man   SFK   7,102
Alnoth, King Edward's man   CAM   *32,8*
Alnoth, Norman the sheriff's man   SFK   7,36
Alnoth of Bray   DEV   *52,36*
Alnoth of Canterbury   NTH   2,6
Abbot Alnoth/of Glastonbury   BRK   8
                                   DEV   4
                                   DOR   8
                                   GLS   8
                                   HAM   11

	KEN	2,31
	SOM	8. 5,12;43;50. 19,9-10. 25,7-8. 37,9
	WIL	7. 24,42. 41,8
Alnoth of Kent	OXF	7,4
Alnoth of London	SRY	6,4
Alnoth (of London)	SRY	5,8. 19,1-2;5;14
Alnoth of Merriot: *see* Harding son of		
Alnoth of Sutton	CAM	AppxP
Alnoth, the Bishop of Durham's man	LIN	3,35;37
Alnoth/Ednoth the constable/steward	BRK	7,7
	SOM	*39,1*
	WIL	22,1-5
Alnoth/Ednoth (the constable/steward)	DEV	*14,1*
	DOR	27,1-4;6;8-11
	GLS	28,5;7
	SOM	18,1. 47,3
Alnoth/Ednoth: *see also* Harding son of		
Alnoth the Kentishman, a royal thane	BKM	4,36. 17,25
Alnoth the monk	SOM	8,20
Alnoth the priest	HAM	17,2
	LIN	CS,19
Alnoth the reeve	SOM	24,24. 25,29
Young Alnoth [= Alnoth Child], a royal thane	BKM	4,29
	HAM	23,57
	KEN	D17;22. C6. P20. 5,4;28;41;44;56;72; 95;100;102;134;175
	SRY	5,1a
	SSX	8,1-2
Alnoth/Aelfnoth/Aethelnoth/Ealdnoth	SHR	4,10,2. 4,25,4
Alnoth: *see also* Aelfnoth, Aethelnoth, Alfnoth, Ealdnoth, Ednoth		
Alnoth's father	LIN	CS,38
Alric	BDF	21,8. 25,1. 32,15. 56,8. 57,9
	BRK	21,9. 36,5
	BKM	B7. 5,12. 14,47-48. 17,16. 29,4
	CON	5,20. 5,2,9;32. 5,3,22. 5,4,15-16. 5,6,1; 3. 5,13,1;12
	DBY	6,24;33;43;46;94. 14,1
	DEV	1,11. 3,66. 16,45-46. 17,52;61;84. 19, 41. 20,10;16-17. 21,1;3;6. 23,23-24. 34,19;48. 35,8;13. 49,5. 51,12. 52,43
	DOR	26,36. 54,4. 55,9
	ESS	6,9. 20,21;58. 33,17. 39,10. 57,1. 80, 1. B3a(x3)
	GLS	3,3. 45,4. 49,1. 50,4. 60,3. 68,7. 69,1. E31;33. WoB16
	HAM	2,1;10. 23,31. 69,9;12;21;38. IoW9,3; 10
	HEF	10,16;32;36;57. 29,20
	HUN	29,4
	NTH	18,24;61;63;72;93-94;97. 29,1. 35,15. 40,6. 56,29
	NTT	2,3. 9,36. 10,30-31;39. 30,29
	OXF	B10. 24,2
	SOM	5,9;24. 19,21. 21,40-42;44;46;62;64; 66;73;84. 22,2;20. 24,30. 25,16;50. 37, 11
	STS	2,22. 8,13. 11,31;53;60;62. 12,9. 17,3; 8;16-17
	SFK	1,44-45. 74,10

Alsi, a royal thane	NFK	1,175
Alsi, Edeva's man	SFK	EC2;14
Alsi, nephew of Earl Ralph	SFK	8,50
Alsi, nephew of Earl R(alph)	SFK	6,216;233
Alsi, wife of	SFK	68,5
Alsi/Aelfsige/Aethelsige	DEV	15,54. 16,41. 23,12;17-21. 34,49. 35, 14. 47,5-6. 48,10. 51,1
	DOR	26,50. 39,2
	SHR	4,8,10-11. 4,11,13. 4,21,13. 6,19
Alsi: *see also* Aelfsige, Aelsi, Aethelsige, Alfsi, Alsige		
Alsige	LIN	7,13. 22,21;24;26;28-29;35. 26,20;33; 37;45. 48,5. 61,5. CS,5
	YKS	C12. 1N117. 1W14. 6N9. 9W35-36;39; 41;44;46;51;63;65;76;89;141. 10W3-4; 16;31;34;43. 11W3. 18W2. 29W3. CW15
Alsige: *see also* Toli son of		
Alsige, brother of Aethelstan and Aelfric	LIN	26,45
Alsige the deacon	LIN	CK,14
Alsige: *see also* Alsi		
Alstan	BDF	23,52
	BKM	12,23
	CHS	14,11
	CON	5,1,19;21. 5,24,19
	DEV	52,9;11-17
	DOR	26,70. 34,9-11;13. 55,3
	ESS	28,3. 30,12. 32,5;8;39. 34,1;8;29. 40, 7. 41,6. 90,33;56. B3a(x2)
	GLS	69,1
	HRT	34,17
	KEN	5,5;18
	NFK	4,3;21. 7,7. 9,8. 12,42. 34,5. 50,1
	NTT	9,90
	SOM	8,18. 21,92
	SFK	6,191;228. 37,4. 67,11. 74,11
	SSX	9,15
	WAR	16,61. 36,2
	WIL	67,29
Alstan, a thane	SFK	37,1
Alstan, Aelmer of Bennington's man	HRT	36,1
Alstan, an Englishman	NFK	9,75
Alstan, Harold's thane	NFK	9,104
Alstan of Boscombe, a royal thane	BDF	18,1;4;6
	GLS	58,4
	HRT	28,1-6;8
	SOM	*19,61*. 26,1-7
	WIL	32,1-14
Alstan (of Boscombe, a royal thane)	BDF	18,2-3;7
	BRK	23,1
	DOR	34,1
	GLS	31,4;7;10-11
	HAM	1,32. 32,4
	HRT	28,7
	WIL	8,12
Alstan, Ordgar's man	CAM	*14,75*
Alstan, reeve of London	KEN	1,1
Alstan Stric	ESS	6,4
Alstan Tilley	DEV	*46,1-2*
Alstan: *see also* Aelstan, Aestan, Aethelstan		

Alswith the nun	LIN	1,9
Alswith (fem.): *see also* Aethelswith		
Altei	HAM	23,6
Altet	KEN	5,190
Aluerle	YKS	1N104 *and note*
Alun	DBY	17,19
Alun: *see also* Adelund, Aethelhun		
Alwaker	HAM	30,1
	SOM	8,9. 24,2;9;18;28;30-32
	WIL	36,2
Alward	CAM	*32,12*
	NFK	9,146
	SFK	6,202. 61,1
Alward Colling	DOR	*1,23*
Alward Colling: *see also* Alfward Colling		
Alward Mart, a thane	DEV	*24,23;24;28. 52,29 note;* 30
Alward of Newton	NFK	1,64
Alward Rufus, a thane	DEV	*15,16*
Alward son of Almund	SHR	4,27,17
Alward son of Toki	DEV	19,*16;19*;35 *and note; 39. 34,14*
Alward (son of Toki)	DEV	19,5-6;14;24-25. 31,1,8
Alward the reeve	DOR	*56,62*
Alward/Aelfward/Aethelward	DEV	1,41. 3,10;15;45;64;75. 15,6;22;25;58; 61. 16,103. 17,31;37;79. 19,5-6;14; 24-25. 24,26. 25,3;9;21. 28,12;14. 34, 1;8. 35,11;18. 36,26. 51,3. 52,29
	DOR	3,1. 26,3;6;29;31. 33,2. 36,*3*;7;10. 39, 1. 40,8-9. 47,11. 48,2. 50,4. 55,20;22; 38;40-42. 56,15;22;25;32;36;62-63. 57, 2
	SHR	3f,2. 3g,10. 4,1,2;36. 4,3,61;64;68;70. 4,4,21. 4,5,15. 4,21,6;10. 4,27,9;23-25; 35
Alward: *see also* Aelfward, Aelward, Aethelward, Ailward, Alfward		
Alware (fem.)	CAM	*44,2*
Alware Pet	DEV	1,63
Alware (fem.): *see also* Aelfwaru, Aelwaru, Aethelwaru		
Alweard	YKS	5W1;2-5. 9W12;27;53;98
Alweard: *see also* Aelward, Aethelward,		
Alwen (fem.)	ESS	24,4. B3a(x2)
Alwen (fem.): *see also* Aelfwen, Aelfwynn		
Alwig	LIN	4,11. 16,41
Alwig: *see also* Alwy(?)		
Alwig, Walter of Aincourt's man	LIN	31,2
Alwin	BDF	21,7. 53,22;36. 55,1. 57,11
	BRK	B6. 7,11;17. 8,1. 17,2;9. 22,1. 31,5. 36, 1. 41,5. 46,7. 60,1. 65,19
	BKM	5,20. 12,25
	CAM	14,6
	CON	1,1. 5,2,2. 5,3,1;3;10;13-15;27. 5,5, 2-3;13. 5,6,5;8. 5,11,7. 5,24,6
	DBY	6,21;98
	DEV	2,15. 3,4;9;20-21;30;76-77;86-87;94; 99. 15,57;72. 16,87. 17,13;17;21;40; 44 -46;59-60;66;71;74;80;90;98. 20,11; 13-15. 21,17. 23,1. 28,9. 29,5-10. 34, 26;43. 35,16. 39,17-18. 52,37;39

DOR	1,22;25. 26,4;17;71. 39,1. 47,8. 55,21. 56,14
ESS	1,6. 4,15;18. 10,5. 18,33. 20,45;50. 21, 9. 23,32. 24,13. 35,14. 37,18. 39,1. 62, 4. B3a(x8)
GLS	1,45. 32,6. 39,9. 42,2. 45,4. 52,6. 65, 1. 69,2-3;8. 73,3. 77,1. EvM112
HAM	2,5. 3,8. 9,1. 23,2;19;26-27;54. 25,1. 29,12,54,1. 60,1. 62,2. 69,27. NF10,1
HEF	1,3;18;70. 9,18. 22,8. 30,1
HRT	34,8. 36,8
HUN	2,9. 29,6
KEN	M4. 5,28;32;35;64-65;68;79;83;85;135
LEC	13,3;28;59;72-73. 14,3. 17,1-3. 29,2;8; 8-9. 32,1-2
NTH	6a,9. 18,10;30;35;55. 23,7;15
NTT	1,61. 4,8. 10,22;34;48;64. 30,1;35
OXF	B10. 7,1. 23,1-2. 27,3. 35,9. 48,1. 55, 1. 58,20
SOM	1,6. 5,*3*;47. *8,31*. 19,11;82. 21,22;27; 72. 25,53. 35,9. 36,3;6. 46,12
STS	1,45. 2,22. 11,10. 12,29
SFK	1,7;77;110. 3,9. 6,38;48;57;207;211; 296. 7,23;85;111;136. 8,8. 16,34;41. 19,14;16. 23,5. 25,73;83-84;90. 33,8. 35,7(x2). 36,5. 38,6;10;27. 40,6. 52,6. 67,11. 74,7;11(x2);13
SRY	5,1g. 8,4. 19,2;17;20;46. 22,2
SSX	9,47;77;112. 10,25;27;56. 11,31;34;38; 49;64;92. 12,38. 13,15;24
WAR	5,1. 16,21;65. 17,39;47;51;59;66;70. 22,14;18. 23,3. 29,2. EBS3
WIL	24,12;25. 25,17. 29,4. 33,1. 41,2;5-6; 8. 42,3. 48,3. 67,38-39;95. 68,9;12;26
WOR	8,10a-10b;17-18. 26,12

Alwin: *see also* Edwy father of		
: *see also* Edwy Young father of		
: *see also* Wulfgeat father of		
Alwin, a royal thane	BDF	41,2
	BKM	16,1;3-7
	ESS	24,1
	HRT	9,9. 15,3
Alwin, a thane	BKM	14,20;35;45. 17,23
	DEV	2,*15*. *15,57*. *17,13*
	ESS	27,8
	GLS	68,9
	SOM	*5,3;47*
Alwin, Aelmer of Bennington's man	HRT	36,5
Alwin Albus: *see* Alwin White		
Alwin, Alstan's man	BDF	18,7
Alwin, Alwin Varus' man	BKM	21,8
(another) Alwin	SOM	5,3
Alwin, Archbishop Stigand's man	HRT	1,10
Alwin, Bishop Wulfwy's man	BDF	28,2
Alwin Black	DEV	*16,27*
	HUN	27,1
Alwin Blond	CAM	*31,2*
Alwin Boy [= Boi]	SRY	5,1b
Alwin, Brictric's man	BKM	17,8

Alwin, brother of Bishop Wulfwy	BDF	16,4
	BKM	41,2
Alwin, brother of Leofwin	WAR	44,11
Alwin, Burgred's man	BDF	3,9;13
	NTH	EB1
Alwin Buxton	LEC	13,21
Alwin Child: *see* Alwin Young, Young Alwin		
Alwin Cobbold	NTH	4,14
Alwin Cock, the beadle	CAM	1,20
Alwin Cock: *see also* Alwin Maimcock		
Alwin Devil	BDF	4,8. E9
	HUN	19,30. D16
Alwin Devil, man of Bishop of Lincoln	BDF	4,2
Alwin Devil, man of King Edward	BDF	4,6-7
Alwin Dod, Aelfric Little's man	HRT	36,4
Alwin Dodson	HRT	36,4. 42,6
Alwin, Earl Algar's man	CAM	*32,8*
Alwin, Earl Edwin's thane	WOR	1,1c
Alwin, Earl Harold's man	BDF	35,2
Alwin, Earl Harold's thane	HRT	24,3
Alwin, Edeva the fair's man	BKM	44,2;5
Alwin, Estan's man	BKM	4,43
Alwin Frost	HAM	IoW3,1
Alwin, Godwin of Benfield's man	HRT	4,18
Alwin Gotton	ESS	22,4
Alwin Horn(e), a royal thane	BDF	30,1
	HRT	42,1-2;5
	KEN	D25
	MDX	4,11
Alwin Hunter, Earl Leofwin's man	HRT	6,1
	NTH	59,1-4. 60,1
Alwin Hunter, Queen Edith's man	HRT	33,4
Alwin, King Edward's man	BDF	53,17-18
	MDX	14,1
Alwin Maimcock, the King's beadle	CAM	*1,20*
Alwin Maimcock: *see also* Alwin Cock		
Abbot Alwin/of Buckfast	DEV	6
Alwin of Gotton, King Edward's man	HRT	10,6. 25,2. 33,17. 42,12. 44,1
Alwin of Mendlesham	SFK	1,77 *note.* 31,51
Alwin of Nuneham	BKM	12,25
Abbot Alwin (of Ramsey)	HUN	D4
Alwin of Rushden	HRT	Appx
Alwin of Wain(?)	HRT	Appx
Alwin Pike	SOM	8,7
Alwin, Queen Edith's man	BKM	4,11. 16,2. 25,1
Alwin Sack, the Bishop of Lincoln's man	BDF	4,5
Alwin, Sired son of Sibbi's man	BKM	12,1
Alwin son of Banna: *see* Alfwy/?Alwin son of Banna		
Alwin son of Brictmer	MDX	3,11
Alwin son of Chipping [rectius Kipping]	BRK	65,6
Alwin son of Edwy	HEF	10,15
Alwin son of Edwy Young	HEF	10,70
Alwin son of Goda	SOM	*24,34*
Alwin son of Goding	BKM	12,27
Alwin son of Ulf	NTH	41,5
Alwin son of Wulfgeat	HAM	69,50
Alwin Stickhare, King Edward's man	MDX	16,1
Alwin (Stickhare, King Edward's man)	ESS	76,1

Alwin Still	ESS	33,18
	HAM	2,8
Alwin, Stori's man	BDF	44,2;4
Alwin, the Abbot (of Ely)'s reeve	CAM	*31,2*
Alwin, the Count of Eu's man	SSX	9,59
Alwin the priest	BDF	57,19
	BRK	7,29
	HUN	D6
	KEN	9,39
	OXF	B10
	SFK	1,13-14. 16,30
	WIL	67,22
Alwin the priest's father	BRK	7,29
Alwin the rat	HAM	69,16
Alwin the reeve	BDF	57,3iii-vi;5
Alwin the sheriff (of Gloucestershire)	GLS	1,2;13. 34,8;12
Alwin (the sheriff, of Gloucestershire)	GLS	34,5-7;9-11
	HEF	10,66
Alwin the sheriff (of Warwickshire)	HUN	19,25
	WAR	6,9. 14,2. 17,6;15;32;62. 23,4
Alwin the sheriff: *see also* Thorkell father of		
Alwin the sheriff's wife	GLS	34,8;12
Alwin the steward	DEV	*3,94*
Alwin, Ulf son of Manni's man	MDX	7,8
Alwin Varus	BKM	4,6-7. 21,8
Alwin White/Albus, Earl Leofwin's man	HAM	69,40
	MDX	25,2
Alwin, wife of	SFK	6,57
	HUN	29,6
Alwin, Wigot's man	MDX	7,3
Young Alwin [= Alwin Child]	HUN	19,14
	NTH	EH5
Alwin Young [= Alwin Child]	WOR	14,2
Alwin/Aelfwine/Aethelwine	SHR	4,3,8. 4,8,4-6
Alwin: *see also* Aelfwin(e), Aethelwine, Alfwine, A(i)lwin, Alwine		
Abbot Alwin's uncle	WOR	26,16
Alwin(e): *see also* Leofwin(e) son of		
Alwine	LIN	2,17;27;36. 4,39. 14,11;32-33;38;40; 44-45;64-65. 18,12. 22,1;5;7. 27,2. 30, 21. 63,15
	YKS	C7;13;15. 1W53. 5W35. 9W42. 13E5. 21E1-2;5-7;9;12. 25W2-2;11-12; 18-19. CE14. CW11;31
Bishop Alwine (of Durham)	YKS	3Y9-10;16-18
Alwine: *see also* Alwin		
Alwold	NFK	8,11. 9,150
	SFK	8,68. 16,45. 69,4. 76,6
Alwold, a lawman	LIN	C2-3
Alwold the priest	SFK	16,22
Alwold/Aelfwold/Aethelwold	DEV	16,28;30;81;139;174. 17,23. 25,8. 35, 9. 36,23-24. *39,16*. 42,11
	DOR	33,1. 57,10
Alwold: *see also* Aethelwold, Alfwold		
Alwulf the priest	SFK	1,122d
Alwulf: *see also* Aethelwulf, Aldwulf		
Alwy	SFK	4,22. 12,6. 19,16
Alwy Tabb	DEV	15,55
Alwy the harper	CAM	17,2

Alwy/Aelfwig/Aethelwig	DEV	25,2. 29,4. 38,1-2. 42,13;21
	DOR	56,31;33. 57,11
	SHR	4,3,43. 4,8,2. 4,16,2. 4,24,4. 6,29
Alwy: *see also* Aethelwig, A(i)lwy, Alfwy, Alwig, Alwin		
Alwynn (fem.)	SFK	6,51
Alwynn (fem.): *see also* Aelfwen, Aelfwynn, Aethelwynn		
Amalfrid	ESS	20,62. 33,10;18
Amalgar	HRT	10,14
Amalric	DBY	6,84;91
	OXF	35,22
Amalric of Dreux	WIL	26,19. 28,10. 66,2
Ambi	LIN	16,39
Ambrose	BDF	22,1
	BKM	16,8
	NTH	35,12-13;26
	NTT	10,28
	OXF	EN12
Ambrose, William Peverel's man	NTT	10,39
Amelina (fem.): *see* Ansketel son of		
Amerland	STS	14,1
Amund	DOR	26,15;27
	SOM	19,84
	SFK	52,1-2;5;8-9
Amund: *see also* Agemund, Agmundr, Anand		
Anand	NFK	6,1. *8,16;46.* 10,33. 34,2
Anand, a thane	NFK	35,10
Anand, a royal Guard	HRT	34,15
Anand the Dane	ESS	18,39
Anand: *see also* Amund, Anund		
Anbold	SFK	33,7
Andrac	HAM	56,1
Andrew	BKM	17,25
	CON	1,1. 5,24,22-23
	SFK	8,11
Ani	SFK	67,11
Anna	GLS	42,3
Ansculf	NFK	12,39
Ansculf: *see also* Giles brother of		
: *see also* William son of		
Ansculf of Picquigny	BKM	17,2
Ansculf of Picquigny : *see also* William of Picquigny		
: *see also* William son of		
Ansculf the sheriff	BKM	17,20
	SRY	21,3
Ansculf Unlike	NFK	1,61
Ansegis	WAR	31,11. 44,16
Ansel(m)	BKM	26,11
Ansel(m): *see also* Anselm		
Anselm	CAM	*14,71*
	ESS	20,73
Anselm, man of Frodo	SFK	14,139
Ansered	KEN	7,17
Ansered: *see also* Ansgered, Aseret		
Ansfred: *see* Ansfrid, Ansgered/Ansfred		
Ansfrid	CHS	9,20
	DEV	24,19
	DOR	34,10;13

	HAM	52,1
	HEF	7,7
	HRT	34,9;10
	KEN	5,198. 9,32
	LEC	17,25;32
	LIN	8,6
	SRY	5,23. 21,3
	SSX	3,4. 10,1;31;69-70;75;79;91-92;97;
		102-104;112;117. 13,6
	WIL	29,5;8-9. 32,17
Ansfrid, a man-at-arms	SSX	3,3
Ansfrid Male, the clerk	KEN	*5,131;146-151;162;189-190;197;201. 7,*
		18;24
Ansfrid Male's father	KEN	5,149
Ansfrid of Cormeilles	GLS	68. 1,59
	HEF	21. 1,1
Ansfrid (of Cormeilles)	HEF	10,36
Ansfrid of Cormeilles' wife: *see* Walter of Lacy's		
niece		
Ansfrid of Vaubadon	NTH	B30
Ansfrid, Ralph's priest	LIN	62,2
Ansfrid the canon	BDF	13,2
Ansfrid: *see also* Ansfred/Ansgered		
Ansgar	NFK	9,26. 35,9
Ansgar/Ansger the cramped	DEV	1,23-24
Ansgar: *see also* Ansger, Åsgar		
Ansger	DEV	3,99. 16,60;73;78-79;81-82;142-144;
		159. 23,15;26. 42,6
	DOR	26,8;11;26;43
	GLS	2,7
	NTT	22,1
	OXF	7,23
	SOM	19,31;36;65;75;81-82
	STS	11,68
Ansger: *see also* Hervey son of		
Ansger Cook	ESS	75
	SOM	1,27. 46,16
	WIL	66,3
Ansger Fower	SOM	*35,19.* 46,12-15
Ansger of Montacute/of Senarpont	DEV	*40*
	SOM	45,18
Ansger of Skidbrooke	LIN	CS,39
Ansger the Breton	DEV	*15,12-15*
	SOM	*1,19.* 19,4;8;46
Ansger the King's chaplain/the clerk	NTH	15. B14
Ansger, the King's servant	DEV	*51,13*
Ansger: *see also* Ansgar, Asgar, Asgeirr		
Ansgered	OXF	6,13
Ansgered/Ansfred	HUN	8,3-4
Ansgered: *see also* Ansered, Ansfred, Aseret		
Ansgot	CHS	1,15. 14,2
	DEV	52,31-33
	ESS	24,56. 59,1
	GLS	E25. EvA119. EvC40. WoB7
	HAM	2,24
	HEF	1,43. 5,2
	KEN	1,2
	MDX	9,5
	NFK	9,162
	SFK	3,67;84

	SRY	4,1. 5,3;6;12;14
	SSX	10,1;27;82;84. 11,96-97
	WOR	2,40. 8,23
Ansgot, a man-at-arms	WIL	2,1
Ansgot, Archbishop Stigand's man	CAM	32,13
	HRT	41,2
Ansgot, brother of Aelmer	HAM	18,3
Ansgot, Earl William's man	GLS	E1 *note*
	HEF	1,46
	WOR	E6
Ansgot of Rochester	BDF	2,2-3
	KEN	2,28. 5,5;*20*;39;68-69;91-92;109
Ansgot of Rots	BKM	4,35
Ansgot the interpreter	SRY	36,8
Ansgot the priest	WAR	31,8
Ansgot: *see also* Asgautr, Asgot, Osgot		
Ansketel	BRK	54,3
	BKM	5,10;16. 53,2
	CAM	32,11
	DEV	16,145. 19,3-4;6. 20,15
	ESS	3,2. 4,6. 18,29. 22,17. 32,2;13;32. 39, 4. 90,55
	GLS	3,5. 41,4. 53,5. 69,5. E11. WoB18
	HAM	23,8;30. IoW7,14
	HEF	1,4
	HRT	2,1-3;5. 20,13
	NFK	4,32;47
	NTH	6a,4
	OXF	7,58. 41,1. 59,5;13;19
	SHR	1,8. 4,27,27
	SOM	21,7;9-10;20-27;35. EBu1
	SFK	7,13. 38,8
	SSX	9,11;128;130. 11,44
	WIL	2,12. 8,7. 68,17
Ansketel: *see also* Roger son of		
Ansketel of Cherbourg/son of Amelina	DOR	54,8 *and note*
Ansketel of Fourneaux	CAM	*14,8*
Ansketel of Graye	OXF	59,14;24-26
Ansketel of Hérouville	CAM	AppxG
Ansketel of Rots/the marshall/a man-at-arms	HRT	16,1
	KEN	2,*11-12*. 5,*13*;16-18;27-28;*35;41;56*;93; 224. *7,13*
	SRY	5,4
Ansketel, Ordric's man	CAM	*32,7*
Ansketel Parker	SOM	46,17-19
Ansketel son of Amelina : *see* Ansketel of Cherbourg/son of Amelina		
Ansketel son of Osmund	HAM	68,3-6. S3
Ansketel son of Ospak	NFK	66,99
Ansketel the archdeacon	KEN	M14
Ansketel, the Bishop of London's man	ESS	48,2
Ansketel the priest	BDF	23,39
	KEN	4,4
Ansketel the priest, Roger Bigot's chaplain	SFK	7,36
Ansketel the reeve	NFK	10,58
Ansketel: *see also* Askell, Asketill		
Anund	SFK	1,9. 2,12. 3,32-33;46-48. 7,15. 13,7. 52,11. 53,1
Anund the priest	SFK	67,11
Anund: *see also* Amund, Anand		

Ape	SOM	5,15
	WIL	53,2
Arcold: *see* Walter son of		
Ardwulf	LEC	14,27
Aretius	OXF	58,20
Arkell	CHS	11,3
	LEC	2,4-6
	NTT	9,44;114. 30,54
	RUT	ELc16
	STS	1,49
	SFK	6,130
	WAR	17,51
Arkell, Earl Harold's thane	HEF	10,28
Arkell, Thorkell's man	WAR	17,16
Arkell: *see also* Arketel, Arnketill		
Arketel	HEF	11,1-2
	SHR	4,16,2
Arketel, a thane	SHR	4,5,3
Arketel: *see also* Arkell, Arnketill		
Arnbern	DBY	7,7
Arnbern the priest	LEC	8,4
Arnbern: *see also* Arnbjorn		
Arnbjorn	LIN	18,11-12;17-20. 27,34. 51,2. 52,2. CK, 9;47
	YKS	1E55. 1W24. 9W72-73;77;98;102; 115-116;120;138;140-141
Arnbjorn, a relative of Wulfgeat	LIN	CK,1
Arnbjorn: *see also* Arnbern		
Arnbrandr	YKS	30W26;28
Arnfastr: *see* Richard son of		
Arngeirr	YKS	1N94
Arngrim	CHS	5,9. 8,14
	HEF	11,1-2
	NTT	6,5. 20,1;5
	SHR	6,26
	WAR	4,5
Arngrim, a thane	SHR	4,5,3
Arngrim: *see also* Arngrimr		
Arngrimr	YKS	1N101. 29E17-18
Arngrimr: *see also* Arngrim		
Arni	CHS	1,18. 9,1-3;6-8. FD2,5. FD4,1
	STS	12,12
Arni: *see also* Earne		
Arnketill	LIN	3,20;35. 4,4. 7,53;57. 12,7. 18,28. 30, 19. 31,9. 56,19. 67,5. 68,26;32;34. CK, 12-13;33
	YKS	C3;34. 1N31;33;38-39;45;47;132;135. 1E15. 1W8;59;61. 5N65. 5E43. 5W30. 6N60-62;72;77;79;117;134;137;139; 141;144-145;149-150;159. 9W24;34; 44;121;123;126;131;144. 10W8;39. 11N15. 11W1. 13W2;22;26. 13N18. 23N2. 24W9. 28W33;37-38. 29N6. 29W34-35;37-38;50. 30W15-16;18; 26-27;29;32-33. CW2. SN,Y8
Arnketill Barn	LIN	16,49
Arnketill, brother of	YKS	13W3 *note*. CW2
Arnketill of Withern	LIN	CS,39
Arnketill son of Ulfr	YKS	CW25
Arnketill (son of Ulfr)	YKS	13W16

Arnketill son of Wulfstan	YKS	CW24
Arnketill (son of Wulfstan)	YKS	25W1;3;6
Arnketill: *see also* Arkell, Arketel		
Arnold	BDF	54,2
	DEV	23,4
	ESS	23,3;8-9. 90,50-51
	KEN	*2,21.* 5,203
	LEC	13,43;45-46;64;66-67
	NFK	21,14
	NTH	45,7-8
	STS	11,8
	SFK	8,9. 38,14;16
	SSX	11,2;17;84;109;112
	WOR	17,1
Arnold: *see also* Roger son of		
Arnold, a man-at-arms	HEF	19,1
Arnold son of Asgautr	LIN	57,12
Arnthorr	LIN	3,27
	YKS	5W25. 9W48. 27W1
Arnthorr the priest	YKS	29W7
Arnthorr (the priest)	YKS	29W8
Arnulf	BKM	14,12
	CAM	*17,4*
	CHS	Y9
	ESS	34,4
	MDX	9,4
	SFK	8,10. 14,26-27;35;52;62;115. 27,12
	WAR	4,5;16,24-25. 17,8
Arnulf of Ardres	BDF	15,1-2;4-6
	CAM	15,2;3
Arnulf of Hesdin	BDF	20
	BRK	50
	BKM	B10. 4,34;37
	DOR	32
	GLS	60
	HAM	26. 7,1
	HUN	18
	KEN	5,15;23;110-111
	MDX	10
	OXF	40. B9
	SOM	41
	STS	11,34;36
	WIL	25. M16. 3,1. 10,3. 32,17
Arnulf of Hesdin: *see also* Ilbod brother of		
Arnulf the priest	GLS	G4
Arnulf: *see also* Earnwulf, Ernulf, Ernwulf		
Arnwin the priest	WOR	2,8
Artald	SFK	8,55
Arthur	ESS	25,17. B3a
	WOR	8,10e
Arulf	YKS	5W28
Asa (fem.)	YKS	13E5;10-11. 29E13. CE15;31
Ascelin	CHS	FD2,3
	ESS	24,30-32. 32,5. 34,23
	STS	8,14-15;17-18
Ascelin: *see also* Azelin		
Aseret	SFK	21,29
Aseret: *see also* Ansered, Ansgered, Asrothr		
Asferth	NTT	9,34
Asferth: *see also* Asfrithr, Asfrothr		

Asford	NFK	1,58. 8,97. 9,174
Asford: *see also* Asfrothr		
Asfrithr	LIN	27,59
	YKS	9W16
Asfrithr: *see also* Asferth		
Asfrothr	LIN	4,3. 8,35;37. 27,7. 49,2. CW,9. CK,4
	YKS	23N28
Asfrothr, Abbot Thoraldr's man	LIN	8,34
Asfrothr: *see also* Asferth, Asford		
Asgar	BKM	21,7
	CHS	FD4,1
	CON	5,2,12
	NFK	31,2;5
	NTH	45,1-9
	SOM	24,1
	SFK	6,217
Asgar/Ansger	DEV	23,15-16;22-24;27
Asgar the constable	BDF	1,5
	BKM	2,3. 14,29-30;45. 21,2-6;8. 28,2
	CAM	14,29. 15,4. 21,5. 22,*1*;2-4;6-10. 26,
		28. 32,11;*16*;17;23
	HRT	B8. 4,7;12-13;15;20;25. 5,11. 17,6-7;
		11-12;14-15. 20,10;12. 24,2. 33,1;5;
		8-9;11;13-15;17-18. 34,11 38,1-2. 42,6
	MDX	9,4-9
	NFK	4,49. 31,5
	SFK	25,73. 66,10
	WAR	30,1
Asgar (the constable)	BRK	38,3;5-6
	ESS	30,2;5;16;22-25;27;31-33;35-36;38-40;
		42-43;45;48-49;51. 90,28
	HRT	17,10. 33,3;6-7;10;12;16;20
	OXF	39,3
	SFK	32,1;3-5;8;19
	SRY	25,1;3
Asgar/Ansger the cramped	DEV	*1,23-24*
Asgar: *see also* Ansgar, Ånsger, Asgeirr		
Asgar's woman	HRT	1,6
Asgautr	LIN	55. 3,48. 26,8
	YKS	9W43
Asgautr: *see also* Arnold son of		
: *see also* Ansgot, Asgot, Osgot		
Asgeirr	YKS	25W29-30 *note*. CW2
Asgeirr: *see also* Ansgar, Asger		
Asgot	CAM	38,5
Asgot, Earl Harold's man	BKM	4,15
Asgot: *see also* Asgautr, Osgot		
Ashred	KEN	5,194
Ashred: *see also* Aescred		
Asi	YKS	5W15
Askell	BDF	18,5. 55,1-2
	BRK	7,2;10;17;38. 19,1. 65,12
	DOR	26,32. 56,66
	ESS	53,2
	GLS	39,5
	HAM	24,1
	HUN	17,1. 19,16
	KEN	5,20;31;39;92
	LEC	42,7
	NFK	65,13

	NTH	22,1-9
	NTT	30,32;41-42
	SHR	4,23,12-14
	SFK	7,109;143. 19,15. 25,53. 30,3. 68,4. 76,14
	SRY	5,1c. 8,29. 26,1
	WAR	17,5
	WIL	25,14
Askell, a Guard	SFK	67,10
Askell, a royal thane	HRT	31,1
Askell, a villager	SFK	68,2
Askell of Beckenham	KEN	D25
Askell of Ware	HRT	4,14;16. 22,2. 25,2. 26,1. 36,11. 37,1
Askell (of Ware)	BDF	17,4. 23,2;13;24;27;42;44;52. 55,9-10
Askell (of Ware), a royal thane	BDF	23,1;3;5-6;11-12;22;33
	HRT	31,1
Askell, the Bishop of Hereford's man	HEF	28,1
Askell the priest	HAM	S2
	SFK	4,14
Askell, Ulf's man	SFK	7,37
Askell: *see also* Ansketel, Asketill		
Asketill	LIN	3,22. 4,11;13-14;53;57;59;72-73. 8,15; 17;23;27-28. 12,7. 26,22-23;49. 28,2. 29,29. 38,14. 51,4. 67,8. 68,31. CS,28.
	YKS	1N136. 6N34;100;152-154. 11N5;14; 16-19;21-22
Asketill, a cook	LIN	22,26
Asketill, a royal thane	LIN	CK,11
Asketill Barn	LIN	12,8
Asketill, brother of Alnoth, Fenkell and Sighvatr/Godwine	LIN	CS,38. CN,30
Asketill, brother of Brandr the monk	LIN	CW,16
Asketill, Gilbert Tison's man	LIN	23,1
Asketill, Jocelyn son of Lambert's man	LIN	28,7
Asketill, Kolsveinn's man	LIN	26,11;30
Asketill, Roger of Poitou's man	LIN	16,43;45
Asketill, the Abbot of Peterborough's man	LIN	8,8
Asketill the priest	LIN	57,34
Asketill: *see also* Ansketel, Askell		
Asketill's father	LIN	CS,28
Aski	CHS	R1,11
	SHR	4,14,27
	WAR	27,4
Aski the priest, the Abbot of Holme's man	NFK	65,13
Aslac	NFK	12,16;19-20. 66,81
	SFK	31,28
Aslac, a thane	NTT	9,69
Aslac: *see also* Aslakr		
Aslakr	LIN	3,35. 8,39. 18,15. 26,47. 28,5;7-8. 57,1
Aslakr: *see also* Aslac		
Aslen	STS	11,18
Asli	LIN	7,36
Asmoth	SFK	6,91
Asmoth: *see also* Brictmer son of		
Asmoth, Toli the sheriff's man	SFK	4,15
Asmundr	YKS	9W23
Asmundr: *see also* Gamall son of		
Asrothr: *see* Ansered, Aseret		

Asulfr	LIN	32,33. 49,1
	YKS	5E55. 6N133-134. 9W52;75;94. 10W15;24;26;28;38. 13W8
Asulfr: *see also* Aescwulf, Aswulf		
Aswulf [erroneous, for Escul = Skuli]	NTT	10,23;52. 30,28
Aswulf: *see also* Aescwulf, Asulfr		
Athelstan	NFK	4,35
	NTT	9,120. 18,6
	SOM	21,76
Athelstan, Alnoth the Kentishman's man	BKM	17,25
Athelstan: *see also* Aethelstan		
Atilic	WOR	26,12
Atilic: *see also* Aethelric(?)		
Atsurr	LIN	S7. 4,34;40. 24,83. 26,35. 51,1;11. 52, 1. CK,3;35;63
	YKS	14E19
Atsurr: *see also* Auti son of		
Atsurr, and his brothers	LIN	7,34
Atsurr, Ivo Tallboys' man	LIN	14,95
Atsurr, Siward's brother	LIN	51,12
Atsurr son of Burg	LIN	T5
Atsurr (Azor) son of Svala (Saleva, Sualeva)	DBY	S5
	LIN	T5
	NTT	S5
Atsurr: *see also* Azor		
Aubrey	DEV	16,36-38;150. 17,68;83;93-94;99-106. 36,25
	LEC	29,15
	NTH	4,3-4
	SSX	11,50
Aubrey : *see also* Humphrey son of		
: *see also* Walter son of		
Aubrey, a man-at-arms	WIL	12,2
Aubrey, a thane	DEV	*17,94*
Aubrey de Vere	CAM	29. 1,16. 26,9. AppxB
	ESS	35. 21,3;8. 90,36-37. B3t. EHu
	HUN	22. 6,18. D7
	MDX	21
	SFK	35. 1,105. 6,216;227. 68,5. 76,21. EE5
Aubrey de Vere's wife	ESS	90,38
Aubrey (de Vere)'s wife	ESS	18,21;24
Earl Aubrey/Aubrey of Coucy	BRK	3,1
	BKM	B12. 1,7
	DOR	E2
	LEC	10
	NTH	21
	OXF	18. B6. 7,36
	WAR	14. B2. 6,9
	WIL	23. 67,61
	YKS	27. SW,Sf13;15
Aubrey the (Queen's) chamberlain	BRK	65,16
	HAM	68,9
	WIL	68,27-28
Aubrey: *see also* Alberic		
Augi	BDF	17,5-6
Augi, Askell's man	BDF	17,4
Augustine	STS	11,24
	SSX	11,108
Augustine: *see also* Austin		

Countess of Aumâle	ESS	54
	SFK	46
Austin	SHR	4,3,44. 4,21,12. 4,28,1
another Austin	SHR	4,3,44
Austin: *see also* Augustine		
Authari: *see* Otheri		
Authbjorn	LIN	4,61
	YKS	29E3
Authgrimr	LIN	4,72
Authgrimr: *see also* Oudgrim		
Authhildr (fem.)	YKS	6N26
Authulfr	YKS	C10. 1N84. 1E48. 6N100
Authulfr: *see also* Othulf		
Authunn	LIN	12,29. 16,12. CK,17
Authvithr	YKS	6N121. 29E16
Auti	CHS	8,11
	DBY	17,11
	GLS	19,2. 53,11. 67,7
	HAM	23,59. 69,7
	LEC	43,9-11
	LIN	C14. 2,17. 7,23;26;28;58. 26,31;44; 49-50;53. 68,33. CK,54
	NFK	38,1
	SHR	4,27,12-13. 7,4
	STS	8,10. EW1
	SFK	37,7
	SSX	13,42
	WAR	12,8
Auti: *see also* Toki son of		
Auti, a thane	SHR	4,5,3
	SFK	37,6. 40,3
Auti, Earl Algar's Guard	BDF	23,20
Auti son of Atsurr	LIN	T5
Auti, the Archbishop of York's man	LIN	CK,16
Avelin	BKM	4,3;21
Avelin, a royal thane	BKM	4,2;4;23
Avenel	SHR	4,27,8
(Avenel), Earl William's cook	GLS	1,6 *and note*
Azelin	BRK	7,27
	DBY	9,2;4
	DOR	1,*18;20*. 40,5. 54,6. 56,19
	GLS	3,5. E14. WoB18
	LIN	13,20
	NFK	9,219
	NTH	6a,22-23
	SHR	7,4
	SOM	5,9-11;21-22;36;49-50;58-60;70. 8, 24-25. 22,28. 45,15
	SSX	10,1;31;66
	WIL	24,27;36. 37,3;6
Azelin, Earl Tosti's man	BDF	53,32-33
Azelin, Gilbert of Ghent's man	LIN	24,86
Azelin of Tetbury	GLS	EvK1
Azelin: *see also* Ascelin		
Azelina, wife of Ralph Tallboys	BDF	55
	BKM	54
	CAM	42
Azo	DOR	55,7
	ESS	32,36
	NTH	6a,25

Azor	BRK	1,28
	BKM	4,24. 12,25-26. 23,13. 41,5. E5
	CAM	AppxN
	DOR	49,14. 56,48;58. E2
	GLS	1,61. E21. WoB5
	HAM	23,28;45;48. IoW8,1;4
	HEF	9,6
	KEN	D17. 5,19;123
	LEC	40,29
	MDX	11,2-4
	NTH	4,20;22. 21,1. 28,1. 48,1-2
	NTT	10,47;61. 25,1. 30,38
	OXF	18,1. 35,17. 52,1. 58,36
	SHR	4,3,7;14-15;47;64. 4,11,1;3;8-9. 4,21, 1. 4,26,5. 6,32
	SOM	45,9
	SFK	67,20-21;33
	SRY	8,30. 19,6;15-16;36;44. 27,1-2
	SSX	9,87;97. 10,34;43;62;107. 11,11;34; 56-57;60-61;88;92;94;99. 12,12;18; 22-23;35;37-39;48;53. 13,5;13;23-28; 45
	WAR	16,6;55. 39,1;4
	WIL	M17. 4,4. 5,3 23,8-10. 24,22;34;42. 67,28;33
	WOR	2,25;59;75. 8,27. 9,1b

Azor: *see also* Henry son of		
: *see also* Jocelyn son of		
: *see also* Swein son of		
: *see also* Ulf son of		
: *see also* William son of		
Azor, a royal Guard	MDX	11,1
Azor, a thane	SHR	4,1,35
Azor, Asgar the constable's man	MDX	9,5
Azor, Burgred's man	BDF	2,4
Azor King Edward's bursar	BRK	41,6
Azor, Leofsi's son	NTH	18,67
Azor of Lessness	KEN	D25
Azor Roote	KEN	9,19
Azor (Atsurr) son of Saleva (Sualeva, Svala)	DBY	S5
	LIN	T5
	NTT	S5
Azor son of Thored, a royal thane	BKM	1,7
Azor son of Thorold [rectius Thorodd]	SOM	*6,2*
Azor son of Toti, a royal thane/Guard/Queen Edith's man	BKM	B5;6;9. 4,25. 14,29. 19,6-7. 41, 1;4;6; 25. 47,1. 49,1
Azor the priest	NTT	9,53
Azor: *see also* Atsurr, Azorin		
Azor's son	NTT	30,38
Azor's wife	WOR	9,1b
Azorin	ESS	44,3
Azorin: *see also* Azor		
Baca	LIN	2,34
Bada	DBY	16,6. 17,8
Baderon: *see* William son of		
Bagot	STS	11,38
Bainard: *see* Geoffrey		
Bairn: *see* Barn		
Bald, four sons of	YKS	6N88
Bald: *see* Bresibalt		

Baldric

BDF	26,1. E4
CHS	15
DBY	6,26;49
HRT	21,2
LEC	15,15
NTT	16,9

Baldric: see also Hugh son of

Baldric, a man-at-arms	KEN	5,128
Baldric, Earl Hugh's man	LIN	13,22;31;39
Baldric, Jocelyn son of Lambert's man	LIN	28,16;33
Baldric, the Bishop of Bayeux's man	LIN	4,76
Baldwin	BRK	22,6-8. 33,1-2. 46,2
	BKM	12,31. 17,15;24;30
	DEV	1,*4;8-12;15-18;29;33-34;45-48;54-55.*
		2,23. 25,25-26. 39,10
	GLS	77. G2. 1,51. 47,1. 62,4-5. EvQ29
	HRT	4,10. 37,23
	KEN	M23
	LEC	13,28
	LIN	40,17. CK,27
	NFK	1,61. 10,28
	NTH	B31. 10,2. 23,5-7;9;13;17;19. 45,6
	OXF	EN9;11
	STS	12,15-16
	SRY	21,4-5
	SSX	3,5
	WAR	16,58. 18,2-3;7-8;10;13-14;16.
		EG14-15
	WIL	24,38
	WOR	1,1d. 2,71. 23,3-4

Baldwin: see also Edwin brother of

Baldwin [error for Baldric]: see Hugh son of

Baldwin, Archbishop Stigand's man	BKM	17,3-4
Baldwin Cook/Baldwin with the beard	CAM	AppxE
Baldwin, Drogo of Beuvrière's man	YKS	14E;48
Baldwin (Drogo of Beuvrière's man)	YKS	14E9;16;28
Abbot Baldwin/of Bury St Edmunds	BDF	6. 53,35
	CAM	6
	ESS	11. B3a
	GLS	19,2
	NFK	1,63;130;144;172;220-221;225-226;
		239. 9,28. 10,93. 21,30. 29,8. 31,14.
		32,7. 35,18. 43,2. 66,7;40-43;46;59
	NTH	8. B3. 18,31
	OXF	1,3. B8
	SFK	14. 1,62;77;88;115. 2,1;3-5;15. 3,2;46.
		4,10. 6,57;62;209-211;214-215;209;
		299-302. 7,1-2. 8,32;35;45-47;55. 9,2.
		10,1. 11,4. 12,1-2;4;6. 15,3;4. 16,1;16;
		33. 18,4. 19,12. 20,1. 21,2;4;9;40,41.
		25,17;19;22;25;27;33-34;40;103;
		78-102;111-112. 26,2. 27,1;3;5;7. 28,
		1b;4. 29,12-13. 30,1. 31,2;40. 33,1-3;
		12-13. 34,1;14. 35,6-7. 37,6. 38,2. 40,
		1-2;5. 41,10. 43,3;9. 46,1. 49,1. 53,1;
		6-7. 54,2-3. 59,2. 61,2. 62,5. 66,1;6;9;
		11;13. 73,1. 75,1 *note*; 2. 76,1;4-5;
		9-11;12 *note*; 19;21

Abbot Baldwin: see also Durand the cleric

: see also Frodo brother of

Baldwin of Exeter: *see* Baldwin the sheriff

Baldwin, Rainer of Brimeux's man	LIN	40,6
Baldwin son of Herlwin	BKM	4,31
	GLS	1,22
Baldwin the Fleming	LIN	65
Baldwin, the king's servant	HRT	42,8
Baldwin the reeve	NFK	10,71
Baldwin the sheriff/of Exeter	CON	Exon fo. 72 [omitted]
	DEV	16. C2. 1,5;30;*36-38;40. 2,24*. 52,33
	DOR	42
	SOM	20
Baldwin (the sheriff/of Exeter)	SOM	5,48
Baldwin the sheriff's daughter	DEV	*16,44*
Baldwin (the sheriff's) wife	DEV	16,94;128

Baldwin (the sheriff's) wife: *see also* Emma

Balki (the Dane)	GLS	78,11
	SFK	16,7;26

Banna: *see* Alfwy/Alwin son of

Bardi	LEC	3,11
	NTH	5,1-4
	RUT	EN7-8

Bardi: *see also* Barthi

Barkr	YKS	1E27. 23N26
Barn [erroneous, for Barne]	LIN	7,52
Barn	SFK	3,61
	YKS	CE2

Barn, Gamall: *see* Gamalbarn

Barn: *see also* Bairn

Barne [= Barni or Bjarni, erroneously indexed Barn]	LIN	7,52

Barni: *see* Barne

Barthi	LIN	T5. 7,38-39;43;48

Barthi: *see also* Bardi

Barthr	LIN	34,24
	YKS	1Y12. 1E9. 9W20;38;48;50-51;58-62; 119. 25W22. 29W25
Basing	YKS	1E2. 3Y7. 5E1. 11E2;5. 14E48;52. 29W27. CE1;12;17
Baswin, Robert of Stafford's man	LIN	59,9;11
Batsveinn	SHR	4,19,5
Baynard	MDX	4,2
	NFK	13,10. 31,6-7;11;14;34;39;44. 66, 35-108
	SFK	7,15. 76,20
	SRY	2,4. 5,17
	SSX	2,1b
Bear	DEV	51,9
Beard	ESS	B3a
Beatrix (fem.)	DEV	34,43
Beatrix, sister of Ralph of Pomeroy	SOM	*30,1*
Beatrix, sister of William (Cheever)	DEV	*19,40;46*

Bell: *see* Aethelward son of

Belling	SSX	12,28. 13,6
Belward of Caerwent	GLS	W7
Benedict	SHR	4,3,28
	STS	8,7
Abbot Benedict/of Selby	LEC	23,2-4
	LIN	63,15
	NTH	B8. 41,3. ELe2
	YKS	2B1

	YKS	8. C15. 7E1-2. 30W3. SW,Bu27;33. SN, L6. SN,D7;10;13;16;20-21. SN,Ma1;6;9-13;15;20. SN,B1-2;5-6;8. SE,Sc4-6;10. SE,Ac1-3. SE,Th2;8-9
Berengar, the Abbot of St Edmunds' man	SFK	76,19
Berenger	NFK	14,16;37
Berewold	LIN	24,32-33
Berewold, Norman of Arcy's man	LIN	32,3
Bergthorr	LIN	14,60;92. 25,8. CS,15
Bergulfr	YKS	9W12
Bernard	BDF	18,6. 23,45. 24,21. 55,10
	BKM	12,17. 17,8
	DEV	16,25;39;126-127. 36,8;17
	DOR	24,5
	ESS	20,18;28;33;70. 28,9. 33,9;17;23. 90, 54
	GLS	1,24;45. 3,7. 67,4. 68,9 *note*; 11. WoB19
	HAM	NF4,1
	HEF	1,24-25;31. 14,4-5. 22,2-4;6-7
	LIN	56,1
	NFK	10,90
	SHR	4,20,26. 4,21,10
	SOM	28,2
	SFK	7,102. 41,5-6
	SSX	10,1
	WIL	32,8;10
Bernard, Alfred of Lincoln's man	LIN	27,3;5;61
Bernard Beard	HEF	1,10b
Bernard Nap(e)less(?)	DEV	*16,125*
Bernard of Alencon	SFK	67,15;29
Bernard of Hill Row	CAM	AppxP
Bernard of London	SFK	6,110
Bernard of St Ouen/a man-at-arms	KEN	5,128
	SFK	47,2
	HAM	39. NF9,10. S2
	SOM	*36,7;13*
	WIL	46
Bernard (Pancevolt)	DOR	33,1;3
Bernard, Roger of Bully's man	NTT	9,57
Bernard the chamberlain	HAM	NF9,13
Bernard the falconer	BRK	60
Bernard the priest	CON	5,24,18
	GLS	1,18
	HUN	D1
Berner	BRK	7,11;14;21
	BKM	14,25. 43,7
	CON	5,8. 4,6;26
	GLS	G4
	HEF	10,22-23
	NFK	15,18
	NTH	54,3
	SHR	4,8,12;15. 4,14,22-23
Berner: *see also* Theobald son of		
Berner, nephew of Robert of Peronne	BRK	65,19
Berner the crossbowman	NFK	51. 1,3. *15,18*
	SFK	21,11
Bernhold	KEN	5,216
Bernwulf	CHS	1,27. 14,8. R1,4
	STS	8,6. 13,1

Bernwulf: *see also* Beornwulf, Bjornulfr

Berold	DOR	55,30
	NFK	29,2
Bersi	CHS	5,6
Bertram	KEN	9,11
	SOM	21,43;70
Bertram of Verdun	BKM	38
Bertunt	SHR	4,23,15

Bertunt: *see also* Beorhthun

Besi	OXF	35,19
	RUT	R13. ELc15
	SFK	6,216. 35,7
Best	ESS	B3a
Bettica, Wulfwin of Eastwick's man	HRT	34,23
Bicca, a thane	DEV	*23,23*
Bicga	SRY	5,22
Bigot of Loges	SFK	4,13
Bigot (of Loges)	CHS	14. 27,1 *note*
Bil	GLS	68,6
Bishop	NTH	2,12. 18,33;83. 35,16. 56,33;66. 58,2
Bisi	BKM	17,21
Bisi, a royal thane	BKM	23,32. 26,8
Bjarni	YKS	1W53

Bjarni: *see also* Barne

Bjornulfr	YKS	C10 *and note.* C18. 6N53;83-84;93; 120;129. 13W20-21;25;44. 13E2-3; 11-12. 13N17;19. CE15

Bjornulfr: *see also* Beornwulf, Bernwulf

Bjorr	YKS	13W35

Bjorr: *see also* Ber

Black	SSX	9,4
Black, Augi's man	BDF	17,6
Black, the Abbot of St Albans' man	HRT	10,17

Black: *see also* Blaec, Blakkr

Black-: *see* Blaec-

Blackman	BRK	7,34-35
	BKM	E4
	GLS	69,1
	HAM	65,1. IoW7,23. 8,7
	KEN	9,12
	OXF	49,1
	SFK	6,94;112. 7,76;99;111;120-121. 16,26. 67,11
	WIL	27,4
Blackman, Earl Tosti's man	BKM	6,1-2
Blackman, Edric's man	SFK	6,93
Blackman, Edric of Laxfield's man	SFK	7,36
Blackman the priest	OXF	9,3
Blackman, wife of	SFK	6,93

Blackman: *see also* Blaecmann

Blackson	SFK	6,32. 7,60;146. 16,35

Blackson: *see also* Blaecsunu

Blackstan	ESS	B3a(x3)

Blackstan: *see also* Blaecstan

Blackwin	SFK	7,60. 25,79. 34,4
Blackwin the sheriff/King Edward's man	CAM	3,2 *note.* 32,34-35;38-39;43

Blackwin: *see also* Blaecwine

Blaec	YKS	13N8 *and note*

Blaec-: *see* Black-

Blaecmaer	SHR	6,20

Blaecmann: *see* Blackman
Blaecstan: *see* Blackstan
Blaecsunu: *see* Blackson
Blaecwine: *see* Blackwin
Blakkr   YKS   13N8 *and note.* 13N10;12-14
Blanc   ESS   B3a
Blancard, Roger of Poitou's man   LIN   16,28;35;44
Bleddyn   HEF   1,49
Bleio, a reeve   GLS   W2
Bletcu   CON   1,1
Blewitt: *see* Ralph
Blize   KEN   3,10
Bloc: *see* Walter son of
Blohin the Breton   CON   *5,25*
Bloiet: *see* Ralph
Boda   HAM   23,43;56. 45,6
                                                    WIL   37,14. 68,33

Boda: *see also* Bodda, Budda
Bodda: *see* Boda, Budda
Bodin   NFK   1,57. 25,25
                                                    STS   11,59
                                                    YKS   6N7;11;18;38-40;44-47;49-51;67;73;
                                                               75-76;78;80;91;122;135
Bodin de Vere   NFK   25,15
Boding the constable   BKM   27,1-2
Boding the constable: *see also* Bondi the
  constable
Bofa   SOM   6,9
Bofa: *see also* Bofi, Bovi
Bofi: *see* Bovi
Boia   HRT   Appx
Boia the priest/clerk of Bodmin   CON   *1,6*
                                                    DEV   1,72 *note*
Boia: *see also* Alwin Boy
Boli   LIN   14,93
Boli: *see also* Bolla, Bolle, Bolli
Bolla   HAM   1,W20. 28,1. 69,32. NF9,8;14;33.
                                                               IoW6,6;13;20. 9,24
                                                    WIL   37,9-10;12. 68,18

Bolla, Alfsi: *see* Alfsi Bowl
Bolla: *see also* Boli, Bolle, Bolli
Bolle   DOR   55,37. 56,8
                                                    GLS   11,14. 51,1
Bolle, a thane   SOM   *19,29*
Bolle the priest   DOR   *13,5;8.* 24,2-3. 56,7
Bolle: *see also* Boli, Bolla, Bolli
Bolle's wife   SOM   47,1
Bolli: *see* Boli, Bolla
Bondi   BRK   21,3;7;20
                                                    CAM   26,17
                                                    DOR   51,1. 57,15
                                                    ESS   29,3-5. 39,8
                                                    GLS   31,2
                                                    HAM   44,2-4. 57,2. 62,1. IoW9,15
                                                    KEN   5,38
                                                    LIN   3,47
                                                    NFK   1,83. 9,111;147. 20,4. 21,22. 23,1-5;
                                                               7-8;10-13;17-18. 36,1;6. 58,2
                                                    NTH   25,2-3. 36,2. 40,5. 48,16. 56,15-18;38
                                                    OXF   24,3-5

	SOM	19,56
	SFK	6,253. 7,29;121. 19,16. *21,94*. 25,56; 103. 67,12. 69,2. 76,1
	SFK	*21,94*
	WAR	16,31. 44,3
	WIL	44,1
	YKS	C19. 14E26. 26E8 *and note*. CE32
Bondi: *see also* Aelfric son of		
Bondi, a thane	NFK	34,18
Bondi, Alric's brother	ESS	30,20
Bondi, Bishop Erfast's man	NFK	10,53
Bondi the constable	BDF	57,4
	BKM	12,29. 17,9
Bondi the constable: *see also* Boding the constable		
Bondi the forester	OXF	1,6
Bondi the smith, Ulf's man	SFK	7,37
Bondi: *see also* L. Bondi		
Bonnard: *see* William son of		
Borda	ESS	32,34-35
Borda: *see also* Brorda		
Bordin	NFK	13,6;19. 66,12;20-21;23
Bosa: *see* Bose, Bosi		
Bose: *see* Leofric son of		
: *see also* Bosa, Bosi		
Boselin	SSX	10,1
	WOR	8,26c
Boselin: *see also* William son of		
Boselin of Dive's wife	CAM	43
Boselin's son	SSX	2,1c
Boselin's son: *see also* William		
Bosi	BRK	33,8
	LIN	56,18
Bosi: *see also* Bosa, Bose, Boso		
Bosker	WAR	16,53
Boso	ESS	90,22
Boso: *see also* Osbern son of		
Boso, Alfred of Lincoln's man	LIN	27,37
Boso: *see also* Bosi		
Bosten	SFK	26,8
Boteric	NFK	21,19;22;28
Bothild (fem.)	NTT	6,7
Bothild (fem.): *see also* Bothildr, Botild		
Bothildr (fem.)	LIN	48,14
Bothildr (fem.): *see also* Bothild, Botild		
Boti	SFK	2,11. 35,7. 38,20
Boti, King Edward's man	SFK	7,33
Botic	SSX	9,57
Botild (fem.)	SFK	76,14
Botild (fem.): *see also* Bothild, Bothildr		
Botolph	SOM	36,2
Botolph: *see also* Botwulf		
Botwulf: *see* Botolph		
Countess of Boulogne: *see* Ida		
Bovi	LEC	44,6
	NFK	49,1-2
	NTH	1,27. 18,27
	NTT	10,17
	WAR	16,16;56
Bovi: *see also* Bofa, Bofi		

Boy: *see* Boia
Brand, a royal Guard   HRT   27,1
Brand: *see also* Brandr, Brant
Brandr   LIN   S3
Brandr the monk (Abbot of Peterborough),   LIN   CW,16
   brother of Asketill
Brandr: *see also* Brand, Brant
Brandulfr   YKS   CE47
Brandwin: *see* Branwin
Brant   NFK   35,12
Brant: *see also* Brand, Brandr
Branting   BDF   23,55
Branting, King Edward's man   BDF   57,3iv
Branwin   DBY   12,4
Branwin: *see also* Brandwin
Breme   SFK   31,50
Bresibalt   KEN   9,3
Bresibalt: *see also* Bald, Beorhtsige, Brictsi
Bretel   CON   5,13,10
    DOR   26,17;29;54-55;60;63;69. E1
    SOM   1,5;9. 19,20-22;45;58;62-64. 46,4
Bretel, a man-at-arms   SOM   19,86
Bretel of St Clair   SOM   *19,15*
Bretel (of St Clair)   DEV   15,20;63
    DOR   26,12;28
Brian   CON   5,9. *4,22*
    GLS   EvN5
    MDX   3,3
    OXF   22,2
    WAR   22,16
Brian: *see also* Evrard son of
   : *see also* Ralph son of
   : *see also* William son of
Count Brian   SFK   2,1-9;13 *note*
Brian of Scales   CAM   *14,15*. AppxF
Brian, Robert of Stafford's man   LIN   59,14-15
Brian: *see also* Bryant
Brict   SFK   39,5
Brict: *see also* Beorht
Brict-: *see also* Beorht-
Brictere   SFK   77,1;3
Brictere: *see also* Beorhthere
Bricteva (fem.)   DEV   52,8
    ESS   1,19. 24,9
    HUN   26,1
    OXF   6,1b;17
    SOM   35,4
Bricteva (fem.): *see also* Beorhtgifu
Brictferth   CON   5,4,11
    DOR   57,1
Brictferth, uncle of Saewin the priest   DEV   *13a,2*
Brictferth: *see also* Beorhtfrith
Brictfled (fem.)   SFK   6,62
Brictfled (fem.): *see also* Beorhtflaed
Brictgeat of Barton   CAM   AppxK
Brictgeat: *see also* Beorhtgeat
Brictheah   BRK   35,1-3. 41,3. 44,2
Bishop Brictheah (of Worcester)   GLS   E20. WoB5
Bishop Brictheah/Beorhtheah (of Worcester)   WOR   2,24
Brictheah: *see also* Beorhtheah

Bishop Brictheah: *see also* Bishop Brictric
Brictith (fem.)   DEV   36,15
Brictith (fem.): *see also* Beorhtgyth
Brictman   SFK   8,6
Brictmer   CHS   2,14
                                               CON   4,1. 5,1,8;13. 5,2,1;11;16;19;21;33. 5,
                                                      4,2;4;12. 5,5,17;20. 5,6,2. 5,7,4. 5,14,
                                                      3-4. 5,24,25
                                               DEV   3,80. 16,4;12;19;31;33;58;65;69;71;83;
                                                      85;96;104;110;116;140;161;175. 19,
                                                      37. 21,19-21. 28,15. 34,41. 40,4. 49,
                                                      1-3. 52,33
                                               DOR   34,7
                                               ESS   20,14;47;49. 32,4. 34,5;7;27. 77,1. 90,
                                                      52
                                               GLS   34,4. 45,1. 68,4
                                               HAM   23,60. 68,5
                                               HEF   1,10b. 9,12. 10,30-31. 16,2
                                               LEC   44,3
                                               SOM   5,58. 19,22. 21,40;45;63. 25,28;32. *35,
                                                      4*
                                               SFK   3,65;101. 6,11;173;201;209;215;271.
                                                      7,98;115;121;133;140;145. 8,65. 21,
                                                      39. 22,2. 32,8. 35,7. 38,16. 39,5;7-9.
                                                      39,2-4;10. 43,6. 61,2. 67,15;27;31. 74,
                                                      13
                                               SSX   12,12. 13,23;45
                                               WAR   16,63
                                               WIL   13,6. 42,5-6. 67,15-16
                                               WOR   2,10. 8,10a-10b;24
Brictmer: *see also* Alwin son of
         : *see also* Queneva mother of
Brictmer, a royal thane   ESS   20,1
                                               WOR   20,6
Brictmer Balehorn   HUN   D5
Brictmer Bubba   SFK   6,226
Brictmer, Earl Harold's man   MDX   11,3
Brictmer son of Asmoth, Brictmer's man   SFK   4,15
Brictmer the beadle   SFK   74,4
Brictmer the Englishman   SOM   *47,17*
Brictmer the priest   CON   *5,25,5*
                                               SOM   *24,16*
Brictmer, the reeve of Robert Malet   SFK   4,15
Brictmer: *see also* Beorhtmaer
Brictnoth   CON   5,3,25
                                               DOR   26,7. 47,2. 54,10
                                               SOM   5,22. 19,38;75. 22,27
                                               SFK   2,20. 6,46;264. 7,80;120. 8,2;*6*. 19,17.
                                                      32,29
                                               WAR   3,4. 16,19;62
                                               WIL   67,38-39
Brictnoth, Earl Edwin's thane   SOM   1,1
Brictnoth: *see also* Beorhtnoth
Brictred   OXF   B10
Brictred, Earl Edwin's thane   WOR   1,1c
Brictred: *see also* Beorhtred
Brictric   BDF   19,3. 32,2
                                               BRK   B6. 35,5. 40,1. 55,1-4. 57,1. 65,10

BKM	4,24. 12,9. 17,8;11-12;14. 19,2. 23,6; 11;13;17-18;21-23;25-28. 26,7. 36,3. 43,4
CHS	9,18
CON	5,23. 1,1. 5,2,31. 5,5,10;14-15;18
DEV	*1,40.* 3,28-29;31;34;51. 16,5-6;9;13; 112;128;162. 17,6;8;55. 19,27;*34.* 20, 1. 23,20. 25,25;27. 28,14. 35,23. 36, 16. 40,*1;3.* 42,1;5-6;16-17;20. 50,1. 51, 8. 52,24;53
DOR	26,23;58. 54,9. 56,51. 57,9
ESS	90,50;58. B3a(x2)
GLS	1,64. 19,2. 36,2. 39,10. 67,3. 78,9; 14-15. E4;8;31-32
HAM	2,5. 38,1. 55,1
HEF	1,74. 17,1-2
HRT	19,1
NFK	19,24. 35,4
OXF	35,12;14
SHR	3e,2. 4,7,5
SOM	5,12-13. 8,2;37. 15,1. 21,1;47;53;69. 25,7;42. 45,2;*5.* 46,6. 47,1;9;22
SFK	7,80;87;95;106;108;117;137. 8,1;6. *16, 31.* 25,105. 32,8. 39,5. 41,9. 67,12(x2)
SRY	5,6
SSX	12,13
WAR	17,16. 22,17. 33,1. 37,8
WIL	7,5. 17,1. 24,5. 25,7;13. 48,4. 67,2-10
WOR	8,7;9b;9c

Brictric: *see also* Aelfric son of		
: *see also* Alfwy brother of		
: *see also* Godiva wife of		
: *see also* Wulfric son of		
Brictric, a royal thane	BDF	19,1
	BKM	19,4. 23,29. 35,1
	GLS	39,6
Brictric, a thane	HAM	1,W1
Bishop Brictric [erroneous for Bishop Beorhtheah, Brictheah]	HEF	1,45
Brictric Black	SFK	25,79. 67,1
Bishop Brictric, brother of Aethelric	HEF	1,45
Brictric, father of Aelfric	SOM	*47,21*
Brictric, Godiva's man	DEV	*52,52*
Brictric, Godman's man	SFK	2,17
Brictric, Queen Edith's man	BKM	23,14;20. 26,3
	HRT	15,5
Brictric, Queen Edith's thane	WOR	19,5
Brictric son of Algar	GLS	1,39-50. 6,1. 31,5. 69,7
	WOR	2,30;37
Brictric (son of Algar)	CON	1,13-19
	DEV	1,57-72. 12,1. 13,1. 24,18-19;21;24. 25,20. 27,1. 40,5-6
	DOR	1,15-17. 10,2. 21,1. 25,1. 41,1. 54,8
	GLS	E1
	HEF	1,42-44
	WOR	EH;EH1
Brictric son of Camm	DEV	*3,32. 19,12*
Brictric son of Doda	WOR	2,63
Brictric, the reeve of St Edmunds	SFK	62,5
Brictric: *see also* Beorhtric, Bishop Beorhtheah		

Brictric's brother	WIL	67,5;10
Brictric's father	WIL	67,6-9
Brictric's widow	BKM	12,14
Brictsi	CON	1,1. 5,7,7-8;10
	DEV	3,47
	ESS	24,65
	GLS	32,4. E3
	HAM	NF9,20
	HEF	1,73
	KEN	5,18;29
	NTT	9,53
	SOM	24,27. 27,1. 46,16
	SFK	71,1
	SRY	5,10. 22,1;5
	SSX	10,11. 11,67. 13,49
	WIL	25,1
Brictsi: *see also* Alfsi son of		
Brictsi, a man-at-arms of King Edward	DOR	49,12
Brictsi, a thane	SOM	*27,1*
Brictsi Child: *see* Young Brictsi		
Young Brictsi [= Brictsi Child]	KEN	D25. 5,8;21;26
	SRY	19,32
Brictsi: *see also* Beorhtsige, (?)Bresibalt		
Brictstan	CAM	*44,2.* AppxM
	SSX	10,80
Brictstan: *see also* Beorhtstan		
Brictward	BRK	1,45. 17,1;5;7. 25,1. 49,3
	SOM	19,32. 45,15. 47,23
	WIL	3,2
Brictward, a thane	SOM	*19,32*
Brictward the priest	DOR	24,1
	SOM	*47,23*
	WIL	*1,23j*
Brictward the priest's father	WIL	1,23j
Brictward: *see also* Beorhtweard		
Brictwin	BRK	7,14
	BKM	17,7
	CAM	*5,11. 17,2*
	DEV	25,10
	DOR	3,10. *11,1;*7. 26,11. 33,6. 37,10
	ESS	20,43. B3a
	HAM	IoW6,18
	NTH	36,3
	SOM	9,6. 19,36;79. 21,65. 25,35
	STS	EN3
	SSX	9,54. 10,72;74. 13,27
	WAR	3,4. 17,68
	WOR	2,28
Brictwin, a royal thane	BKM	12,24
Brictwin, a thane	DOR	*11,1*
	SOM	*21,65*
Brictwin, Earl Harold's man	BKM	12,37
Brictwin the reeve	DOR	*56,9-11;17;35-38*
Brictwin (the reeve)	DOR	56,39-41
Brictwin: *see also* Beorhtwine		
Brictwold	CON	5,3,4
	DEV	3,53;58-59. 17,43. 19,31. 20,3-5. 28,4; 11. 38,1. 48,9
	DOR	37,5
	SHR	4,17,3

	SOM	22,7. 47,23
	SFK	6,10;271. *8,23.* 16,16;36. 52,1;3-5;9. 67,3. 74,5
Brictwold, a thane	DEV	*38,1*
Brictwold Muffle	SFK	32,28
Brictwold son of Leofmer	SFK	*14,5-6;21;28;65;106*
Brictwold the priest	HEF	8,9
	WOR	2,60
Brictwold: *see also* Beorhtweald		
Brictwulf	ESS	20,75-76. 90,63
	NFK	*14,35*
Brictwulf: *see also* Beorhtwulf		
Brictwy	DOR	33,4
	SOM	19,69
	SSX	10,51
	WIL	41,3
Brictwy son of Camm	DEV	*17,13*
Brictwy: *see also* Beorhtwig		
Brisard, Earl Hugh's man	LIN	13,30
Broddi: *see* Brode, Brodo		
Brode	NFK	8,55
Brode: *see also* Broddi, Brodo		
Broder	CON	5,5,5
	DEV	17,20
	STS	11,18;44-45
Broder: *see also* Brother		
Brodo	BDF	55,5
	NFK	66,67
Brodo: *see also* Broddi, Brode		
Broklauss	LIN	4,39. 12,86
Brorda: *see* Borda		
Brother	SFK	1,53. 3,89
Brother: *see also* Broder, Brothor		
Brothor, Brothir: *see also* Broder, Brother		
Brown	CHS	1,30. 9,28. 13,5. 14,5;7
	DBY	1,30. 6,24;62. B7
	DOR	26,1
	ESS	24,66. 34,24
	HEF	14,4
	NTT	10,28;31. 30,55
	SOM	45,3
	SFK	1,119. 8,8. 16,43. 67,10
	WAR	31,9
Brown: *see also* Aelfric son of		
: *see also* Leofwin son of		
Brown, a thane	DBY	13,2
Brown, Roger Bigot's reeve	NFK	1,2
Brown the priest	OXF	14,4
Brown, the reeve of Ipswich	SFK	7,63-66
Brown: *see also* Brun, Brunn		
Brown's son [erroneous, for Brunsunu]	KEN	5,10
Browning	HAM	IoW6,2. 9,17
	HEF	1,15;25. 8,1. 10,26
	HRT	5,4
	KEN	5,9
	SHR	4,17,1-2
	SOM	21,37. *46,4*
	WAR	17,12;55. 44,16
	WIL	29,9
Browning, a thane	SOM	*46,4*

Browning: *see also* Bruning		
Browning's brother	HAM	IoW6,2
Brumage	NTH	18,18
Bruman	BRK	B7
	BKM	12,23
	CAM	1,2
	ESS	B3a
Bruman: *see also* Brunmann		
Brun: *see* Brown, Brunn		
Brunard	NFK	19,9
	SFK	9,1
Brunel, Kolsveinn's man	LIN	26,36-37
Brungar	DEV	3,78. 16,123. 20,8
	DOR	26,5
	ESS	B3a
	SFK	6,215. 7,62. 16,35. 27,7
Brungar the Englishman	SOM	*5,28*
Brunhyse	LIN	28,15
Brunier	LIN	68,33
Bruning of Chesterton	CAM	AppxO
Bruning: *see also* Browning		
Brunloc	ESS	B3a
	SFK	14,152
Brunloc: *see also* Brunlocc		
Brunlocc: *see* Brunloc		
Brunmaer: *see* Brunmer		
Brunman	SFK	7,108. 67,32
Brunman Beard, half man of Brunmer and Norman	SFK	7,36
Brunman of Burgh	SFK	6,110
Brunman the reeve	KEN	C8
Brunman: *see also* Bruman, Brunmann		
Brunmann: *see* Bruman, Brunman		
Brunmer	SFK	2,18. 7,36;109;111
Brunmer the priest	SFK	66,12
Brunmer: *see also* Brunmaer		
Brunn	YKS	1N76. 1E4. CW8
Brunn the priest	YKS	C16
Brunn the priest, mother of	YKS	C16
Brunn: *see also* Brown, Brun		
Brunsunu: *see* Brown's son		
Brunwin	ESS	B3a(x2)
	SFK	16,23. 35,4. 67,14
Brunwin, Manulf's man	SFK	4,15
Brunwin: *see also* Brunwine		
Brunwine: *see* Brunwin		
Bryant	BKM	15,2
	OXF	EBu1
	STS	11,15-16;66
Bryant: *see also* Brian		
Bucca: *see* Buck		
Buck [MS. Boche, = Bucca]	KEN	5,196
Buck: *see also* Bucca		
Budd	ESS	20,3
Budd: *see also* Budda		
Budda: *see also* Boda, Bodda, Budd		
Buga	YKS	5W12
Buga: *see* Buggi		
Bugg	NTT	6,7. 14,2. 30,8
Bugg: *see* Buggi		

Buggi: *see* Buga, Bugg		
Bui	YKS	30W6
Bului	HUN	18,1
Bului: *see also* ?Burgwig		
Burcard	SFK	*14,72*
Burcard: *see also* Burgheard		
Burde	DOR	37,9
Burg: *see* Atsurr son of		
Burghard	ESS	32,3
	NFK	1,61
	SFK	1,83-84;86;95. 4,12;24;26;28-31;33;35;
		38 -39. 6,215. 7,42-43. 16,15;26. 31,
		21-24;26-30;32-33;35-36
Burghard: *see also* Peter brother of		
Burghard, a royal Guard	BKM	13,2
Burghard, a royal thane	BKM	13,3
Burghard, a thane	NFK	6,6
Burghard of Mendlesham	SFK	14,152
Burghard (of Mendlesham)	SFK	1,76-77. 14,146
Burghard of Shenley	BKM	B4
Burghard: *see also* Burgheard		
Burgheard: *see* Burcard, Burghard		
Burghelm	HAM	6,3
	WIL	24,31-32. 29,5
Burghi: *see* Burgi		
Burgi, Asgar's man	HRT	33,12
Burgi: *see also* Burghi		
Burgnoth	KEN	5,147
Burgred	BDF	2,4. 3,1-7;9;13-15;17. 25,6. 54,4
	BKM	5,12-14;16. 12,34. 41,3
	CON	5,23,2. 5,26,1
	DEV	16,86;172. 19,30. *28,2.* 34,18;22. 51,
		13
	NTH	4,1-2;4;8-9;11-13;15;17;23-24. 35,1j.
		56,65
	STS	11,62-63
Burgred: *see also* Edwin son of		
: *see also* Ulf son of		
: *see also* Wulfsi son of		
Burgred, a royal thane	BDF	3,16
Burgred, a thane	BKM	5,17
	DEV	*28,2*
(another?) Burgred	DEV	28,2
Burgred the priest	HUN	B12. 19,9
Burgred's son	NTH	4,29
Burgric	SFK	3,100. 7,79;106. 16,43. 46,7;9. 67,10
Burgwald son of Leofwine, a lawman	LIN	C3
Burgwig: *see* ?Bului		
Burnin	SFK	4,32
Burnin: *see also* Warin son of		
Burnt Albert	SFK	8,15
Burrer	SHR	4,11,17
Burro	CAM	25,2
Buterus	LEC	29,10
Cabe	CAM	5,37
Cabe: *see also* Algar Cappe		
Cadiand	HEF	1,53
Cadio	DEV	16,16
	STS	11,9-10
Cadiou	LIN	12,47

Cadwallon	CON	4,6
Calcebuef(?)	HEF	A10 *and note*
Calebot	ESS	B3a
Camm: *see* Brictric son of		
: *see* Brictwy son of		
Cana	SRY	5,5
	SSX	9,30;48;83;85. 10,8;36;88;101;113
Canute	DBY	17,15
	NTT	30,43
	SFK	28,3-4
King Canute	CHS	2,1. B13
	ESS	3,9
	SHR	3c,2
	WIL	2,1
Canute: *see also* Knutr		
King Caradoc	GLS	W2
Carl	DBY	14,9
Carl: *see also* Karl, Karli		
Carlmann: *see* Carman		
Carman	WIL	26,17
Carman: *see also* Carlmann		
Cave the reeve	HAM	4,1
Ceolmer	WOR	20,1
Ceolred	SOM	19,23;67
	WAR	16,22
Ceolred, Thorkell's man	WAR	17,16
Ceolric	SOM	9,2;6. 21,2. 36,4. *47,4*
	SFK	*32,14*
Ceolstan	WIL	68,9
Ceolwin	GLS	E16
	WIL	45,2
Ceolwold	SFK	25,64
Charbonnel	HEF	33
Cheping [rectius Keping]	SOM	22,16. 25,47
Cheping [rectius Keping]: *see also* Chipping		
Chipping [rectius Kipping]	BRK	EH1
	CHS	1,17
	HAM	1,26;W19. 3,1. 29,1-3;5-11;13-14;16. 69,6. NF1,1. 9,15. S2. IoW1,8
	SFK	6,216
	WIL	67,41
Chipping [rectius Kipping]: *see also* Alwin son of		
Chipping [rectius Kipping], a thane	BRK	46,3
Chipping [rectius Kipping]: *see* also Cheping		
Christina	OXF	54
	WAR	42. B2
Clamahoc: *see* Eudo son of		
Clarebald	LEC	15,15
Clarebald: *see also* Clarenbold		
Clarenbold	ESS	24,44
	SFK	42,2
Clarenbold of le Marais	BKM	19,1
Clarenbold: *see also* Clarebald		
Claron	NTT	9,28;32
Clibert	YKS	2B19. 29E6;8-9;27. 30W39
Clodoen	STS	11,46;60
Cniht [mistaken for Knutr]	YKS	1W25
Cniht [erroneously rendered 'knight']	DEV	16,125-126. 25,8
Cock Hagni	NFK	9,83-84
Cola	BRK	65,10;13

	CON	5,3,5;8;18;23. 5,24,3
	DBY	6,10;45
	DEV	*3,12*. 17,35. 24,20
	ESS	20,7. 27,16. 33,22. 62,2
	GLS	54,2
	KEN	*2,11*
	LIN	26,7
	NFK	4,49
	SOM	25,54. 27,3
	SRY	19,39;47. 36,8
	SSX	9,95. 10,12;26;105. 12,30;54;56
	WIL	24,17. 34,1. 37,4. 67,42
	YKS	9W107
Cola, a thane	DEV	*3,12*
	SOM	*27,3*
Cola, Henry of Ferrers' man	DBY	6,2
Cola Hunter (son of Wulfgeat)	HAM	69,32;52
Cola, nephew of Kolsveinn	LIN	C22
Cola of Basing's son	HAM	69,13
Cola the Englishman	BRK	41,5
Cola's father	WIL	67,42
Colben	CHS	9,27. 26,12
Colbern the priest	NFK	45 *and note*
Colbert	CHS	2,21. 8,4;8;10
	DEV	15,26. 17,47;75. 36,21
	LIN	57,46
Colbert the priest	NFK	*L45 and note*
Colbran	DEV	16,77. 36,18
	DOR	28,3
	WAR	44,7
Colbran: *see also* Kolbrandr		
Coleman	NFK	9,98. 20,13. 24,7
	SFK	6,216. 7,77;80. 14,24. 35,7. 62,2
Coleman: *see also* Colman		
Colgrim	DBY	6,82;85
	HAM	NF3,7
	HEF	33,1
	NTT	22,1
	SOM	21,16
Colgrim the Englishman	SOM	*7,11*
Colgrim: *see also* Kolgrimr		
Colle	DBY	4,2. 6,76. 10,18
Colling	DBY	6,49
	SHR	4,7,5
Colman	BRK	17,1
	ESS	23,30. 90,53. B3a
	HAM	35,1
	NTT	30,18
	OXF	B10. 58,36
	SRY	19,17
Colman, Brictric's man	BKM	23,6
Colman Hunter	SRY	19,39
Colman: *see also* Coleman		
Coln	DBY	1,15. 6,72
Coln, father of Edric	DBY	B8
Colsege	ESS	23,28
Colswein	CAM	14,28;30;32-33. AppxJ
	KEN	5,193
	SOM	5,41
	WIL	26,20

Colswein: *see also* Aelmer son of
Colswein, the Bishop of Coutances' man   DEV   25,3
Colswein: *see also* Kolsveinn
Columban the monk   OXF   6,6-8
Colwin   DEV   16,13;37;41
Colwin the reeve   DEV   *42,3. 52,4*
Colwin (the reeve)   DEV   C2. 1,25. 52,1-8
Conan   OXF   6,9
Conded, Kolsveinn's man   LIN   26,27;30;38
Constantine   GLS   3,1. WoB15
Constantine: *see also* Hugh son of
            : *see also* William son of
Corbelin   NTH   56,51
                                                SRY   8,22. 36,4
                                                SSX   11,23;31

Corbet: *see* Robert son of
       : *see* Roger
       : *see* Roger son of
Corbin   KEN   5,59
                                                WAR   4,2

Corbucion: *see* Robert son of
          : *see* William son of
Corp   ESS   32,33
Costelin   HEF   1,58
Costelin's son   HEF   1,58
Crawa   SFK   25,78
Crin   YKS   6N74
Croc   WIL   10,2. 24,14. 68,14;31
Croc: *see also* Reginald son of
Croc Hunter   HAM   60
Culling   ESS   B3a
Culling, a burgess of Ipswich   SFK   1,122d
Cus   SFK   6,44. 7,37
Cuthwulf   GLS   6,8
                                                HAM   28,6. NF4,1. IoW1,4
                                                SOM   *45,7*
                                                SSX   11,14
                                                WIL   42,4;9. 67,39
Cuthwulf, a thane   SOM   *45,7*
Cwengifu (fem.): *see* Queneva
Cwenhild the nun   GLS   78,8
Cwenleofu (fem.)   LIN   42,16
Cwenthryth the nun   LIN   67,27
Cynegar   DEV   20,6
Cyneric: *see* Cynric
Cynesi   CON   5,4,7
Cynesi: *see also* Cynesige
Cynesige: *see* Cynesi, Kinsey
Cynestan   CON   5,2,25-26
                                                DEV   17,5;7

Cynewig: *see* Cynwy
Cynric   SFK   3,57. 7,99. 53,3. 77,2-3
Cynric, Edric son of Ingold's man   SFK   4,15
Cynric: *see also* Cyneric
Cyneweald: *see* Cynwold
Cynwold   SFK   67,9
Cynwold: *see also* Cyneweald
Cynwy   OXF   24,6
                                                SOM   19,77
Cynwy Chelle, a royal thane   GLS   1,58. 66,1

Cynwy: *see also* Cynewig
Cypping: *see* Cheping, Chipping

Dachelin	DOR	33,2
Daeging	SHR	4,4,17
Dagobert	GLS	W11
Danemund, Asgar the constable's man	CAM	26,28
David	CHS	9,8
	DOR	37,4
	ESS	20,48
	NTH	58
	RUT	EN21
David of Argenton	BDF	50
	CAM	39
David of Balsham	CAM	AppxD
David the interpreter	DOR	54,7
Dedol	CHS	1,19. 2,25-26. 5,4
Deincora	LIN	20,4
Dela	ESS	B3a
Demiblanc	ESS	35,8;13. B3a
Dena	LIN	3,3. 18,15. 25,19;25. 59,4-6
	NTT	9,64
Dena, a royal thane	GLS	42,1

Dena: *see also* Dene

Dene	WIL	50,4

Dene: *see also* Dena
Deorc: *see* Derch
Deoring: *see* Dering
Deormann: *see* Derman
Deorsige: *see* Dersi
Deorstan: *see* Derstan
Deorwulf: *see* Derwulf
Deorwynn (fem.): *see* Derwen

Derch	CHS	8,14;28

Derch: *see also* Deorc

Dering	KEN	5,15
	LIN	12,48. 24,100
	SFK	7,118
	SRY	5,9
Dering son of Sired	KEN	M19

Dering: *see also* Deoring

Derman	ESS	B3a
	HRT	42,1-5
	KEN	*3,1*
	OXF	B10
	WAR	16,8
Derman of London	MDX	23

Derman: *see also* Deormann

Dersi	SFK	74,13

Dersi: *see also* Deorsige

Derstan	SFK	7,112

Derstan: *see also* Deorstan

Derwen [= Deorwynn (fem.)]	OXF	B10
Derwulf	ESS	90,60
	SFK	21,39. 77,4

Derwulf: *see also* Deorwulf

Doda	BRK	B4
	CHS	17,5
	CON	1,1. 5,4,18. 5,12,2-3. 5,24,9
	DEV	3,18;23;25;43;65. 16,7;114;118;120. 25,4. 36,10

	DOR	1,18. 33,3. 50,1. 54,12. 56,2;50
	GLS	39,12. E20. WoB5
	HAM	1,34
	SHR	4,23,7;14. 4,24,2. 4,26,6
	SOM	46,2
	SSX	10,24
	WAR	22,15
	WIL	30,2
	WOR	2,24;63
Doda: *see also* Brictric son of		
Doda, a forester	SOM	*46,3*
Doda, a thane	DEV	*16,7*
Doda, Alfred of Lincoln's man	LIN	27,60
another Doda	GLS	39,12
(another) Doda	DEV	16,7
Doda of Curry	SOM	*47,12*
Doda the monk	DOR	56,20-21 *note.* 57,8
Doda the priest	DEV	*16,135*
	SSX	10,1
Doda's son	GLS	E20. WoB5
	WOR	2,24
Dodin	NTH	B34. 39,1-3. 40,4. 48,17. 56,52. 60,4
Dodin: *see also* Doding		
Doding	ESS	29,1. 42,3
	MDX	3,2
Doding, Alfred of Lincoln's man	LIN	27,51;53
Doding, Asgar the constable's man	BKM	21,2
Doding: *see also* Dodin		
Dodman	DOR	26,14;35-37;48. *36,6*
	SOM	9,7. *10,2.* 19,32;87. 21,98. 25,33-36; 45-46
Dodman: *see also* Dudemann		
Doleswif	DEV	16,67
Dolfin	DBY	17,3;8-9
Dolgfinnr	YKS	1W40. 9W110. 29W39-41
Domnall	YKS	6N119
Domnic	BDF	21,11
	BRK	21,19
Domnic: *see also* Dunnic		
Donald	HAM	IoW8,5
Dot	BDF	57,11
	BKM	25,2
	CAM	*14,71*
	CHS	1,15. 2,7;17. 6,2. 8,17;23;32;34. 9,12. 14,4. 17,7-8;10. 18,5. 24,8-9. R1,3
	ESS	24,11. 32,32
	SHR	4,27,26
	SFK	3,100. 29,3
Dot, a thane	CHS	2,20
Dove	ESS	22,5. 90,57
Drengr	YKS	25W32-33
Drodo of Beuvrière	NFK	1,57 (*but see note*)
Drodo: *see* Drogo		
Drogo	BRK	B9. 18,2. 47,1
	BKM	16,10
	CHS	2,7;9-10;17;20
	DBY	7,3
	DEV	*1,11.* 3,2. 7,4. 15,23-24;*25*;34;62
	ESS	48,1
	HEF	1,21. 6,9. 8,1. 24,8

LIN	CN,22;28. CW,20. CK,6;40;58
NFK	8,82. 11,3
NTH	35,17-19
OXF	15,5. 28,9;16. EBe3
RUT	ELc9
SOM	5,5-7. 19,9;23-25;30;34;55-57;74;77.
	20,2-3. 22,14
STS	11,66. 12,27-29
SFK	19,12
WAR	22,25. 27,4. EBS2-3

Drogo de (la) Beuvrière: see Drogo of Beuvrière

Drogo, a man-at-arms

SOM	19,86

Drogo of Beuvrière [de la Beuvrière]

LEC	36
LIN	30. 2,36. 51,10. 64,1. CN,5. CK26;50
NFK	30. 8,134;137. 10,61
NTH	53
SFK	48
YKS	14

Drogo (of Beuvrière)

NFK	1,57
YKS	2E33. CW39. CE52. SE,Hu4

Drogo of Beuvrière: see also Drodo of Beuvrière

Drogo of Montacute

SOM	45,12

Drogo (of Montacute)

DEV	15,23-24
DOR	26,2;66. E1
SOM	19,86

Drogo, Ralph's man

LIN	64,2

Drogo, Robert Malet's man

NFK	66,59

Drogo son of Mauger

DEV	3,9-85

Drogo son of Poyntz

GLS	54
HEF	23. 1,29-30;38
WIL	49. M14
WOR	21. 8,9d

Drogo (son of Poyntz)

GLS	3,5. 45,6. WoB18

Druward

HEF	1,39
WOR	E1

Dubhan

YKS	1L8

Dubhan: see also Dwan

Dubhghall

YKS	1N133

Dublel

ESS	B3a

Dudeman: see Godwin son of
: see Dudemann

Dudemann: see Dodman, Dudeman

Duncan

DOR	E1

Duncan, a man-at-arms

SOM	19,86

Dunn

BRK	39,1
DEV	15,67;70;77. 52,32;34-35
GLS	50,1-4. 78,13
HAM	IoW1,15
SOM	1,6. 21,44;81. 22,12;21. 25,19;33-34.
	35,14. 39,2-3. 47,19
WIL	48,1;5;9. 67,28

Dunnic: see Domnic

Dunning

CHS	14,10. 25,1-3. 26,3;6
DBY	6,34;71;77. 12,3. 17,9
DEV	15,57
GLS	G4. 1,43. 39,14
HUN	19,29
NTT	9,62. 30,52
SHR	4,18,1. 4,21,6. 4,24,3. 4,27,1;4. 6,20
STS	1,61. 11,27. 17,7

	WOR	8,4;7
	YKS	10W16
Dunstan	DBY	9,2. 11,4
	NTT	9,72
	SOM	19,24
	YKS	C10. 1W26. 9W3;16;113;118;122; 128-129;136;139. 13W1. CW5
Dunstan, a thane	SOM	*19,24*
Durand	CAM	26,6;11;14-15;31;34;37
	CHS	8,9
	HAM	2,1;21. 35,4. NF3,3-4;12-13
	KEN	D8
	LEC	16,3. 35,2
	NFK	9,216
	NTH	18,88
	SOM	25,12;21-23;*36*(?)
	SFK	6,128. 7,84;111;118;121. 14,77;119. 16,25. 39,12. 67,18. 74,3
	SRY	28,1
	SSX	6,3. 10,15;48. 11,48
	WIL	2,11. 56,3
	WOR	2,29
Durand, a thane	NTT	9,69
Durand, brother of Roger (of Pîtres)	HEF	1,61
Durand, Edric's man	SFK	67,12
Durand, half man of Edric	SFK	67,17
Durand, Hugh de Montfort's man	NFK	*23,9*
Durand Malet	LEC	35
	LIN	44. CN,12
	NTT	26
Durand Malzor: *see* Adam son of		
Durand of Gloucester/the sheriff	GLS	53. G4. W8;15. B1. 2,10. 3,7. 35,2. E15. EvM4. WoB19
	HAM	37. S3
	HEF	22. 1,31;38
	WIL	30. M7. 26,19
Durand (of Gloucester/the sheriff)	GLS	3,4. 4,1. 16,1. WoB17
	WIL	28,10
Durand of Gloucester: *see also* Walter nephew of		
Durand of Offton	SFK	67,23
Durand the barber	HAM	65
Durand the canon	MDX	3,15
Durand the carpenter	DOR	*55,48.* 57,20-21
Durand the cleric, of St Edmunds and of Abbot Baldwin	SFK	*14,119*
Durand the reeve	NTH	B33
Durand the sheriff: *see* Durand of Gloucester		
Dwan	CHS	Y9
Dwan: *see also* Dubhan		
Dynechaie	SFK	6,191
E.	SFK	8,11
Eadgar: *see* Edgar		
Eadgifu (fem.)	LIN	18,25. 26,26. 34,1;3;8-9;27. 36,1-2;5
	YKS	15E1-4;7-10;12;14-16. CE14
Eadgifu (fem.) : *see also* Godric son of		
: *see also* Edeva		
Eadgyth (fem.): *see* Edith		
Eadhild (fem.) : *see* Edhild		
Eadlufu (fem.) : *see* Edlufu		
Eadmaer: *see* Edmer		

Eadmund	YKS	11N3-4;6-7;9-11;20
Eadmund: *see also* Edmund		
Eadnoth: *see* Ednoth		
Eadraed: *see* Edred		
Eadric	LIN	3,53. 12,29;88. 13,33;44. 25,15. 27,22; 24-25. 32,31. 48,10
Eadric: *see also* Godwine son of		
Eadric, Godric's brother	LIN	CS,6
Eadric: *see also* Edric		
Eadsige	LIN	S6
Eadsige: *see also* Edsi		
Eadweald: *see* Edwald, Edwold		
Eadweard	YKS	9W44
Eadweard: *see also* Edward		
Eadwig: *see* Edwy		
Eadwine	LIN	44,2;4
Eadwine: *see also* Adwin, Edwin		
Eadwulf	YKS	5E39. 9W52;87
Eadwulf: *see also* Edwulf		
Ealdbeorht: *see* Aldbert		
Ealdceorl: *see* Aldchurl		
Ealdgar: *see* Algar		
Ealdgifu (fem.): *see* Aldeva		
Ealdgyth (fem.): *see* Aldgyth, Aldith		
Ealdhild (fem.)	WIL	67,90
Ealdhild (fem.): *see also* Aldhild		
Ealdhild's husband	WIL	67,90
Ealdnoth: *see* Alnoth		
Ealdormann	LIN	4,1
Ealdred: *see* Aldred		
Ealdwine	LIN	64,17
Ealdwine: *see also* Aldwin, Aldwine		
Ealhhere: *see* Alchere		
Ealhmund: *see* Alhmund, Almund		
Eardwulf	YKS	1W5-6. 13N18
Earn-: *see also* Ern-		
Earne	YKS	1N61. 24W18
Earne: *see also* Arni		
Earngeat: *see* Erngeat		
Earnsige: *see* Ernsy		
Earnwig: *see* Ernwy		
Earnwine	LIN	2,21. 4,17. 12,93. 16,2;4;7-8. 28,5. 30, 5. 47,2. 68,30
	YKS	C2 *and note.* C12. 9W2;4;25;67;97. 13W12. 14E15;31. SW,An5. SE,How9
another Earnwine	YKS	C12
Earnwine Catenase	YKS	CW32
Earnwine (Catenase)	YKS	25W13
Earnwine, Roger of Poitou's man	LIN	16,1;33;47
Earnwine the priest	LIN	C6;16. S6. 1,9. 4,1. 12,7;29. 68,25;31; 42. CN,16
	YKS	29W2;9. 29E7;12. 30W40. CE18;27. CW32
Earnwine (the priest)	YKS	5E7. 25W16. SW,BA7. SW,Sf22. SE,Wa3. SE,Bt1-2
Earnwine: *see also* Ernwin		
Earnwulf	LIN	30,28
	YKS	1L8. 9W54
Earnwulf: *see also* Arnulf, Ernulf, Ernwulf		
Ebbi, Brictric son of Algar's man	GLS	6,1

Ebrard	WIL	3,2. 8,11
Ebrard, and his two brothers	LIN	26,25
Ebrard: *see also* Eburhard, Ev(e)rard		
Eburhard	YKS	13W16;26;35
Eburhard, William of Percy's man	YKS	1W53. SW,Bu49
Eburhard: *see also* Ebrard		
Ecbeorht, Gilbert of Ghent's man	LIN	24,22;76
Ecbeorht: *see also* Ecgbeorht		
Eccha, the King's reeve	DEV	1,4
Ecgbeorht	YKS	C10
Ecgbeorht: *see also* Ecbeorht		
Ecgfrith	YKS	1E30-32. CE42
Ecgwulf	LIN	12,29
Edda	DEV	42,12
Edelo, Robert of Stafford's man	LIN	59,12
Edeva (fem.)	BKM	4,1. 5,2;7-8
	CON	5,9,3
	DEV	15,38. 23,9. 25,1
	DOR	50,2
	ESS	5,1. 20,17;54. 22,1
	HAM	1,W12. 69,34
	HRT	15,6
	KEN	5,60;62
	MDX	25,1
	SOM	1,20. 21,66
	SSX	11,10;18-19. 12,11;19;51
Edeva : *see also* Richard son of		
: *see also* Wulfward son of		
Edeva/Aldeva (fem.)	WOR	28
Countess Edeva	SFK	4,17
Countess Edeva: *see also* Edeva		
Edeva Puella, Archbishop Stigand's man	HRT	5,16
Edeva Puella/the fair/the rich	BKM	13,1. 17,9. 44,2;5
	CAM	1,12. *13,8-10.* 14,1-2;7;9;*11*;13;*14-16;*
		*19-20;22;24;27;31;33-36;37;38;41;*44;
		*45-46;48;56-57;61;*74. 19,4. 26,*16*;38.
		29,10. 31,3;7. 32,*8;32*;44
	HRT	4,22;25. 5,16. 16,1-7;10-12. 35,3. 37,
		19
	SFK	1,61;63-64;67-73. 3,67-69. 4,17. 4,17.
		31,54. 46,4. EC1
Edeva (Puella/the fair/the rich)	CAM	14,3-6;8;10;17-18;21;23;25-26;28;32;
		42-43;49-55;58-60;62-71;73;75-78;
		80-82. 19,4. 26,16;38;40;49. 32,31. 35,
		1
	ESS	1,30. 4,16. 21,2-5;11-12
	SFK	1,64. 3,68-69;71-74;76-77;81;84. 25,
		104. 46,5. EC2
Edeva the nun	HRT	15,4
Edeva, wife of Edward son of Swein	ESS	85,1
Edeva, wife of Sired	BKM	B8
Edeva, wife of Wulfward	BKM	5,1. 14,14
Edeva (fem.): *see also* Eadgifu, Edgifu		
Edgar	HUN	11,1-2
	SFK	43,1. 76,20
	WIL	1,11
Earl Edgar	CAM	EE1
Earl 'Edgar': *see* Earl Algar		
Prince Edgar	HRT	38
Edgar the priest	WIL	67,52

Edgar's father   WIL   1,11
Edgar: *see also* Eadgar
Edgifu (fem.): *see* Eadgifu, Edeva
Edhild (fem.)   DEV   3,95
                                            SFK   3,91. 7,137

Edhild (fem.): *see also* Eadhild
Edith (fem.)   BRK   7,16. 65,14
                                            BKM   14,13
                                            DEV   19,37. 23,2
                                            GLS   78,7
                                            HEF   8,8;10. 9,10;19
                                            KEN   5,78;202
                                            LEC   21,1-2
                                            OXF   B10
                                            SHR   C13. 4,27,6;26. 6,2;9;30-31;33
                                            SOM   25,48
                                            SFK   1,88-90. 74,13
                                            SSX   9,26
                                            WAR   43,2
                                            WOR   2,12
Edith, a nun   SOM   16,12
                                            WOR   2,67
Edith of Asholt   KEN   D25
Queen Edith   BDF   1,4. 2,1. 23,28-29;32. 49,4. 57,6
                                            BRK   1,4;14-16;47. 20,3. 21,20. 65,5;15-17
                                            BKM   4,11;16;18. 5,1-2;6. 14,6;13;27;40. 16,
                                                     2. 19,1-2. 21,1. 23,14;20. 25,1. 26,3;8.
                                                     29,2. 41,1. 43,11. 55,1. 56,1-2. 57,13
                                            CON   *5,1,14*
                                            DEV   C2. 1,25-28
                                            DOR   2,6
                                            ESS   20,8. 27,15. 42,7-9
                                            GLS   1,20
                                            HAM   1,4-5;7;24;W22. 6,1;9. 10,1. 13,1. 23,
                                                     7. 69,6;26
                                            HEF   1,9-10a;39. 9,7. 10,29
                                            HRT   7,1. 15,5. 18,1. 32,2. 33,2;4. 34,4. 42,7
                                            KEN   C6. 13,1
                                            LEC   1,6-9
                                            LIN   S9. T2;5. 1,9;14;35;81;91. 68,24;31
                                            MDX   9,1
                                            NTH   B36. 1,3;32
                                            OXF   20,4. 34,2. 35,2
                                            RUT   R17;19-20. EN3. ELc2
                                            SHR   E3
                                            SOM   1,26-31;32-35. 5,46. 11,1. 32,2-3. 47,
                                                     20. EDo1
                                            SFK   1,122a-122b. 6,26. 25,56. 37,2. 41,
                                                     1-2. 52,1. 76,15
                                            SRY   1,7;10;12-13
                                            SSX   9,35. 10,44;63;90. 12,3
                                            WIL   1,15-17. 59,1
                                            WOR   15,13. 18,2. 19,5. E1
Queen (Edith)   GLS   1,7
                                            SFK   6,112
(Queen) Edith   WIL   19,1
Edith, sister of Earl Oda   HEF   18,1
Edith (fem.): *see also* Eadgyth
Edlufu Thief   DEV   25,1
Edlufu (fem.): *see* Eadlufu, Edlufu Thief

Edmer	DEV	3,24;52;56-57;94. 15,33-38. 16,7;34;
		82;133;173. 17,77. 19,7. 34,23. 35,3;
		12;19;24. 36,11-12. 41,2. 42,19;24.
		44. 48,11. 50,3-5
	ESS	20,15. 24,48. 51,1
	GLS	G3. 1,4. 17,1
	HUN	19,14
	NTH	2,7. 18,5-6;9. EH5
	SHR	4,8,14. 4,9,2. 4,24,4
	SOM	5,8. 21,63
	SFK	6,8
	SRY	5,7. 19,38
	WAR	3,4
	WIL	26,21
Edmer, a thane	GLS	1,3
Edmer Ator, a royal thane	BKM	12,3
	DEV	15,*12-13;14-30;*31;*32-33*
	HRT	15,12. 19,1
	MDX	8,6
	SOM	8,*31. 19,44;46. 37,5;12. 47,10*
Edmer (Ator, a royal thane)	CON	5,2,3. 5,24,13-14
	DOR	26,44;46;49;52;63
Edmer, brother of Aelfric	SOM	2,7
Edmer, Earl Algar's thane	SFK	8,33
Edmer, Earl Harold's thane	HRT	15,1
Edmer the priest	SSX	9,5. 10,1
Edmer: *see also* Eadmaer		
Edmund	BRK	B7. 14,1. 45,1-2
	DBY	17,11
	GLS	39,17
	HAM	69,20;54. NF9,45
	SHR	4,8,7. 4,27,15
	STS	8,18;26-27
	SFK	3,70-71. 25,67
	SSX	10,9
	WIL	67,55-57
Edmund, a royal thane	BKM	20,1
Edmund, Earl Harold's man	HRT	1,14. 5,5
King Edmund	SFK	14,167
Abbot Edmund (of Pershore)	WOR	9,4
Edmund son of Aiulf	WIL	67,58-59(?)
Edmund son of Algot	ESS	61
	MDX	3,10
Edmund son of Payne	HAM	69,51
	NFK	46
	SOM	46,21-23
Edmund the priest	SFK	47,2-3
Edmund the priest, wife of	SFK	47,3
Edmund: *see also* Eadmund		
Edmund's father	HAM	69,20
Ednoth	BRK	18,1
	CON	5,18. 5,6,4
	DEV	2,10. 3,36. *14,3.* 16,8. 23,7
	DOR	37,6
	ESS	20,28;70. 33,15. 41,10
	GLS	1,65
	HAM	3,5. 45,8. 69,13. NF9,30. IoW7,21. 8,6
	SOM	18,3-4. 21,59
	SFK	7,85. 16,37. 36,10

SSX	9,109-110;129
WIL	37,16. 48,12

Ednoth: *see also* Alnoth/Ednoth, Eadnoth
Edred

SOM	8,20. *19,72*. 35,8
SFK	8,58
WIL	24,28

Edred, Asgar's man

HRT	33,6

Edred the priest

BRK	1,10

Edred: *see also* Eadraed
Edric

BRK	1,24. 7,38. 22,9
BKM	14,29
CHS	7,4. 8,33;36
DBY	6,7;34;39;49;98. 17,2. B8
DEV	3,8;*12*;41;91;93;96-97. 15,27-29;56; 69. 16,42;88;137. 19,29. 23,24. 31, 1-4. 34,28. 40,7. 41,1. 43,3. 44,2. 52, 22-23
DOR	*12,16*. 27,5. 32,1. 33,2. 56,42-47;49
ESS	18,18;35. 20,38-39. 24,14. 25,21. 26, 5. 39,2. B3a(x4)
GLS	19,2. 39,1. 60,4-7. 68,7. 69,1
HAM	1,35. 2,24. 7,1. 23,42-44;46. 26,1. 29, 15. 37,2. 51,1. NF3,14. 9,17. IoW8,9. 9,6
HEF	36. 1,29. 9,5;11;15-16. 10,74
HUN	6,14
KEN	5,129;186. 7,6. 9,37
LEC	21,1-2
NFK	1,104;114-120;128;131;172;188. 4,4; 42. 7,3;9;11;16-19. 8,123-125;127; 132. 9,18;21;48;148;166;181. 10,56. 12,5. 17,18;51. 19,35. 21,29. 25,1;12. 26,1. 29,8. 30,2. 44,1. 66,80
NTH	18,22;30. EH3
NTT	9,70
OXF	B10
SHR	4,1,28-29. 4,3,19;32;37;39;65. 4,4,4; 10-11;14;16. 4,8,3. 4,10,1. 4,11,5;12; 15-16. 4,14,12. 4,15,2-4. 4,19,12. 4,20, 6;8;12;22-23. 4,21,4;8;19. 4,22,1. 4,23, 3. 4,24,1. 4,25,1. 4,27,33. 5,7. 6,13-14
SOM	5,18;21;32;60. 6,1. 21,33;56;59. 30,2. 32,4;6. 41,1-3. 42,1-3. 46,*4*;24
STS	11,23;40. 17,8. EW3
SFK	1,50;111;123f. 2,16. 3,45;95;98;101. 4, 15;18(x2). 6,3;5-6;10;11;14-16;32-34; 36 -37;42;44-46;48;57;60-61;64-65; 67-69;78-79;82;87;90;93-95;97(x3); 102;106;110-111;115-118;123; 126-127;130;132-141;143;145; 149-157;153;156;159;161-162; 164-165;170-172;174-180;183-184; 187-190;191(x2);192-203;205;236-249; 251;253-257;261-262;264-271; 276-278;280-293;296;308;311. 7,13; 15;38;56;58;76-77;79(x2);90;98;105; 111;121;123;125;131;142(x2);143; 145-146;151. 8,8;*23*;25;30. 16,14;16; 24;26-30;33;38;43. 21,67;90. 22,3. 25, 59;87. 26,12a;12d;13;15. 29,4. 30,2.

		31,16-18;27. 32,1. 35,7. 38,4;6;22. 39,
		5;9. 51,1. 64,1. 67,2;5(x2);8;11-12;
		15-16;20-22;26;28;30-32. 74,4;11;13.
		77,4
	SRY	1,13. 8,12
	SSX	9,103. 11,29
	WAR	12,10. 16,13;50. 25,1. 28,14. 44,4
	WIL	1,5. 25,4-5;24. 27,4;12;26. 29,1;8. 49,
		3. 66,1. 67,50. 68,21;30
	WOR	8,23. 15,6;12
E(dric)	SFK	6,119-120;122;124;134;143;151-152;
		154-155;157;173;197;199-200;203;
		238;240-241;243-244;252;255-256;
		290-292. 52,1. 67,10;17
Edric : *see also* Aelfric brother of		
: *see also* Aelfric father of		
: *see also* Coln father of		
: *see also* Godric brother of		
: *see also* Ketel father of		
: *see also* Odo son of		
Edric, a thane	DEV	*3,12*
	NFK	9,71. 36,5
	SOM	*46,4*
(another) Edric	SHR	4,21,8
Edric, Asgar the constable's man	HRT	4,7
Edric Blind	WIL	67,53
Edric, brother of Aelfric	SFK	76,3
Edric, brother of Godric	GLS	53,10
Edric, Count Alan's man	NFK	1,197. 4,51
Edric, Earl Algar's man	HRT	35,3. 37,18
Edric, Edric of Laxfield's man	NFK	4,39;42
Edric, G. of Laxfield's man	NFK	4,41-42
Edric Grim	SFK	3,21-23;*24-27*;28;*29*; 34-42;*49*;50-52;
		89;94-95. 8,26. 31,15. 34,15. 46,10.
		67,25
Edric, Harold's man	SFK	6,92
Edric, King Edward's man	BDF	53,28
Edric Lang, Earl Harold's thane	GLS	1,62
Edric of Easthorpe	ESS	37,20 (cf 20,40)
Edric (of Easthorpe)	ESS	20,40
Edric of Elsham	KEN	5,185;210
Edric of Laxfield	NFK	1,203;205. 4,38;39;40;51;53. 7,4;5-8;
		9-13. 9,88;105. 35,16
	SFK	1,31. 3,34;39;41. 6,28;58;62;79-80;
		83-84;110;114;128-129;135;148;260;
		264;272-273;295;303-304. 7,23;36. 8,
		29. 14,68. 16,6;15;25. 19,16. 31,20;
		27. 64,3. 67,15;28-29;33
Edric (of Luxfield)	SFK	6,305-306. 7,114
Edric of Marlow	BKM	7,2
Edric Snipe, a royal thane	CAM	21,*5 note.* 31,*1*;2
Edric son of Aelfric	SHR	3c,8
Edric son of Ingold	SFK	4,15
Edric son of Ketel	GLS	78,5;16
Edric Spud	SFK	25,78
Edric the bald	BDF	55,8
Edric the cripple	DEV	1,11
Edric (the cripple): *see also* Edward son of		
Edric the deacon	SFK	76,20
Edric the falconer	NFK	63

Edric, the King's reeve	SFK	6,217
Edric the priest	CAM	*31,1*
Edric the sheriff (of Wiltshire)	GLS	E16
	WIL	45,2
Edric the steersman	NFK	10,76
	WOR	2,52
Edric the Wild	HEF	9,3
	SHR	4,1,14;18;20. 4,5,13. 4,10,3. 4,22,3
Edric, wife of	SFK	6,57
Edric Young	SOM	*5,39*
Edric, Young Aelfric's man	CAM	32,3
Edric: *see also* Eadric		
Edric's brother	HAM	23,44
Edric's wife	WIL	M15. 25,4-5
Edsi	BRK	21,1
	CAM	32,18. *35,2*
	CON	5,8,1
	DEV	16,99. 19,33
	ESS	21,8. 30,15
	HAM	23,24. 29,4. 68,4
Edsi, man of Godith	HRT	4,23
Archbishop Edsi	KEN	*2,39*
Edsi the sheriff	HAM	6,10. 47,1
Edsi: *see also* Eadsige		
Edwald	SOM	21,47. 24,4. 25,12
Edwald, a thane	SOM	*21,47*
Edwald: *see also* Eadweald, Edwold		
Edward	BDF	56,5. 57,5
	BRK	8,1. 13,2. 41,1. 58,1. 63,1;3-5. 65,9;12
	CAM	AppxB
	CHS	9,4;16;22-23;25. 24,5;7;9
	CON	5,2,14
	DBY	6,34. 17,22
	DEV	16,165. 17,81. 30,2
	DOR	2,2;6. 56,12
	ESS	18,27. 20,63;65. 30,7-8. 35,11
	GLS	78,6
	HAM	2,1. 21,10. 32,3. 40,1. 43,5. 68,2
	KEN	*1,3*. 5,99;183;199
	LIN	4,42. 30,31. 57,6
	NTH	35,9. 56,25-26;36
	OXF	6,13. 14,5. EBu1
	RUT	EN12;17-18;20
	SOM	5,53. 24,7
	SFK	4,4. 7,109
	SSX	9,61;112. 10,18;25. 13,34
	WIL	2,3. 3,4. 7,7. 8,12. 13,3;16. 15,2. 22,3. 26,6;19. 32,7. 41,3;10. 67,15;24;43; 54. 68,33
	WOR	8,8;10a;10e
Edward, a man-at-arms	WIL	14,1
Edward, a royal thane	BKM	14,36. 15,1
(another) Edward	WIL	8,12
Edward Child: *see* Edward Young		
Edward, Earl Tosti's man	BKM	15,2
Edward Hunter	DOR	56,66
King Edward	CHS	B7
	DEV	2,2
	DOR	34,8
	ESS	24,23;25;29;35

	HEF	1,41
	HRT	17,15
	KEN	*5,149*
	SHR	3d,7. 4,26,3
	SFK	33,15. 34,5. 40,2
	WIL	1,3
Edward Lip	DOR	57,19
Abbot E(dward, of Cerne)	DOR	*11,10*
Edward of Pirton	HRT	1,10
Edward of Salisbury/the sheriff/a man-at-arms	BKM	24
	DOR	31
	GLS	E14
	HAM	27. 12,1. NF7
	HRT	32
	MDX	20
	OXF	41. B9
	SOM	40. *1,31*. EW1
	SRY	27. 19,25
	WIL	24p. 24. M5. B4. 12,2. 67,100. 68,14;
		23
Edward (of Salisbury, etc.)	GLS	1,63
	WIL	7,4;12-13
Edward of Stone	KEN	D25
Edward Snook	KEN	5,139
Edward son of Edric (the Cripple)	DEV	1,11
Edward son of Swein	ESS	85
Edward son of Swein, King Edward's man	MDX	25,1
Edward son of Swein: *see* Edeva wife of		
Edward son of Wulfward(?)	SOM	*9,3*
Edward, the Abbot of Ely's man	CAM	*13,11*
Edward, the Abbot of St Albans' man	BDF	53,25
Edward the Breton/Edward the Briton	SOM	*24,5*
Edward the clerk	DOR	6,2
Edward the priest	DEV	*51,6*
	ESS	B3a
Edward the sheriff: *see* Edward of Salisbury		
Edward White	BDF	20,2
Young Edward [= Edward Child]	BKM	12,8. 14,38;45
Young Edward, Earl Harold's man	BKM	12,7
Young Edward, a royal thane	BKM	14,22-23. 15,1
	LIN	S8. 2,34. 56,1
Edward: *see also* Eadweard		
Edward's father	WIL	67,54
Edwin	BKM	5,4. 23,30
	CAM	*14,70*
	CHS	2,7-12. 6,1. 17,1;12. 24,2. FD2, 6.
		FD7,1-2
	CON	5,4,8-9
	DBY	1,9. 7,4. 14,7. 16,4
	DEV	3,89. 15,30. 15,35;97. 19,11. 24,32.
		34,14;37;46. 35,6. 52,38-39
	DOR	56,3;14
	ESS	30,13. B3a(x6)
	HAM	23,8. 69,4-5
	HEF	1,23. 14,2-3;5-6;8;12. 23,3. 25,2;4
	KEN	M12-13. 5,80;103;120
	LEC	13,49. 35,2
	NFK	1,183;229. 9,30;139. 10,49. 12,4;7-15;
		17-18;22-25;27;32. 19,23;36. 35,8. 66,
		82

	NTH	4,5;25-26. 18,9;14;42;76-77. 26,5;7. 41,9
	OXF	35,10. 45,1-3
	SHR	4,3,13. 4,14,23;28. 4,21,7. 4,23,18
	SOM	5,5. 9,5;8. 19,39. 21,17;64
	STS	12,11
	SFK	3,72-73;83;86. 7,18. 8,58. 13,2;7. 21, 51. 25,70. 32,8
	SRY	5,14. 19,22
	SSX	10,33. 11,13. 13,51
	WAR	17,14;18-26;28-29;56
	WIL	24,33. 27,9-10;16. 67,51. 68,2
	WOR	20,5
	YKS	C36 *and note.* 6N128 *and note*
Edwin a free man	BRK	20,1. 41,4
Edwin, a free priest	ESS	32,9
Edwin, a royal thane	BKM	5,3
	MDX	21,1
	NFK	12,16
Edwin, a thane	BRK	46,3
	BKM	14,35
	CHS	2,20
	NFK	12,30
	YKS	2B8
Edwin Alfrith	LEC	19,12-14
Edwin, Asgar the constable's man	BDF	1,5
Edwin, Azor's man	BKM	12,26
Edwin, brother of Baldwin	KEN	*M23*
Earl Edwin	BKM	14,25. 17,7
	CHS	1,1;8;13;22;24-26;34. 2,1-6;21. 14,1. 17,2. S1,1. FD1,1-2. FD6,1. FT1,1. FT3,1
	DBY	6,25;59
	DOR	1,2 (*but see note*)
	HEF	1,40;47
	LIN	1,38
	OXF	1,7a;7b;12
	SHR	3b,3. 4,1,16;19;21-22;25-27;30. 4,6,5. 4,7,4. 4,11,6. 4,18,3. 4,19,1;3
	STS	8,5. 11,6;67-68
	WAR	1,1;6-7. 16,44. 17,60;63. 26,1. 27,1;3. 42,1. EBW1
	WOR	C1. 1,1a;1c-1d;3b. 19,6. 23,10. 26,4. E2;7
	YKS	C36 *note.* 1Y2. 1W73. 5W14. 6N1;52. 6W1. 9W1. 10W1
Edwin Groat	ESS	32,31. 68,1
Edwin Hunter	DOR	*56,31-33*
	HAM	69,41
Edwin, King Edward's man	MDX	22,1
Edwin of Butterleigh	DEV	*52,38-39*
Edwin son of Burgred, a royal thane	BKM	5,9;20
	NTH	4,32;36
	OXF	EN3;7
Edwin the priest	BRK	7,22
	CAM	AppxE
	ESS	B3a. 32,9
	HAM	69,8
	STS	7,13
	SFK	8,81

Edwin the sheriff	OXF	24,5
	WAR	4,3. 17,10
Edwin the smith, in Carlewuda	SFK	6,110
Edwin the smith in Carlewuda: *see also* Aelfric son of (? Edwin) the smith		
Edwin: *see also* Adwin, Eadwine		
Edwold	ESS	4,2;4
	SFK	8,11-12. 39,6
Edwold, King Edward's reeve	ESS	18,11
Edwold, wife of	SFK	8,11
Edwold: *see also* Eadweald, Edwald		
Edwulf	BKM	23,30
	DBY	6,64
	DEV	16,60;93;115;124. 19,45
	HEF	15,1
	SOM	46,21-22
	STS	4,8
	WAR	17,25
	WIL	4,1-2
Edwulf, and his father	HAM	69,25
Edwulf: *see also* Eadwulf		
Edwy	BRK	B7
	CON	*1,1. 4,22.* 5,3;21. 5,4,6. 5,5,1;11-12. 5, 8,4;6-10. 5,13,3
	DEV	3,44. 15,12. 16,62;100;113;154;160. 20,1. 34,55
	DOR	26,62
	ESS	90,83
	GLS	19,2. 32,13. 39,21. 53,9. 56,1
	HAM	69,13. NF3,7. IoW9,12
	HEF	1,16. 10,9;16;23;46;59;72. 25,6
	NTT	9,6;16
	SHR	4,26,7. 6,22
	SOM	*19,13.* 36,13
	SFK	*8,9.* 16,41;47
	WOR	15,1. 20,3;5
Edwy: *see also* Alwin son of		
Edwy, a thane	DEV	*15,12*
Edwy Child: *see* Edwy Young		
Edwy, father of Alwin	HEF	10,15
Edwy, the Abbot of Ely's man	CAM	27,1
Edwy, the King's reeve	NFK	4,20
Edwy the priest	KEN	5,172
Edwy Young [= Edwy Child]	HEF	2,58. 10,10-11;21;24;47-49;54-55;73
Edwy Young [= Edwy Child]: *see also* Alwin son of		
Edwy Young, father of Alwin	HEF	10,70
Edwy: *see also* Eadwig		
Egbrand	CHS	9,11;13
	YKS	1W49-50. 6N98. CE17
Egelfride (fem.)	YKS	1N113. 23N33
Egelfride (fem.): *see also* Aegelfride		
Ehelo, Robert of Stafford's man	LIN	59,19
Eilafr	LIN	2,6;8. 47,4-7. CN,9;11
	YKS	C17. 1N131. 1E14. 14E43
Einarr	LIN	48,4
Einarr's stepmother	LIN	48,4
Einbold	NFK	31,10;43
Eingar, Earl Harold's man	BKM	37,2
Einulf	YKS	C7

Erchenger the priest	SOM	*16,3*
Erchenold, the Bishop of Lincoln's man	LIN	7,14-15;38
Erembald	YKS	14E27
Erfast	NFK	1,57
Bishop Erfast (of Thetford)	NFK	1,59;61;69. 10,21;27;29;43;53-54;69; 78;81;90;93
	SFK	1,119. 25,60. 75,3
(Bishop) Erfast (of Thetford)	SFK	19,1-2
Bishop Erfast: *see also* Heloise niece of		
Erfast: *see also* Herfast		
Erhard: *see* Stephen son of		
Eric	DEV	15,14
	HUN	29,3. D27
	RUT	R8. ELc12
	SFK	21,22
Eric, brother of Tosti	HUN	D27
Eric: *see also* Eirikr, Yric		
Erland	SFK	3,56;62
Erlebald	HAM	23,13
	SOM	21,90. 25,55
	WIL	37,1
	WOR	2,61. 26,1-2;5;7;15
Erlechin	CHS	8,27
	WIL	67,49
Erling	ESS	30,14
	HAM	23,29
Ermenald	DEV	5,1
Ermenfrid	WAR	6,20. 17,18-19;49;56;65. 44,6
Ermenfrid, Osbern of Arques' man	YKS	25W13;16
Ermengot	SFK	3,67
Ermenhald	CON	3,1-6
Ernburgis	WIL	37,8
Ernebald	SOM	23,1
	WIL	E3
Ernegis	YKS	6N118
Erneis	CON	5,3,19
	GLS	31,12. 45,6. 54,1. 66,3-6
	LEC	13,40;52
	SOM	6,1;10. 8,35. 21,91
Erneis, a thane	GLS	39,8
Erneis, Earl Hugh's man	LIN	13,20
Erneis of Buron/Burun	LIN	34. CS,24;26. CW,18
	YKS	24. C13
Erneis (of Buron/Burun)	YKS	30W30. SW,Sk18. SW,An2-3. SW,Bu3-5;7-14;25-26;28;31;35;40-44. SE,C9. SE,Sn2. SE,Wa7
Erneis, the Bishop of Bayeux's man	LIN	4,23
Erngeat	CHS	7,1-3. 10,4. 20,4
	DBY	6,32
	SHR	4,14,19-21. 6,25
	SFK	7,83. 61,1
	WOR	26,9
Erngeat, Earl Edwin's thane	WOR	1,1c
Erngeat: *see also* Earngeat		
Ernsy	HEF	1,20;30. 10,68
	WOR	15,9
Ernsy: *see also* Earnsige		
Ernucion	BRK	12,1
	SHR	4,27,4
	SSX	11,56;85

Ernucion: *see also* John son of
Ernulf   ESS   20,13
Ernulf, Roger of Bully's man   NTT   9,89
Ernulf: *see also* Earnwulf, Ernwulf
Ernwin   CHS   2,18. 8,1;5. 23,1-2
                                              DBY   14,10. 16,2
                                              HEF   7,7
                                              NTT   30,35;42-43;51-52;54
                                              SHR   4,4,13
                                              WAR   28,17-18
                                              WOR   21,4
Ernwin, a thane   CHS   2,20
Ernwin the priest   BDF   14. 4,3
                                              CHS   Y13
                                              NTT   9,109. 30,41;49
Ernwin the priest's father   BDF   14,1
Ernwin's mother   WAR   21,18
Ernwin: *see also* Earnwine
Ernwulf   HAM   69,6
                                              SFK   6,32
Ernwulf: *see also* Earnwulf, Ernulf
Ernwy   CHS   1,15. 9,10. 26,7. FD3,2
                                              DBY   6,63. 7,10. 17,10;22
                                              HEF   8,5. 10,12;54-55. 14,9. 20,2. 21,1. 25,8
                                              LEC   43,9-11
                                              NTH   34,1
                                              NTT   16,5;12. 30,56
                                              SHR   4,3,11. 4,4,12;15. 4,5,4;7. 4,20,1. 4,26,
                                                    3
                                              SOM   25,56
                                              STS   17,6
                                              WAR   22,26. 28,3;6. 35,1-2
Ernwy, a thane   GLS   37,3
Ernwy, Earl Harold's thane   HEF   22,1
Ernwy Foot   CHS   1,7
Ernwy of Childerley   CAM   AppxO
Ernwy the priest   NTT   30,11
Ernwy: *see also* Earnwig
Ertald   LIN   C20
                                              SFK   8,22
Ertein   SHR   4,27,22
                                              DBY   17,9
                                              ESS   47,3
Esbern   CHS   FD8,2
                                              KEN   5,42
                                              LEC   14,23. 40,1-7
                                              NTT   30,35
                                              SSX   11,36
                                              WAR   4,2
                                              WIL   67,93
Esbern Big   KEN   D17. C5-6. 5,37;57;86-87;168. 7,6. 9,
                                                    16
Esbern Crook   NTT   21,1-2
Esbern of Chelsfield   KEN   D25
Esbern: *see also* Esbjorn
Esbjorn   LIN   3,16. 12,17;19. 14,3;84. 22,33. 26,3;
                                                    10. 47,1. 48,2. 57,5
                                              YKS   1N71
Esbjorn: *see also* Esbern
Escul: *see* Skuli

Esmeld the priest: *see* Smelt
Esmellt the chaplain: *see* Smelt
Essocher   SSX   13,17
Essulf son of Ringulf   GLS   EvQ29
Essulf: *see also* Aescwulf
Estan   BKM   4,43
                                              HAM   69,44. IoW7,1
                                              NFK   4,22
                                              NTH   18,29
                                              SOM   22,9. 35,6-7
Estan: *see also* Leofwin son of
Estan, a thane   BKM   17,22
Estan the canon   HEF   6,2
Estan: *see also* Aestan, Aethelstan
Estgar   NFK   8,13
Estmund   SFK   1,102
Estred   CAM   26,14-15
                                              SFK   74,13
Estrild, a nun   MDX   17,1
Eudo   BKM   49,1
                                              GLS   3,4. WoB17
                                              LIN   3,15;22;25. 4,55. 12,86. CS,22
                                              NFK   20,1;7;31-32. 66,90
Eudo, a man-at-arms   KEN   5,128
Eudo Clamahoc   NFK   66,94
Eudo, Count Alan's man   LIN   12,40;80;82;85;93;96
Eudo, Earl Ralph's man   NFK   1,7
Eudo son of Clamahoc   NFK   1,11;218. *20,18.* 22,11
Eudo son of Hubert: *see* Eudo the steward
Eudo son of Nigel   SFK   2,16-20 *note*
Eudo son of Spir(e)wic   LIN   29. CS,21. CN,30
                                              NFK   29. 1,221. 9,100
                                              SFK   53. 6,210
Eudo the steward/son of Hubert   BDF   21. 8,4-5. 25,7. 28,1
                                              BRK   32. 1,1
                                              CAM   25. AppxL
                                              ESS   25. 1,25;27. 10,1. 28,8. 30,41. B3d;7
                                              HAM   30. 6,16 *note*
                                              HRT   31. B3
                                              HUN   15
                                              LIN   S6
                                              NFK   24. 9,184. 66,100
                                              NTH   42
                                              SFK   28. 16,41. 29,11
Eudo (the steward/son of Hubert)   ESS   10,3
                                              HRT   B5
Euen   SFK   67,1
Euremar, Godfrey of Cambrai's man   LIN   51,6
Eurold [= Evrold], Jocelyn son of Lambert's LIN   28,32
  man
Eustace   NTH   6a,13;17;24;26. 35,15. 48,12. 56,46.
                                                     EH2
                                              SSX   12,17
Count Eustace (of Boulogne)   BDF   15
                                              CAM   15. AppxK
                                              ESS   20. 1,24. 3,2. 12,1. 28,9. B1;3g
                                              HAM   20
                                              HRT   17. 24,2. Appx
                                              HUN   9

	KEN	10
	NFK	5. 8,31. 66,86
	OXF	19
	SOM	17. 1,28
	SFK	5. 76,16 *note*
	SRY	15. 5,28. 25,2
Count E(ustace, of Boulogne)	ESS	1,3;27. 17,2
Count Eustace: *see also* Geoffrey son of		
Eustace of Huntingdon/the sheriff	BDF	E6-7
	CAM	30. 39,2. Ehu
	HUN	19. D20
	LIN	S4
	NTH	55. EH4
Eustace (of Huntingdon/the sheriff)	HUN	B1;10;12-13. 2,2. 5,2. 6,3;7-8. 13,3;4. 20,3;4. D1;2;12;19-21;25
Eustace the sheriff: *see* Eustace of Huntingdon		
Eustace the cleric	SSX	9,72
Count Eustace, wife of	DOR	58,1
Count Eustace's cleric	ESS	1,28
Everard	LEC	38,1
Everard, the Abbot of Ramsey's man	HUN	6,7
Everard: *see also* Evrard		
Everbold: *see* Odo son of		
Everwacer	DEV	16,109
	SOM	27,3. 37,2-4;6;10
Everwacer: *see also* Aelfric son of		
Everwin	NFK	1,61
	OXF	27,5. 28,29
Evrard	CAM	29,2
	ESS	30,51
	SOM	8,30. 17,3
Evrard son of Brian	CAM	*29,1.* AppxB
Evrard, William of Percy's man	LIN	22,35-36
Evrard: *see also* Ebrard, Eburhard, Everard		
Count of Evreux	BRK	17. B5
	HAM	S3
	OXF	17. B9. 7,51
Evrold: *see* Eurold		
Ewein	WAR	22,15
Ewen the Breton	HEF	10,41;50
Ewicman	NFK	1,62. 21,37
Ewing	WIL	47,1
Ewing: *see also* Ifing		
Eyiolfr: *see* Aiulf		
Fafiton	HUN	D13
Fafiton: *see also* Robert Fafiton		
: *see also* Robert son of		
Falc	SFK	14,59. 21,2
Fargrimr	YKS	13E5
Fargrimr: *see also* Fragrin		
Farman	CAM	AppxC
	SFK	7,68. 21,75
Farman, a man-at-arms	KEN	*2,10*
Farthegn	YKS	25W2
Farthin	NTH	18,15
Fastrad	SOM	6,1;9;14
(another?) Fastrad	SOM	6,1
Fastulfr	LIN	S12
Fatherling	HAM	23,22-24;68. 52,1
Fathin	NFK	*4,2*

Fathir	NFK	19,11;13. 20,8
	SFK	25,24
Fathir, a royal thane	NFK	20,2
Fech	SHR	4,11,13
Feche	WOR	16,3
Fech(e): see also Fiacc		
Feggi	LEC	40,34
Feigr	YKS	30W1;31
Fellow	ESS	67,2. 90,65-66
Fenkell	LIN	3,43
Fenkell's father	LIN	CS,38
Fenkell, brother of Alnoth, Asketill and	LIN	CS,38. CN,30
Sighvatr/Godwine		
Fermeus	SFK	35,3
Ferron	NTH	6a,27
Fiacc	LIN	T5
Fiacc: see also Fech(e)		
Filiman	ESS	B3a
Fin: see Finn, Finnr		
Finch	NFK	66,101
Finn: see also Fin, Finnr		
Fin(n) the Dane	BKM	19,5. 57,16
	ESS	84 note. 23,38;43
Finn (the Dane)	SFK	8,59. 25,19;51-53;56-57;59;61;63;72;
		75;77. 35,3
Finn the Dane: see also Wulfeva wife of		
Finnghall	YKS	6N11
Finnr	LIN	34,4
Finnr: see also Fin, Finn		
Firmatus	CAM	29,10-11
Firmin	CAM	AppxF
Fish	NFK	34,20
Flint	SFK	74,11
Flohere	DEV	41,1. 22
Flotmann	YKS	1W41. 6N143;157
Forne, a thane	GLS	32,7
Forni	YKS	C17. 1E1;4. 9W30. 13E5. 14E52.
		26E1-2;4;8-10 and note. 26E12. 29E4
Forthred, a thane	SOM	5,65
Fragrin	STS	2,20
Fragrin: see also Fargrimr		
Frambold: see Godwin Frambold		
Fran	CHS	8,20
	LEC	17,20
	NTH	4,28. 26,10
	NTT	4,6. 6,10. 9,10;88;96. 13,7
	STS	2,20
	SSX	10,8;37;88;104
	WOR	2,18
Fran: see also Oswulf son of		
: see also Frani		
Fran, Earl Edwin's thane	WOR	1,1c
Franco, Drogo of Beuvrière's man	YKS	14E33;37;47;51
Frani	LIN	16,22. 26,11;14;23
	SFK	67,16
	YKS	14E45;48 and note. CE45
another Frani	YKS	14E48
Frani, brother of	YKS	14E48 note. CE45
Frani son of Thorr	YKS	CE41
Frani (son of Thorr)	YKS	14E43

Frani: *see also* Fran
Frank   DEV   28,4
                                                   SHR   2,1
                                                   SFK   48,1
Frank, Drogo of Beuvrière's man   NFK   8,137
Frawin   CON   5,24,21
                                                   DEV   *15,47*. 35,2. 43,5. 51,14
                                                   SSX   11,23
                                                   WIL   68,18
Frawin, a thane   DEV   *15,47*
Frawin of Kirtling   CAM   AppxB
Fredegis   NTH   18,31. 35,9. 43,1
                                                   NTT   2,1. 10,53-55;57. 16,8
                                                   RUT   EN12
Fredegis: *see also* Fredregis, Fregis
Frederic   NFK   8,6-7;22;33;47;62-63;66-67;94-95;98;
                                                            111;113;116-118;130;132;137. 66,68
                                                   SSX   12,43. 13,4
Frederick   KEN   9,1
                                                   SFK   26,4;9
Frederick, brother (of William of Warenne)   CAM   18,7 *note*
Fredregis   NFK   8,67
Fredregis: *see also* Fredegis, Fregis
Fregis   NTH   18,18;20;26;90
Fregis: *see also* Fredegis, Fredregis
Frenchman   NFK   31,16-17
Freond   ESS   B3a
Frewin   ESS   20,64
                                                   SFK   7,121
Fridbert, Earl Leofwin's man   BKM   4,20
Frideb..., a priest   SFK   74,16
Fridebern   ESS   30,44;50
                                                   SFK   25,82
Fridebern, a royal thane   SFK   32,6
Fridebert   CAM   *5,24*. 32,5
                                                   ESS   1,22. 18,36
Fridebert, a thane   ESS   30,4
Frienday   LEC   2,7
Frithgestr   LIN   2,37. 51,2. 59,9
                                                   YKS   1N79;101;123;136-137
Frithgestr, Kolgrimr's man   LIN   67,20
Frodo   NFK   14,19;22;35;42-43
                                                   SFK   1,1. 2,7. 7,56. 14,33;68;86
                                                   ESS   56. 90,85
Frodo, brother of Abbot (Baldwin)   SFK   12. *14,21;28;65;106;137-139. 21,40.*
                                                            25,79
Froger the sheriff   BRK   1,10;43
Frumold, Drogo of Beuvrière's man   YKS   14E44 *and note*
Fugel   HAM   S2
Fuglo, Alric son of Goding's man   BDF   24,2;7
Fulbert   BDF   18,7
                                                   KEN   5,138;144;159-160. 9,40
                                                   LEC   13,34
                                                   NFK   13,10;17
Fulbert: *see also* Hugh son of
Fulbert (a priest of Hermer's)   NFK   1,61
Fulbert, Gilbert of Ghent's man   LIN   24,84
Fulbric   WAR   32,1
Fulcald: *see* Fulcwald
Fulcard   SFK   6,195. 35,7(x2)

Fulcard: *see also* Fulchard
Fulchard

BRK	21,12. 65,18
CON	2,7

Fulchard: *see also* Fulcard
Fulcher

NFK	8,59. 14,10;23;30
SFK	*14,82*
YKS	13N15 *and note.* 23N29

Fulcher of Mesnières
Fulcher, the Abbot's man
Fulcher the Breton

SFK	*Notes to* 14,11;78;80;89-90;99
NFK	1,66
NFK	*14,10*
SFK	*14,22*

Fulcher: *see also* Fulchere
Fulchere

NTH	18,76-78. 39,4-6. 56,40
SHR	1,8. 4,3,11;20. 4,25,4

Fulchere Malsor
Fulchere of Paris
Fulchere the bowman

RUT	R18
BDF	16,7. 24,25-26. 53,17-18
DEV	*49*

Fulchere: *see also* Fulcher
Fulco

YKS	10W27;33;39. 13W13. 13N14

Fulco, Drogo of Beuvrière's man
Fulco, Gilbert Tison's man
Fulco, Osbern of Arques' man
Fulco, William of Percy's man

YKS	14E53
YKS	21E4
YKS	25W6;29-30
LIN	22,25;28;33

Fulco: *see also* Fulk
Fulcold: *see* Fulcald, Fulcwald, Fulkhold
Fulcran
Fulcred

SOM	5,17;19;30-31;41;63
DOR	*1,7;10-12;14.* 54,3-4. E3
HAM	6,3
MDX	3,13
SFK	1,10. 6,83;92;95-96;289. 25,9;90
WIL	10,2. 66,5

Fulcred: *see also* Robert son of
    : *see also* Stephen son of
Fulcric

LIN	2,9. 32,3;9;13;15;17;21. 63,8;20;24. 68,38. CN,23
SFK	3,70-71
YKS	23E12
LIN	12,4

Fulcric, and his 2 brothers
Fulcwald: *see also* Fulcald, Fulcwold, Fulkhold
Fulcwin

SOM	24,10;18

Fulcwin: *see also* Fulkwin
Fulcwold

DEV	19,18
HRT	15,6

Fulcwold: *see also* Fulcold, Fulcwald, Fulkhold
Fulcwy

DEV	*19,18*
SHR	4,27,2-3

Fulcwy: *see also* Fulkwy
Fulk

BKM	41,4;7
CAM	AppxE
CHS	2,19
DBY	16,1-2
DEV	17,38-40;42. 39,3
HAM	69,2
HRT	35,3. Appx
HUN	11,1
LEC	13,54. 36,1. 44,7
OXF	29,4;7
SHR	4,3,46. 4,20,20;24-25;27
SFK	30,1;3
SRY	27,3

	SSX	10,106. 11,14;31-32. 14,1
	WAR	16,38-39;63
Fulk of Ditton	CAM	AppxE (omitted: cf ICC 25)
Fulk of Lisors/Lusore	DBY	16,1
	YKS	CW14
Fulk, Roger of Bully's man	NTT	9,18;20;41;55;64;70;126-127
Fulk Waruhel	CAM	AppxK
Fulk: *see also* Fulco		
Fulkhold [erroneous for Fulcold]	BKM	12,18
	HAM	35,5
Fulkhold [for Fulcold]: *see also* Fulcwald, Fulcwold		
Fulkwin	BKM	30,1
	HAM	NF3,2;6;8-10
Fulkwin: *see also* Fulcwin		
Fulkwy	CAM	14,25;43;45
Fulkwy: *see also* Fulcwy		
Fursa	BDF	E7
	HUN	19,11. D15
G.	ESS	90,57
	NFK	1,61 *note*
G. of Laxfield	NFK	4,41
Gadio	OXF	27,7
Gaimar: *see* ?Gamas		
Gamalbarn	YKS	C10 *and note*. 1W42-46;56-57;62; 65-66. 13W13;17;24;28;30-33. 21W5; 7-15;17. 30W11-12
Gamalbarn: *see also* Barn, Gamall		
Gamalkarl	YKS	C15
Gamalkarl: *see also* Gamall, Karl		
Gamall	LIN	4,5;23;74. 11,9. 14,16;23-26;41;63. 16, 32. 17,2. 25,7. 32,31. 34,7. 45,1
	YKS	C3. 1N3;32;57-58;67-68;72;74;82-83; 86;88. 1E16;45. 1W17 *note*; 18-19;39; 59-60. 2N5. 5N63;73. 5E4;21;29;31; 32;42;44;67. 6N30;56;71;90;103;105; 107;132. 8N2-7;11. 8N12-20. 8N21-22. 8W2. 8E2;4-5. 9W24;26; 47-48;56;65-66;76-78;100;103;112; 115-116;129-130;138;142-143. 11E1. 11N16. 11W2. 13W4-5;25;45. 13N15. 14E35;48. 21W16. 23N10-11;15-16. 23E2-6;8-10;13;15-17. 24W11. 25W24-25. 26E4-5;12. 29E2;13;19-20; 24. 29N11. 29W48. 30W3;13-14;36. CE33. CW2. SN,Bi1
Gamall, brother of	YKS	29E20
Gamall, mother of	YKS	29E20
Gamall, Norman of Arcy's man	LIN	32,7;27
Gamall son of Asmundr	YKS	CW2
Gamall (son of Asmundr)	YKS	13W3
Gamall son of Osbert	YKS	C36
Gamall, sons of	YKS	6N103
Gamall: *see also* Gamalbarn, Gamel		
Gamas	SFK	14,114
Gamas: *see also* ?Gaimar		
Gamel	CHS	24,3. 26,9-10
	DBY	6,7;12;83;91;94-96;98
	LEC	14,33

	NTT	16,1
	SHR	4,8,9. 4,14,25. 4,21,3
	STS	17,2;12-14
Gamel, a man-at-arms	CHS	R5,6
Gamel, a thane	CHS	R5,3
Gamel: *see also* Gamall		
Gamel's father	CHS	26,9-10
Gamelin: *see* Odo son of		
Gamilo	SFK	*14,24*
Gaosfrid: *see* Geoffrey		
Garthulfr [? Gardulf]	LIN	32,24
Garwine	LIN	C16
Garwine: *see also* Godric son of		
Gaufrid, Gausfrid: *see* Geoffrey		
Gautarr: *see* Gotre		
Gauti	NFK	65,13
	SFK	3,56. 7,15
Gauti, Earl Harold's Guard	MDX	8,3
Gauti, Earl Harold's thane	HRT	17,13
Gauti: *see also* Goti		
Gelder	NTH	39,15
Genred	NFK	9,29;32
Genust	SHR	4,21,6;14
Geoffrey	BDF	4,1
	BRK	27,3
	BKM	14,12. 23,16
	CAM	14,63;70;72;77
	CHS	R1,43
	DBY	10,6
	DEV	3,93. 5,1;3-4;8. 34,53-54
	DOR	36,9
	ESS	20,14. 24,20. 33,2;22. 47,3
	GLS	32,13. 34,7. 38,4-5
	HAM	2,5;10;14-15. 3,6. 23,47;60. 37,2.
		IoW7,23. 8,5;7;9
	HEF	7,6. 15,5
	HRT	9,9. 10,13
	KEN	2,10. 7,26
	LEC	16,4-5. 17,10
	LIN	8,33;39. 14,85. 59,1. CS,39
	NFK	4,18;44. 10,37. 29,1;3. 31,8;17;31;44
	NTH	4,1;14-15. 6a,5-6;13. 43,2;9-10. 46,1
	NTT	13,8
	OXF	35,17;30. 58,15
	RUT	R6
	SHR	4,3,27. 6,8
	SOM	2,6. 21,15-16;48;74-77. 25,24. 36,
		9-10. 37,9
	STS	8,25. 11,29. 12,4
	SFK	25,57. 53,5-6. 67,12
	SRY	5,8
	SSX	3,1;7. 8,1. 9,14;109-110. 11,15;36;66;
		113
	WAR	28,11
	YKS	6N60;82;85;108. 13E2;7;9

Geoffrey [representing Galfrid, Gaosfrid,
  Gaufrid, Gausfrid, God(e)frid, Gosfrid]: *see
  note in introduction*
Geoffrey: *see also* Osbern son of
     : *see also* William son of

Geoffrey, a man-at-arms   CHS   9,17. R5,6
                                               NTH   6a,6
                                               SHR   4,4,20
                                               SSX   11,1
Geoffrey Alselin   DBY   9. 6,27;81. B5
                                               LEC   28
                                               LIN   64. C4;20
                                               NTH   44. B25
                                               NTT   12. B13
                                               YKS   18. CW16;19;33-34. SW,Sf21. SW,An9
Geoffrey Alselin: *see also* Ralph nephew of
Geoffrey Bainard/Baynard   ESS   68,2
                                               NFK   31,1-5
                                               YKS   1Y14 *and note*
Geoffrey de Mandeville   BRK   38. 1,14
                                               BKM   21. 38,1
                                               CAM   22. AppxA
                                               ESS   30. 5,2. 8,9. 90,20-28;34. B31. ESf2
                                               GLS   G4
                                               HRT   33. B8. 9,3;10
                                               MDX   9. 2,3. 25,2
                                               NTH   45
                                               OXF   39
                                               SFK   32. 8,4. 61,1. 67,11
                                               SRY   25
                                               WAR   30. B2.
G(eoffrey) de Mandeville   ESS   1,3. 10,5. 20,71. 25,16. 34,7. 52,1. 77,
                                                       1
                                               SFK   6,112. 21,58;95
Geoffrey de Mandeville: *see also* William
  nephew of
Geoffrey (Delamare)   GLS   64,2
Geoffrey, Drogo of Beuvrière's man   LIN   30,17-20
Geoffrey, Gilbert of Ghent's man   LIN   24,36;80;83
                                               RUT   R15. ELc5
Geoffrey, Gilbert Tison's man   YKS   21E9
Geoffrey, Hugh son of Baldric's man   YKS   23E14
Geoffrey, Ivo Tallboys' man   LIN   14,11;13;84. CN19
Geoffrey Mallory   DOR   *36,1*
Geoffrey Malregard   SOM   *5,46*
Geoffrey Martel   ESS   30,3
(Geoffrey) Martel   ESS   30,24;31-32;35;43
Geoffrey Martel: *see also* Martel
Geoffrey, Norman of Arcy's man   LIN   32,4;6;8
Geoffrey of Baynard: *see* Geoffrey Bainard,
  Baynard
Geoffrey of Beauchamp   YKS   CE9. SE,Ac2
Geoffrey of Bec   HRT   34. B4. 1,9;13. 10,12;17;19
Geoffrey of Chesfield   HRT   Appx
Bishop Geoffrey/of Coutances/of St Lô   BDF   3. 31,1
                                               BRK   6
                                               BKM   5. B3. 40,1
                                               DEV   3. 1,1 *and note*; 11
                                               DOR   5
                                               GLS   6. W13. 1,21. E9
                                               HAM   S3
                                               HUN   3. B13
                                               LEC   4
                                               LIN   6
                                               MDX   21,1

	NFK	*15,22*
	NTH	4. B2. 35,1j. 41,5. 56,65. EB1-2. EH1
	OXF	B8. EN1-4
	SOM	5. 1,7;28. 8,2;25;38. 20,1. 44,2. EBe, 1-3. EBu1-2
	SFK	21,17 *and note.* 29,9
	WAR	5. B2
	WIL	5. 7,5;10
	YKS	C9;16
Geoffrey of Flocques	SSX	9,105
Geoffrey of la Guerche	LEC	29. C14
	LIN	63. CW,17
	NTH	47. B24
	NTT	19
	WAR	31. B2. 14,1-6
	YKS	17. SW,St2
Geoffrey of Rots/a man-at-arms	KEN	*2,4;10-11.* 5,8;26;83. 13,1
Geoffrey of Runeville	HRT	34,22
Geoffrey (of Runeville)	HRT	34,23
Abbot Geoffrey/of Tavistock	CON	*3*
	DEV	5
	DOR	*16 and notes*
Geoffrey of Trelly	BDF	3,4;10
	DEV	*3,97*
	SOM	EBe2
Geoffrey of Vautortes	SOM	*21,5;14;81*
Geoffrey of Westbrook	HRT	Appx
Geoffrey Orlateile	GLS	51
	SRY	26
Geoffrey Ridel	NFK	9,88
Geoffrey, Robert of Stafford's man	LIN	59,4-5;7
Geoffrey, Roger of Bully's man	NTT	9,6;33;36;116;118-119
Geoffrey, Roger of Poitou's man	LIN	16,9
Geoffrey son of Count Eustace	SRY	25,2
Geoffrey son of Count Eustace, wife of	SRY	25,2
Geoffrey son of Hamo	SFK	25,86
Geoffrey son of Modbert	KEN	*D8 and note*
Geoffrey son of (Roger of) Malleterre	KEN	*5,124*
Geoffrey Talbot	ESS	47,1
Geoffrey, the Abbot of Ely's constable	CAM	AppxP
Geoffrey, the Archbishop's man	YKS	2A3
Geoffrey the canon	SSX	9,126
Geoffrey the chamberlain	HAM	67. 1,42
Geoffrey the cleric	SSX	9,11
Geoffrey the little	SRY	36,1
Geoffrey the marshall	HAM	62. 56,3
	WIL	M12. *68,21*
Geoffrey, the reeve of Ely's Hundreds	CAM	AppxP
Geoffrey [of] Tournai, Count Alan's man	LIN	12,89
Geofu (fem.): *see* Ieva		
Gerald	DOR	26,41
	ESS	24,24. 39,4-5
	HEF	10,12-13;20;23. 15,9
	SFK	8,51. 25,105. 38,14;22-23
	SSX	10,1;56
	WAR	4,3-4
	WIL	27,13
Gerald: *see also* Robert son of		
Gerald, a man-at-arms	SSX	9,1
G(erald), a thane	DEV	*45,1*

Gerald of Wilton	WIL	18
Gerald the chaplain	DEV	45
Gerald the marshall	SFK	65
Gerald the priest, of Wilton	WIL	1,19
Gerard	BKM	43,6. 51,2
	CHS	R6,4
	DEV	46. 23,5;7-8;12. 32,8-9
	ESS	33,1. 41,1;10-11
	GLS	W16. 39,19
	HAM	3,1
	HEF	10,33. 21,7
	LEC	17,22;24;30-31
	NTH	56,62
	SHR	4,23
	SOM	19,6. 24,15. 46,20
	SFK	40,3
	SRY	22,3
	WIL	13,9. 26,5
Gerard, a man-at-arms	NFK	*8,37;44*
	SSX	9,6;8
Gerard Ditcher	SOM	*8,15;17. 21,38*
Gerard, Hugh son of Baldric's man	YKS	23N9-11;13;15-16
Gerard (Hugh son of Baldric's man)	YKS	23N4
Gerard of Lorraine	CAM	*14,18-19.* AppxG
Gerard, Rainer of Brimeux's man	LIN	40,7
Gerard, Roger of Poitou's man	LIN	16,39
Gerard the chamberlain	GLS	19,2. EvM79
Gerard (the chamberlain)	GLS	W10. 1,24;40-41
Gerard the watchman	NFK	1,61
Gerard, William of Warenne's man-at-arms	NFK	*8,37;44*
Gerbert	LEC	34
Gerbodo	YKS	9W56;98
Gerbodo, Drogo of Beuvrière's man	YKS	14E36
Gerhelm	SHR	4,23,13
Geri	SHR	4,3,18;71
Gerin	HAM	S2. IoW9,18
	WAR	34
Gerling	DOR	55,16
Germanus	HAM	3,8. 23,14
Germund	BDF	16,8
	BKM	21,5
	ESS	23,15. 30,48. 33,13;15. 90,53
	HRT	33,7-8;12
	SFK	25,55
Germund of St Ouen	HRT	Appx
Germund, Walter Giffard's man	NFK	66,63
Gernand	YKS	6N26;58;148
Gernio	OXF	B9. 58,16
Gero	DEV	37,1
Geron	SOM	EDe1
Gervi	HAM	1,37
Gervi: *see also* Gerwy		
Gerwy	GLS	67,3
Gerwy: *see also* Gervi		
Gerwy of Loge's wife	GLS	76,1
Gest, Saeric's brother	WIL	67,96
Gethne	SHR	4,21,11
Giefu (fem.): *see* Ieva		
Gifard	NFK	35,3 *and note*; 16-17
	SFK	40,6

Giffard of Dry Drayton	CAM	AppxO
Gilbert	BDF	53,11
	BRK	1,7. 7,10;26;36-37;42-44. 22,1. 34,1
	BKM	18,1-2
	CHS	27,2. S1,7. R1,43. Y12
	DBY	11,1
	DEV	16,31;88;141. 28,5;12. 35,12. 42,9
	DOR	27,1
	ESS	3,2
	HEF	1,16. 8,1. 10,16;42. 19,9
	HRT	4,15
	KEN	7,19. 9,34
	LEC	15,13;15. 17,19
	LIN	C20. 30,32. 63,25. CK,63
	NFK	8,66
	NTH	21,5. 56,53;63
	OXF	6,13. 9,7. 27,10. 28,13-14;18-19. 29, 12. 34,1
	SHR	4,4,18
	STS	11,11-13;53. 12,5;10;13
	SFK	6,19-21;29-30;34-37;40;52;83;92;100; 279;283. 25,8;78. 29,8. 31,38
	SSX	3,6. 10,3;15;22;27;57;114. 12,6;36. 13, 15-16
	WAR	16,34;49;51;54;57;59. 17,33;36. 37,7
	WIL	1,20. 5,4. 7,8. 8,12. 20,2-4. 24,30. 26, 2. 49,2
	YKS	9W17;50
Gilbert: *see also* Robert son of : *see also* Walter Cook son of		
Gilbert, a man-at-arms	HEF	19,1
	SSX	13,9
Gilbert Blunt	SFK	6,84-88;105;133;254
G(ilbert Blunt)	SFK	6,134 *note*
Gilbert, brother of Robert the clerk	HAM	2,10
Gilbert Cook	NTH	57
Gilbert (de Eskecot)	GLS	39,7. 63,4
Gilbert, Hugh son of Baldric's man	LIN	25,13
Gilbert Hunter	CHS	18
Bishop Gilbert Maminot/of Lisieux	BRK	1,1
	BKM	6. 4,5;14;33;41-42
	DOR	6. 1,31
	GLS	30. E9
	HRT	6
	KEN	5,29;36-37
	MDX	3,7
	OXF	8
	SRY	1,5. 5,10;13. 6,1
	WIL	6
	YKS	C14. SE,Ac2
Gilbert of Blosseville	BDF	53,15
	BKM	53,4
Gilbert of Bouillé	WAR	B2
Gilbert of Breteuil/Bretteville	BRK	36
	HAM	43. 11,1. S3
	OXF	59,1-2
	WIL	29. 68,23
Count Gilbert (of Brionne): *see* Richard son of		
Gilbert of Coleville	SFK	6,127;180;236;272
Bishop Gilbert/of Evreux	SFK	22

Gilbert of Ghent	BDF	27
	BRK	37. B3
	BKM	22. E1
	CAM	23. AppxM
	DBY	13. 9,5. 16,1
	HUN	21. B2
	LEC	33
	LIN	24. C7. 4,1. 8,9. 18,19. 25,19. 42,8. 57,40. CS,13;18-19;23;30;33;36-37. CN,1. CW,6;11;17-18. CK,6;35-36;44
	NTH	46
	NTT	17
	OXF	38
	RUT	5. R15. EN14-15. ELc5
	WAR	32. B2. EN7.
	YKS	20. CW4. SE,Tu1-2
Gilbert of Histon	CAM	AppxO
Gilbert of Linden End	CAM	AppxP
Gilbert of Maine	GLS	EvK1
Gilbert of Venables	CHS	17
Gilbert of Wissant	SFK	6,30;143;239;244;281;286-287
Gilbert, Roger of Bully's man	NTT	9,52
Gilbert son of Richere of L'Aigle	NFK	42
	SFK	ENf5
	SRY	24
Gilbert son of Solomon	BDF	48. 29,1
	ESS	73. 15,1
	HRT	40
Gilbert son of Thorold	CAM	24
	ESS	58
	GLS	52. 3,1. 19,2. WoB15
	HEF	25. 1,51
	SOM	42. 1,21
	WAR	33. EW3
	WOR	20. 2,47. 8,10c;23;25. 11,2
Gilbert son of Thorold: *see also* Walter son-in-law of		
Gilbert son of Warin	ESS	1,13
Gilbert, the Abbot of Peterborough's man	LIN	8,9;22
Gilbert, the Archbishop of York's man	LIN	2,3;21
Gilbert, the Bishop of Bayeux's man	ESS	18,34. 48,2
Gilbert the crossbowman	NFK	52. 1,61
	SFK	68
Gilbert the priest	BKM	2,1
	ESS	82
	HUN	20,5-6
	SFK	32,4
	SRY	6,1
Gilbert the sheriff	HEF	8,1
	SSX	10,1
Gilbert the watchman	NFK	1,61
Gilbert Tison	LIN	23
	NTT	18
	YKS	21. CE14;16;28. SW,Sk16. SW,Sf27. SW, Bu17;26;31-32;34;37-41. SE,He1-3;6;8-9;11. SE,C7-8. SE,How7-9. SE,Wei2-3. SE,P3
Gilbert with the beard	CAM	*20,1*
Giles	GLS	WoC4
Giles, brother of Ansculf	BRK	34

	BKM	51
	NTH	43. B26
	OXF	37
Gilleandrais	YKS	13N12
Gillebride	YKS	29E30
Gillemicel	YKS	1N135. 1L7. 30W39
Gillemicel: *see also* Gillemichael		
Gillemichael	CHS	Y8;12
Gillemichael: *see also* Gillemicel		
Gillepatric	YKS	6N28;87;90;94;99;102
Gilli	YKS	1E46. 6N29;131;137-138
Ginni	ESS	B31
	SFK	8,64
Gislold, a man-at-arms	SHR	4,20,8
Bishop Giso/of Wells	SOM	6. 1,2;21. 22,20
Givold	SOM	22,20
Gladiou	ESS	22,13
Gladman	SFK	67,12
Gladwin	DBY	17,15
	LEC	14,24
	NTT	9,90. 10,16;65
	STS	13,7
Gladwin, the Abbot of St Albans' man	BKM	12,18
Gladwin: *see also* Gladwine, Glaedwine		
Gladwine	LIN	4,76
Gladwine: *see also* Gladwin, Glaedwine		
Glaedwine: *see* Gladwin, Gladwine		
Gleman of Levington	SFK	6,110
Gleu, Alfred of Lincoln's man	LIN	27,12;14;47-48
	RUT	ELc6-7
Gleu, Godfrey of Cambrai's man	LIN	51,10
	RUT	ELc9-10
Gleu: *see also* Glew		
Glew	BDF	31,1
Glew: *see also* Gleu		
Glewin	CHS	17,4
Gluniairnn	YKS	C12. 1W13;17 *note*; 18-19;29. 6N92.
		9W14;16;39-40. 10W39. 30W30
Gobert: *see* Robert son of		
God(...)	NFK	9,86
Goda (fem.)	CAM	13,1-2;4-7. 26,22
	DEV	3,72. 17,53;96. 34,35;39. 35,28. 42,7
	DOR	1,30
	ESS	B3a(x6),m
	KEN	9,53
	OXF	58,21
	RUT	R5-6
	SOM	22,11
	SFK	7,22;75;80;82;105;108-109;110(x2);
		112. 16,29. 25,81. *39,10*
	SSX	9,22-23;78;80;96;100-101. 10,42;110
	WIL	24,40. 25,26. 67,48
Goda (fem.), Earl Algar's man	CAM	*13,1*
Goda (fem.): *see* Gode, *see also* Countess Goda		
Countess Goda/King Edward's sister	BKM	37,1. 38,1. 53,5
	DBY	3,2
	DOR	1,30-31
	GLS	21,1. 23,2. 24,1. 72,1
	MDX	13,1
	SRY	14,1. 32,1

	SSX	5,3. 9,34;37;40;44-45;49-50;52;66-68;
		70;72-73;82;99;122. 11,77
(Countess) Goda	DEV	33,1-2
	GLS	72,2-3
Goda (masc)	CAM	14,53
Goda: *see also* Alwin son of		
Goda, brother of Aelfwin, Ulf's man	SFK	7,37
Goda of 'Struostuna'	SFK	6,110
Goda the priest	DEV	*45,2*
Godard	SFK	25,84
Godard, Jocelyn son of Lambert's man	LIN	28,20
Godbald	BRK	22,8. 65,18
Godbald: *see also* Godbold		
Godbold	BKM	14,48
	ESS	24,19;45;57
	SHR	3g,5-6;8. 4,21,7. 4,27,7
	SOM	43
Godbold the bowman	DEV	47
Godbold (the bowman)	SOM	43,1
Godbold the priest	SHR	3g,3
Godbold: *see also* Godbald		
Godday	ESS	B3a
Gode (fem.)	HRT	18,1. 32,2. 34,4
	WIL	27,24
Gode, King Edward's man	HRT	17,4
Gode, Queen Edith's man	HRT	42,7
Gode (fem.) : *see also* Countess Goda		
: *see also* Goda		
Gode (masc.): *see* Goda (masc.), Golde		
Godefrid: *see* Geoffrey, Godfrey		
Godel	KEN	5,18
Godelind (fem.)	YKS	C10
Goderun (fem.)	OXF	B10
Godesa (fem.)	HAM	IoW9,11
	KEN	5,200. 7,24
Godescal	DOR	54,7
	SOM	8,10
	WIL	65. 36,1
Godfrey	BDF	4,1;3
	BRK	7,12. 28,2
	BKM	41,6
	CON	2,11
	DEV	*1,23. 15,67.* 19,13. 25,7;13;20
	DOR	3,11
	ESS	24,40. 30,51. 41,9
	HEF	1,8. 21,3
	HRT	36,3;4
	LEC	3,12. 16,1
	LIN	8,36;38
	NTH	5,4
	OXF	29,8;10;15;23. 46,1
	SRY	4,1
	SSX	2,1a;1d. 10,3;79. 11,105. 12,8;11;
		20-21;44
	WIL	24,7;38
	WOR	2,12;52
	YKS	13W17-19;32;37
Godfrey, a man-at-arms	DOR	3,17

Godfrey of Cambrai	LEC	30
	LIN	51
	RUT	ELc9
Godfrey of Pierrepont	SFK	26,12c;14
Godfrey (of Vautortes)	DEV	*15,67 and note*
Godfrey Scullion	DOR	57,22
Godfrey Scullion, father of	DOR	57,22
Godfrey, the Abbot of Peterborough's man	LIN	8,36
Godfrey the arblaster	KEN	*2,21*
Godfrey the chamberlain	DEV	*16,53-54*
Godfrey the cleric	SSX	10,71
Godfrey the priest	SSX	10,27
Godfrey the steward/Godfrey of Malling	KEN	*2,15-16;36-37. 3.5*
Godfrey: *see also* Geoffrey		
Godfrid: *see* Geoffrey, Godfrey		
Godgifu (fem.): *see* Godiva		
Godgyth (fem.)	CHS	20,5;7-8;12
Godgyth (fem.): *see also* Godith		
Godhere	ESS	4,17. 66,2
	SFK	8,4
Godhild (fem.): *see* Godil, Gothild, Gotild		
Godhyse (fem.)	YKS	5W17. CW20
Godil (fem.)	KEN	5,98
Godil (fem.): *see also* Godhild		
Goding	BKM	17,20
	ESS	23,36. 28,4. 90,73. B3a(x3)
	HAM	23,34
	NFK	1,144
	STS	11,35
	SFK	3,73. 7,89(x2). 16,35. 74,13
Goding : *see also* Aelfric son of		
: *see also* Aelmer son of		
: *see also* Alric son of		
: *see also* Alwin son of		
: *see also* Godingson, Alric		
Goding Bolt	CAM	*31,2*
Goding, Edric the Bald's man	BDF	55,8
Goding, Osbern the monk's man	HRT	10,12
Goding Thorbert, Edeva the fair's man	CAM	26,38
Godith (fem.)	DBY	1,34
	ESS	5,6. 24,8. 30,26. B3a
	HRT	4,23. 33,19
	SHR	4,25,6
Godith, Asgar's man	HRT	17,10
Godith, Asgar the constable's man	HRT	17,6-7;14. 33,13;18
Godith (fem.): *see also* Godgyth		
Godiva (fem.)	CAM	38,1
	CHS	R1,33
	DBY	16,6
	DEV	25,11. 42,12. 52,52-53
	ESS	90,55. B3a(x2)
	HRT	33,7
	NTH	18,34
	SOM	8,25
	STS	8,21. 11,4;13;23;37;42
	SFK	7,90. 11,4. 25,33. 67,29
	WAR	17,42
	WIL	29,5. 50,3
Godiva (fem.): *see also* Countess Godiva		
Godiva (fem.), Edeva the fair's man	CAM	*14,24*

Godiva (fem.), wife of Brictric	DEV	*52,52-53 and note*
Countess Godiva/wife of Earl Leofric	DBY	S5
	LEC	11
	NTT	S5. 6,1;13;15
	SHR	4,1,31. 4,7,1. 4,11,11. 4,19,2;8
	STS	4,2. 12,5;21-22
	WAR	15. 43,1
	WOR	26,13
Godiva: *see also* Godgifu		
Godiva's husband	SOM	8,25
Godlamb	CAM	14,34. 41,8
Godleofu (fem.): *see* Golleva		
Godlid of Longstanton/Godlive	CAM	AppxN
Godlive: *see* Godlid, Guthlif		
Godman	CAM	32,17
	DEV	16,171
	ESS	24,54. 75,1. 83,2
	HAM	1,W8. 49,1
	LIN	48,12
	NTH	18,34
	SOM	19,60. 33,1
	SFK	2,17. 3,68. 6,65-66. 7,90;117;119. 8,
		56. 25,55. 29,4. 67,4
Godman, a thane	SFK	59,2
Godman, Earl Algar's man	CAM	*32,8*
Godman, Edeva's man	CAM	14,34
Godman the priest	DEV	*16,51;129*
Godmer	CAM	*32,11*
	SFK	3,59
Godmer, Alstan's man	BDF	18,3
Godmer of Girton	CAM	AppxN
Godmund	BDF	56,7
	DOR	40,3. 56,1
	ESS	20,62
	HEF	1,10b;17. 10,51;53
	HRT	42,15
	NFK	23,16 *and note*
	WAR	27,1
	WIL	65,2
Godmund, brother of Thorkell	WAR	17,7
Godmund, Earl Waltheof's man	CAM	39,3
Godmund, King Edward's man	BDF	3,8
Godmund son of Saeric	HEF	10,71
Godnir, a royal Guard	BKM	12,36
Godnir: *see also* Goldnir		
Godo	SSX	9,115
Godram	NFK	4,26
Godram: *see also* Aethelstan son of		
Godred	YKS	5N57 *and note*
Godred: *see also* Guthrothr		
Godric	BRK	B4;7. 21,6;12;16. 29,1. 31,1. 36,2
	BKM	12,10
	CAM	1,12. *18,8. 29,11.* 32,1
	CHS	1,9;28. 2,31. 8,12;23. 11,1-4. 12,5-8.
		27,4
	CON	4,11-12;16. 5,3,11-12;28
	DBY	1,30-31. 6,12;29-30;34;55;73;97. 14,
		2-3;8. 16,2. 17,2;6

DEV	*3,12*. 16,83;101. 19,2-3;*4*. 23,3;13. 34, 24;32. 39,4;9. 40,6. 43,1. 51,2. 52,4-7; 20
DOR	26,1;47. 36,1-2;8. 55,2. 56,27;54
ESS	4,12. 14,1. 18,9;41. 20,73. 24,12;29; 43;46;59-61. 32,33. 33,5. 34,14. 63,2. 71,2. B3a(x6),e
GLS	19,2. 26,1. 36,1;3. 39,18. 43,1-2. 60,3. 68,5. E31-32
HAM	23,41. 45,4. 58,1. 69,11. NF3,16. 9,7; 9;32. IoW6,5;11-12;15-16. 7,15. 9,5; 14;20
HEF	2,26. 8,7. 22,6. 29,1. 31,3-4;6. 36,1
HUN	2,5. 6,17. D8
KEN	5,7;45;47;77;90;94;100;162;171;187; 208
LEC	3,5-10;12-13. 14,16. 43,2;4
LIN	C15. T4. 12,1. 13,21;24;30;33;41-42; 44-45. 14,9. 16,27;36. 22,34. 26,5;23. 28,2. 29,18. 31,15. 32,29. 43,1;5. 45, 4. 49,4. 55,1. 58,8. 60,1. 67,18-19. CS, 15;37;39. CW,5. CK,30
NFK	1,10;57;71-75;77-78;80;87;90-91;96; 111;120;122;124;131-132;133a;144; 174;195;201;209;213. 4,10;31. 6,1. 8, 5;37;71. 9,193-194;196-198;200;204; 232. 10,39;71;81. 12,38. 15,18. 17,55; 63. 20,19-20. 25,18. 26,5. 29,1. 31,11. 32,3. 66,42;64;82;84-85;91;92
NTH	6a,32. 15,1. 18,57. 22,8. 23,10
NTT	2,10. 5,12. 9,28;40;59;82;89;94;105; 129. 10,1;27;59;61;66. 16,5. 20,7. 28, 3. 29,1. 30,22;24
OXF	B10. 7,51. 55,1. 56,3-4
SHR	4,4,3;24. 4,16,1. 4,23,8. 4,27,3;23. 6,8
SOM	*5,3*. 9,4;8. 19,3;29;65-66;70. 21,10-11; 25;28;37;67;*80*;85. 37,11. 45,8
STS	5,2. 11,19;25;33;65. 17,10;13-14. ED5
SFK	1,19;111;123e-123f. 3,95. 4,2. 6,36;84; 159;176-177;186;191;193;202;234; 245. 7,8-9;24;57;77(x3);80(x3);85;91; 97-98;108-109;117-118;120-121; 148(x2). 8,3;*17*;81. 11,1-3. 13,6. 16,*8*; 23;26;36. 21,52. 25,57;67;69-70;75. 32,26. 35,7(x2). 39,1;5-6. 45,1. 66,13. 67,10. 68,3-4. 74,13(x2). EC1
SRY	36,7
SSX	12,44-45
WAR	16,22-23;25;42-43. 17,4;41. 29,5
WIL	1,21. 2,7. 22,6. 24,11. 25,17. 26,16. 27,22. 28,5. 37,15. 39,1-2. 41,9. 66,2. 67,46;98. 68,18. E2
WOR	2,17;32;61;73. 8,9b;9d-9e;10a;10d;19; 22. 18,1-2. 26,1
YKS	1W22;25. 2N29. 9W4;42-43;74;82;87. 10W7;10;16;37

Godric: *see also* Alric nephew of

Godric, a forester	SOM	*46,3*
Godric, a royal thane	BDF	4,1;3
	ESS	24,16;25

	GLS	39,16
	WOR	9,1e. 23,9
Godric, a thane	BKM	4,30. 5,21
	DEV	*3,12. 19,4. 23,3. 40,6. 43,1. 51,2*
	DOR	*36,5*
	GLS	26,3. 37,3
	HAM	19,1
	HEF	19,2
	NTT	9,26
	SOM	*5,3. 21,85. 22,28*
Godric, Aelmer of Bennington's man	HRT	20,8
Godric, Algar's man	CAM	*32,7*
Godric, Alric's uncle	HAM	69,38
Godric, and his two brothers	LIN	3,41
Godric, Archbishop Stigand's man	HRT	10,11
Godric, Asgar the constable's man	BKM	28,2
Godric, brother of Bishop Wulfwy	BKM	3a,2
Godric, brother of Edric	GLS	53,10
Godric Clock	GLS	E31
	WOR	8,9b
Godric, Count Alan's man	LIN	12,53;57
Godric Cratel	BKM	57,13
Godric, Eadric's brother	LIN	CS,6
Godric, Earl Algar's thane	WOR	15,4
Godric, Godman's man	SFK	2,17
Godric, Godric of Ross's man	NFK	66,91
Godric, Harold's man/a thane	BKM	17,22
Godric Hunter	DOR	*56,4*
	WIL	67,45
Godric Karlson	KEN	D17
Godric, King Edward's man	CAM	29,6
Godric Latimer	KEN	*M24*
Godric Long	SFK	7,77
Godric Malf, and his sons	HAM	69,39. NF9,36-39
Godric Mapson	HEF	1,60
Godric of Bishopsbourne	KEN	D17. 9,42
Godric of Calverleigh	DEV	*52,21*
Godric of Colchester	ESS	20,42
Godric (of Colchester)	ESS	B1-2
Godric of Croxton	CAM	AppxL
Godric of Fowlmere	CAM	AppxH
Godric of Heigham	NFK	65,7
Godric of Peyton	SFK	6,238 (cf 27,13)
Godric of Ringshall	SFK	29,8
Godric of Ross	NFK	66,91
Godric, Oswy's man	BKM	17,29
Godric Poinc	ESS	22,18
Godric Skipper	ESS	22,16
Godric son of Agmundr	LIN	68,45
Godric son of Eadgifu, a lawman	LIN	C2-3
Godric son of Garwine, a monk	LIN	C16
Godric son of Herebold	SFK	6,108
Godric son of Karl	KEN	D17. 5,25
Godric son of Thorfrothr	LIN	T5
Godric the burgess	ESS	B3a
Godric the canon	KEN	P1
Godric the deacon	CAM	*29,6*
	KEN	*2,42*
	LIN	68,31;35
Godric the falconer	CAM	*32,28*

OXF	B10. 58,26;38
RUT	R10
SHR	4,3,12;58. 4,8,12-13;15. 4,14,9;15-16. 4,23,2
SOM	2,7. 5,33;56. 8,1. 16,10. 19,29;71. 21, 21;91;94. 22,28. 47,6-7;9
STS	8,19;22;29;31-32. 11,16;32;41. 12,9; 20. 13,7-8. 14,2. 17,11. EN2
SFK	1,49;53. 2,19. 3,82. 6,12;116;120; 165-168;191;307. 7,14;51;82;92;98. 8, 63. 14,164. 16,35;44. 21,39;71. 25,60; 79;86. 35,7. 38,8;11. 40,3. 66,13. 67, 10-12. 74,12-13
SRY	19,42
SSX	9,15-16;69;116-118. 10,20-21;49;55; 58;95;111;118. 11,5;38;71;79;86;100; 108-109;112. 13,21
WAR	17,31;40. 22,3. 44,14
WIL	20,2-4. 24,36. 25,9. 41,9. 46,1. 67,36; 40. 68,17
WOR	2,25-26

G(odwin?)	NFK	1,61
Godwin: *see also* A(e)lmer son of		
Godwin, a freeman of Edric's	NFK	29,8
Godwin, a royal thane	BDF	29,1
	ESS	24,10. 25,5
	HRT	34,21
	SFK	28,1
Godwin, a thane	BKM	43,11
	DEV	2,15. 16,7
	HAM	1,W1
	NFK	1,198
	SOM	19,29
	SFK	33,3
Godwin Aelfeth: *see* Godwin (son of?) Aelfeth		
(another) Godwin	DEV	16,7
Godwin, Aelfric the priest's man	SFK	2,17
Godwin, Aelmer of Bennington's man	HRT	20,5
Godwin, Alric son of Goding's man	BKM	23,31
Godwin, Alstan's man	BDF	18,2
Godwin, Archbishop Stigand's man	CAM	32,8
Godwin, Askell's man	BDF	23,13
Godwin Benfield	HRT	4,14. 2,11
Godwin Benfield: *see also* Godwin of Benfield		
Godwin, Bishop Wulfwy's man, a thane	BKM	14,48-49
Godwin, brother of Alfward	KEN	5,33
Godwin, Burgred's man	BDF	54,4
Godwin Child: *see* Young Godwin		
Godwin Clack	WIL	67,47
Earl Godwin	DOR	1,2
	GLS	1,63. E4
	HEF	1,74. 19,8
	HAM	1,13-14;19;W12;W14. 18,2. 20,2. 21, 6-7;10. 23,32. 28,2;7. 66,1. 69,1. IoW7,1. ESx
	HEF	1,74. 19,8
	KEN	D1. 2,41;43. 4,16. 5,40;64-65;79; 84-85;89;93;109;128;142;178. 7,10. 9, 4;10. 10,1-2
	SRY	5,28. 24,1

	SSX	1,1-2. 8,3. 9,1;104;106-108;121. 10,27; 31;39-41;43;45-46;61;93;115. 11,3;5; 8-10;13-14;16;30;36-37;41;45;65; 75-76;95-98;105. 12,9-10;13;28;30;33; 36;42;48. 13,6;13;17-18;20;31;35;42; 46-47;51;53
	WIL	48,12
	WOR	19,12
(Earl) Godwin	HEF	19,3
	KEN	2,5
Earl Godwin: *see also* Gunhilda, daughter of		
Godwin, Earl Gyrth's man	BDF	54,1
Godwin, Earl Harold's man	BDF	53,7;9
	HRT	1,13
Godwin, Earl Leofwin's man	BKM	4,9;22;40
Godwin, Earl Tosti's man	BDF	47,3
Godwin, Earl Waltheof's man	CAM	41,13-14
Godwin, Edeva's man	CAM	14,6
Godwin, Engelric's man	HRT	15,5
Godwin Foot	KEN	5,34
Godwin Frambold, a royal thane	BDF	31,1. 32,7. 46,2. 47,2
Godwin, Gyrth's freeman	NFK	29,8-9
Godwin Haldane	NFK	61. 1,216
Godwin Halden [indexing error for above]	NFK	1,216
Godwin Hunter	DOR	56,24;27
Godwin, King Edward's man	BDF	53,19
	BKM	44,3
Godwin Nabson/Godwin of Fulbourn	CAM	AppxE
Godwin of Benfield	HRT	4,18-19. 20,3;12
Godwin of Benfield: *see also* Godwin Benfield		
Godwin of (Chittlehampton)	DEV	52,9-19 *and notes* (cf 52,10)
	SOM	47,7
Godwin of Fulbourn: *see* Godwin Nabson		
Godwin of Hormead	HRT	Appx (cf 38,1-2)
Godwin of Letchworth	HRT	34,7
Godwin of Linacre	CAM	26,9
Godwin of Scotton	NFK	9,87
Godwin of Soulbury, a royal thane	HRT	20,7
Godwin of Stanton	GLS	1,67
Godwin of Sutton	SFK	6,165-169
Godwin of Weston	HUN	19,28. D13
Godwin Sech	ESS	90,28
Godwin Shield	CAM	41,14
Godwin (son of?) Aelfeth, Wigot's man	MDX	7,7
Godwin son of Alfhere	SFK	6,1-2;112-114
Godwin son of Algar	SFK	7,36
Godwin son of Alsi, Queen Edith's thane	SFK	6,26-27
Godwin son of Dudeman	ESS	EKt
	KEN	5,104
Godwin son of Harold	SOM	1,14;16
Godwin son of Karl	KEN	5,105
Godwin son of Leofwin	BDF	24,9
Godwin son of Toki/Tokeson	NFK	29,2
	SFK	7,22;47-48
Godwin son of Wulfstan	HRT	20,9
Godwin, the Abbot (of Ely)'s man	CAM	5,2. 26,50. 30,3
Godwin the beadle	BKM	57,18
Godwin the burgess	BDF	56,2
Godwin the deacon	ESS	88. 30,11

Godwin the Englishman	ESS	76,1
	SOM	*16,10. 47,15*
Godwin the falconer	HAM	69,49
Godwin, the King's reeve	SOM	*1,20.* 19,33
Godwin the priest	BKM	12,20. 57,5
	CAM	*30,3. 31,1.* AppxM
	DBY	B12
	DEV	*15,7*
	ESS	68,8
	HAM	5,1
	LEC	8,1
	NTH	B32. 17,2-3;5
	NTT	10,27;56
	SOM	*8,33*
	SFK	38,11
	SSX	6,4. 12,33;42
Godwin the priest, a thane	BKM	17,22
Godwin the priest, Harold's man	SFK	7,122
Godwin the priest: *see also* Aelfric brother of		
Godwin the reeve	DOR	56,26
Godwin Tokeson: *see* Godwin son of Toki		
Godwin, Ulf's man	BKM	17,28
Godwin, uncle of Earl Ralph	NFK	1,61 *note*; 144;185
G(odwin), uncle of Earl Ralph	ESS	ENf
	NFK	38,2-3
Godwin Weakfeet	ESS	B3a
Godwin Weakfeet's son	ESS	B3a
Godwin Wombstring	CAM	22,7
Godwin Woodhen	ESS	9,5. 90,1-3
Godwin (Woodhen)	ESS	60,1
Young Godwin (Abbot of Westminster)	BKM	12,12
Young Godwin [= Godwin Child]	CAM	14,1;80. 18,3. 35,2
Young Godwin, Edeva the fair's man	CAM	14,1;6
Godwin: *see also* Godwine		
Godwin's mother	SOM	47,15
Godwin's wife	HRT	16,1
Godwine	LIN	2,16. 3,5;42. 4,39. 14,8-9. 18,28;31. 19,1. 23,1. 26,40. 29,1;3-4;8-9;11;18; 28;30. 32,8. 58,1-2; 6. 61,9. 62,1. CS, 27
	YKS	1W27-28. 2B3. 6W3. 9W106;109-112. 25W6 *note*; 8. CW34
Godwine, Guy of Craon's man	LIN	57,18;55
Godwine, Robert of Stafford's man	LIN	59,20
Godwine son of Beorhtric, a lawman	LIN	C3
Godwine son of Eadric	YKS	CW27
Godwine (son of Eadric)	YKS	25W1;3;6
Godwine, Waldin the Breton's man	LIN	46,1
Godwine: *see also* Godwin		
Godwine/Sighvatr: *see* Sighvatr		
Godwy	CAM	14,43
	SFK	16,22;28-29. 25,57. 30,1
Godwy Dear, of Bedford	BDF	57,14
Godwy the Englishman	BDF	15,3
Goisfrid: *see* Geoffrey		
Goismer	ESS	23,7. 90,49
Gold	CAM	32,29
Gold: *see also* Hugh son of		
Gold, the Abbot of Ely's man	CAM	*32,27*
Golde/Gode	HUN	19,21. 29,5

Golde: *see also* Gode
Golderon (fem.), Leofnoth's man   BDF   24,20
Golderon (fem.): *see also* Goldrun
Goldhere   ESS   B3a(x2)
Golding   ESS   B3a
Golding, Earl Harold's man   MDX   5,2
Goldman   ESS   B3a
Goldnir: *see* Godnir
Goldric   ESS   B3a
Goldrun (fem.): *see* Golderon
Goldstan   ESS   1,8. 90,49. B3a
                                                   KEN   M11
Goldwin   ESS   B3a(x2)
                                                   OXF   B10
                                                   SSX   9,16. 10,28
Golleva (fem.)   HAM   69,35
Golleva (fem.): *see also* Godleofu
Gorham: *see* W. son of
Gos   HUN   B14. D3
Gosbert   DEV   36,3-6
                                                   GLS   G4
                                                   OXF   27,3;9
                                                   STS   8,13
                                                   SFK   8,66;69-70
Gosbert: *see also* Hugh Gosbert
Gosbert of Beauvais   HRT   35. Appx
Gosfrid: *see* Geoffrey
Gosmer   GLS   6,3
Gospatric   YKS   28. C11;13;18. 1N42;46;48-51;53-56;
                                                          93-96;104-107. 1W42;54. 5N28-29.
                                                          6N31-32;47-48;61-62;65;67;70;72;79;
                                                          89;112-113;116-118;135;139;149-150.
                                                          9W15. 24W1-2;4-7;12-16. 29E22.
                                                          29W47;49. 30W22-23;30. SW,Sk3.
                                                          SW,An17. SW,Bu2;4-6;11-12;14-15;
                                                          20-26;30;32;34;37;49. SW,H6. SN,
                                                          Bi2-3. SE,D6
Got Chill   ESS   B3a
Got Fleet   ESS   B3a
Got Hugh   ESS   B3a
Gothild (fem.): *see* Godhild, Gotild
Goti   ESS   13,1. 28,1;9;11
Goti: *see also* Gauti
Gotild (fem.)   ESS   28,13-14;16
Gotild (fem.): *see also* Godhild, Gothild
Gotre   ESS   32,14;45
Gotshelm   CON   7
                                                   DEV   25. 1,*57-59;61-62;64-65*;70. 16,138;
                                                          161. 24,32. 36,7. *42,6*
Gotshelm, brother of Walter of Claville   DEV   24-25 *and notes*
Gotshelm Cook   DOR   8,1
Gotshelm of Exeter/the canon   DEV   25,28 *and note*
Gozhere: *see* Hugh son of
Gozo   SSX   12,16
Grapinel   ESS   24,22
Green   SSX   13,41
Greifi   LIN   12,56;58
Grento   SSX   10,66
Grento, a man-at-arms   DEV   *5,13*
                                                   SHR   4,4,20

Griffin	CON	1,1. 5,7,1
Grim	CAM	*31,1*
	CHS	1,4
	CON	5,2,4;20. 5,4,10;13
	DEV	17,3;9
	ESS	25,17. 35,5. 40,3. 90,51;55
	GLS	53,4
	HEF	1,71. 27,1
	NTT	9,62;70;112. 10,45
	SHR	4,1,22
	SFK	7,56;87;89. 14,123. 36,6-7
	WAR	22,12. 34,1
	WOR	15,5
Grim: *see also* Leofric son of		
Grim, Edeva's man	CAM	14,76
Grim, Edric son of Ingold's man	SFK	4,15
Grim, King Edward's man	MDX	9,3
Grim of West Wratting	CAM	AppxD
Grim the reeve	ESS	83. 1,18
Grim: *see also* Grimr		
Grim's sons	GLS	EvQ29
Grimbald	BRK	62
	ESS	71,4
	LEC	40,26-27;39
	LIN	14,5;12-14. 16,5. 41,1. 48,2. 68,38
	NTH	56,26-29
	RUT	EN18-19
Grimbald: *see also* Svertingr son of		
Grimbald, Bisi's man	BKM	17,21
Grimbald, King Edward's man	BDF	41,1
Grimbald Krakr	LIN	12,9;13
Grimbald the goldsmith, Edeva's man	CAM	*14,66*
	WIL	67,43-44
Grimbald: *see also* Grimbold		
Grimbert	LIN	56,6;8
Grimbold	SFK	*8,8*
Grimbold: *see also* Grimbald		
Grimkel	CHS	24,1
	ESS	32,42-43
Grimkel: *see also* Grimkell, -ketel, -ketill		
Grimkell	NTT	9,45;126. 10,33;43;46;62
	WAR	18,1
Grimkell: *see also* Grimkel, -ketel, -ketill		
Grimketel	HEF	1,71. 9,17
	NFK	8,123
	NTT	10,47
	SHR	4,14,7
Grimketel: *see also* Grimkel(l), -ketill		
Grimketill	LIN	3,7;40. 4,43. 7,26. 14,6. 16,35;44. 22, 8;31-32. 25,2;9;11. 27,7;14. 29,22. 32, 4;7. 35,2;16. 47,1. CN,25. CW,12
	YKS	C12. 1E33. 9W5;19;22. 14E46. CE51
Grimketill, a thane	LIN	25,1
Grimketill: *see also* Grimkel(l), -ketel		
Grimr	LIN	34,2;4-6
	YKS	C12-13. 1N73;75;78. 1E10;56. 1W9. 5W21. 6N27;31. 13W20-21. 24W3. 24E1-2. 25W29-30 *note*. CW2
Grimr: *see also* Grim		
Grim's sons	GLS	EvQ29

Grimulf	WAR	22,19
Grimulf: *see also* Grimwulf		
Grimwulf	ESS	B3a
	SFK	4,4. 8,12. 52,9
Grimwulf: *see also* Grimulf		
Grip: *see* Hugh son of		
: *see* Walter son of		
Gris: *see* Hagris		
Gross: *see also* William son of		
Grucan	YKS	29W2 *and note*
Gruffydd	CHS	9,18. 19,1
	HEF	9,14. 10,50
	STS	1,33
Gruffydd: *see also* Aldith wife of		
Gruffydd Boy [= Puer]	HEF	1,34-35
Gruffydd (Boy)	HEF	1,38
King Gruffydd	CHS	B7. FT3,7
	GLS	W4
	HEF	1,49
Gruffydd son of King Maredudd	HEF	31 *note*. 29,1
Guard: *see* Huscarl		
Gudrun: *see* Guthrun		
Guerlin	WIL	8,11
Guerri	NFK	37,2-3
Gulfer?	LIN	59,17
Gulfer: *see also* Gulfered, Ulfarr, Wulfer		
Gulfered, Robert of Stafford's man	LIN	59,16-17
Gulfered: *see also* Gulfer, Wulfred		
Gundrada	SSX	11,72
Gundulf	GLS	2,6
	SSX	10,47
Bishop Gundulf/of Rochester	CAM	4
	ESS	EKt
	KEN	4. 1,1-2. 5,58
	SFK	20
Bishop Gundulf: *see also* William brother of		
Gundwin	ESS	80
	LEC	40,31
	WIL	48,12
Gundwin the chamberlain	SFK	58
Gundwin, the keeper of the granaries	WIL	68,29
Gunfrid	BDF	23,51
	HEF	9,1. 10,27
	NFK	10,18. 35,2;4-5
	NTH	26,10
	SHR	4,5,6. 6,14
	SOM	45,6
	SRY	8,17
	WIL	8,3. 12,6. 26,10
	WOR	26,9;16
Gunfrid: *see also* Ralph son of		
Gunfrid, a man-at-arms	WIL	12,2
Gunfrid Mawditt	WIL	53
Gunfrid of Chocques	BDF	37
	BKM	50
	LEC	31
	LIN	52. S7. CK,3
	NTH	48. B27. 1,10
Gunfrid, Robert of Tosny's man	LIN	18,17;20
Gunfrid the archdeacon	NFK	10,16

Gunhard	DEV	24,10
Gunhild (fem.)	SSX	13,29
Gunhild (fem.): *see also* Gunhilda, Gunnhildr		
Gunhilda (fem.)	SOM	*1,18.* 5,17
Gunhilda (fem.): *see also* Gunhild, Gunnhildr		
Gunhilda, Earl Godwin's daughter	SOM	*1,24*
Gunnar	BRK	43,2
	CON	5,24,11
	DEV	24,31
	HEF	22,2-4
	WIL	58,1
Gunnar: *see also* Gunnarr		
Gunnarr	YKS	1W35;37. 6N106-107. 9W19. 14E14 *and note*
Gunnarr: *see also* Gunnar, Gunner		
Gunner	CHS	3,2. 10,3
	ESS	24,63;67
	SFK	7,17;117
Gunner: *see also* Gunnarr		
Gunnhvati	SFK	74,13
Gunnhvati: *see also* Gunnhvatr		
Gunnhildr (fem.): *see* Gunhild(a)		
Gunnhvatr	LIN	3,42. 12,1;3. 22,30. 29,1;4;8-9;28. 68, 2. CW,10
Gunnhvatr: *see also* Gunnhvati		
Gunni	NFK	4,23
Gunni, Aelfric son of Goding's man	BKM	57,17
Gunni the Dane	SOM	*29,1*
Gunning	CHS	8,22
Gunnketill	LIN	26,43. 48,8;15
Gunnulf	SFK	7,42. 77,4
Gunnvarthr: *see* Gunward		
Gunnvor (fem.)	YKS	5N31;53-54
Guntard	SOM	37,6
	YKS	14E16
Gunter	DEV	32,2
	WIL	27,6
Guntram	SSX	11,95
Guntram: *see also* Siward Guntram		
Gunward [= Gunnvarthr]	SHR	4,3,46. 4,20,24. 6,23
Gutbert	ESS	30,27
Guthfrithr	LIN	47,8
Guthfrithr, brother of Aelfric and Harold	LIN	CS,21
Guthfrithr's father	LIN	CS,21
Guthfrithr's sons	LIN	CS,22
Guthlac [probably for Guthleikr]	CHS	1,5
Guthleikr: *see* Guthlac		
Guthlif	CAM	*14,81*
Guthlif: *see also* Godlid, Godlive		
Guthmund	ESS	26,2
Guthmund, brother of Abbot Wulfric/thane	ESS	27,2;4-5;11;13-14 *and note*
	SFK	29,1. 31,8 *note*; 9-14;38;40-43;45-48; 60. 41,11
another Guthmund	ESS	28,5
Guthmund: *see also* Guthmundr		
Guthmundr	LIN	4,56
Guthred	ESS	38,3
Guthrithr (fem.)	YKS	29E16
Guthrothr, a lawman	LIN	C2-3;21. CW,3
Guthrothr: *see also* Godred		

Guthrun, Gudrun (fem.)	SOM	19,60
Guy	CAM	7,2. AppxL
	DOR	47,8
	ESS	20,30-31;72-73
	LIN	EN,2
	NFK	8,31
	NTT	1,66
	SOM	22,17
	SSX	11,5
Guy: *see also* Osmund uncle of		
: *see also* Thurstan son of		
: *see also* William son of		
Guy, and his daughter	HAM	44,4
Guy d'Oilly	OXF	44
Guy of Anjou	CAM	*15,2*
	NFK	1,1. 5,1
Guy of Craon	LEC	24
	LIN	57. 2,42. 24,61;81. 46,2. CW,15. CK, 49;53;58;60;66;69
Guy of Raimbeaucourt	CAM	31. 5,33. *32,30*
	LEC	23
	LIN	39. S11. CK,57
	NTH	41. B18. ELe2
	OXF	36. B9
Guy of Raimbeaucourt: *see also* Ingelrann, son of		
Guy, son-in-law of Hugh	LIN	25,19;25
Guy the priest	HRT	34,21
	SOM	5,34
Gyrth	BRK	30,1
	ESS	3,11
	HAM	35,2
	NFK	1,29;45-46;59-60;148;155;192;195. 4, 9-10;15;34;54. 6,6. 8,8. 9,3a;89;146; 159-160;169-170;182;234. 10,20;22; 44;67;69;78;81. 12,6-7;18. 14,17. 19, 20;36. 25,23. 29,8-9. 33,2;6. 34,9. 48, 2. 50,9. 52,3. 53,1. 57,1. 58,3. 61,2-3. 64,1-2. 66,89. ESf2
	SFK	1,7;18-19;32;34;44-49;51;103. 3,19. 4, 20;34-35;37;40;41 *note*. 6,13;125. 7,40; 47;75. 8,14-15. 16,35. 19,18. 21,30; 62. 25,67;71. 31,25;31;34. 36,6. 38, 11. 50,1. 67,14. 69,2;4. 74,7
	SSX	11,110. 13,19
Earl Gyrth/brother of Harold	BDF	53,5. 54,1
	CAM	*14,18*. 25,4;6-7. 26,13;18. 32,10. 41, 5-7
	HRT	24,1. 26,1. 37,1
	NFK	14,16;*17*. 66,16
	SFK	1,23;101-102;122a. 3,55
	SSX	13,9
(Earl) Gyrth	BRK	10,1
	HRT	37,19
Gyrth the canon	MDX	3,16
Gyrth: *see also* Gythr		
Gyrthr, Count Alan's man	LIN	12,90. CK,69
Gytha (fem.)	CON	5,7,6;9
	DOR	17,1
	LEC	2,7

	LIN	63,6
	NTH	35,1-7;10;22-26
	OXF	EN12
	WAR	16,10
	YKS	5E35-36
Gytha (fem.): *see also* Countess Gytha		
Countess Gytha/mother of Earl Harold/wife of	BDF	22,2
Earl Ralph	BRK	10,1
	BKM	16,8-10
	DBY	S5
	DEV	1,29-35;*50*. 11,1
	DOR	1,14
	GLS	1,63
	HAM	1,19;W14
	NTT	S5. 10,5. 23,1
	SOM	*1,22-23*
	SRY	15,1
	SSX	11,4;6-7;33;41. 12,41. 13,22
(Countess) Gytha	SOM	1,11
	WIL	1,9-10;13
Gythr: *see also* Gyrth		
H. Malemayns	NFK	65,16
Habeinn	LIN	3,39
Habeinn: *see also* Aben		
Haca	DEV	21,9-10
Hademar	DEV	15,2;18;60
Hademar, Edmer Ator's man	DEV	*15,18*
Hademar: *see also* Haemar		
Hadwic	HEF	10,62. 15,2
Hadwic: *see also* Hadwig		
Hadwig	GLS	E8
Hadwig: *see also* Hadwic		
Hadwin	GLS	G4
	HEF	8,5
Haemar	CON	5,23,5
Haemar: *see also* Hademar		
Hafgrim	WAR	22,5
Hag of Linton	CAM	AppxF
Hagebern/Hagebert	ESS	70. 1,27
Hagen	HEF	21,4
Hager	ESS	27,17
Hagni: *see also* Ralph son of		
Hagni, a thane	NFK	1,182
Hagni the reeve	NFK	56. 1,81-82;84;86-87. 6,2. 9,2. 12,42
Hagni: *see also* Cock Hagni, Wulfric Hagni		
Hagris	SFK	6,229
Hagris: *see also* Gris		
Haimard	BKM	41,3
Haimer	NFK	1,33
Haimeric of Arques	DEV	*50*
Haimo	WIL	22,2;4;6
Haimo: *see also* Hamo		
Haket	LIN	32,19
Hakon	CHS	8,29;37. 13,5
	DBY	6,37. 12,1-2. 17,9
	ESS	33,1. 36,11. B3a
	HAM	1,18
	LIN	7,14-15
	OXF	32,1. 53,1-2
	SFK	1,18;47

	WIL	29,2
	YKS	5W13
Hakon, Ralph Paynel's man	LIN	35,11
Hakon, Roger of Poitou's man	LIN	16,12
Haldane	BRK	33,6-7
	CHS	8,22;28;42
	DBY	7,3. 17,9
	ESS	36,6
	GLS	39,4
	LEC	3,15. 40,14
	NTH	40,1;4-5
	NTT	4,1. 10,25;40. 21,3. 30,2-6;30;33;36; 45;47-48
	SFK	4,16. 6,112;118;165. 7,40;50. 8,4;6. 26,12b;12d. 32,2;9;11-16;19;21-31. 67,11
Haldane: *see also* Haldane's mother		
Haldane, a royal Guard	BKM	46,1
Haldane, Earl Harold's man	BKM	23,10
Haldane of Tewin, a royal thane	HRT	36,19. Appx
Halden: *see* Godwin Haldane, Halden		
Halewise (fem.): *see also* Heloise		
?Halewise (fem.)	DEV	25,7
Halfdan	LIN	2,18;29. 3,6;50. 7,16;20;22;27;30;32. 12,89. 14,42. 27,41;44-45;59. 59,7. 61, 6. 68,32;34. CK,45;67. EN,3
	YKS	C12. 1E19. 9W77;86;96;101;115;138. 10W6;35-36. 13W17. 13E6-7. 14E45; 47. 22W4. CE26. CW31
Halfdan, a thane	LIN	25,1
Halfdan, and his brothers	LIN	31,17
Halfdan [son of] Topi	LIN	7,18
Halfdan the priest	LIN	68,28
Halfdan the priest, a lawman	LIN	C2-3
Halfdan: *see also* Haldane		
Halldorr	YKS	1N113;117. 5N74. 6N28-29. 25W24. 29N1
Halsard	SRY	20,1-2
Hamelin	CON	5,5. 1,1. 2,14
	DEV	15,8;43
	LIN	25,5
	SSX	11,27-28
	YKS	C7. 9W57. CE5
Hamelin, Hugh son of Baldric's man	LIN	25,6;11
Hamelin of Ballon	GLS	EvK1
Haming	BKM	23,15
Haming, a royal thane	BKM	23,3-4
Hamo	CHS	1,22;34. 27,2
	DEV	19,21-22;26;36
	DOR	26,1;61
	KEN	*2,4*
	SFK	3,88-89;94;98-102 *and note.* 25,12
Hamo: *see also* Geoffrey son of		
: *see also* Ralph son of		
: *see also* Robert son of		
Hamo of (Mascy)	CHS	13. FD7
Hamo of St Clair	SFK	*6,271. 7,133. 16,3-6;8;27-34*
Hamo of Valognes	SFK	3,15;87

Hamo the sheriff/steward	ESS	28. 1,2. 66,1. 90,31-33. 133b
	KEN	12. C1. 1,1-3. 2,16;31. 5,30;42;96;127
	SRY	30. 8,15;23-25
Hamo (the sheriff/steward)	ESS	1,3. 89,3
	KEN	5,126
Hamo (the steward)'s son	ESS	20,6
Hamo: *see also* Haimo		
Harald, Haraldr: *see* Harold		
Hardekin	ESS	B3a
	NFK	9,102
	SFK	25,57. 67,12
Harding	BRK	65,17
	BKM	57,14-15
	DOR	43,1
	GLS	78,15
	HAM	6,1
	LEC	10,1-17
	OXF	B10
	SOM	8,32
	SFK	7,25. 29,9
	WAR	14,1;3;6. 17,30
	WIL	12,1. 20,1-6. 23,6. 67,60-62
Harding [for Erding]	SRY	19,11;23-24;26
Harding son of Alnoth/of Merriot	SOM	47,3 *note*
Harding (son of Alnoth/of Merriot)	SOM	47,4-8
Hardred: *see* Heardred, Nardred		
Hardwin	CHS	9,7;17
	ESS	49,1
	HRT	16,5
	NFK	19,20;27-28;36. 28,2
	SFK	6,46. 9,1-2. 21,16. 23,1. 39,5
Hardwin, brother of Earl Ralph	SFK	2,10 *note*. 7,67
Hardwin of Scales	CAM	26. 5,2;7;*10 and notes to*; 5;17;19;
		21-22;26;29-30;32;35. 13,2. *14,22. 19,*
		4. EE1. AppxC; G; H; M
	ESS	1,9
	HRT	37. B10
Hardwin, Walkelin's man	NTH	4,7
Hardwulf	DEV	3,79
	NTT	9,18
Hardwulf: *see also* Heardwulf		
Haret	SFK	66,6
Harold	BRK	1,34-36;39-40;44. 18,1. 33,4. 65,7
	CAM	AppxC
	GLS	EvK116
	HEF	6,10
	KEN	C4. P20. 5,14;18. 9,50
	LIN	3,13;27. 14,43
	NFK	1,1;2;4-6;15;45;53;55;57;61;141;169.
		4,15;18-20;22;53. 5,1. 8,8. 9,29;33;40;
		46;88;124;138. 9,104;117;143;149;
		151;172;174;176;178;231;233. 10,38;
		40;55-58. 20,9;19;24;31. 21,16-17;22;
		33-34. 22,1;10-13;16;21-23. 24,5-6.
		25,10-11;20. 26,3;5. 27,2. 29,1. 31,17;
		44. 34,13. 35,1-2. 36,1;6-7. 37,3. 41,
		1. 48,2. 51,5-6. 66,79;99;93;97
	NTT	3,1;3. 9,88

SFK	2,16;19-20. 4,16. 6,17;92;191;226. 7, 57;73;102;119;122;147. 8,3;7;11;31; 48;55-56. 16,2;20;40. 20,1. 25,60. 27, 13. 29,11. 31,20. 32,14;16. 36,3;5-7; 15. 38,22. 39,1;17. 40,4. 41,7. 43,1;3; 5-6. 48,1. 49,1. 55,1. 67,7;10;12;27. 76,6;20;23
SSX	3,1. 5,2. 10,23. 11,26. 12,29. 13,7;11; 23;25;28-29
WIL	28,3. 50,2
YKS	9W119 *and note.* 14E8;54
NFK	10,43

H(arold)
Harold : *see also* Godwin son of
    : *see also* Gyrth brother of
Harold, a man-at-arms

Harold, a thane

Harold, a thane: *see* Aelfeva wife of
Harold, Alfwy Hiles' man
Harold, brother of Aelfric and Guthfrithr
Earl Harold

SSX	3,3
WIL	2,10
BKM	17,22-23
HAM	1,W1
GLS	69,6
LIN	CS,21
BDF	23,4. 35,2. 50,1. 53,7;9. E1;8
BRK	1,19. 4,1. 7,34. 15,1. 18,2. 49,1
BKM	1,3-5. 3a,3-5. 4,13;15. 12,2;6-7;11;13; 24;37. 17,2;5-6. 23,5;10. 26,11. 30,1. 37,1-2. 43,11. 45,1. 51,1-2
CAM	1,17. 3,1;6. 12,1. *14,75.* 17,1;5-6. 21, 1. 26,4;*5*;7;18. 32,5. 41,1;3-4. EE2
CHS	8,21;41
CON	1,1-13. 4,2;21. 5,1,5. 5,2,17. 5,4,17
DEV	1,36-49. 3,6. 11,2-3
DOR	1,7-13;30. 17,2. 19,14. 27,2. 48,1. 54,6
ESS	B3k
GLS	B1. 1,1-5;14;54;60;62-63;66. 5,1. 6,4. 28,4. 39,2. 45,3. 50,3. 53,5. 60,1. 68, 2. E5
HAM	1,1;20;40;W11;W15. 20,1. 21,2;9. 23, 35. 28,6. 29,14. 30,1
HEF	C11-12. 1,7-8;56;65;67-69. 2,8;12;26; 31-33;37;50. 8,3;6. 10,25;28;30;32;34; 44;51;56. 14,7. 15,6-8. 17,2. 19,2-5; 7-10. 21,7. 22,1. 23,2. 24,6. 25,5;9. 29, 17-18. 31,1-2
HRT	B6. 1,1-15;17. 5,5;23;25. 15,1. 17;2-3; 8-9;13. 20,13. 23,4. 24,3. 30,1. 33,17. 34,5;12-13;24. 35,1-2. 36,11. 37,8;11; 14;22. 44,1
HUN	13,1. D10;14;17
KEN	5,29;108
LEC	43,1-6
LIN	C8. T5. 13,1;10;17;28;34;38-39. 15,1. CK,38
MDX	5,1-2. 8,3-4. 11,3. 18,2
NFK	3,2
OXF	1,6;8-9. 10,1. 15,4. 58,29-30
RUT	R16. ELc4
SHR	4,13,1. E1-2
SOM	1,12-13;15;19;21;25. 5,51. 6,9. 19,35. 35,11
STS	1,12

	SFK	68,1;3-4 *note*
	SRY	1,4-5;11. 2,3. 5,17;20. 6,1. 20,1-2. 26, 1. 36,5
	SSX	9,18;21;42-43;59;74. 10,59;63;83;86. 11,93. 12,4-5. 13,33;41
	WIL	B5. 1,8;12;14;18-19. 18,2. 23,7. 24,4. 28,2;11. 30,7. 41,1. 47,2. 68,15
	WOR	3,3
	YKS	C36-39. 4E1-2. 12W1
	CAM	EE1
(Earl) Harold	DOR	34,8
	ESS	1,1-4;19-21;23-24;26-29. 6,8;11;15. 7, 1. 19,1. 20,5-6;9;11;51;66. 28,1;6;8. 30,16;34. 31,1. 34,28. 40,1. 41,3. 49, 3. 68,2. 90,35. ESf1
	HAM	1,12-14
	HRT	17,4
	HEF	1,68-69
	NFK	4,26;35
	SFK	1,96;100;102;119. 36,1. 38,21. EE1
	SRY	5,13;16;27. 6,5. 11,1. 15,1. 17,1;4. 36, 4
	WOR	26,16
Earl Harold: *see also* Aelfeva sister of		
: *see also* Countess Gytha mother of		
Harold, Edric's man	SFK	7,13
(Earl) Harold's priest	ESS	1,24
(Earl) Harold's reeve	ESS	1,24
Harold son of Earl Ralph	GLS	61
	MDX	9,1
	WAR	38. B2
	WOR	22
Harold the constable	LIN	T5
Harold's concubine	KEN	C4
Harold's father	LIN	CS,21
Harthacanute	SFK	7,85
Harthacanute: *see also* Harthaknutr		
Harthaknutr, a lawman	LIN	C2
Harthaknutr : *see also* Svertingr son of		
: *see also* Harthacanute		
Harthgripr	LIN	4,15
Harvey	KEN	9,12;24;49
Harvey: *see also* Hervey		
Hascoit (Musard)	BRK	35
Hascoit Musard	BKM	49. B9
	DBY	12
	GLS	66
	OXF	56
	WAR	39
Hasten	CHS	9,29
Hato	ESS	20,65
	SFK	5,7
Havarthr	YKS	1N22-24;118;120-122. 29N8. CN3
(Hawise) wife of Hugh son of Grip	DOR	55
Heahwine: *see* Nawen		
Heardred: *see* Hardred, Nardred		
Heardwulf	YKS	29W42
Heardwulf: *see also* Hardwulf		
Heca	DEV	17,32;49;64;69;95. 21,18
Heca the sheriff	DEV	*17,38*

Hedned	YKS	C11 *and note*
Heinfrid	NFK	29,8;11
	SFK	53,1
Heinfrid: *see also* Herfrith		
Helbod: *see* Hildbod		
Heldred	HAM	23,16;32. 28,2
	SRY	21,3
Heldred: *see also* Aldred		
Heldric	CON	5,24,25
Heldwin	LEC	15,15
Helgi	NTT	9,98;111
	SSX	10,65. 11,46;116
Helgot	BKM	43,4-5
	DEV	34,*16*;26. *49*,7
	SHR	4,21. 4,11,1;9. 6,27;29;32
	STS	8,24. 11,24;43
Helgot: *see also* Algot		
Helio	STS	11,26;47
Heloise (fem.): *see also* Halewise		
?Heloise (fem.)	DEV	17,9. 25,7
Heloise (fem.), niece of Bishop Erfast	NFK	10,81
Helto	BKM	4,1-3;21
	KEN	5,2
Helto the steward	KEN	1,1
Helto the steward's nephew	KEN	1,1
Heming	NTT	11,26
	SSX	10,6;19;29;46. 12,10
Heming, King Edward's man	CAM	14,40
Heming: *see also* Hemming, Hemingr		
Hemingr	LIN	T5. 31,11;16
Hemingr: *see also* Heming, Hemming		
Hemming	GLS	64,2
Hemming: *see also* Heming, Hemingr		
Henry	DBY	4,2. B10. S5
	NFK	32,7
	SFK	14,16
	YKS	14E13
another Henry	BRK	21,15;17;19
King Henry I	YKS	31N10
Count? Henry, of Eu	GLS	EvK *note.* Ev
Henry of Ferrers	BRK	21. B1;4. 1,25-27;32;37-38;42
	BKM	27
	DBY	6. 1,27;35. 8,2
	ESS	29. 90,81
	GLS	59. 31,2
	HEF	13
	LEC	14. C16. 19,6;9
	LIN	21. CW,17
	NTH	25. B13
	NTT	24. S5
	OXF	24. B9. 1,6
	STS	10. B9. 8,23. ED3-4
	WAR	19. B2
	WIL	39. 1,2. E1;2
Henry of Ferrer's steward	ESS	29,5
Earl (Henry), of Warwick	GLS	EvK *note.* EvQ29
Earl? Henry, of Warwick	GLS	EvK *note*
Henry son of Azor	BDF	43
Henry, the Abbot of St Edmund's man	SFK	21,4
Henry the steward	BRK	21,18

Henry the treasurer	HAM	56
Henry's wife	ESS	39,10
Heppo the crossbowman	LIN	61. CK,41
Her	DOR	47,12
Herbert	CHS	1,34. 3,6
	DBY	6,65
	DEV	21,15
	GLS	31,8;10
	HAM	23,48. 47,2-3
	HEF	1,22. 8,1. 10,9-10. 24,7
	HUN	19,10;14. ELc18
	KEN	5,145;156;183-184;195
	LEC	2,2. 42,1-4
	LIN	35,4
	NTH	EH5
	OXF	28,27
	SHR	4,3,57. 4,8,4;6;10-11. 4,21,15
	SOM	21,30;96. 26,4. 35,6-7;16
	SFK	6,191
	SRY	33,1
	SSX	3,8
	WIL	3,3. 37,11
	WOR	15,12. 19,7;11
Herbert: *see also* Hugh nephew of		
Herbert Blacun	SFK	75,3
Herbert, Countess Judith's man	LIN	56,18
	RUT	ELc15
Herbert, Eustace the sheriff's man	HUN	19,13
	NTH	EH4
Herbert, Norman of Arcy's man	LIN	32,12;28;31
Herbert, Odo the crossbowman's man	LIN	48,9;11
Herbert, Roger Bigot's chamberlain	NFK	66,86
Herbert son of Ivo	BDF	2,6-9
	HRT	10,9
	KEN	D10. P19. 5,54;138;155-156. 9,35
Herbert son of Ivo: *see also* Hugh nephew of		
Herbert son of Remigius	HAM	54
Herbert, the Archbishop of York's man	LIN	2,6;11;18
Herbert the chamberlain	HAM	55. 6,16. 23,35
	NFK	66,86
Herbert the forester	HAM	1,31
Herbert the reeve	BDF	57,1
Herbert's nephew	KEN	D10
Herbrand	BKM	14,4
	HAM	IoW9,5
	WOR	8,16. 26,12
Herbrand of Pont Audemer	HAM	58
Herch, Brictric's man	BKM	23,23
Herch: *see also* Herki		
Hereberd the ditcher	NFK	1,61
Herebold	SFK	6,108
Herebold: *see also* Godric son of		
Hereward	GLS	E28. EvA120. EvC41. WoB7
	SFK	14,152
	WAR	16,26;46;48. 17,33
	WOR	2,43
Hereward: *see also* Hereweard		
Hereweard	LIN	8,34. 42,9. CK,4;48
Hereweard: *see also* Hereward		
Herewig	YKS	6N11;35. 9W42

Herewig: *see also* Hervey
Herewold   SFK   6,106;289
Herewulf   NFK   66,42
                            SRY   5,29
                            SSX   5,1. 9,23. 11,95
Herfast, Nigel of Aubigny's man   BDF   16,3. 24,6;8;29-30
Herfast: *see also* Erfast
Herfrid [?error for Heinfrid]   KEN   5,155;170;195. 9,41
                            SRY   1,13. 5,11;26
Herfrid: *see also* Heinfrid, Herfrith
Herfrith   NFK   29,7
Herfrith: *see also* Herfrid
Heringod   KEN   2,*21*
Herki   HAM   2,15
Herki: *see also* Herch
Herling   BRK   58,2
                            DOR   6,3
Herlwin   BRK   36,6
                            GLS   E9
                            HUN   19,19
                            NFK   21,15;29;34
                            NTH   4,32. 32,1. EH7
                            OXF   EN3
                            SOM   5,12-13;20;27. 8,2
                            WAR   16,32
Herlwin: *see also* Baldwin son of
         : *see also* Ralph son of
Herlwin son of Ivo   NFK   66,51
Herman   HEF   1,45;50. 10,69
                            LIN   28,31
                            NFK   21,8
                            STS   11,50
                            SFK   7,99
                            WIL   3,2. 30,7
                            WOR   18,3. E5
Herman, Jocelyn son of Lambert's man   LIN   28,29
Herman of Dreux   HEF   27
                            WIL   66,1
Bishop Herman (of Salisbury)   BRK   3,2-3
                            WIL   3,1
Bishop (Herman) (of Salisbury)   WIL   67,11
Bishop Herman's nephew   WIL   3,1
Hermenfrid: *see* William son of
Hermer   BRK   7,23
                            DEV   23,14. 25,8;24
                            GLS   1,45
                            NFK   1,66. 8,18. 9,187;191;227. 15,2. 66,
                                         48-49;106
Hermer, Ivo Tallboys' man   LIN   14,3
Hermer of Ferrers   NFK   13. 66,1-34
                            SFK   10
Hernetoc   SSX   9,10
Herpolf   HAM   IoW2,1
Herstan   ESS   B3a
Hertald   MDX   5,2
Hervey   BRK   1,7
                            BKM   17,28. E7-8
                            CAM   32,6
                            LIN   12,49
                            NFK   4,49

	OXF	1,11. 7,7-8;31;60. 58,11-13
	STS	11,57-59;61;64
	SFK	21,29-30;83;86-87. 31,36;42
	WAR	22,23
Hervey Bedruel/of Berry/of Bourges	SFK	67 *and note.* 8,59. 21,*36*,50-*51;*55-*56; 58;66-68;*85;87;96;*97-100.* 32,28
Hervey, Count Alan's man	LIN	12,51
	NTT	2,4
Hervey de Vere	NFK	1,61. 25,15
Hervey of Berry: *see* Hervey Bedruel		
Hervey of Bourges: *see* Hervey Bedruel		
Hervey of Helléan('s wife)	DEV	44
Hervey of Helléan('s wife): *see also* Emma		
Hervey of Sawston	CAM	AppxG
Hervey of 'Spain'	ESS	21,9-11
Hervey (of 'Spain')	ESS	21,2;4;12
Hervey of Wilton/the chamberlain	DOR	57,9
	WIL	68,1
Hervey (of Wilton/the chamberlain)	WIL	B1. 1,18. 15,1. 24,6. 68,2;15
Hervey son of Ansger	DOR	*12,14*
Hervey the chamberlain: *see* Hervey of Wilton		
Hervey the commissioner	BKM	48
Hervey: *see also* Harvey, Herewig, Hervi		
Herwulf: *see* Herewulf		
Hervi: *see* Harvey, Herewig, Hervey		
Hezelin	BRK	7,35
Hilary	SFK	16,3
Hildbod, Hildebod: *see* Helbod, Ilbod		
Hildebert	SOM	6,10;14. 44,1;3
Hildebert: *see also* Ilbert		
Hildebrand the lorimer	NFK	1,61
Hild(e)ger: *see* Ilger		
Hildferth	SFK	7,112
Hildwin	NTH	26,8-9
Hildwine	DEV	21,11
Hoc	LIN	27,24
Hoc: *see also* Hoch		
Hoch	CAM	36,1
Hoch: *see also* Hoc		
Hofward	NFK	47,2 *and note*
Hofward: *see also* Howard		
Hoga	NTT	9,98
Hoga: *see also* Swart Hoga		
Hold	ESS	90,60
Holdfast [= Holefast]	ESS	22,3
Holland	WOR	23,14
Holmger	HAM	NF3,15
Holmketill	LIN	12,85;96
Honday, Earl Harold's man	BDF	50,1
Horling	BRK	22,2;5
Horrap	ESS	B3a
Horwulf	CAM	14,62. 15,2. 32,6
	ESS	1,10. 14,2
Horwulf, a royal thane	CAM	15,3
Horwulf, Edeva's man	CAM	*14,75*
Howard	ESS	5,7
	SFK	1,111
Howard [rectius Huard]	LEC	13,32-33;52;74
	WIL	24,5-6
Howard of Noyers	HRT	33,15 *note.* Appx

Howard: *see also* Hofward
Hraefn(-), Hrafn(-): *see* Raven(-)
Hrafnketill: *see* Rafnketill, Ravenkel
Hrafnsvartr: *see* Rafnsvartr, Ravensward,
Huard of Vernon   SFK   9,2-3
Huard: *see also* Howard [rectius Huard]
Hubald   WIL   25,28
Hubald: *see also* Hugh Hubald; Nubald
Hubert   BRK   7,3
                                             DEV   23,21. 42,19
                                             DOR   26,39-40
                                             ESS   30,5. 44,1-2
                                             HEF   1,40
                                             NFK   7,9;11
                                             SOM   24,14
                                             STS   10,6
                                             SFK   6,1;26-27 *note*; 30;53;57-58;62;109;
                                                      196;235;248-249;260;280;299;302
                                             SSX   10,16
                                             WAR   18,8
                                             WOR   E2

Hubert: *see also* Adam son of
      : *see also* Eudo (the steward) son of
      : *see also* Ralph son of
Hubert (of Curzon)   BRK   21,11
Hubert of Mont-Canisy   SFK   57. 6,190;260
                                             YKS   C19
Hubert of Port   ESS   32,29. 83,2
                                             HAM   24
                                             SFK   16,34. 77,4
Hubert of St Clair   SOM   *19,10*
Hubert (of St Clair)   DOR   26,33
Hubert, Ralph Paynel's man   YKS   16W3
Hubert the Breton   SFK   *14,68*
Hubert the Breton: *see also* Reginald brother of
Hugh   BDF   25,3;12. 32,3;5;8;12;16. 33,2. 53,2;6;
                                                      9-10;12;14;16;31;33-34
                                             BRK   1,7. 34,2
                                             BKM   13,2-3. 14,6;27;30-32;34;41-42;44;
                                                      46-47
                                             CHS   1,22. 27,3-4
                                             DBY   6,38
                                             DEV   5,1. 15,38. 16,117;154
                                             DOR   10,1. 34,4;7;14-15. 47,6. *55,1-2;4-6;
                                                      8-9;12;16;18-22;24-28;31;35-36;38;
                                                      40-42;45;47*
                                             ESS   3,16. 4,1;17. 18,28;30-33;35. 20,
                                                      39-40. 24,37. 30,26;44. 32,3;6;18. 40,5
                                             GLS   W16
                                             HAM   2,8. 23,61-62;65;67. 28,6. 36,2. 51,2.
                                                      69,51
                                             HEF   1,75. 10,8;14;64-67
                                             HRT   33,9. Appx
                                             HUN   12,1. 20,7
                                             KEN   5,168;193;195
                                             LEC   2,7. 6,7. 13,55-56;68;72-73. 14,17;33.
                                                      17,7-8;12;26-27. 40,10-11. 43,2;7
                                             LIN   56,12;21. 68,39-40. CN,5
                                             MDX   19,1

	DEV	14
	DOR	27
	GLS	28. 2,10. EvK1;159. EvM4;108;112
	HAM	22
	HUN	11
	LEC	43. C8
	LIN	13. C8;20. 36,4. CS,2;6;12;14-16;24; 35. CK,17
	NFK	6. 66,97-98
	NTH	22. B10
	NTT	3. S5
	OXF	15. B9. EBe3
	RUT	6. R16. ELc4
	SHR	4,2
	SOM	18
	SFK	4. 6,19-20;21-22 *note*. 16,34. 31,2;34. 67,3. Also folio 291a
	WAR	13
	WIL	22
	YKS	4. C2;10. CN1. SN,L1-5;10;12-13; 19-24;33-37. SE,P4. SE,Hu1;8
(Earl) Hugh	GLS	31,9
	SFK	1,110. 67,4
Hugh, Earl Hugh's man	LIN	13,41-42
Hugh Farsit	CAM	AppxN
Hugh Gosbert	DOR	57,2;5-8
Hugh Got	ESS	B3a
Hugh Grant, of Scoca	BRK	B3;9
	OXF	EBe3
Hugh Hubald	BDF	44,1-4
	CAM	*24,1*
Hugh, Hugh son of Baldric's man	YKS	23E6
Hugh, Ivo Tallboys' man	LIN	14,9
Hugh, King Edward's chamberlain: *see* Hugh the chamberlain		
Hugh Latimer	HAM	NF10,3
Hugh Maci	HAM	22,1
Hugh Maltravers	SOM	26,5
Hugh (Maltravers)	DOR	34,5
	SOM	26,6
Hugh Maminot	GLS	30,1-3
Hugh Mason	HAM	3,1
Hugh Musard	LEC	40,40-41
	LIN	S5
Hugh, nephew of Herbert (son of Ivo)	BDF	2,9
	ESS	18,25 *note*
	KEN	5,38;63-66;79-82;145;184
	NTT	7,6
Hugh of Beauchamp	BDF	23. 4,2. 17,2;4;6. 21,6;10. 25,7. 54,2. 55,9
	BKM	25
	HRT	27. 44,1
Hugh of Bernières	CAM	27
	ESS	*10,5*. 30,28-30. 90,29
	MDX	3,2. 15,1
Hugh of Beuerda	SFK	31,40
Hugh of Bolbec	BDF	16,1;3-4
	BRK	B3;5;9
	BKM	26. B7. 14,1-2;16

	CAM	*17,2-3*
	HUN	14
	OXF	25. EBe3
Hugh of Boscherbert	DOR	53. *36,3. 55,46*
Hugh (of Boscherbert)	DOR	55,17-18
Hugh of Bréboeuf	KEN	5,98
Hugh of Corbon	NFK	9,48. 66,83
	SFK	7,18;37;75
Hugh of Delamere	CHS	10
Hugh of Dol	DEV	*20,7*
Hugh of Exning	CAM	AppxA
Hugh of Flanders	BDF	34
Hugh of Gournai	ESS	47
Hugh of Gouville	LEC	C12
	NTH	B35. ELe1
Hugh of Grandmesnil	BDF	29,1. 54,1;4
	GLS	62
	HAM	S3
	HRT	26. 5,26. 43,1
	LEC	13. C5;11-12. 40,8-11;22. 43,4
	LIN	30,22
	NTH	23. ELe1
	NTT	23
	OXF	EN8-12
	SFK	49
	WAR	18. B2. EG13-16
	WOR	2,71
Hugh of Grandmesnil: *see also* Adelaide wife of		
Hugh of Ham	GLS	EvK116
Hugh of Hotot	RUT	R11
Hugh of Houdain	ESS	43,6
	NFK	9,182-183
	SFK	7,2 *note*; 60;62;103-105. 30,3. 76,14
H(ugh) of Houdain	SFK	1,60
Hugh of Ivry	DOR	54,1 *and note*
	NTH	24
	OXF	26
Hugh of Ivry: *see also* Hugh Butler		
Hugh of Ivry: *see also* Roger, ?brother of		
Hugh of Lacy	GLS	EvK1;116. EvN11
Hugh (of Lacy)	GLS	32,1. 39,5;16
Hugh of Montgomery	STS	9
Hugh of Port	BRK	52. 10,1-2
	CAM	28
	DOR	51
	HAM	23. 1,27;29. 2,23. 3,9. 4,1. 6,4;6-7;13; 16. 9,2. 43,6. 47,1. 53,2. NF6. NF10, 1. S3
	KEN	1,1;3. 5,1;7;45-47;70;115-118;143;153; 174;*185-188*
	NFK	2,3
	NTH	1,3
	RUT	EN3
	SRY	5,24-25
Hugh of Rennes	DEV	*16,116*
Hugh of St Quentin	DOR	52
	ESS	60. 90,1
	HAM	23,51. NF6,1-2. NF9,16-17;19;23. NF10,2
Hugh of 'Spain'	SOM	*35,8*

Hugh of Teversham	SOM	*35,9*
Hugh of Vautortes	DEV	*15,74*
	SOM	*1,11. 19,67. 45,13*
Hugh of Verly	ESS	30,50
Hugh of Wanchy	SFK	26,9
Hugh, Osbern of Arques' man	YKS	25W20
Hugh Pedefold	CAM	*26,30;33.* AppxJ
Hugh, Robert of Stafford's man	LIN	59,2
Hugh Rufus	LIN	7,48
Hugh Silvester	DOR	54,2
Hugh son of Baldric/the sheriff	BRK	51
	HAM	44
	LEC	1,2
	LIN	25. C20;25. 24,66. CN,8;24
	NTH	1,4
	NTT	22. B3
	RUT	EN4
	WIL	51
	YKS	23. C11;26. SW,An1. SW,Bu1.
		SN,L14;41. SE,He4. SE,Wel3;7.
		SE,C2-3. SE,How9. SE,Sn5. SE,Dr4-5.
		SE,Wa7-8. SE,P4-6. SE,Sc1-7. SE,Ac7;
		12. SE,Th1-2;8
Hugh son of Baldric: *see also*		
Hugh son of Baldwin		
Walter (of Rivers) son-in-law of		
Hugh son of Baldwin [error for Baldric]	LEC	1,2
Hugh son of Constantine	WAR	18,15
Hugh son of Earl Roger	STS	B5
Hugh son of Fulbert	KEN	5,159
Hugh son of Gold	SFK	26,8
Hugh son of Gozhere	BKM	57,7
Hugh son of Grip/the sheriff	DOR	B1 *and note*; 2;3-4. 1,22-29. *11,5.* 13,*1*;
		4. 23,1 *and note. 55,3;8;17;34.* 56,36
Hugh (son of Grip/the sheriff/of Wareham)	DOR	8,4. 10,1. 55,*1-6;9;12;16;18-22;24-28;*
		31;33;35-36;38;40-42;45;47
Hugh son of Grip, wife of	DOR	55. 2,6. 13,1;4. 19,11. *36,3.* 37,13
Hugh (son of Grip), wife of	DOR	3,15. 8,2-4. 11,6. *55,23.* 56,58
Hugh son of Grip, wife of: *see also* (Hawise)		
Hugh son of Mauger/a man-at-arms	ESS	27,16-17
Hugh son of Norman/Northmann	CHS	11. FD5,3. FT3,1-2
	SFK	4,6;35-39
	YKS	4N3. 4E1
Hugh son of Osbern	CHS	12. 16. FD5
Hugh son of Osmund	HAM	68,2. NF9,1
Hugh son of Ranulf	SSX	6,1. 12,42
Hugh son of Thorgils	SHR	4,22
Hugh son of William, a man-at-arms	KEN	5,128
Hugh, the Archbishop of York's man	LIN	2,29
Hugh, the Bishop of Lincoln's man	LIN	7,54
Hugh the bowman	SSX	9,14
Hugh the chamberlain (of King Edward)	BRK	56,1
	HUN	D1
	OXF	15,3
	WAR	13,1
Hugh the cleric	SSX	3,3
Hugh/Hugolin the interpreter	SOM	1,31 *and note.* 7,*11.* 45,9-11
Hugh the servant	LIN	CS,40
Hugh the sheriff	HAM	30,1
	YKS	C10

Hugh, William of Écouis's man	NFK	1,61
	SFK	9,2
Hugh, William's man	SRY	21,7
Hugh's wife	WIL	7,1
Hugolin	ESS	4,11;14
	WIL	7,7
Hugolin the steersman	BRK	58
Humphrey	BDF	3,15
	BKM	12,35;38
	CHS	2,18;21
	CON	5,24,19
	DEV	*3,70*
	DOR	26,21-22. 37,14
	ESS	3,11. 4,4. 27,5;18. 34,5;36. 37,2
	GLS	1,43;47-48;50
	HAM	IoW1,7. 6,9;18;20. 9,11
	HRT	4,1;24. 15,5;12. 31,8. 36,12
	HUN	11,2
	LEC	39,1
	LIN	CS,39
	NFK	1,57;192. 7,6. 8,137. 33,1. 34,18. 35,
		6-7;10-11;15. 36,1-2;5-7. 66,103
	NTH	18,13-16;53
	OXF	6,12. 7,44-45. 35,27
	SOM	1,34. 5,62. 19,70. 37,11
	STS	10,9
	SFK	3,56;59;69. 6,13;17;125;175;261-263;
		295;311-315;319. 14,114. 26,5;7. 52,2
	SSX	10,91;117. 11,102
	WAR	39,2-4
	WIL	7,14. 28,3;8
	YKS	9W27;52;97
Humphrey, a man-at-arms	CHS	9,17
Humphrey, brother of Aiulf the chamberlain	HAM	S3
Humphrey Cook	GLS	71
	WIL	*68,16*
Humphrey de l'Isle	WIL	27. M9
Humphrey, Erneis of Buron's man	YKS	24E2
Humphrey Flambard	SSX	11,1
Humphrey, Gilbert Tison's man	YKS	21E11
Humphrey Goldenbollocks	ESS	90,30
Humphrey, nephew of Ranulf Ilger's brother	NFK	1,192
Humphrey of Anneville	CAM	25,7. *31,3. Notes to* 25,4-6;8. 31,7.
		AppxJ
	HRT	B5
Humphrey (of Anneville)	HRT	31,1
Humphrey of Bohun	NFK	40
Humphrey of Bouville	HEF	28
Humphrey of Carteret	DOR	*3,10*
Humphrey of Culey	NFK	9,5;84
Humphrey of Kinsbourne	HRT	Appx
Humphrey of Maidenhill	GLS	70
Humphrey (of Maidenhill)	GLS	1,2
Humphrey of St Bertin's	SFK	48,1
Humphrey of St Omer	NFK	8,8
Humphrey son of Aubrey	NFK	39. ESf7
	SFK	56. 34,9
Humphrey son of Rodric	SFK	26,1
Humphrey son of R(odric)	SFK	6,172
Humphrey (son of Rodric)	SFK	21,1

Humphrey Strapfoot	KEN	D9
Humphrey the chamberlain	BRK	53
	DOR	50
	GLS	69. E17
	HAM	57. S3
	HEF	1,75
	LEC	32. 1,5
	SOM	45,1-5. *8,19*
	SFK	52. 8,22
	SRY	31. 1,8. 31,1
	WIL	52
Humphrey Visdeloup	BRK	54. B1
	HAM	69,40
Humphrey, William of Warenne's man	SFK	21,1
Hun	SFK	25,67
Huna	SFK	3,99. 6,39;45;48;251;271. 7,117
Huna of Ely	CAM	AppxP
Huna: *see also* Huni		
Hunald	ESS	71,1;4
Hunbald	GLS	60,7
Hundger	HAM	15,1. 69,7
Hundger son of Odin	DOR	57,15-16
Hundigrimr	YKS	1N42. 6N27
Hunding	CHS	2,30. 24,4
	DBY	7,7
Hunding: *see also* Hundingr		
Hundingr	YKS	1E56
Hundingr, three sons of	YKS	1W17
Hundingr: *see also* Hunding		
Hundulf	CHS	2,26
	DBY	1,10. 7,10
Hunebot	SFK	8,16
Hunef	HUN	B14. D3
	KEN	5,108
Hunepot	SFK	3,95
Huneva (fem.)	HUN	20,3
Huneva (fem.): *see also* Hungifu		
Hungifu (fem.): *see* Huneva		
Huni	YKS	14E36
Huni: *see also* Hun, Huna		
Hunman, Alli's man	BKM	53,3
Hunning	ESS	B3a
	SHR	4,3,56. 4,4,1-2. 4,19,6;9-11. 4,20,
		15-16. 4,26,4. 4,27,8;27. 6,7
Hunning's brother	SHR	4,19,9
Hunta	HAM	NF9,22;26
	STS	11,46
Hunuth	CAM	*44,2*
Hunwin	CAM	*44,2*
Hunwin: *see also* Hunwine		
Hunwine	DOR	55,36
	WIL	50,5
Hunwine: *see also* Hunwin		
Hunwulf	WOR	26,6
Huscarl	CAM	*17,2*
	GLS	34,3
	NFK	1,192
	SFK	*16,8*
Huscarl [translated Guard]	SOM	25,6. 47,24
	SRY	21,6-7

	SSX	3,5
	WAR	EG11
Huscarl of Swaffham/King Edward's man	CAM	*14,64*. AppxC
Husteman	SFK	7,105
Hwaetman: *see also* Aelfeva wife of		
Hwaetman of London	MDX	25,2
Hwaetman: *see also* Hwaetmann		
Hwaetmann	DOR	54,3
	HEF	1,75
Hwaetmann: *see also* Hwaetman		
Hwata	CON	5,24,15
Hwelp	YKS	14E19 *and note*
Iarnagot	SFK	53,3;7
Countess Ida/of Boulogne	DOR	58
	SOM	17,7
	SRY	16
Ieva (fem.)	SFK	6,264
Ieva (fem.): *see also* Geofu, Giefu		
Ifing	DEV	16,167
	SOM	40,2
	WIL	47,1
Ifing: *see also* Ewing		
Ilbert	CHS	23
	DOR	55,21
	HEF	1,10b;32-33;38;62
	HRT	34,13. 38,2
	LIN	4,5-6;37;73;80-81. CS,10
	OXF	7,20;26;30;33;55;57;59;61-64
	WIL	27,12
	YKS	2W1
Ilbert, brother of William	HEF	8,7
Ilbert de Lacy: *see* Ilbert of Lacy		
Ilbert of Hertford/the sheriff	CAM	32,10
	HRT	1,6;8-9;11-13
Ilbert of Lacy	BRK	B9
	BKM	4,38. E2
	LIN	20. 40,24. CS,11
	NTT	20
	OXF	1,6. 7,5. EBe3
	YKS	9
Ilbert (of Lacy)	YKS	CW1-3;23. SW,Sk4-12. SW,BA5-11. SW,Sf37. SW,O2-14;16. SW,St1;3-8; 10-16. SW,Ag1-8;13;15-16. SW,M1-10
Ilbert (of Lacy?)	SRY	5,19
Ilbert son of Thorold	HEF	26. 1,3;5
Ilbert, the Bishop of Bayeux's man	LIN	4,3-4;10-16;36;42-43;46;54;56-57;67; 72
Ilbert the sheriff	HEF	1,1
Ilbert: *see also* Hildebert		
Ilbod	ESS	69. 1,2. 90,77
Ilbod, brother of Arnulf of Hesdin	OXF	48
Ilbod: *see also* Helbod, Hilbod, Hild(e)bod		
Ilbold	LIN	CK,10
	NTH	ELc4
	RUT	ELc19
Ilger	ESS	32,9;23-24;31
	GLS	6,1
	NTH	4,34
	OXF	EN5

Ilger: *see also* Ranulf brother of
  : *see also* Hild(e)ger
Ilving   DBY   6,77
                                                   STS   1,42

Ilving: *see also* Ylfing
Ingelrann   DOR   40,6
                                                   HAM   29,15
                                                   HEF   10,11;21
                                                   HUN   19,15;19
                                                   NTH   18,75. 43,7. EH7
                                                   SHR   4,11,12;16. 6,7;10;18;20
                                                   SOM   41,3
                                                   SSX   8,14. 9,9;14;19-20
Ingelrann, a man-at-arms   SSX   9,1
Ingelrann, Drogo of Beuvrière's man   LIN   30,28
Ingelrann son of Guy of Raimbeaucourt   LIN   39,1-4
                                                   OXF   36,1
Ingelrann, the Abbot of Ramsey's man   HUN   6,7
Ingelrann: *see also* Ingran
Ingenwulf   LEC   44,1
                                                   WAR   16,24-25;30

Ingifrithr (fem.)   YKS   1E42
Ingimundr   LIN   12,29. 16,9. 32,6
Ingimundr, and his brothers   LIN   12,31. CN,26
Ingirithr (fem.)   YKS   1E10. 29E7
Ingjaldr   YKS   C36
Ingjaldr: *see also* Ingold
Ingold   BKM   12,2
                                                   LEC   8,3. 17,16-17;21

Ingold: *see also* Edric son of
Ingold, a thane   NFK   48,3
Ingold: *see also* Ingjaldr
Ingran   DBY   16,6-7
Ingran, Roger of Bully's man   NTT   9,45
Ingran: *see also* Ingelrann
Ingulf   ESS   27,12. 32,41
                                                   HAM   27,2
                                                   LIN   67,8
                                                   NFK   10,20. 19,15;21
                                                   NTT   17,7
                                                   SOM   9,8. 45,10
Ingulf, a Guard   SFK   67,13
Ingulf the monk   SRY   9,1
Ingvar   CAM   15,2
                                                   DEV   15,62. 16,23. 21,7. 39,19-20
                                                   ESS   20,71. 37,3;10;12;14;16
Ingvar, a royal thane   CAM   34,1
Ingvar, a thane   ESS   18,2
                                                   SFK   19,16

Ingvar: *see also* Ingward
Ingward [erroneous, for Ingvar]   HUN   24,1
Ingward: *see also* Ingvar
Iolf   CON   5,25,1-2
Iovin   CON   5,7. 1,*1*;4
Isaac   NFK   47. 1,66. 9,26;32;86
                                                   SFK   62. 7,4. 8,67. 21,64
Isambard   HRT   34,14
Isambard: *see also* Isenbard
Isenbard   NTH   6a,18

Isenbard: *see also* Isambard

Isolde	DOR	55a
Isward	OXF	6,9;17
Iudhael	DEV	1,55;71
	WAR	28,3
Iudhael, a reeve	GLS	W2
Iudhael of Totnes	CON	6
	DEV	17. 1,71 *note*
Iudichael	BDF	55,4
	WAR	22,26

Iudichael: *see also* Judic(h)ael

Ivar	SHR	4,27,34
	STS	1,54-55
Ivo	BKM	12,34. 14,39
	LEC	13,35;44;50-51;65. 15,12
	LIN	1,9;14. 8,10;28. 24,33. 28,21. 58,4. CW,13. CK,63
	NTH	6a,34. 23,9;12
	SFK	39,12
	SSX	11,5;32;55;79

Ivo: *see also* Herbert son of
: *see also* Herlwin son of
: *see also* Reynold son of
: *see also* Robert son of

Ivo, Eudo son of Spirewic's man	LIN	29,27
Ivo, father of Reynold	NFK	8,29
Ivo, Gilbert of Ghent's man	LIN	24,27;73
Ivo, Robert of Tosny's man	LIN	18,15;24;32
Ivo, steward of Hugh of Grandmesnil	BDF	54,4
Ivo Tallboys	BDF	1,1a;2a;3. 4,5
	LIN	14. C10. 1,80. CS,20;27;35. CN,3; 19-20;28. CK,22
	NFK	27. 1,131. 4,44;51
	SFK	1,123f
Ivo the sheriff	LIN	CW,4
Iwain	ESS	20,12;50
Jacob	OXF	6,9

Jacob: *see also* James

Jagelin	DEV	36,20. 47,13
James	SFK	14,24

James: *see also* Jacob

Jaulfr	LIN	40,1-2;4-6;10;12;15;17;20;26
Jocelyn	BRK	23,1;3. 36,2
	CHS	19. 1,1
	DBY	4,2. 6,4
	DEV	*1,55.* 16,148. 36,15
	HAM	23,17. 45,2
	HUN	19,18
	LIN	3,33. 7,2;20;26;58. 13,38. 27,21. CN,7; 18
	NFK	14,*35*;36;42
	NTH	22,9. EH6
	NTT	10,46
	OXF	6,12
	SOM	33,1
	SFK	6,19
	SRY	8,21
	SSX	10,22;27;31. 12,53
	WAR	17,27
	WIL	27,27. 42,1

Jocelyn: *see also* Ralph son of		
Jocelyn, Alfred of Lincoln's man	LIN	22,20;22;25;57-59
Jocelyn Bernwin	DEV	*16,118*
Jocelyn, Drogo of Beuvrière's man	LIN	30,3
Jocelyn, Earl Hugh's man	LIN	13,38
	RUT	R16. ELc4;8
Jocelyn, Frodo's man	LIN	*14,137-138*
Jocelyn Hunter	HEF	1,40
	WOR	E2
Jocelyn, Ivo Tallboys' man	LIN	14,25;40
Jocelyn Lorimer	ESS	64. 1,2. 9,7
Jocelyn of Cormeilles	HAM	61
Jocelyn of Loddon	NFK	*14,7-8*
Jocelyn of Norwich	NFK	65,15
Jocelyn, Ralph of Buron's man	NTT	15,9
Jocelyn Rivers/of Rivers	SOM	*1,9*
	WIL	64
Jocelyn son of Azor	HAM	IoW8. IoW1,7
Jocelyn son of Azor: *see also* William brother of		
Jocelyn son of Lambert	LIN	28. 3,4. 24,53. CS,3. CN,17;19. CW,3
Jocelyn, the Bishop of Durham's man	LIN	3,3
Jocelyn, the Bishop of Lincoln's man	LIN	7,19;28
Jocelyn the Breton	BDF	52
	BKM	44
	GLS	74. W12
Jocelyn, the Count of Mortain's man	SFK	21,1
Jocelyn's son	GLS	EvO8
Johais	WAR	28,8;10
John	DBY	6,62-63
	DEV	17,22;33. *48,11*
	DOR	10,2;4
	ESS	24,24;34
	GLS	73,2
	HUN	2,6-7. 19,4-5
	LEC	14,26
	LIN	34,24
	NTH	48,13
	SOM	21,32
	SFK	14,63
	SRY	19,9;14;17;29-30
John: *see also* Waleran father of		
John, Erneis of Buron's man	LIN	34,24
John, nephew of Waleran	ESS	65
	NFK	49. 8,51. 15,12. 17,18. 49,6 *note*
	SFK	15,3
John of les Roches	BDF	8,2. 24,12
John, Osbern of Arques' man	YKS	25W24
John son of Ernucion	ESS	40,1
John son of Waleran	CAM	35
	ESS	40. 1,4. B1;3p
	SFK	55. EE6
John (son of Waleran)	ESS	90,46
John the chamberlain	GLS	1,44;50
John the Dane	SOM	6,14. *44,1*
John (the Dane)	DOR	46,1-2
John the sheriff	HEF	10,19
John the usher	DOR	*57,10*
	SOM	2,8. 6,7. 8,26. 46,6-7;8 *note; 9-11*
	WIL	68,18-19
Joli	YKS	1Y9

Joseph	OXF	1,6
Josteinn	LIN	68,41
Josteinn: *see also* Justan, Justin		
Judicael	CAM	B1. 12,4
	WIL	25,27
Judicael, King Edward's huntsman	CAM	12,2-3
Judicael the priest	NFK	44
	SFK	64. 75,3
Judicael: *see also* Judichael		
Judichael, the Earl's falconer	NFK	1,131
Judichael: *see also* Iudichael, Judicael		
Judith (fem.): *see* Countess Judith		
Countess Judith	BDF	53. 21,1. 54,3
	BKM	53
	CAM	41. *37,2*
	ESS	55
	HUN	20. B5;14. 19,27. D18
	LEC	40. C17. 14,16
	LIN	56. C10;20. S8. 34,12. CK,2;19;25
	MDX	24
	NTH	56. B11;16;34;38. 2,2-3. 9,6. 18,1. 40, 2. 53,1. ELc2-3
	OXF	53
	RUT	2. R7-8;11-13. EN16-20. ELc10-18
	YKS	10W41. SW,Sf35
Juran	HAM	IoW6,7
Justan	NTT	9,100
Justan, a thane	NTT	9,69
Justan: *see also* Josteinn, Justin		
Justin	HAM	3,8. NF5,1
Justin: *see also* Josteinn, Justan		
Kafli	SOM	21,61
Kalmann	YKS	1W38
Kari	LEC	14,28
Karl	BRK	54,1
	CHS	1,10. 8,19
	HAM	36,1-2
	SHR	4,3,5. 4,14,2
	SOM	34,1
	SRY	33,1
	SSX	10,60;114. 13,14
	WIL	26,1-15
Karl : *see also* Godric son of		
: *see also* Godwin son of		
Karl of Cheveley	CAM	AppxB
Karl: *see also* Carl, Karli		
Karli	LIN	12,52;55. 59,4-6. 68,23. CK,23;51
	YKS	1N41. 1E12-13;17-18;22-23;25-26;41; 54. 1W15. 5E45-46. 13E15-16. 13N9-11;19. 14E18. 20E1. 29E5;10. 30W9
Karli: *see also* Carl, Karl		
Kaskin	DBY	1,33
	NTT	9,35;53
Kaskin: *see also* Alfsi son of		
Kene	NFK	25,24
Kenesis	GLS	W4
Kenias	DEV	25,14-15;23
Kening	HAM	43,2-3
Kenmarchuc	BRK	35,1

Kenna	HAM	NF10,4
Kenred	CON	1,1
Kenric	NTH	30,19
Kenting	ESS	B3a
Kentish, Leofnoth son of Osmund's man	BKM	12,38
Kentwin	WAR	16,3;11;29
Kenward	GLS	52,1
	WAR	33,1
	WOR	2,13;19;73. 20,4
Kenward, a royal thane	GLS	39,7
Kenwin	STS	17,1
	WIL	24,23. 27,14
Keping: *see* Cheping		
Ketel	BDF	24,20
	BKM	57,12
	CHS	26,1. R1,38. Y6
	CON	5,7,5
	DBY	1,32. 6,1;43;75-76;78;95;101
	DEV	24,27. 34,15
	DOR	8,1-2. 19,9. 56,2
	ESS	34,34
	GLS	32,2. 78,2-3
	HAM	6,6. 21,4. 22,1. 34,1. NF9,2;42. S2. IoW1,10. 6,1;3;14
	HEF	1,13
	NFK	1,29;92;147;183. 8,124;126;133. 9, 146. 10,90. 13,9. 19,15. 21,2;24-25; 27-28;32. 26,2. 32,3-5. 48,1-3. 49,8. 60,1
	NTH	22,7
	OXF	35,34
	SHR	3e,1. 4,5,1. 4,21,5. 4,22,2. 4,26,3
	SOM	24,19. 36,2
	STS	1,34
	SFK	7,49. 56,1. 66,10;13. 69,3. 76,19
	SSX	11,42
	WAR	28,7
	WIL	20,5. 25,11-12. 67,40
Ketel: *see also* Edric son of		
Ketel, a royal thane	SFK	34,6
Ketel, a thane	SFK	37,6
Ketel, father of Edric	GLS	78,5;16
Ketel Friday	NFK	1,208. 65,17
Ketel Hunter	SRY	36,9
Ketel Hunter's father	SRY	36,9
Ketel, Stigand's thane		
Ketel Uva	SFK	7,104
Ketel's father	LIN	22,26
Ketel, Ketel-: *see also* Ketill, Ketill-		
Ketelbern	LEC	3,16
	NFK	4,46
	NTT	16,2
	WAR	12,5. 16,53. 17,56
	WOR	8,10c
Ketelbern: *see also* Ketilbjorn		
Ketelbert	HUN	12,1. 29,1
	NTH	56,31
	WOR	8,10a. 19,14
Ketelbert, Queen Edith's man	BDF	57,6
Ketil-: *see also* Ketel-		

Ketilbern: *see also* Ketilbjorn		
Ketilbjorn	LIN	69. C20. 4,16;23;65. 53,2. 68,5-8; 10-15. CS,17;20;34;37
	YKS	1E20;24;32-33 (*but see note*); 60. 5E57-59;68-69;71;72 *and note.* 9W77. 10W19;21;30. 20E2. 29W3. 29E21;28
Ketilbjorn, brother of	YKS	1E60
Ketilbjorn: *see also* Ketil-, Ketelbern		
Ketilfrothr	YKS	1N4. 14E29;31;39
Ketilfrothrs, two	YKS	14E28
Ketill	LIN	4,2. 26,1. 32,8;11. 57,5. 68,37
	YKS	1W7;37;48. 1L5. 2E11. 6N27. 9W31; 105;110. 11E3-4. 21E1-2;7-8. 23E1. 29W15;28;45-46;50. 30W22. CW3
Ketill, brother of	YKS	CW3
Ketill, brother of Thorfrothr	LIN	22,26
Ketill of Sutton	LIN	CK,70
Ketill the priest	YKS	C6
Ketill: *see also* Ketel		
Killi	YKS	13E5
Kinsey	SOM	24,35
Kinsey: *see also* Cynesige		
Kip	HRT	33,17
Kipping	DEV	15,11. 16,79. 47,9-10;13
Kipping, a thane	DEV	*15,11. 16,79*
Kipping: *see also* Cheping, Chipping		
Klakkr	LIN	16,14. 25,13. 27,21. 29,22. 47,10. CS, 25
Knight [for Cniht]	DEV	16,125-126. 25,28
Knutr	LIN	12,42. 26,10;16
	YKS	C36. 1N59-60;62;68-69;85;89-90;103. 1E15;45. 5E10;39. 6N58;82;119. 9W94. 13N16. 14E33;37. 21E1;3-4. 23N27. CE37-39
Knutr [erroneous, for Cniht]	YKS	1W25
Knutr: *see also* Canute		
Koddi	LIN	14,18;20. 27,10. 40,7;9. CS,29
Kofsi	LIN	36,3-4. CK,28
	YKS	C36 *and note.* 6N36. 23N1
Kolbrandr	YKS	1N66. 29E30
Kolbrandr: *see also* Colbran		
Kolgrimr	LIN	67. 1,9. 3,35. 8,12. 11,5;7. 12,48. 30, 26;32. 68,19. CK,60-61
	YKS	5E18-20;44
Kolgrimr, Count Alan's man	LIN	12,52;55;91-92
Kolgrimr, Drogo of Beuvrière's man	LIN	30,25
Kolgrimr, Odo the crossbowman's man	LIN	48,13
Kolgrimr, Robert of Stafford's man	LIN	59,18
Kolgrimr: *see also* Colgrim		
Kolsveinn	LIN	26. C22. 3,1-3. 8,13. CS,7. CN,26. CW,2;8. CK,31;34;54;64
Kolsveinn: *see also* Cola nephew of		
Kolsveinn, Drogo of Beuvrière's man	LIN	30,36
Kolsveinn, Earl Hugh's man	LIN	13,26
Kolsveinn, Gilbert of Ghent's man	LIN	24,2
Kolsveinn, Jocelyn son of Lambert's man	LIN	28,3
Kolsveinn, Rainer of Brimeux's man	LIN	40,2
Kolsveinn, the Bishop of Bayeux's man	LIN	4,2
Kolsveinn, the Bishop of Durham's man	LIN	3,36
Kolsveinn: *see also* Colswein		

L. Bondi	NFK	23,12
Lagmann	YKS	1E40;54
Lagmann: *see also* Lawman		
Lambakarl	LIN	2,11. 13,22;26;31
Lambert	CAM	18,5-6
	CHS	3,2
	DOR	3,1;6
	ESS	20,52-53;55-56. 30,33
	KEN	P9
	LEC	17,13
	LIN	CS,3
	NFK	8,102;109
	SOM	37,1;8
Lambert : *see also* Jocelyn son of		
: *see also* Modbert son of		
: *see also* Walter son of		
Lambert, Jocelyn son of Lambert's man	LIN	28,38
Lambert, the Bishop of Durham's man	LIN	3,31
Lambert the priest	BRK	B7
Lambert: *see also* Lanbert		
Lambi	LIN	14,58
Lanbert, Drogo of Beuvrière's man	YKS	14E46
Lanbert: *see also* Lambert		
Lancelin	NTH	56,37-39
Landri	BRK	34,2
Landri: *see also* Landric		
Landric	LIN	12,84
	NTH	41,6. 43,6;8;11
	YKS	29W27-28. CW30
Landric, Count Alan's man	LIN	12,7;37
	YKS	6N36;53
Landric (Count Alan's man)	YKS	6N37;131
Landric the carpenter	YKS	C20
Landric: *see also* Landri		
Archbishop Lanfranc/of Canterbury	BRK	B3;9
	BKM	2
	CAM	4,1
	HRT	2. 16,1
	KEN	2. D19. C1;8. P15. 5,38;128. 13,1
	MDX	2
	OXF	2. B8. EBe3
	SFK	15. 20,1 *note*
	SRY	2
	SSX	2
	WIL	67,44;100
Lang	SFK	7,22
Langabein	HUN	19,13
Langfer	NTH	3,1. EH4
	RUT	EN6
	SFK	7,109. 32,2
Lank	BDF	57,7
	BRK	1,47. 63,2
	HAM	1,6;45
	SRY	21,1
Lank, Leofnoth's man	BDF	32,6
Lank's wife	BRK	1,6
Laurence	LEC	16,7
Laurence: *see also* Lawrence		
Lawman	ESS	68,6
Lawman: *see also* Lagmann		

Lawrence	BRK	42,1
	STS	11,54
Lawrence: *see also* Laurence		
Ledhard	WIL	24,42
Ledhard: *see also* Osbern/Osbert son of		
Ledman	SFK	7,15
Ledman the priest	CAM	AppxP
Ledmer	CAM	26,9
	DBY	6,34;94
	DEV	34,5;7
	DOR	28,7
	ESS	20,25-26. B3a
	SHR	4,4,19
	SOM	*5,67*
	SFK	5,6. 16,36
	SRY	21,2
Ledmer [? Leofmer]	ESS	B3a
	HRT	36,3
Ledmer, Archbishop Stigand's man	HRT	7,3. 23,1-2
Ledmer, Earl Tosti's man	BDF	23,47
Ledmer of Dry Drayton	CAM	AppxO
Ledmer of Hempstead/the reeve	ESS	90,48 *note*; 76
Ledmer of Whittlesford	CAM	AppxG
Ledmer of Witchford	CAM	AppxP
Ledmer the priest	ESS	20,77. 23,4
	SFK	25,1
Ledric	OXF	51,1
Ledwin	DEV	34,4
	SOM	*24,13*
Ledwin: *see also* Leodwine		
Ledwy	SHR	4,23,5
Lefleda [? Elfleda] (fem.)	CAM	*26,21*
Leith, a royal thane	BKM	4,32
Leodflaed (fem.)	LIN	26,48. 59,5
Leodmer: *see* Ledmer		
Leodwine	LIN	16,30. 27,12;35. 68,29
	YKS	13W22 *and note*
Leodwine son of Rafn, a lawman	LIN	C3
Leodwine: *see also* Ledwin		
Leofa	HAM	IoW8,9
	HUN	23,1
	SOM	16,8
Leofcild	ESS	23,36. 36,10. 57,2. 90,59
	SFK	7,60;62. 29,2
Leofcild, a royal thane	ESS	24,15
Leofcwen (fem.)	SFK	35,8
Leofday	ESS	30,2
	SOM	5,55. 36,12
	WIL	37,5
Leofeva (fem.)	BDF	23,17
	BRK	B6. 42,1
	DOR	49,1
	ESS	18,24. 23,29. 28,15. 33,4. B3a(x4)
	HRT	1,6;12. 34,12
	HUN	D2
	KEN	5,97
	OXF	B10
	SOM	2,7
	SFK	15,3. 16,20;48. 21,70. 32,9. 74,13

	SSX	9,84
	WAR	17,47
Leofeva, a widow	HRT	37,21
Leofeva (fem.), Edeva's man	CAM	*14,25*
Leofeva (fem.), Edeva the fair's man	CAM	*14,45*
Leofeva, King Edward's man	BDF	53,8
Abbess Leofeva/of Shaftesbury	BRK	15,2
	DOR	19. 1,30. 49,17. 55,21. B4
	SOM	14. 37,7
	SSX	8a
	WIL	12
Leofeva the nun	WAR	B2. 43,1
Leofeva (fem.): *see also* Leofgifu		
Leofflaed (fem.): *see* Leofled, Loefled		
Leofgar	DEV	3,50. 15,66. 16,130;144. 21,13. 34,13. 35,4. 36,6. 42,3. 43,4
	DOR	57,13
	SOM	21,23. 24,3
	SRY	5,27
Leofgar, King Edward's man	BDF	53,23
Leofgeat	BDF	23,32
	CAM	AppxF
	CHS	9,9
	DOR	40,2
	ESS	B3a
	HEF	9,16. 29,19
	HRT	16,3. Appx
	NTH	4,35
	NTT	2,6. 9,40
	OXF	58,37. EN6
	SHR	4,4,17. 4,16,1
	SOM	36,7
	SFK	7,76. 25,34;80
	STS	12,13 (*but see note*)
	WAR	16,13. 17,40. 28,11
	WIL	4,3. 67,86
	WOR	26,3
Leofgeat [mistake for Leofgyth (fem.)]: *see* Leofgeat's husband		
Leofgeat the priest	BDF	13,1
Leofgeat: *see also* Lovett		
Leofgeat's husband	WIL	67,86
Leofgifu (fem.)	LIN	68,48
Leofgifu (fem.): *see also* Leofeva		
Leofgyth (fem.): [mistaken for Leofgeat]: *see* Leofgeat's husband		
Leofgyth (fem.): *see also* Leofith		
Leofhard	ESS	1,14
Leofhelm	SRY	19,17
	SSX	12,31
Leofhild (fem.)	ESS	30,3
	STS	17,20
Leofing	CAM	26,25
	CHS	8,6. R1,20
	DBY	1,30;32. 6,2;94. 7,8. 10,13
	DOR	*55,8*
	ESS	27,10. 41,5
	HAM	3,11. NF3,9. 9,42. IoW7,18
	HEF	20,2. 23,5
	NTH	18,33

	NTT	9,57. 20,6
	SOM	9,6. 19,64. 21,54;71. *22,18*. 25,21. 45,
		2. 46,20
	STS	17,8-9
	WAR	22,28
	WIL	35,1
	YKS	9W113
Leofing, a thane	SOM	*19,64*. *21,54*
Leofing, brother of Ordric	SOM	*45,1*
Leofing, King Edward's man	BKM	17,13
Bishop Leofing (of Worcester)	HEF	1,44
	WOR	E4
Leofing, the Abbot of St Albans' man	BKM	12,22
Leofing the priest, Edeva's man	HRT	16,5
	YKS	C3
Leofith (fem.)	ESS	30,43
Leofith (fem.): *see also* Leofgyth		
Leofkell	NTT	9,34
Leofkell: *see also* Leofketill		
Leofketill	YKS	5W21
Leofketill: *see also* Leofkell		
Leofkollr	YKS	9W39
Leofled (fem.)	BRK	B7. 1,13
	CAM	14,82
	HEF	1,11. 7,1-3;5. 29,3-8;10;15
	HRT	5,19
	SHR	8,1-2
	SFK	1,123f. 7,111. 52,1
Leofled (fem.): *see also* Leofflaed, Loefled		
Leofman	HAM	1,12-13
Leofmer	DEV	21,15
	DOR	55,15
	ESS	90,61
	SHR	4,27,19
	SOM	5,67. 21,57
	SRY	19,2
	SSX	10,80
Leofmer: *see also* Brictwold son of		
Leofmer, a royal thane	BDF	25,12
Leofmer, Brictric's man	BKM	23,21
Leofmer, Earl Gyrth's man	CAM	*41,5*
Leofmer of Hinxton	CAM	AppxG
Leofmer the beadle	BDF	57,3v
Leofmer: *see also* Ledmer [? Leofmer]		
Leofnoth	BDF	24,20. 32,4;9
	CHS	1,36. 3,3;5;7-10. 5,4;8. 8,13. 9,24. 20,
		2;9. 26,4. FD2,1;4
	CON	1,1. 5,24,4-5
	DBY	1,30. 6,26;28;34;53;55;101. 10,1;4-7;
		9-11;16-19;21-22;24-25;27. 17,21
	DEV	16,49
	GLS	27,1. 28,2. 53,12
	HEF	1,22;28. 22,5. 26,2
	KEN	*2,39*. 5,73
	LEC	3,14. 14,28
	NTH	13,1. 18,40;64. 19,1-3. 39,1-18. 48,11
	NTT	13,6;9;11-12
	OXF	35,20
	RUT	R18

	SHR	4,3,35. 4,4,18-19. 4,6,3. 4,8,8. 4,18,2. 6,10
	STS	2,11
	SSX	9,13;53. 10,94. 12,26
	WAR	16,24;27;31. EN3
	WIL	6,1. 27,2;5;17. 28,1;6-7;13
	WOR	15,7
	YKS	1N13. 9W140
Leofnoth, a royal thane	BDF	32,1;3;5-6;8. 33,1-2
	WOR	23,8
Leofnoth, King Edward's man	BKM	43,1
Leofnoth of Sutton	KEN	D25
Leofnoth son of Osmund	BKM	12,38
Leofnoth Star	DBY	6,65
Leofnoth the priest	WOR	8,13
Leofred	DEV	24,12
	KEN	9,29
	SFK	38,18
Leofred of Ruckinge	KEN	5,165
Leofric	BDF	15,1
	BKM	25,3
	CAM	*35,1*
	CHS	1,5. 8,27. 9,19. 26,7
	CON	5,5,21. 5,23,4. 5,24,8
	DBY	6,7;19;86;91. 7,1-2;5. 10,8-11;17;20; 22;24. 17,1. B6
	DEV	3,98. 16,26;53-54;57. 21,4. 34,47. 39, 7 52,46
	ESS	18,19. 23,34. 30,12. 40,6;8. B3a(x3)
	GLS	31,8. 39,1. 62,6. 68,7
	HEF	10,55;61. 15,1. 20,2
	HUN	2,6. D29
	KEN	5,27;54
	LEC	14,23. 15,15-16. 23,2;5-6. 41,2-3. 44,9
	LIN	4,39. 18,27. 31,9. 39,1;3. 59,16. 61,1. 68,16. CK,42
	NFK	12,19-20. 21,10. 31,44
	NTH	18,4;13;28;43;45-48;52;58;75. 23,6. 41,3;7. 43,2;4;6;9-10. 47,1c. 54,3. 56, 35. ELe2
	NTT	7,1;4. 9,57;112. 13,1;8;10. 19,1. 29,1. 30,37
	OXF	B10. 35,9. 44,1
	RUT	R14
	SHR	4,3,2;55. 4,5,9;12. 4,19,12. 4,20,2. 4, 27,7
	SOM	8,17. 21,77. 25,30;51
	STS	15,1-2. 16,2
	SFK	1,11;58. 3,95(x2). 6,8;49;58;116;209; 227. 7,15;56;77;80(x2);82;86;94;97-98; 101;108;111;117-118;138-139;143. 8, 56(x2);63. 12,4. 14,128. 16,6;15;24. 21,49;69. 25,70;74;77;103. 29,8. 34,9. 35,7. 62,4-5. 67,10;12. 74,4;13. 75,5. 76,1
	SRY	5,16
	SSX	9,113
	WAR	16,51;54. 22,15-16. 28,13. 40,1. 41,2. EG16

	WIL	26,21. 50,2
	WOR	8,8;9g. 26,4
Leofric: *see also* Osmund son of		
: *see also* William (son of)		
Leofric, a rider	GLS	E33
Leofric, a thane	LEC	15,7
	SFK	5,1
Leofric, Azor's man	BKM	41,5
Leofric, Brictric's man	BDF	19,3
Leofric, Burgred's man	BDF	25,6
Leofric Child: *see* Leofric Young		
Leofric Cobbe	SFK	7,36
Leofric Cook	SFK	6,107
Earl Leofric	SHR	3b,2. 4,28,4
	STS	EW3
	WAR	3,4. 8,1. 12,10. 29,3. 43,1
Leofric, Earl Edwin's man	BKM	17,7
Leofric, Earl Harold's man	BKM	3a,3;5
Leofric, Earl Leofwin's man	MDX	25,3
Leofric, Earl Leofwin's Guard	HRT	34,7
Leofric, Edwin's man	BKM	5,4
Leofric Hobbeson	SFK	7,59. 29,7. 30,3
Bishop Leofric (of Exeter)	CON	2,2;15
	DEV	*2,7-8;14;16-23*
	OXF	5,1
Leofric of Hemley	SFK	6,110
Abbot Leofric/of Peterborough	DBY	3,2 *note*
	LIN	56,4
	NTH	ELc2
	RUT	ELc10
Leofric of Thorndon	NFK	7,14
Leofric of Wateringbury	KEN	D25
Leofric, Oswulf's man	HRT	15,5
Leofric Snipe	SFK	7,143
Leofric son of Bose, a royal thane	NFK	20,23
Leofric son of Grim	CAM	AppxG
Leofric son of Leofwin	LEC	29,3;18
Leofric son of Osmund, a royal thane	BDF	22,1
Leofric, the Abbot of Ramsey's man	BDF	34,3
Leofric, the Bishop of Lincoln's man	BDF	4,4
Leofric the deacon	SFK	7,31
Leofric the monk	BRK	33,5
Leofric the priest	WIL	1,13
Leofric the priest, a thane	SOM	*9,3*
Leofric the reeve	WAR	EW3
	WOR	2,47
Leofric Young [= Leofric Child]	LIN	63,1. CK,61
Leofric: *see also* Loernic		
Leofrun (fem.)	CON	5,2,23. 5,14,6
	DOR	54,2. 56,54
	SOM	*19,72*
Leofrun, Aelmer of Bennington's man	HRT	36,8
Leofrun, Archbishop Stigand's man	HRT	34,14
Leofsexe	ESS	B3a
Leofsi	BKM	12,15
	CAM	21,1
	DBY	6,43
	ESS	20,48;76. 25,2. 38,3
	HAM	3,8. 23,33
	HEF	10,67;69;74

	HRT	28,1. 34,17. Appx
	NFK	8,61
	NTH	41,6. 51,1
	SOM	25,37
	SFK	6,92;193. *8,1.* 67,12
	SSX	9,122. 11,33

Leofsi: *see also* Azor son of

Leofsi, a thane	DBY	6,42
Leofsi, Brictric's man	BKM	23,26-28
Leofsi, Earl Tosti's man	BDF	53,2
Leofsi, Earl Waltheof's man	CAM	21,8-9
Abbot Leofsi (of Ely)	CAM	*28,2. 35,2*
Leofsi the reeve	HRT	31,8

Leofsi: *see also* Leofsige

Leofsida (fem.)	WIL	5,7

Leofsida (fem.): *see also* Leofsidu

Leofsidu (fem.)	SFK	14,138

Leofsidu (fem.): *see also* Leofsida

Leofsige	LIN	4,51. 12,20. 26,2. 28,38. 59,19. CK,16
	YKS	5W21-22. 9W105

Leofsige: *see also* Leofsi

Leofson	ESS	10,3. 25,20. 30,12;18-19. B3a(x3)
	SFK	7,59;90. 29,1. 38,16
Leofstan	ESS	20,53;55;68. 24,6-7;9;42;44. 32,13;44.
		52,3. B3a(x3)
	HEF	15,3
	KEN	5,4;174
	NFK	1,195. 9,86. 35,5. 37,1-2
	NTH	B31. 18,65
	SFK	2,19. 6,111;155;202. 7,41;65;76;87;89;
		93;98;110;121. 8,57. 16,26. 25,72. 34,
		5;8;14. 35,8

Leofstan of Falkenham	SFK	6,110
Leofstan of Loes	SFK	29,1
Abbot Leofstan (of St Edmunds)	SFK	25,1. 68,5
Leofstan the priest	SFK	1,122d. 7,40
Leofstan the reeve	ESS	52,2
Leofswith (fem.)	ESS	B3a
Leofwara (fem.)	HRT	4,8
	SOM	32,1
	STS	12,27
	WAR	EBS2

Leofwara (fem.): *see also* Leofwaru

Leofward	BRK	33,9
	KEN	5,152
	NTT	30,17
	SSX	10,70
Abbot Leofward/of Muchelney	SOM	9. 21,54(?)-55
Leofwaru (fem.)	SFK	25,84

Leofwaru (fem.): *see also* Leofwara

Leofwin	BDF	8,6. 24,25
	BRK	7,9. 17,3. 21,21. 45,3
	BKM	12,10. 41,5. 57,10
	CAM	*32,43*
	CHS	8,35;38. 9,14. 10,1-2. 14,12. 20,3
	CON	5,26,2
	DBY	1,9. 6,39;44;63. 7,9;12. 16,3;5. 17,5-6;
		20
	DEV	23,11
	DOR	4,1. 26,57;65. 28,4. 57,20

ESS	1,7. 20,43;45;52. 21,8. 24,62. 26,3. 27, 17. 30,12. 33,13. 34,37. 46,3. 54,1. 76, 1. 90,61;86. B3a(x12)
GLS	11,14. 19,2. 28,6-7. 30,1-2. 39,18-20. 53,5;7. 68,10. 78,1
HAM	2,19. 3,6;8. 69,3;43-44
HEF	10,13;21;59
HRT	13,2. 15,8. 30,3
HUN	15,1. 19,17
KEN	M2. 5,43;66;122;174;189. 9,25
LEC	1,12. 9,1. 13,19. 17,4. 29,14. 43,3. 44, 2
MDX	11,2
NFK	20,10-11
NTH	18,45;54;80;96. 28,3
NTT	3,4. 6,5. 9,79. 10,2
OXF	8,1-4. 58,24-25;30
SHR	4,14,4. 4,15,2-3
SOM	5,68. 17,1-2. 19,32. 21,38. 24,13. 25, 23-24
SFK	6,3;191;209(x2). 7,15;56;76. 8,60. 16, 15-16;24;33;38. 25,103. 26,6. 41,5;17. 74,4;13
SRY	1,15
SSX	9,27;61-62;98;110. 10,58;64;112. 11, 21;45;54;68;85. 12,40;55. 13,20;36-40; 43;56
WAR	3,4;7. 4,1. 5,1. 16,2;7;22;30;32;53. 31, 1-12. 44,11-12
WIL	24,29. 68,9;13
WOR	2,29. 15,6

Leofwin : *see also* Alwin brother of	
: *see also* Burgwald son of	
: *see also* Godwin son of	
: *see also* Leofric son of	
Leofwin, a man-at-arms	SSX 13,9
Leofwin, a royal thane	BDF 32,10;12-13;15
	BKM 14,42
	HRT 29,1. 33,2. 40,1
	SFK 8,32
Leofwin, a thane	DEV *35,9*
	GLS 68,9
	HAM 19,1
	SOM *19,32*
	SFK 41,15
Leofwin, Alric son of Goding's man	BKM 12,28
another Leofwin	GLS 68,9
Leofwin Benne	SFK 35,7
Leofwin, brother of Alfsi	BKM 17,1
Leofwin, brother of Swein	SRY 25,3
Leofwin, Burgred's man	BKM 41,3
Leofwin Cave	BKM 57,8
Leofwin Child: *see* Leofwin Young, Young Leofwin	
Leofwin Crist	ESS B3a
Leofwin Croc	ESS 46,2
	SFK 8,49
Leofwin Doda	WAR 37,2

Earl Leofwin	BKM	B11. 2,2. 4,3;5;7-10;13-14;19-20;22; 27;33-35;37;40-42. 12,12. 14,19. 26, 10. 28,3. 43,4. 51,1
	DEV	1,51-55
	HRT	B6. 5,1;9-10;20. 6,1. 15,2;10-11. 34,1; 7. 42,14
	KEN	5,48;52-53;58-59;67;71;106-107
	MDX	2,2-3. 9,6. 14,2. 18,1. 25,2-3
	SOM	4,1
	SRY	5,11;19
	SSX	9,27-29
Leofwin, Earl Harold's man	HRT	30,1. 36,11. 44,1
Leofwin, Earl Waltheof's man	BDF	40,3
Leofwin, Edwin's man	BKM	23,30
Leofwin, Godwin of Benfield's man	HRT	20,12
Leofwin Gric'	CAM	AppxM
Leofwin Latimer	HEF	1,10c;36
Leofwin (Latimer)	HEF	1,38
Leofwin of Bacton, a royal thane	SFK	6,212;217. 41,10;?11 *note* (cf 41,7)
Leofwin of Bottisham	CAM	AppxC
Bishop Leofwin (of Lichfield)	STS	11,12
Leofwin of Mentmore	BKM	43,4
Leofwin of Nuneham	BKM	57. B13. 40,1
Leofwin of Nuneham's mother	OXF	EW2
	WAR	37,9
Leofwin Sock	DEV	*51,7*
Leofwin son of Brown	SFK	6,110
Leofwin son of Estan	BKM	12,31
Leofwin son of Ringwulf	SFK	6,216
Leofwin the bald	SFK	57,1
Leofwin the forester	HAM	1,2
Leofwin the goldsmith	BRK	7,8
Leofwin, the King's reeve	BKM	57,8
Leofwin the priest	CAM	*31,1*
	NTH	17,1
Leofwin Wavre	BKM	57,9
Young Leofwin [= Leofwin Child], a royal thane	BDF	12,1. 24,18. 25,14. 48,1. E2
	DBY	6,29. 16,1
	ESS	38,4. 42,4
	HRT	13,1
	SHR	4,1,23
	SFK	16,4;30
(Young) Leofwin	ESS	42,2;6
Leofwin: *see also* Leofwine		
Leofwin(e) son of Alwin(e)	DBY	S5
	LIN	T5
	NTT	S5
Leofwine	LIN	S11. 25,13. 42,2. 63,2;5. CW,3
	YKS	5E51. 5W33. 9W55;88
Leofwine: *see also* Burgwald son of		
Leofwine, father of Burgwald, a monk	LIN	C3
Leofwine the priest, a lawman	LIN	C2
Leofwine: *see also* Leofwin, Leofwin(e)		
Leofwold	ESS	B3a
	NFK	35,2
	SFK	8,68
Leofwold, a thane	NFK	13,24
Leofwold: *see also* Livol		
Leofwy	GLS	53,7
	OXF	56,1

	SHR	4,3;22. 4,6,4
	SOM	2,7
Leofwy, Archbishop Stigand's man	OXF	29,16
Leofwy, Asgar the constable's man	CAM	14,29
Leofwy of Duxford	CAM	AppxG
Leohtgifu (fem.): *see* Licteva		
Leohtwine: *see* Lictwin		
Leowulf: *see* Livol		
Let	GLS	1,41
Letard	HRT	Appx
Lethelin	WIL	25,3
Lethi	SHR	5,3
Leysingr	LIN	28,33
	YKS	1N12;26-30;37-38. 1W37. 11N1-2
Liboret	BDF	23,55
Licteva (fem.)	SFK	21,25. 52,6
Licteva (fem.): *see also* Leohtgifu		
Lictwin	SFK	8,4
Lictwin: *see also* Leohtwine		
Ligulf	DBY	1,30;36. 6,9;61. 16,1
	STS	16,2
Ligulf: *see also* Ligulfr, Livol		
Ligulfr	YKS	C3. 1N1;3;67;70;98;124;130-131. 1E4; 21. 1W3-4;13. 5N53;59-60;69-70. 5E48;50;52. 5W6-7;18;36. 6N29-30. 9W28;32;54;95;99;121. 13W12;15. 13N7. 14E20. 23N9;11. 25W29-30 *note*. 28W30. 29W24. 29E14. 29N5. CW4;6;33
Ligulfr: *see also* Ligulf		
Ligulfrs, two	YKS	1N110
Lindbald the monk	BRK	7,25
Linxi	HAM	60,2
Liseman	WIL	67,89
Lisois of Moutiers	CAM	25,9
Lisois (of Moutiers)	BDF	21,13
	ESS	25,2 *note*; 5
	NFK	24,1-4;6. 66,100
	SFK	28,2
Lithwulf	GLS	EvQ29
Livol [= Leofwulf, Leofwold or Ligulf]	HAM	IoW8,4
Locar	NTT	9,32
Lodi, a thane	BKM	14,45
Lodowin	OXF	B10
Lodric	BRK	49,2
Loefled (fem.)	ESS	B3a(x3)
Loefled (fem.): *see also* Leofflaed, Leofled		
Loefred	ESS	32,9. B3a
	SSX	9,106. 13,31
Loefred: *see also* Leofred		
Loernic	NFK	8,6
	SFK	6,305-306;308;310
Loernic: *see also* Leofric		
Lokki	NTH	18,82
Lorce Bret	ESS	B3a
Lord	NFK	4,31
Losoard	LIN	C20. CS,13. CN,14
Losoard, the Bishop of Bayeux's man	LIN	4,8;41;61
	NTT	7,2-3;5
Lothen	CHS	8,2

Lother	SFK	25,87
Lovell	NFK	31,28;33
	SSX	3,9
Lovell, a man-at-arms	SSX	3,3
Lovett	HRT	34,2;8
	LEC	13,58
	STS	12,13
Lovett: *see also* Leofgeat		
Lovettot	YKS	CE36 *and note*
Ludi	HEF	32,1
	SHR	4,11,2
Ludo	DEV	23,13;22. 25,23
	SOM	24,12;22
Ludo, a man-at-arms of Walscin's	DEV	*23,17-20. 42,16*
Ludric	HEF	10,58
	WAR	37,5
Ludric, Earl Algar's thane	HEF	10,58
Lufa	DEV	35,17
Lufa the reeve	SRY	5,3
Lunden	SFK	7,80
Lundi	ESS	B3a
Lunen	HUN	6,21. 9,1-4
Lurk	SFK	31,13
Lustwin	SFK	6,118;184. 7,56. 8,12;66. 52,1
Lustwin, wife of	SFK	6,118
Lutting	ESS	90,68
Luvede	CHS	7,4
Mabon	YKS	9W18
Maccus	CON	4,17
	LIN	27,25;27;33
	YKS	14E48 *and note.* 29W14
Machel	CHS	Y11
Machel: *see also* Machelm		
Machelm	YKS	30W38
Machelm: *see also* Machel		
Machern	CHS	Y12
	YKS	30W39 *and note*
Madalgrim	YKS	1N116;125-129. 6N10
Madalred	YKS	29N1
Madoc	SHR	4,27,31
Madoc: *see also* Madog		
Madog	GLS	78,17
	HEF	36
Madog: *see also* Madoc		
Maelcolumban	YKS	29W14
Maelcolumban: *see also* Northmann son of		
Maelmaedhog	YKS	1N123
Maerwynn (fem.): *see* Marwen, Merwen		
Magbanec	YKS	1N18-19
Maghere	SOM	6,10
Magne/Manne: *see* William son of		
Magni	HUN	23,1
	SFK	3,101
Magnus Swarthy: *see also* Manni Swart		
Mainard	LIN	16,20;41
Mainard, Roger of Poitou's man	LIN	16,3
Mainard: *see also* Maynard		
Maino	KEN	9,3-4;6
Maino: *see also* Mainou		
Mainou	OXF	6,14. 56,4

Mainou the Breton	BKM	43. B8
	HRT	39
	LEC	37
	NTH	54
Mainou: *see also* Maino		
Maiwulf	NTH	40,6
Malemayns	NFK	65,16
Malet	BDF	22,2
	NFK	20,29 *note*
	NTH	EB4
	SFK	1,102. 3,86;89. 4,42. 6,11;33;38-39; 46-47;49;57;211;217-218. 7,71;136; 140;144-145;148. 16,16;30. 28,6. 45,1
Malet: *see also* Robert Malet		
: *see also* William Malet		
Malger	YKS	9W53. 13W2-4;8-9
Malus Vicinus	SFK	76,1
Man	YKS	14E43 *and note*
Manasseh	OXF	B9. 58,27
Manasseh Cook	DOR	*3,6*
Manasseh Cook's wife	SOM	46,24-25
Manasseh's wife	SOM	6,1
Manbodo	YKS	14E29
Manegot	WAR	18,15
Manfred	DEV	19,23
	NTT	20,3
	SOM	25,14;40;47
Manfred, Ralph of Limsey's man	NTT	14,7
Manfrid	CAM	AppxD
Mann	NFK	34,7
	SFK	1,102
Mann: *see also* William son of		
Manni	SOM	25,22
	SFK	7,19;54. 44,3-4
Manni: *see also* Ulf son of		
: *see also* William son of Magne/Manne		
: *see also* William son of Manni		
Manni Swart	SRY	29,2
Manni Swart, a thane	SFK	3,1;3
Manni Swart: *see also* Ulf son of		
Manning	ESS	18,29
Manno	HAM	3,1. 45,5
Manson	ESS	B3a,c
	SFK	7,28;76;84;86
Manstan	ESS	B3a(x2)
	SFK	7,58
Manwin	ESS	B3a(x9)
Marcher	KEN	7,19
Marchiud	CHS	FT1,9
Marculf	SFK	16,6. 77,4
King Maredudd	HEF	29,1. 31,1;7
King Maredudd: *see also* Gruffydd son of		
Martel	ESS	30,24;31-32;35;43
Martel: *see also* Geoffrey Martel		
: *see also* Martell		
Martell	BDF	E3
	HRT	19,2
Martell: *see also* Martel		

Martin	BKM	47
	LIN	45. CK,30
	NTH	18,79
Marwen (fem.)	NFK	30,5
Marwen (fem.): *see also* Maerwynn, Merwen		
Mascerel	ESS	23,14. 90,58
Mathilda, Matilda (fem.)	DEV	24,1. 40,4. 52,25
	SOM	17,8
Queen Matilda	BKM	52
	CON	1,13-19
	DEV	1,57-72. *13a,2.* 27,1
	DOR	1,15-29. 17,1
	GLS	1,47;50
	HAM	1,8
	NTH	8,4
	WAR	3,4
	WIL	17,1
Queen (Matilda)	DOR	*50,2.* 54,8. 56,19
	ESS	1,11-12;23. 60,3. 82,1. B3j
	GLS	1,24;37;42;44;51. 69,6-7
	HAM	6,12. 53,2
	LIN	68,30
	SRY	1,8. 31,1
	WAR	EG2-3
Matilda, the King's daughter	HAM	67,1
Matilda (fem.): *see also* Mathilda		
Matthew, Kolsveinn's man	LIN	26,20-21;46
Matthew of Mortagne	BRK	59
	DOR	46
	ESS	53
	GLS	73
	SOM	44
	WIL	63
Mauger	DBY	13,1-2
	DOR	26,34;60
	ESS	18,26-27. 20,51. 41,12
	HAM	2,14. 3,5. IoW2,1
	KEN	2,30. 5,9-11;22
	LIN	7,17;24;35-36
	NFK	9,212
	NTH	45,5
	NTT	11,3
	SOM	1,12. 19,2-3;11;48;59. *21,92*
	SSX	6,1
Mauger: *see also* Drogo son of		
: *see also* Hugh son of		
: *see also* William son of		
Mauger of Carteret	DEV	*15,57*
	SOM	*10,1.* 19,*16*-19. *68.* 46,21
Mauger, the Archbishop of Canterbury's man	ESS	6,8
Mauger, the Bishop of Lincoln's man	LIN	7,16;34
Bishop Maurice (of London)	DOR	7. 1,31
	ESS	3-4. 20,4. 48,2
	HRT	4. Appx
	MDX	3. 15,1. 16,1
	SOM	15. 1,19;21. 8,37
Mawa, a free man	SFK	36,3
Mawa, a half free woman	SFK	*32,26*
Maynard	ESS	24,12
	HAM	45,9

	NFK	9,160. 66,51
	SFK	3,9. 6,169
	WIL	68,27
Maynard, the Abbot of Ramsey's man	NFK	1,61
Maynard the watchman	NFK	1,61
Maynard: *see also* Mainard		
Meginta	LEC	14,18
Menleva (fem.)	SFK	35,7
Merdo, a thane	LIN	25,1
Merefin	NTH	18,39
Mereswith (fem.)	SOM	21,24
Merewine	YKS	13N1
Merewine: *see also* Norman son of		
: *see also* Ulfketill son of		
: *see also* Merwin		
Mergeat: *see* Aelfric son of		
: *see* Alric son of		
Merken	CON	5,24,23
Merlesveinn	LIN	C5. T5. 35,1;3-4;6-9;11-12;14-15. CK, 5;11;31
	YKS	C1a;36. 6N151. 16E1;3-5. 16N1-2. 16W1-5. CW,38
Merlesveinn the sheriff	LIN	CW,12
	SOM	1,4 *note*
Merlesveinn: *see also* Merlesweinn		
Merlesweinn	CON	5,1,1-2;10. 5,2,18. 5,3,20;24. 5, 17,4. 5,24,4
	DEV	32,1-10
	GLS	44,1
	SOM	1,4. 24,21-23;29. 31,1-5
Merlesweinn: *see also* Merlesveinn		
Merra	LIN	18,32
Merwen (fem.)	BDF	13,2
	ESS	65,1
	HAM	23,33
Merwen (fem.): *see also* Maerwynn, Marwen		
Merwin	CAM	14,37
	HEF	1,54
	SRY	19,39
	WAR	16,35. 37,7
Merwin, Earl Oda's thane	HEF	10,39
Merwin: *see also* Merewine		
Count of Meulan	LEC	9. 44
	NTH	19
	WAR	16. B2;5. 17,60. EN2-3
Mild (fem.)	SFK	35,7
Miles Crispin	BDF	19. 53,7
	BRK	33. B1
	BKM	23
	GLS	64. 1,2. E15
	OXF	35. B9
	SRY	29
	WIL	28. 30,5. 68,25
Miles (Crispin)	BRK	B1
	HAM	69,40
	OXF	EBe1
Miles de Belefol	SFK	38,25
Miles (de Belefol)	SFK	38,6;19-20
Miles Molay	BRK	B8
Miles the porter	HAM	68,7-8

Modbert	DEV	16,11;26;130-132
	ESS	33,8
Modbert: *see also* (Geoffrey) son of		
Modbert son of Lambert	DEV	*16,50*
Modgeva (fem.)	SFK	11,4
Modgeva of Colcarr	SFK	6,110
Modgeva (fem.): *see also* Modgifu		
Modgifu (fem.)	NFK	4,50
	YKS	C5
Modgifu (fem.): *see also* Modgeva		
Moding	ESS	25,8;10
Moding, Queen Edith's man	BDF	23,32
Modwin	ESS	68. 70,2
Molleva (?fem.)	KEN	5,191-192;217;220-222. 9,36
Moran	CHS	26,12
Morcar	BKM	5,18. 12,31. 53,9-10
	DBY	16,7
	LEC	18,3
	LIN	T3. 1,6. 3,31. 27,3;5;57. 30,25;27;29.
		56,9. CN,5. CK,5;50
	NFK	7,10
	NTT	9,74;110. 10,18
	SHR	4,27,26
	SOM	EBu2
	SFK	7,77
	YKS	C28;30;32;36. 1Y1;4;6-11;14. 3Y1-2.
		5W20;23-25. 6W2;5-6. 6N162.
		9W17-18. 14E2;4-5;7;9. CE11
Morcar: *see also* Aelfeva mother of		
Earl Morcar	BKM	23,2
	CHS	2,21. 8,16. 20,11
	HEF	1,6
	HRT	5,24
	LEC	1,1-2
	LIN	C6. T5. 1,1;4-5;26;65. 2,37;39. 30,1;
		22;26;28. 35,13. 42,1. CK,34;40
	NTH	1,4. 32,1
	NTT	1,58
	RUT	EN4
	SHR	4,1,17;24. 4,3,16. 4,4,6;20. 4,9,1. 4,11,
		4. 4,23,16
	STS	10,3
Earl Morcar: *see also* Aelfeva mother of		
Morcar, Earl Harold's man	BKM	45,1
Morcar the priest, of Luton	BDF	1,2b. 40,1-2
Mordwing	BDF	23,44
Moregrim	SFK	7,82;89
Morel	NFK	10,11
Morewin	SFK	6,247. 21,37;91
Morfar	CHS	26,1
Morfar: *see also* Morfari		
Morfari	YKS	9W10;18;121;124
Morfari: *see also* Morfar		
Morganwy	GLS	37,2
Moriland	LEC	16,6
Morin	CAM	12,4-5. 14,9
	DEV	16,169
	GLS	W4. 3,5. WoB18
	SSX	10,8;36;88;113. 11,2;9;29;90. 13,49-51
Morin: *see also* Roger son of		

Morin of Caen	DEV	*16,173-174. 51,14*
Count of Mortain: *see* Robert of Mortain		
Morulf	YKS	C3
Morvan	NFK	29,7
Morvan: *see also* Morvant		
Morvant	SFK	53,1
Morvant: *see also* Morvan		
Moses	SOM	5,53-54
Mucel	CAM	32,39
Mulagrimr	YKS	5E29-30. CE3
Muli	YKS	3Y5. 5E56. 11E2. CE17
Munding	SFK	7,58
Mundred: *see* Mundret		
Mundret	CHS	C24. 1,22;34. 2,13. 26,3
	SHR	4,1,19
	SFK	4,30-31
Munulf	SFK	4,15;42
Munulf the priest, the Abbot of Ely's man	SFK	26,5
Murdac	YKS	C14. 14E3;34;53
Murdoch, a man-at-arms	SSX	3,3
Murdoch: *see also* Robert son of		
Muriel, wife of Roger of Bully	DEV	27,1 *note*
Mylnugrimr	YKS	1E58. 5E73. CE10
N.	SFK	31,13. 39,5
Nardred [? for Hardred]	SFK	3,57
Nawen [? Hawen, for Heahwine]	STS	4,9. 5,1
Nicholas	SOM	34,1
	STS	16,1
	SFK	26,3-4;6
	WAR	15,1-6
	WIL	26,21
Nicholas, Earl Hugh's goldsmith	NFK	66,98
Nicholas of Kennett	CAM	*18,8.* AppxA
Nicholas the bowman	DEV	48
Nicholas the goldsmith	NFK	66,98
Nicholas the gunner	WAR	40. B2
Nicholas: *see also* Nicolas		
Nicolas	BRK	7,22
Nicolas: *see also* Nicholas		
Nigel	BRK	B1. 21,8. 64,1
	BKM	23,19-20;29. 53,7
	CON	5,6. *4,22*
	DBY	6,17. 10,15
	DEV	5,10. 17,4-5;10-14;82
	DOR	*36,6*
	ESS	27,13. 32,25;27;39. 41,2;9
	HAM	NF3,3;5;11;14-16. IoW6,16. 7,4;19. 8, 3
	KEN	2,15. 9,47
	LEC	14,10;23;30;34
	LIN	3,9. 56,7-8
	MDX	14,2
	NFK	31,45. 35,8;13-14
	NTH	2,3. 18,90. 56,63-64
	SHR	4,24
	SOM	5,18-19;30;55. 25,28;43
	SFK	2,7
	SRY	5,23
	SSX	11,2;16;44;62;102-103. 12,9;22;45;52
	WAR	19,6

	WIL	1,1
	YKS	3Y8 *note*
Nigel : *see also* Eudo son of		
: *see also* Robert son of		
: *see also* Roger son of		
: *see also* William son of		
Nigel, a man-at-arms	CHS	R5,6
	DEV	5,4
Nigel, a servant of Count Robert (of Mortain)'s	SFK	2,8
Nigel, Countess Judith's man	LIN	56,6
Nigel Fossard	YKS	C5;9. CN5. CE1;10-11;13;18. CW11; 18;37
Nigel (Fossard)	YKS	5N1-8;22-23;27;30;32;53-54;58-61; 66. 5E1;3-11;15;17-19;21-25;29-44; 58-59;68-69;71-73. 5W6-8;11;13;15; 30-31;35. CE2-4;8;19-21;27. CW12-14;21
Nigel, Ivo Tallboys' man	LIN	14,16;32;38;45
Nigel of Aubigny	BDF	24. 8,2. 16,3
	BRK	12,1
	BKM	39
	LEC	39
	WAR	41
Nigel of Berville	BKM	40
Nigel (of Burcy)	CHS	25. R5,6
Nigel of Gournai	SOM	*5,30;32;38;44-45*
Nigel of le Vast	BDF	24,9-11;22-23
	BKM	39,2
Nigel of Muneville	YKS	C4
Nigel of Stafford	DBY	14
	STS	16. ED5
Nigel (of Stafford)	STS	2,6-7;17-19;22. 13,1-2;4;6. 15,2
Nigel, the Bishop of Durham's man	LIN	3,5;8;39;51
Nigel, the Bishop of Lincoln's man	NTT	6,13;15
Nigel the doctor	GLS	1,2
	HAM	63. S3
	HEF	7
	KEN	M21
	SHR	9. 3d,6
	SOM	*8,30.* 13,1
	WIL	56. 1,18
	WOR	12,1-2
Nivelung	YKS	9W11 *and note*; 18
Norigold	NTH	56,58
	SFK	33,2
Norigot	NTH	4,19. 41,4;9
Norman	BDF	21,13. 23,52
	BRK	7,2;9;15;19-20;46. 35,2
	CAM	38,2
	DEV	14,2. 15,65;68. 16,14;102. 20,4. 36, 17. 42,8
	ESS	1,19. 20,30;79. 25,7. 33,14
	HAM	23,14. 54,2. 68,6
	HUN	20,4;7
	KEN	D17. 5,96. 9,44;46;48. 12,3-4
	LEC	10,6;11-13. 16,2. 28,1-5
	LIN	31,3. CN,8. CK,39;55
	NFK	31,38;42
	NTH	18,21. 30,1-6;9-11. 55,1-2. 57,4
	SHR	4,25

	SOM	1,4. 20,2. 21,47;85;92. 36,11-12
	SFK	2,19. 3,61. 6,28;84;135;258. 7,3;10-12; 28;30;32;37-39;70;76-77;79-96;112; 114;126-128;136-143. 8,46;51. 14,1; 41. 21,105. 25,23. 31,13. 39,9-10. 41, 6. 43,3. 74,13. 76,19
	SRY	30,2
	SSX	9,32;86. 10,38. 12,4. 13,8
	WIL	37,8
N(orman)	SFK	7,81-90;92-94;97-101;103-111;113; 115;117-121;128-129;132

Norman/Northmann: *see also* Hugh son of
         : *see also* William son of

Norman, a man-at-arms	SSX	9,8
Norman, a thane	SFK	7,18
Norman Crassus, a lawman	LIN	33. C3;21. CW,3-5;17
Norman of Arcy	LIN	32. 3,7. CS,30. CW,20
Norman of Lincoln	DBY	B7
Norman of Nosterfield End	CAM	*29,7-8.* AppxF
Norman Parker	DEV	*1,64*
Norman Pigman	HEF	1,4
Norman son of Merewine	LIN	CK,21
Norman son of Siward the priest	LIN	C14
Norman son of Tancred	SFK	8,35;46-47;49
Norman the priest	NTT	9,1
Norman the sheriff	SFK	63. 6,91;290. 7,36
Norman (the sheriff)	SFK	16,34
Norman, William of Percy's man	LIN	22,3;8;13

Norman: *see also* Northmann

Northmann	YKS	C10. 1N2;14;75;77. 1E47. 5N22-23;27; 30;53;58;65. 5E17;39-40;42-43. 6N54; 113;115. 9W39;68;83. 10W16. 11E3. 13W6-7;9-11. 13E1-2;7;9-10;12-13. 13N2;4-5. 14E29. 21E10. 25W21;26. 29E11;13;25. 29W43. CE8;26;31. CW13;17;30
Northmann son of Maelcolumban	YKS	CE23. CW26
Northmann son of Ulfr	YKS	CE13

Northmann: *see also* Norman

Not	ESS	B3a
Novi	HEF	1,59
Nubold [MS. Nuboldus, for Huboldus = Hubald]	WIL	25,24
O.	NFK	10,13
Ocsen	HAM	46,1-2
Oda	STS	1,47. 11,29
Earl Oda	HEF	1,44. 10,39. 23,6
	WOR	E4

Earl Oda: *see also* Edith sister of

Odard	CHS	9,18-19. 26,2
	ESS	24,65
	LEC	15,15
	SFK	14,93
	SFK	*14,71*
	WAR	16,64
Odard, a man-at-arms	CHS	9,17
Odard the gunner	SRY	35
Odbert	BKM	17,3-4

	NTH 36,2. 39,7-8;10-11. 43,11
	SRY 1,1f. 5,6. 6,4
Odbert: *see also* Otbert	
Odbold	DOR 2,6. 3,16
	WIL 3,3
Odda	BRK 6,1
Oddi	YKS 9W3;11;17. 14E16. CW31
Oddi the deacon	YKS 25W14. CE52
Oddi (the deacon)	YKS 14E49
Oddi the priest	YKS CE49
Oddi (the priest)	YKS 14E19
Odelard	BRK 46,6-7
	OXF 30,1
Odelard: *see also* Odilard	
Odelin	KEN 7,19
Odelin: *see also* Otelin	
Oder	NFK 19,13;27;31;40. 20,4;9;26;28
	NTH 4,24. 41,8
Odeva [= Odgiva]	DEV 52,1 (*but see note*)
Odfrid	YKS 29E30
Odfrida (fem.)	YKS 5N37 *and note*
Odger	LIN CK,40-41;43-44;46;48
Odger: *see also* William son of	
Odger of London	HUN D2
Odger, Ralph Paynel's man	LIN 35,13
Odger the Breton	LEC 38
	LIN 42
Odger: *see also* Oger	
Odgiva: *see* Odeva	
Odilard	HAM 29,8;13. NF5,1
	HEF 9,2
	HUN 19,16-17
	SHR 6,21
	WIL 41,2
Odilard the larderer	HUN 19,22
Odilard the steward	KEN *7,19*
Odilard: *see also* Odelard	
Odin	CHS FT1,8. FT3,1
	SRY 8,22. 19,2
Odin: *see also* Hundger son of	
Odin of Windsor	HAM 3,8
Odin the chamberlain	WIL 68,25
Odin the Dane	ESS 18,37
Odincar	LEC 40,35
	NTT 9,1;76;92;96;100;106;108
Odincar, a thane	DBY 13,2
Odincar: *see also* Othenkarl	
Odo	BRK 48,1
	BKM 43,3
	CAM 14,65-66. 32,43
	CON 5,14. 4,26;28
	DEV 16,92;171. 17,41;70-77
	ESS 24,19;25;50-51;66. 30,45. 37,8;10
	GLS 39,3
	HAM 1,W1;W2. 23,25. 51,2. NF9,2
	HEF 1,61. 10,32;34;39
	HUN 19,25
	KEN 5,88;112-113
	LIN 14,35;59-60;62;92. 32,20
	NFK 27,1

	SHR	4,18. 4,3,9-10;17-19. 4,8,5
	SOM	22,10
	SFK	3,68. 67,22;30-31
	WAR	22,22
	WIL	3,4. 4,1-2. 66,6
	WOR	2,78. 12,2. 19,10
Odo: *see also* Aldred brother of		
: *see also* William son of		
Odo, Brictric's man	BKM	26,5
Odo, Count Alan's man	YKS	6N56
Odo (Count Alan's man)	YKS	6N59-60 *note*
Odo, Ivo Tallboys' man	LIN	14,12;14-15;31;34;43-44;58;87;93
Odo, Norman of Arcy's man	LIN	32,9
Bishop Odo/of Bayeux	BDF	2. 40,3
	BRK	41,3. 44,2;5. 65,19
	BKM	4. B11. E2
	CAM	28,2. 37,1. 43,1
	DOR	4
	ESS	18. 1,27. 4,9-10. 9,1. 20,1. 36,9. 48,2
	GLS	1,22-23;65. 41,5. E29;34. EvN1
	HAM	23,56-68. NF10,2. EL
	HRT	5. 10,9. 31,8. 37,19. 42,11
	KEN	5. D7-8;10. M1;3;13-14. C3;5;8. P19.
		1,3. 2,5. 3,3. 4,16. 7,5-6;10. 9,1;42. 13,
		1
	LEC	1,10
	LIN	4. 27,11. 30,14. 40,24. CN13;15-16.
		CS1-2;13;24;28
	NFK	2. 1,111;120-122. 4,44. 66,82
	NTH	2. B16;30
	NTT	7
	OXF	7. B8. 1,6
	SOM	4
	SFK	16. 75,5. 77,1;6
	SRY	5. 1,1c-d;5;11;13. 6,1. 8,29. 14,1. 36,1
	SSX	1,2
	WAR	4. 20,1
	WIL	4. M2. 13,21
	WOR	11. 2,44. 10,12
Odo of Flanders	SOM	45,6
Odo of Winchester	BRK	65. 10,1
	HAM	21,1. 67,1. 69,1-3;7. S2
	SSX	14
	WIL	67,1
Odo, Ralph of Mortimer's man	LIN	36,2
Odo son of Edric/the Englishman	DEV	*52,22-25*
Odo son of Everbold	DOR	54,11-14
Odo son of Gamelin	DEV	42
	SOM	38. *21,65*
Odo son of Gamelin: *see also* Theobald		
father-in-law of		
Odo, Swein's man	ESS	9,14
Odo the chamberlain	CAM	*14,21;26;31*
Odo the chamberlain, son of	DOR	36,8
Odo the crossbowman	LIN	48. 1,36
	YKS	26. C17. CE32. SE,P8. SE,Bt2;7.
		SE,Ac3;6-8;11-12
Odo the steward	HAM	6,16 (*but see note*)
Odo the treasurer	DOR	*1,21*
Odo, Walter of Aincourt's man	LIN	31,8

Odolina (fem.)	WIL	67,83
Odulf: *see* Authulfr, Othulf		
Oepi	SRY	5,12
Oepi, Brictric's man	BKM	36,3
Offa	GLS	39,20
	SFK	53,5. 74,13
	SSX	11,8
Offa, Stigand's thane	NFK	9,168
Oger	DOR	40,9
	NFK	8,89
	NTH	41,6
	RUT	4
Oger son of Ungomar	RUT	R14
Oger the Breton	NTH	52
Oger: *see also* Odger		
Ogga	NTT	15,8
Ogis	DOR	*36,3*
	SOM	*1,1.* 21,55;63;72. 25,8
Oia	NFK	*1,147*
Oio?	NFK	*1,147*
Oirant, and his father	HAM	IoW9,7
Olaf	HAM	IoW7,4
	MDX	7,4
	NTH	60,3
	SSX	9,10
Oliver	DEV	36,16;18;26
Olova (fem.)	NFK	21,19
Orcus	SRY	1,5
Orde	CHS	9,26
	SOM	19,25
Orderic	NTH	18,32
Orderic: *see also* Ordric		
Ordgar	BRK	B9
	CAM	12,1. 14,21;75. 32,5
	CAM	14,75
	ESS	13,2. 56,1. 57,5. 90,85
	NFK	5,1-3. 39,1
	NTH	18,43;57-58
	OXF	35,24-25. 58,38
	SOM	21,7;75. 46,7
	WIL	7,8
Ordgar, Edmer Ator's man	DEV	*15,17*
Ordgar, King Edward's sheriff	CAM	22,6. 28,1
Ordgar in Kyluertestuna	SFK	6,110
Ordgar, Robert (Gernon)'s thane	ESS	32,7
Ordgar, the reeve of the Abbot (of St Edmund's)	SFK	14,152
Ordgar's father	OXF	35,25
Ordgeat	ESS	B3a
Ordgrim	SHR	4,11,19
Ordheah	WAR	22,5
Ording	CHS	1,23
	KEN	5,18
	NFK	20,34
Ording of Horton	KEN	D25
Ordlaf	ESS	B3a
Ordmer	BRK	65,11
	CAM	*31,2*
	DBY	6,32
	ESS	39,4

	LEC	29,10
	NTH	18,92. 55,3
	SHR	4,27,19
	STS	11,12;31;53;58
	SFK	12,3. 74,15
Ordmer, Brictric's man	BKM	12,9
Ordmer, Edeva's man	CAM	14,65
Ordmer of Badlingham	CAM	14,67. AppxA
Ordmer, the Abbot of Ramsey's man	HRT	37,13
Ordmer the priest	SSX	10,1
Ordnoth, Robert son of Wymarc's man	CAM	30,1-2
Ordric	BKM	14,48
	DEV	15,64. 23,8. 48,1;3-8
	ESS	35,14
	GLS	3,3. 71,1. 78,9. WoB16
	HEF	10,72
	NTT	9,19
	SFK	6,210. 7,92. 31,58. 35,7
	WAR	16,34. 17,31;37;50-57;59;61. 28,4. 44, 13
	WOR	2,32;55-56
Ordric: *see also* Leofing brother of		
Ordric, a thane	SHR	4,16,2
	SOM	1,21
Ordric, brother of Aelfric	KEN	5,110
Ordric, brother of Leofing	SOM	*45,1*
Ordric, King Edward's man	CAM	*32,7*
Ordric, Leofnoth's man	BDF	32,9
Ordric: *see also* Orderic		
Ordwold	HAM	41,1
	SOM	*5,62*
	WIL	67,65. 68,7
Ordwold, a thane	SOM	*5,62*
Ordwulf	BRK	38,1-2
	CON	5,1,9;12
	DEV	1,56 *and note*. 2,9. 15,3-5;8-10;39-53. 30,1. 35,1;10
	SOM	6,9. 19,16
	WIL	27,13
Ordwulf, a thane	DEV	*15,11*
	SOM	1,21
Ordwulf's sister	DEV	15,41
Ordwy	BDF	53,27
	HUN	19,23
	SHR	4,14,6. 4,23,18
	SRY	21,5
	WAR	22,13. 36,1
Ordwy, a thane	SHR	4,16,2
Ordwy, burgess of Bedford	BDF	6,1. 56,3
Ordwy, King Edward's man	BDF	57,10;12
Ordwy, Wigot of Wallingford's man	BKM	23,33
Orm	CHS	9,17. Y1;10
	DBY	6,59;92
Orm: *see also* Ormr		
Ormketill	LIN	12,96
Ormr	LIN	12,14

Osbern Male: *see also* Osbert Male

Osbern of Arques	LIN	41. CK,26
	YKS	25. C16. CW1;24;26-29;32;36;38;41. SW, BA4;8;13. SW,An4-15. SW,Bu1-2; 6-7;10;18
Osbern of Cherbourg	GLS	71,1
Osbern of Eu	HAM	2,25 *note.* ESr
	SRY	1,9. 3,1
Bishop Osbern/of Exeter	BRK	5
	CON	2. 5,1,3
	DEV	2
	DOR	35,1
	GLS	5. G3-4. 1,56
	HAM	5
	NFK	11
	OXF	5
	SRY	4
	SSX	6
	WIL	1,5;23f

Bishop Osbern : *see also* Bishop Osbert
           : *see also* Earl William brother of

Osbern/Osbert of Sacey	DEV	43 *and notes*
Osbern of Wanchy	SFK	25,59
Osbern, Osbern of Arques' man	YKS	25W19
Osbern/Osbert Paisforiere	KEN	2,*26*. 5,12;138;*152;171*-173;*213-214*
Osbern son of Boso	YKS	C3
Osbern son of Geoffrey	SSX	9,52;70
Osbern/Osbert son of Ledhard	KEN	2,38. 5,135-136;200 *and note*; 205-207; 216;*218*. 7,19
Osbern son of Richard	BDF	44
	GLS	1,11. 48,3. EvK10
	HEF	24. 1,12. E1
	NTT	27
	OXF	EW2
	SHR	5. E4
	STS	7,2
	WAR	37. B2. 6,5
	WOR	19. 2,14;49. E35
Osbern son of Tezzo	CHS	24. FD5,3. FD6
Osbern son of Walter	BDF	45
Osbern, the Archbishop of York's man	LIN	2,38
Osbern, the Bishop's clerk	LIN	7,29
Osbern the falconer	HAM	68,11
Osbern the Frenchman	ESS	24,3
Osbern the monk	HRT	10,12
Osbern the priest	LIN	53-54. 2,16
	WIL	57. 1,6. 19,3
Osbern, uncle of Alfred (of Marlborough)	HEF	19,2-3
Osbern, William of Percy's man	LIN	22,10;29
Osbert	BDF	32,1;6-7
	BKM	17,31. 21,7. 23,5
	DEV	*17,34*. 24,7
	ESS	24,58. 30,17. 47,2
	HRT	34,5;25
	LIN	57,35
	NFK	8,128. 9,225. 33,1-3;5-6. 37,1-3. 49, 4-5
	NTT	11,6
	SFK	7,120-121. 13,3
	WIL	5,5

Osbert: *see also* Gamall son of
   : *see also* Osbern
   : *see also* Osbern/Osbert son of Ledhard

Bishop Osbert [for Osbern, of Exeter]	NFK	L11 *note*
Osbert Male	SFK	34,6
Osbert Male: *see also* Osbern Male		
Osbert of Breuil	BDF	23,27;31
Oscar [rectius Osgar] of Bedford	BDF	56,1
Oseva (fem.)	DEV	*52,1 (but see note)*
Oseva (fem.): *see also* Osgifu		
Osferth	CON	5,13
	DEV	16,3;11;15;55;80;107-108;157;176. 21,
		16. 35,27
	NFK	9,154
	SFK	1,31. 7,85;91
Osferth, Toli's man	SFK	6,106
Osfram	LIN	27,55-56;57,12;41;45;57. 67,23. 68,
		21-22. CK,47;49
Osgar: *see* Oscar		
Osgeard	KEN	5,17;180. 9,45
Osgeat	ESS	B3a
	SFK	7,143
Osgeat, King Edward's man	BDF	23,56
Osgeat the reeve	BDF	57,18;20
Osgifu (fem.): *see* Oseva		
Osgot	BRK	28,1-3
	CAM	*32,13*
	CHS	4,1-2
	ESS	B3a
	GLS	38,1-5. 60,1
	HAM	IoW7,10. 8,1
	HEF	10,35
	LEC	1,9
	NFK	6,3. 12,1
	NTH	40,2. 58,1
	NTT	30,14;20
	RUT	EN21
	SFK	7,108. 16,17;36
	WIL	67,82
Osgot, Archbishop Stigand's man	CAM	*32,8*
Osgot, Edeva's man	HRT	16,3
Osgot: *see also* Ansgot, Asgautr, Asgot		
Oslac	DEV	*28,2*
	ESS	18,45. 37,1. 38,2
	LEC	2,4. 17,7-8
	NFK	9,221-222. 25,17
	NTH	23,2. 60,5
	SFK	3,91. 4,7. 6,114
	WAR	17,29
Oslac, a thane	DEV	*28,2*
	SHR	4,1,35
	SFK	31,3
(another?) Oslac	DEV	28,2
Oslac White	NTH	1,21
Osmelin	HAM	34,1
	SSX	2,5. 11,80;110
Osmer	CHS	5,5;7;10-13. 8,31;35;38. FD5,2
	DBY	6,8
	DEV	16,127. 17,50
	DOR	3,18

	LEC	44,5
	SOM	47,25
Osmer, a man-at-arms	DOR	3,17
Osmer the priest	DBY	B11
Osmer's father	SOM	47,25
Osmund	BDF	22,1
	BRK	54,4
	CAM	32,38. AppxM
	CHS	FD7,2. R3,1
	DBY	6,88-89. 11,3. 17,16;18
	DEV	25,9-10;12
	DOR	56,53
	ESS	40,3
	HAM	21,3;5. 69,15
	HUN	D8
	LEC	2,4. 15,14
	LIN	7,48;50. 30,18. 59,3;12;15;20
	NFK	1,72. 5,2. 8,18;91-93
	NTH	4,22. 18,2;25;88. 21,1. 35,13;21. 43,8
	NTT	9,22. 15,1;3
	OXF	40,2. 58,5
	SHR	4,3,58
	SOM	5,56. 6,12. 19,41
	SFK	3,100. 6,186;238. 10,1
	SRY	18,2-4
	SSX	12,50
	WAR	28,6
	WIL	15,1. 24,16-17. 26,20. 66,8
Osmund : *see also* Ansketel son of		
: *see also* Hugh son of		
: *see also* Leofnoth son of		
: *see also* Leofric son of		
: *see also* Ralph son of		
: *see also* William son of		
Osmund, a thane	LEC	15,7
	WIL	21,2
Osmund Bent	DBY	17,13
Osmund, Edric of Laxfield's man	SFK	7,36
Osmund, father of Ralph	HUN	D8
Osmund Little	CAM	AppxE
Osmund of Anjou	ESS	1,3
Bishop Osmund/of Salisbury	BRK	3. B6. 1,34
	DOR	2. 3,1-18
	LIN	5. CK,62
	LEC	14,23
	OXF	4
	SOM	3. EDo1
	WIL	3. 1,23h. 25,2. 32,2. 67,11
Osmund of Stretham	CAM	AppxP
Osmund of Vaubadon	HRT	1,13
Osmund of Witcham	CAM	AppxP
Osmund, Ralph of Buron's man	NTT	15,4;7
Osmund, Stigand's thane	NFK	6,7
Osmund son of Leofric	NTH	18,1
Osmund Stramin	SOM	5,6-7. 22,15
Osmund the baker	DOR	57,17-18
Osmund the canon	BDF	13,1
Osmund the Dane	NTH	43,7
Osmund the priest	OXF	14,3
Osmund, uncle of Guy	NFK	8,31

Oswy, the Abbot of Ely's man	CAM	40,1
Oswy Wild the priest	KEN	*M24*
Otbert	YKS	C10 *and note*
Otbert: *see also* Odbert		
Otelin	DEV	16,23;55;86;111;121-122;124;176
Otelin: *see also* Odelin		
Othenkarl	LIN	4,65. 24,74. 48,1
Othenkarl: *see also* Odincar		
Othere	DEV	15,53. 17,26;28;56. 19,10
Othere: *see also* Walter son of		
Othere, a thane	SHR	4,3,10
Othere: *see also* Otheri, Ottarr		
Otheri	SFK	19,19
Otheri: *see also* Authari, Othere, Ottarr		
Otho	SRY	19,33
	WIL	67,92
Otho's father	WIL	67,92
Othulf	SFK	13,3
Othulf: *see also* Authulfr, Odulf		
Ottarr	YKS	1E17;25;36
Ottarr: *see also* Toki son of		
: *see also* Othere		
Otti	SFK	7,84
Otto	STS	17,19
Otto the goldsmith	CAM	1,18
	ESS	81. 1,11-12. B3j
	SFK	1,97-99
Otto (the goldsmith)	SFK	14,13
Oualet	SSX	14,2
Oudgrim	NTT	9,3
Oudgrim: *see also* Authgrimr		
Oudkell	NTT	7,4
Oudkell: *see also* R. Oudkell		
Owen	CHS	8,27;31
	HEF	31,7
Owen: *see also* Owin		
Owin	DBY	7,8
	ESS	B3a
Owin: *see also* Owen		
Ows, King (William)'s reeve	GLS	W11
Padda	SFK	7,7
Palli	GLS	58,3
	WAR	18,4
Papald	HAM	43,3
Pat	CHS	27,2
	SFK	1,111
Pata	STS	13,5
Patrick of Chaworth	GLS	EvK1
Paulinus	SOM	25,26
Payne	BRK	36,4-5
	BKM	16,3. 17,9-12;14;26;29. 41,2
	CAM	26,44-47;49
	CHS	5,4. 9,24-26
	DOR	2,2
	ESS	24,5;33
	GLS	70,1
	HAM	NF9,3;19;26
	HRT	4,13;17. 37,20
	LEC	25,3
	NFK	9,130. 46,1

	NTH	35,8
	OXF	29,18. 59,12
	STS	12,14
	SFK	25,81-82;84
	SSX	11,30;97
	WIL	27,2;5
	WOR	23,13

Payne: *see also* Edmund son of		
: *see also* Ralph son of		
: *see also* Roger son of		
Payne, a man-at-arms	SSX	11,3
Payne, Hardwin of Scale's steward	CAM	*26,16*. AppxG
Payne, William Peverel's man	NTT	10,51
Payne's daughter	NFK	46,1
Peacock	ESS	B3a
Peret the forester	HAM	NF9,24
Perlo	SOM	21,47
Pesserera	SFK	31,42
Peter	DEV	20,6
	ESS	32,17;44
	HRT	1,12. 5,9;25. 28,1;5. 37,19
	NFK	8,113
	OXF	28,10-11. 59,9
	SFK	14,17;36;43;61. 67,23
	SRY	19,2
	WAR	27,3
	WIL	24,40
Peter, a burgess	HRT	42,7
Peter, brother of Burghard	SFK	*14,17*
Peter, Ivo Tallboys' man	LIN	14,20;41
Bishop Peter (of Lichfield & Chester)	BRK	B4. 1,9;11;42
	SOM	16,6-7;14. 47,1
Bishop Peter: *see also* Ranulf nephew of		
: *see also* Reinbald son of		
Peter of Palluel	SFK	67,18
Peter of Valognes/the sheriff	CAM	33. 1,17
	ESS	36. 1,2;4. 5,2. 49,3. ESf1
	HRT	36. B7;11. 1,9;12-13;19. 9,10. 28,1.
		36,9;13. 37,19
	LIN	60. C3;15;20
	NFK	34. 8,106. 10,22. 66;87;89
	SFK	37. 1,96. 14,78;81-83;*85;96-97*. 75,2
Peter (of Valognes/the sheriff)	ESS	1,19;25-27
P(eter of Valognes/the sheriff)	SFK	EE1
Peter, the Abbot of St Edmunds' man	NFK	1,61
Peter the cleric	SFK	14,13;*87*
Peter the cleric: *see* Walter nephew of		
Peter the steward	SFK	*14,53;61;70*
Peverel	HAM	IoW7,3;8
Peverel: *see also* Ranulf Peverel		
: *see also* William Peverel		
Phanceon	NFK	4,2 *and note*; 16
Pic	ESS	B3a
Picot	BKM	41,1
	CHS	2,14
	HAM	1,34. 23,3. 69,34-35
	HEF	25,3
	HRT	EC1-2
	LIN	12,14;17;19
	NTH	41,6

	SHR	4,20. 3d,5. 4,4,20
	STS	2,6
	SRY	19,20-22;28
	SSX	11,74
	YKS	13W7. 13E12
Picot, a man-at-arms	SHR	4,20,8
Picot, Count Alan's man	LIN	12,14
	YKS	6N58
Picot (Count Alan's man)	YKS	6N27-30 note
Picot of Cambridge/the sheriff	CAM	32. B12-13. 1,14-16 note; 23. 3,2;4-5. 5,11;24. 13,8. 14,39;41;58. 21,7-9. 29, 12. 31,7. 33,1. 36,1. 41,9-12;16. EE1. AppxA; K; L
	ESS	1,9
Picot (of Cambridge/the sheriff)	ESS	1,13. 32,35;43
	SFK	1,120-121
Picot the sheriff: see also Roger brother of		
Picot: see also Pirot		
Picot's wife	CAM	21,9
Pilwin	NTT	6,5. 20,1
Pin	GLS	2,7
Pinna of Balsham	CAM	AppxD
Pinson	ESS	35,5
Pipe	SOM	8,2
Pirot [? Picot]	BDF	21,14-15. 24,18;24
	CAM	25,1-3
	ESS	25,11 (but see note)
	SFK	28,6 (but see note)
Pirot [?Picot]: see also Picot		
Pirot's [? Picot's] wife	BDF	24,18
Pleines, the Abbot of Ramsey's man	HUN	6,7
Pointel: see (Theodoric) Pointel		
Pote	ESS	B3a
Poyntz: see Drogo son of		
: see Walter son of		
Queneva/mother of Brictmer	SFK	14,117 note. 39,7 note; 8-10
Queneva (fem.): see also Cwengifu		
Quentin: see also Quintin		
Quentin's wife	LEC	8,2
Quintin	NFK	19,20;32
	WIL	3,2-3
Quintin: see also Quentin		
R.: see Humphrey son of		
Bishop R.	SHR	4,4,23
R. Halebold	WAR	17,60
R. Oudkell	SFK	66,16
Abbot R** [= ?Rhiwallon]/of Winchester	BRK	10. B9 and note
	DOR	9
	HAM	6. IoW7,13
	SRY	7
	SSX	7. 11,8
	WIL	10. 25,6
R(...) son of Walter	LEC	3,15
Rabel	CON	5,24,16-17
	NFK	1,61
Rabel the carpenter	NFK	66,101-102
Rabel the engineer	NFK	55
Rada	NFK	1,128-131
	SFK	48,1
Radbod	SFK	74,4

Radbod Lang?	NFK	*9,100*
Radbod the reeve	NFK	20,31
Radbod: *see also* Ratbod		
Rademar	DEV	23,5
	SOM	24,5;7-8;25-27;33
(another) Rademar	DEV	23,5
Rademer, Gilbert of Ghent's man	LIN	24,61
Radfred the priest	HAM	1,7
Radfrid	NFK	14,41. 15,11. 16,5. 19,2;6;9
	SFK	*14,139*
Rafn	YKS	1W30. 6N17
Rafn: *see also* Leodwine son of		
Rafnketill	YKS	C8;12. 1W30;69. 9W133;136. 13W35.
		14E18;39;43;49. 23E11. 29W18-19;35;
		44. CE46;48
Rafnketill: *see also* Ravenkel		
Rafnsvartr	YKS	1W64;68
Rafnsvartr: *see also* Ravenswart		
Rafwin	STS	1,41;45. 2,22. 11,30
	SSX	11,62
Ragenald	CHS	1,35
Ragenald [mistranscribed Reginald]	NTT	9,127. 14,2. 17,2
Ragenhild (fem.)	BRK	46,5
Ragenot	YKS	25W17 *and note*
Ragnaldr	LIN	48,13. 68,4;17
	YKS	2W9 *and note.* 5W16;26-27. 9W11.
		10W14. 29W10
Rahere	SOM	*47,22*
Raimer the clerk/brother of Walter of Douai	DEV	*23,5 note*
	SOM	*24,35*
	SSX	3,3
	SRY	1,1b
Raimer the clerk: *see also* W(alscin) brother of		
Rainald	LIN	CS,39
	YKS	2W9 *and note*
Rainald, Geoffrey of la Guerche's man	LIN	63,2
Rainald, Kolsveinn's man	LIN	26,43
Rainald, Walter of Aincourt's man	LIN	31,3;5
Rainalm	ESS	30,19;39
	SFK	32,6
Rainard: *see also* Roger son of		
Rainer	DEV	16,8;22;95-96;119;133-135. 47,14
	ESS	20,32
	KEN	5,95
	LEC	29,17
	LIN	CS,11
	NFK	8,100;110. 66,108
	SHR	4,3,8
	SSX	9,103
	WIL	42,2-3;8
	YKS	2N25
Rainer, Drogo of Beuvrière's man	LIN	30,6
	YKS	14E30;39
Rainer, Jocelyn son of Lambert's man	LIN	28,25;37;43
Rainer of Brimeux	LIN	40. CS,9;14;25;29. CN,10;23
Rainer the deacon	LIN	CN,9;11;13;18;23
Rainer the steward	DEV	*16,56*
Rainer: *see also* Rayner		
Rainfrid, a man-at-arms	SHR	4,4,20
Rainfrid, Ivo Tallboys' man	LIN	14,17

Rainward

Rainward: *see also* William son of
Ralph

DBY	10,5
SOM	24,3-4;16;23-24;27(?)
BDF	21,16. 23,19. 25,4. E7
BRK	27,2
BKM	12,2;16;20-21;24-25;31;36. 14,14;19; 33;35-36;43;48. 16,7. 17,2. 19,5. 23, 2-4;32. 29,4. 44,5. 53,5. 57,10
CAM	14,16. 26,48. 32,37
CHS	9,9;27. FT3,4. R3,1. R6,4
CON	5,24,24
DBY	6,34-36;53-54. 10,10-11. 11,3
DEV	*1,37*. 5,1;4-5 *note*. 17,9;24;36-37; 45-46;55-57;63-67;91-92;94;102-105. 19,9;14;20;25;39. 21,6;10;13-14. 23, 22;26. 42,8 48,4. 51,4
DOR	2,6. 10,3. 37,1-2. 47,7. 54,1;9. 55,12; 29. 56,29
ESS	3,1. 4,7;13. 20,45. 24,42;55-56. 25,14. 28,2-4;13-15. 30,12. 32,29. 35,2-4. 36, 4;7. 39,12. 45,1. 90,56
GLS	3,7. 34,11. 39,4;15. 44,1. WoB19
HAM	2,15. 23,46;49;52. 37,1. 43,1. 45,3-4
HEF	1,27. 7,2. 10,25-26;31. 14,6. 19,1. 22, 1. 29,14
HRT	4,11;12. 5,24. 15,7;11. 16,7. 21,1. 33, 1;13. 34,1;11
HUN	19,11
KEN	M7. *2,11*. 5,4. 7,6. 9,30
LEC	3,5-10;14. 10,7;14. 13,46. 29,16. 40, 32-33;38. 43,2. 44,4;10;12-13
LIN	3,4;47. 12,7;62. 13,20. 64,18
MDX	9,2
NFK	1,57;140. 8,15;24;37;107-108;122. 9, 196;198. 10,19. 12,45. 12,4;6;18;34. 21,11-13. 23,17-18. 24,3;7. 34,6-7. 61, 3
NTH	4,23. 18,31-41;84-87. 21,4. 25,3. 30, 16. 36,3. 41,5
NTT	6,8;11
OXF	7,50;56. 16,1. 20,4. 24,1. 29,6. 34,2. 35,19. 59,11;15. ES1
SHR	4,3,67-68. 4,6,3
SOM	5,69. 6,1. 22,5-7. 24,20;30-32. 25,17; 53. 28,1
STS	2,22. 12,8;30. EN3. EW3-4
SFK	3,79. 6,177-178. 7,145-148. 14,3;35; 53. 25,88. 31,42. 38,16;23
SRY	2,1. 3,1. 5,8-9;19;21;28. 19,38;46
SSX	2,7. 3,5;8. 6,1. 9,19;120. 10,1;12;21; 26;30;32;34-35;54;58;62;65;78;95; 105-106. 11,2;13;17;24-25;47;78. 12, 13;33-34;40;49-50. 13,13;23-25;28;31; 37-39;41-42;44;48
WAR	12,10-11. 16,66. 17,43;45-46. 19,2. EN5
WIL	7,11. 8,9. 26,11;14. 32,9;12. 36,2. 55,2
WOR	2,79. 20,2
YKS	9W4-5 *note*;46;54;58;140

R(alph)

NFK	9,196;198. 10,19. 12,45

	NFK	1,63-64;75;95;111;131;152;172;
		201-202;216. 4,1;26;52;56. 8,5. 9,4;13;
		30;49;160. 10,59;69;71. 12,1;42. 15,
		18;17,1;30. 19,25. 21,14. 26,5. 38,2-3.
		51,9. 52,3. 65,8;17. 66,42;80-81;83-84
	SFK	1,10. 3,1;40-41. 4,32. 6,169. 7,19;44;
		133. 16,2-3. 46,8. 74,8-9. 76,13;17.
		ENf4
Ralph (Earl/Wader)	NFK	1,7;77-78;136;181-182;194-195. 4,42.
		6,1. 19,20. 27,2. 47,7. 58,3. 66,98
	SFK	3,59. 16,33. 25,104. 31,53 note
R(alph, Earl/Wader)	NFK	1,73;97;106;120-121;161. 4,51. 66,64;
		102
	SFK	3,57
Earl Ralph/the Elder/the constable	CON	5,1,6
	LIN	T5. 1,8. 12,21;43;47-49;60;91. CK,23;
		51;66
	NFK	1,151;153;202-204. 4,23;37. 8,8;10;
		124. 10,21;66. 17,21;24;33;37. 20,31.
		48,4
	SFK	1,101. 3,15;61;98-100. 4,14. 14,101.
		31,53. 46,7
	NFK	1,94;96;97 note; 98-99. 10,80. 55,2
	SFK	3,10;17-18. 13,6. 32,10
Earl R(alph/the Elder/the constable)	NFK	1,95
	SFK	3,10;17-18. 13,6. 32,10
Earl Ralph : see also Alsi nephew of		
: see also Countess Gytha		
: see also Godwin uncle of		
: see also Harold son of		
: see also Hardwin brother of wife of		
Earl Ralph's wife	NFK	8,10
Ralph, Erneis of Buron's man	YKS	24W4
Ralph Fat/the fat	NFK	34,9
	SFK	14,35;37
Ralph Framen	LEC	42,9
Ralph, Gilbert of Ghent's man	LIN	24,41;74
Ralph, Godric the steward's man	NFK	9,42
Ralph, Hugh son of Baldric's man	LIN	25,2
	YKS	23N28
Ralph Hunter	CHS	21. FD8
Ralph, Kolsveinn's man	LIN	26,40
Ralph Latimer	CAM	5,37
	ESS	90,42
Ralph, nephew of Geoffrey Alselin	LIN	C4. 64,1-2;7-8;10;15
	NTH	B25
Ralph of Bagpuize	BRK	21,3;14
Ralph of Bapaume	LIN	C20
Ralph of Beaufour	NFK	20. 1,11;66;215;218;239;241. 6,7. 15,
		19;20. 19,40. 22,11. 48,5-6. 50,13. 65,
		16. 66,90-91
	SFK	11
Ralph of Berkeley	GLS	43
Ralph of Bernay/the sheriff	HEF	1,2;39;70. 19,1;4
	WOR	2,36. E1
Ralph of Bruyère	DEV	16,12;35;48-49;153;163
Ralph of Buron	DBY	11
	NTT	15. B10
Ralph (of Cardiff)	GLS	1,24;38
Ralph of Chartres	LEC	10,15-17

Ralph of Sacey	GLS	EvK116
	HEF	1,61
Ralph of St Samson	KEN	M2
Ralph of St Wandrille	KEN	7,6
Ralph of Savenay	SFK	16,4;6-8;13;23-24;30;34-35;48. 21,39.
		34,7;10;12;17
Ralph of Shephall(?)	HRT	Appx
Ralph of Tilly	DEV	*5,1*
Ralph of Tosny	BRK	47
	ESS	51
	GLS	45. EvN12
	HAM	S3
	HEF	8. 1,21-22;38;62
	HRT	22
	NFK	22. 1,211. 21,15. *22,1.* 66,69-70
	WOR	15
Ralph of Tourleville	NFK	9,8
	SFK	7,73;86;98
R(alph of Tourleville)	SFK	7,99-101
Ralph Pagnell/Paynel	DEV	32
	GLS	44
	LIN	35. C5;20. CW,19. CK,5;31;53
	NTH	31
	SOM	31
	YKS	16. C25. CN2. CW38. SW,BA9.
		SW,Bu1;8-9;27;43. SN,Ma5;20-22.
		SN,B22. SE,How10-11. SE,Bt6.
		SE,Th1
Ralph Passwater	BDF	25,1
	BKM	40,1
Ralph Paynel: *see* Ralph Pagnell/Paynel		
Ralph Piercehedge	BRK	B6
Ralph Pinel	ESS	77. B3a
	SFK	61. 39,3. 73,1
Ralph Pippin	LEC	17,33
Ralph, Roger of Bully's man	NTT	9,110
Ralph Rufus	SOM	*5,2;48;66-67*
Ralph son of Brian	ESS	3,5. 4,15;18. 34,26;30. 90,12
	SFK	34,8
Ralph son of Gunfrid	SSX	10,9
Ralph son of Hagni	NFK	57. 50,9
Ralph son of Herlwin	NFK	9,8-9;12;73;231. 19,8. 66,75
Ralph son of H(erlwin)	NFK	9,118
R(alph) son of H(erlwin)	NFK	9,120
Ralph son of Hubert	DBY	10. 2,1. 6,99. B6
	LEC	22
	LIN	62
	NTT	13. B12
	STS	15
	WOR	23,8
Ralph son of Jocelyn	DEV	21 *note*. 21,6;13-14 *notes*
Ralph son of Osmund	HUN	27. 6,17. 22,2. D8
Ralph son of Ospak	KEN	2,29
Ralph son of Payne	DEV	*19,43*
Ralph son of Richard	KEN	9,29
Ralph son of Robert	KEN	5,202
Ralph son of Siegfried/Sifrid	BRK	49. B3
	HAM	3,5;10
Ralph son of the Earl	BRK	48
Ralph son of Theodoric	SSX	13,45

HRT	4,14;15;20. 15,2;13
HUN	24. 1,1-2;5-8. 23,1
KEN	5,120-122;147
LEC	3,11
LIN	CW,8
NFK	6,2. 9,161. 10,19. 21,6-8;18;21;25;29. 35,1. 66,97
OXF	58,6. EG2
SHR	4,4,1-2
SOM	21,29. 25,27;44. 35,4;13;20
STS	2,22
SFK	6,39. 7,71-72. 33,6. 67,4;20
SRY	5,16. 27,2
SSX	10,10;31;58;66;76;80
WAR	11,4. 16,29
WIL	27,20
WOR	10,13

Ranulf : *see also* Hugh son of		
: *see also* William son of		
Ranulf, a man-at-arms	KEN	5,138
Ranulf, Alfred of Lincoln's man	LIN	27,23-24
Ranulf, brother of Abbot Walter	GLS	EvO1
Ranulf, brother of Ilger	BDF	29. 53,30
	CAM	34
	ESS	37. 1,1;27. 7,1
	HRT	25
	HUN	24
	MDX	22
	NFK	36. 1,192. 66,103
	SFK	39
R(anulf), brother of Ilger	SFK	67,15
Ranulf brother of Ilger: *see also* Humphrey		
nephew of		
Ranulf, Erneis of Buron's man	LIN	34,9
Ranulf Flambard	BRK	3,3
	HAM	66. NF8
	MDX	3,4
	OXF	B9. 14,6
	SOM	7,12
	SRY	1,14-15
	WIL	8,6;9
Ranulf, Geoffrey of la Guerche's man	NTT	19,1
Ranulf, Guy of Craon's man	LIN	57,22;24
Ranulf (Mainwaring)	CHS	20 *note*
Ranulf, nephew of Bishop Peter	SOM	*16,7*
Ranulf, nephew of William of Warenne	SFK	26,13
Ranulf of Colombières	KEN	D8-9. *C3*. P19. 5,48;95;101;123;133; 219. 7,19
Ranulf of St Valéry	LIN	43
Ranulf of Stringston	SOM	*35,4*
Ranulf of Vaubadon	KEN	5,223. 7,19
Ranulf of Vaubadon's brother	KEN	5,223
Ranulf Peverel	BRK	B3
	ESS	34. 1,2;17;25. 9,14. 10,3. 20,56. 32,8. 90,10-14. B3q. EKt
	KEN	5,104
	MDX	4,4
	NFK	32. 9,184;189. 66,105
	OXF	31

	BKM	35,3
	CAM	14,40. 29,6
	DEV	*1,23.* 5,11. 15,26-30;36-37;45-46;48; 50-53;64-65;67-72;75;78-79. 16,149; 172. 20,16-17. 21,1. 35,9;13;19-22;27; 30. 42,15;18
	ESS	30,2;45. 35,14
	GLS	3,7. WoB19
	HAM	2,23. 36,1. IoW6,14
	HRT	34,24
	NTH	17,4. 55,2
	OXF	1,10. 6,9. 27,8. 28,23-24. 29,9;13;20. 34,1. 35,12;14;34. 59,16-18;22. EBe2
	SHR	4,1,11;19. 4,28,1
	SOM	37,12
	SFK	67,2;16
	SRY	8,16
	SSX	11,46;67;116
	WAR	12,3-5;7
	WIL	28,2;6-7;12-13
Reginald [error for Ragenald]	NTT	9,127. 14,2. 17,2
Reginald: *see also* William son of		
Reginald (Balliol)	CHS	22. 27,3
	STS	14. 8,4-6 *note*
Reginald, brother of Hubert the Breton	SFK	*14,68*
Reginald Canute	WIL	62. *28,9*
Reginald of Downham	CAM	AppxP
Reginald of Vautortes	CON	*5,2. 2,14*
	DEV	*15,44. Notes to* 1,23. 15,26-30;48;67
	SOM	*19,28;43*
Reginald son of Croc	HAM	59. S3. IoW1,6
Reginald son of Erchenbald	SRY	33,1
Reginald the archer	OXF	58,2-3
Reginald the baker	HAM	IoW6,10
Reginald the Breton	SFK	70. *14,68*
Reginald the chaplain	GLS	1,42
	WAR	EG3
Reginald the gunner	ESS	79
Reginald the sheriff	SHR	4,3
Reginald Wadard	OXF	7,10-11
Reginald, Walter of Aincourt's man	NTT	11,25 [error for Reynold]
Reginald: *see also* Reynold		
Reginwal	DEV	*23,5*
Reinbald	BRK	1,22. 7,14;18-19
	BKM	E4
	OXF	49
	WIL	25,23
	WOR	8,9b-9c
Reinbald: *see also* Alfward son of		
Reinbald of Cirencester/the chancellor/	BRK	61. B6. 1,3. EB1
the priest	BKM	11
	DOR	24,4
	GLS	26
	HEF	1,46
	SOM	1,8;*10.* 45,14
	WIL	1,23c-d. 18,2
	WOR	E6
Reinbald (of Cirencester/the chancellor/	GLS	1,1. 19,2. E31
the priest	SOM	16,1
Reinbald son of Bishop Peter	BRK	1,42

Richard of Clare: *see* Richard son of Count
  Gilbert
Richard (of Clare): *see also* Ro(t)hais wife of

Richard of Courcy	OXF	32. B9. 1,2
Richard of Guilden Morden	CAM	22,7. AppxJ
Richard of le Marais	KEN	5,145
Richard of Merri	SOM	*35,3;17*
Richard of Neville	DEV	*16,57*
Richard of Reviers	DOR	54,5
Richard of Sackville	ESS	20,8
	HRT	31,6
Richard (of Sackville)	ESS	25,1
Richard of St Clair	NFK	1,61;63
	SFK	11,4
Richard of Sollers	GLS	EvK116
Richard of Sourdeval	YKS	C8. 5N9. CE6-7;31. CW6
Richard (of Sourdeval)	YKS	5N11-14;17-18;20;24;26;28;45;76.
		5E20;27-28;45;54. 5W1-5;14;16-25;
		32-34;36

Richard of Tonbridge: *see* Richard son of
  Count Gilbert

Richard of Vernon	CHS	5
	NFK	6,1
Richard Poynant/the reeve	BDF	39
	BRK	43. 1,7
	HAM	42. S3
	NFK	1,217. 9,167
	OXF	33
	WIL	58. 13,9
Richard, Ralph of Mortimer's man	LIN	36,1

Richard Reckless: *see* Richard Sturmy, Sturmid

Richard, Robert Blunt's man	SFK	75,2
Richard, Roger of Bully's man	NTT	9,37
Richard Scrope	HEF	12,1. 24,7
	WOR	19,1-2;7;10
Richard (Scrope)	HEF	12,2

Richard Scrope: *see also* Osbern son of
          : *see also* William son of

Richard son of Alan	NFK	10,43-44
Richard son of Arnfastr	YKS	23. C18. SW,An1;8;13-14;16
Richard son of Count Gilbert/of Clare/of	BDF	38
Tonbridge	CAM	19
	DEV	26
	ESS	23. 1,11;13;27. 25,12 *note*. 30,23. 90,
		49-78
	HAM	1,8
	HRT	42a
	HUN	28
	KEN	11. *C8*. 2,*3*-4;9-10;28-29. 3,2;4-5. 4,
		1-2. 5,6-7;26;40;56;60;62;93;103;106;
		209
	MDX	13
	SFK	25. 8,63. 16,15. 21,44. 33,1. 67,1. 76,
		1-7. EE2. Cf 25,1
	SRY	19. 1,6;13. 36,4
	SSX	E1
	WIL	40
Richard (son of Count Gilbert/of Clare/of	SFK	8,35;47;59. 29,1
Tonbridge)		

Richard son of Count Gilbert: *see also* Ro(t)hais
  wife of

Richard son of King William	DOR	50,2
	HRT	36,19
Richard son of Thorold/Thorolf/Thorulf	CON	2,5. 5,3
	DEV	30. 15,42. 16,115. 30,1 and note
Richard son of William	KEN	5,119
Richard Sturmy/Sturmid/Reckless	HAM	41. 3,3
	SRY	8,18
	WIL	61. 13,2. 68,3-7
Richard Talbot	BDF	16,2
Richard, the Abbot of Peterborough's man	LIN	8,15
Richard, the Archbishop of Canterbury's man	KEN	2,34
Richard the artificer	BKM	42. E6
	HUN	D24
	NTH	B21
	OXF	58,1
Richard the bald	SFK	14,54
Richard the commissioner	GLS	49
Richard the constable, the Archbishop's man	KEN	2,34-35
Richard the forester	STS	13
	WAR	44. 1,9
Richard the forester: see also Richard Hunter		
Richard the interpreter	SOM	5,54. 45,14
Richard, the reeve of Cheveley Hundred	CAM	AppxB
Richard, the reeve of Staine Hundred	CAM	AppxC
Richard the young man [iuvenis]	WOR	25,1
Richard the young man: see also Richard a young man		
Richere	HAM	2,16;19. 3,6
	HEF	16,2
	SFK	33,2
	WIL	2,9;12
Richere: see also Gilbert son of		
: see also Walter son of		
Richere of l'Aigle: see also Gilbert son of		
Richere of les Andelys	HAM	S3
	SOM	16,2
Richere the clerk	HAM	3,15-16
Rictan	SFK	74,13
Riculf	DEV	24,27;32
	HRT	4,19. Appx
	KEN	5,184
	LEC	25,4
Ricward [mis-transcribed as Richard]	HAM	33,1
Ricwold	NFK	29,4-5
Ringulf: see also Essulf son of		
: see also Ranulf son of		
: see also Ringwulf		
Ringwulf	NFK	9,14;21. 50,8
	SFK	6,216
Ringwulf: see also Leofwin son of		
: see also Ringulf		
Ripe	SOM	36,3
Roald	HAM	6,5
	LEC	14,11
Roald Dubbed	DEV	35
Roald: see also Roaldr		
Roaldr	LIN	67,13
Roaldr: see also Thorir son of		
: see also Roald		
Roaldr, Kolgrimr's man	LIN	67,1

Robert

BDF	23,49;54. 34,3. 39,2. 40,2. 53,24-25
BRK	1,12-13. 7,28. 18,2. 21,10. 31,5. 37,1
BKM	4,4;9;22-23;25. 5,1. 6,2. 13,1. 14,17; 26;49. 16,2. 17,21. 19,6. 23,23. 32,1. 44,4
CAM	3,1. 12,2-3. 14,38;46. *26,24*. 32,32;44
CHS	1,22. R1,43. R6,4
DBY	1,36. 6,37;46;64;69;96-97. 7,1;13. 10, 4;7-8
DEV	2,14. 3,96. 5,1;10. 16,32;40;61-62; 83-85;87. 17,43. 18,1. 19,10;41. 21,18; 21. 34,27;40. *51,2*
DOR	2,3. 26,13;16;18-19;25;30-31;32(?); 56-57;67. 30,3. 36,7. 37,11. 55,26-28. 56,28
ESS	20,35;41-42;67. 23,6. 24,29;41;56;60. 27,14. 32,20;28;41-42. 34,29. 71,4. 90, 8
GLS	3,5. WoB18
HAM	2,1;9. 23,55. 28,9. 45,1. NF7,1. IoW2, 1. 6,3
HEF	1,23. 10,24;46;54;58-59. 31,1
HRT	36,1
KEN	5,99-100;215. 9,15
LEC	2,3-4. 3,4. 10,9-10. 13,63. 14,19-22; 29. 15,15. 17,9;23-24. 22,1. 23,5-6. 29, 7;19. 40,23;25. 43,6;10-11. 44,5-6;8-9
LIN	8,36. 22,12;34
MDX	7,2
NFK	9,61;86;88;103;107-108;110;124;134. 31,15. 66,57
NTH	4,1;17-18;30;36. 6a,31. 18,79-81. 22, 1-2. 30,15;18. 35,20-22. 36,1. 43,9. 46, 7. 56,25;59-60. ELc2. ELe2
NTT	2,3. 3,1. 10,16
OXF	6,10;12-13;15. 7,16. 9,4. 15,1;3;5. 24, 2;5. 27,6. 28,22. 34,1. 38,1-2. 59,3-4; 6-9;19-20;28-29. EN1
RUT	EN13;17
SHR	4,1,11;17. 4,3,10;33;39;49;70. 4,8,8. 4, 17,1. 4,23,14-15
SOM	2,6. 5,54;61. 19,73. 21,3-4;11;17-18; 28;31;45;78-79;86. 22,13;18;21;25. 25, 5;40. 35,16;21. 36,14. 46,7;9
STS	2,3;22. 8,12. 11,42;49-50;67. 12,6;9; 18-19;24-25
SFK	6,50;55;306. 14,14;62;64. 25,3;78. 31, 42. 41,15
SSX	8,1. 9,1;14;19;31;99;107. 11,8;10-14; 17-25;27;31;47-53;55;57-58;60-61; 69-73;78-79. 12,36;41;43. 13,30;33-36; 40;42-43;47;56-57
WAR	1,6. 16,31;33;40;52. 17,28;53. 18,10, 28,1. 31,10. 44,15. EBS1. EBW5. EG12. EN7
WIL	5,6. 7,2;4. 8,2;6. 24,21;24. 25,2;11-14; 18. 26,17. 27,7-10;14;24. 37,10. 42, 5-6;10. 68,6
WOR	2,53. 23,5;8. 26,10-11;14;17
YKS	3Y9. 9W11;13;44;47-48

Robert: *see also* Ralph son of
    : *see also* Unfrid son of
    : *see also* William son of

another Robert	OXF	6,12-13
	SHR	4,6,4
(another) Robert	SOM	5,54
	SSX	9,1
Robert Baron	NFK	1,61
Robert Bastard	DEV	29. 21,18 *note*
Robert Black	KEN	D8. M9
Robert Blanchard/Blunt	ESS	35,5. 90,83. ENf
	MDX	17
	NFK	1,7;66;87;136;206;209; 231. 19,20. 26, 3. 38,3. 47,1. 66,64;80;84
	NTH	33
	SFK	66. 6,57. 14,92;100-101;123. 25,22. 75,1-2
	WIL	60
R(obert) Blanchard/Blunt	NFK	1,113;216. 8,5. 10,69. 51,9. 58,3

Robert Blunt: *see also* Ralph brother of
    : *see also* Robert Blanchard
    : *see also* (Robert of Aumâle)
        son-in-law of

Robert Boy [= Puer]	DOR	*55,38-39*
Robert Brutin	KEN	*2,12*
Robert Burdet's son	LEC	13,41;53
Robert Burdet's wife	LEC	17,29
Robert Butler	GLS	40,1 *note*
	SHR	4,6
Robert Cook	CHS	4
	KEN	9,33
	SSX	9,4;14
Robert, Count Alan's man	LIN	12,4
	YKS	6N147;151
Robert (Count Alan's man)	YKS	6N128;148;158 *note*
(Robert) Count of Eu	ESS	31
	HUN	10
	KEN	*C8.* 2,25;32. 5,67;175
	SSX	9. 8,4;7-15
Robert d'Oilly	BDF	28. 19,2. E3
	BRK	41. B3;5-6;9. 1,39. 8,1
	BKM	19. B5. 4,31
	ESS	30,30
	GLS	48. 1,36
	HRT	19
	NTH	28
	NTT	27,1
	OXF	28. B9. 1,7b?2,1. 7,19;49;56. 9,10. 58, 31. EBe3. EG1
	STS	8,32
	SRY	19,25
	WAR	21. 4,5. 17,13;15;48;55;70
	WOR	19,3
Robert d'Oilly's wife	BKM	19,1-2
Robert, Drogo of Beuvrière's man	LIN	30,7;9;12;33
	YKS	14E32
Robert, Earl Hugh's man	NTT	3,3
Robert Fafiton/son of Fafiton	BDF	30
	CAM	38. *12,2-3. 32,15*

	HUN	25
	MDX	15
(Robert) Fafiton	HUN	D13
Robert Farthing, Godric the steward's man	SFK	14,146
Robert, father of Berengar	OXF	34,3
	YKS	7E2
Robert Fossard	YKS	31E3
Robert, Geoffrey of la Guerche's man	LIN	63,1
Robert Gernon	BKM	20
	CAM	21. 22,5
	ESS	32. 1,3;24;28. 3,10. 6,12. 8,9. 9,5. 34, 8. 49,3
	HEF	12
	HRT	20
	MDX	14
	NFK	33. 66,99
	SOM	*21,89*
	SFK	36. EE3
Robert, Gilbert of Ghent's man	LIN	24,10;12;92
	NTT	17,16
Robert Herecom	SOM	*21,8*
Robert, Hugh of Port's steward	BRK	10,1
Robert, Hugh's nephew	DOR	*55,45*
Robert Hunter	WAR	21,1. 22,10
Robert, King William's officer	GLS	G4
Robert Latimer	KEN	*2,4.* 5,19;49-50;84-85;89;102;209. 7,2
Robert Malet	ESS	44
	LIN	58. CK,20;35
	NFK	7. 1,197;205;208. 4,39. 9,180;211. 17, 51. 20,29 *and note.* 35,16. 36,5. 44,1. 66,58;61;107
	NTT	25
	RUT	3. R10
	SFK	6. 1,103;105. 3,94-95. 4,15. 7,11; 15-16;138-140;143. 8,42. 16,14-15;29. *18,1.* 19,9. 21,16;35;45-46. 26,12d; 13-14. 31,15. 32,1. 34,12. 38,6. 43,5. 51,1-2. 64,1. 67,2-4;10;19;27. 75,4-5. 76,23. 77,2. ENf3
	SRY	28
	YKS	11. C12. CE9;15;17;29. CW32. SW, Sk16. SW,An1;3. SN,L19;25;27;29; 31-34;36;43. SN,Ma17. SN,Bi1;3. SN,A9-11.SE,Wel6. SE,C1;3-5;10. SE,Wei1. SE,P2
Ro(bert) Malet	SFK	21,85;100. 39,12
R(obert) Malet	ESS	90,84
	NFK	4,53. 8,129. 9,100;179. 14,31. 66,60
	SFK	1,10;14. 2,17-18;20. 3,28;41. 7,6;13; 17;21;26;30;33;36;75;79. 8,8. 16,26. 21,48;65;*71-79;88-92;94.* 32,28. 34, 15. 52,1. 53,6. 67,5;15. 77,4
(Robert) Malet	SFK	3,98-102. 6,177. 7,144. 16,25;33 *note;* 38 *note*
Robert Malet's father: *see* William Malet		
Robert Malet's mother	NFK	7,14
	SFK	77. 6,76-77. 6,8;11;156;161;176;191; 193-195;199-201;209-229 *note;* 230; 232;251;253;271;311. 34,13,75,5
Robert Marshall	WIL	59

Robert Marshall: *see also* the Marshall
Robert, Norman of Arcy's man   LIN   32,15
Robert of Armentières   BRK   B9
                                                OXF   EBe3
Robert of Auberville   SOM   1,2. *8,17*. 24,8. 46,1-5
Robert of Aumâle   DEV   28
(Robert of Aumâle), son-in-law of Robert Blunt WIL   60,1
Robert of Auvers   NTH   B22
Robert of Barbes   KEN   5,193
Robert of Beaumont   DEV   *16,40;65-68;137*
Robert of Belleme   GLS   EvK116
Robert of Blythburgh   SFK   7,5. 33,8
Robert of Braose?   WIL   *33,1* (*but see note*)
Robert of Brus   YKS   31
Robert of Bucy   LEC   17. 13,27-30. 40,15-21
                                                NTH   30. B17
                                                STS   15,1-2
Robert of Cherry Hinton   CAM   14,4 *note*. AppxE
Bishop Robert/of Chester   CHS   B. 2,1-2;5. S1,7. R4
                                                DBY   2. S5
                                                HRT   7
                                                NTT   S5
                                                SHR   1. C13
                                                STS   2. B2. EW5
                                                WAR   2. B2. 28,19. EBS1. EBW3
                                                WOR   23,1
Bishop Robert: *see also* Rayner father of
Robert of Claville   SFK   6,46-47
R(obert) of Claville   SFK   6,110
Robert of Courson   NFK   9,29;100;178
                                                SFK   7,6-7;23;51. 76,17-18
Robert (of Courson)   NFK   9,31
R(obert) of Courson   SFK   4,14. 7,8
Robert of Criel   SSX   9,7;11
Robert (of Doynton)   GLS   6,5;7-8
Abbot Robert (of Evesham)   GLS   EvE10. EvO26
Robert of Ferrers   GLS   EvK116
Robert of Fordham   CAM   AppxA
Robert of Gatemore   SOM   22,*11-12*
Robert of Glanville   NFK   17,51
                                                SFK   6,3;5;51;54;157;291;308-309
R(obert) of Glanville   SFK   6,124;160 *note*;179;181. 26,16;19-20
Robert (of Glanville)   SFK   26,17
Robert of Hardres   KEN   *2,16;26*
Robert of Harford: *see* Robert of 'Hereford'
Robert of Hastings   SSX   5,1
Bishop Robert/of Hereford   ESS   19. 1,24
                                                GLS   4. 1,55. EvK116. E5-6
                                                HEF   2. C9. 1,10c. 10,5;37;48;75
                                                OXF   B8. 5,1
                                                SHR   2. 4,1,4. 4,14,12. 7,4
                                                WOR   3. 2,16. E9;21-26
Robert of 'Hereford'   DEV   *28,10* (*but see note*)
Robert of Jort   LEC   42,5-6
Robert of Lacy   GLS   EvK116
Robert of Montbegon   ESS   89,2
Count Robert/of Mortain   BRK   19
                                                BKM   12
                                                CAM   12. B1

CON	5. 1,1;4;6-7. 2,2;6;14. 3,7. 4,1-2;*3*; 7-15;19-20;*21*;22-23;25-29
DEV	15. 1,11;23;25;50. 2,9-10. 7,4. 34,2. 35,10
DOR	26. 19,14. 56,36. E1
GLS	29
HAM	19. 1,47. S3
HRT	15. 10,6;9. 39,1
MDX	8
NFK	3
NTH	18. B9
NTT	4
OXF	16. B9
SOM	19. 1,4-5;9;*11*-12;19-20. 2,8. 8,30-31; 39-40. 10,1;6. 21,92. 46,4
SFK	2. 1,1 *note.* 21,1. 31,48. 76,16
SRY	17. 1,4. 6,1
SSX	10. 2,1a. 8,6. 12,2;10-11
WIL	20. 16,5
YKS	5. C3;27. CE6. CW37. SW,Sk18-20. SW,BA3. SW,Sf21;23-24;26;28-34. SW,O2. SW,St8-9. SW,An5. SW,Bu8; 44. SW,H8-9. SN,L5-10;12;15-18; 20-26;28;38-39;41-44. SN,D3;14-15; 17. SN,Ma2;4;6;14-15;17-19;21;23-24. SN,B2-16;26-27. SN,Bi6;8. SN,A8-9. SE,He2;4;7;9-10. SE, Wel6. SE,C2; 5-9. SE,How7-9. SE, Wei2;4-5;7. SE,Sn1-7;10. SE,Dr4-5. SE,Wa2. SE,P3. SE,Hu1-7. SE,Tu5;7-8. SE,Bt4-7;9. SE,Sc1;4;7;9-10. SE,Ac4-5;7-11. SE,Th1-3;5-7

Robert of Moutiers, Count Alan's man	NTT	2,9
Robert of Noyers	BKM	4,42. 6,1
Robert of Peronne: *see* Berner nephew of		
Robert of Pierrepont	SFK	26,12a
Robert of Pont-Chardon	DEV	1,5. *16,69-72;74*
	HRT	20,28
Robert of Rhuddlan	CHS	3. C25. FD2. FT2. G
Robert of Romney	BKM	4,40
	KEN	D8. P19-20. 2,43. *3,21.* 5,176-182
Robert of Stafford	BRK	42
	LIN	59. CK,12;16;20;23;51;64
	NTH	27
	OXF	27
	STS	11. B6-7;12
	WAR	22. B2. EN4
	WOR	17
Robert of Stratford	SFK	71
Robert (of Stratford)	SFK	27,9
Robert of Thaon	BKM	4,36
Robert of Tilleul	GLS	28,1
Robert of Tosny	BDF	26. E4
	BKM	18
	CAM	20
	ESS	50
	GLS	46
	HRT	21
	LEC	15. 1,4. 40,20
	LIN	18. CW,11. CK,9;19-20;22;46

	NTH	26. B12;33
	RUT	EN11
	SFK	44. 7,19
	YKS	7. SE,Wa1-2
Robert of Ulcombe	SSX	9,105
Robert of Vatteville/Watteville	ESS	23,41
	SRY	1,1g. 19,3;6-8;15;23-25;37(?)
Robert of Vaux	ESS	43,4-5
	NFK	9,2-4;46-47;53;56;64-67;67;99;116; 233-234. 14,40. 19,36
	SFK	6,84. 7,14-15;19. 9,3
R(obert) of Vaux	SFK	1,22. 7,16-17;24;40;44-45;49-50;54
Robert of Verly	ESS	32,14-15;26 note; 37;45. ENf
	NFK	38
	SFK	60
Robert (of Verly)	ESS	32,26
Robert of Vessey/a man-at-arms	LEC	16. C13
	LIN	37. CK,36
	NTH	29
	SHR	4,11,4
	WAR	24
Robert of Watteville: see Robert of Vatteville		
Robert Parler	WOR	8,25
Robert, Roger of Bully's man	NTT	9,2;22;70
Robert St Léger	SSX	9,11
Robert son of Alfred	GLS	EvO10
Robert son of Corbet	SHR	4,5
Robert son of Corbucion	ESS	41. 1,4
	NFK	35. 1,229. 31,11-12;17;44
	SFK	40
Robert son of Fafiton: see Robert Fafiton		
Robert son of Fulcred	SFK	6,46-49
Robert son of Gerald	BRK	40
	DOR	30
	HAM	28
	SOM	33. 1,9
	WIL	42
Robert son of Gilbert	SOM	25,5
Robert son of Gobert	ESS	78
Robert son of Hamo	GLS	EvK1;116
Robert son of Hugh	CHS	2. B13
Robert son of Ivo	DEV	15,10;14
	DOR	26,7 note; 24
	SOM	19,13-14;35;66;85
Robert son of Murdoch	HAM	68,10
	OXF	50
Robert son of Nigel	BDF	29,1
Robert son of Ralph	OXF	58,8-9
	WIL	68,8
Robert son of Ralph of Hastings	ESS	B7
Robert son of Rolf	BRK	65,20
	WIL	43
Robert son of Rozelin	BDF	15,7
	ESS	76
	HRT	17,2
	MDX	16
	SOM	31,5
Robert (son of Rozelin)	HRT	17,4;8-9
Robert son of Stigand	LIN	CS,30

Robert son of Theobald	SHR	4,9
	SSX	11,2;8
Robert son of Thurstan	OXF	58,4-5
Robert son of Walkelin	OXF	6,12
Robert son of Walter	BKM	19,3
	SOM	*19,37*
Robert son of Warin	CAM	AppxM
Robert son of Watson, a man-at-arms	KEN	*2,26. 3,18*
Robert son of William	DBY	15
	NTT	28
	NTT	3,1
Robert son of William the usher	LEC	43,9
Robert son of William: *see also* Adam son of		
Robert son of Wymarc/the sheriff	CAM	13,*8-9*;11. 25,5;10. 26,35-36;39. 30,
		1-2. 32,10;12;*18*;20;24
	ESS	18,6. 24,4;*20 note*; 23;25;29;31;35;43;
		49;53;55;64;83,1. 90,35. B3n
	HEF	22,7. 25,3
	HRT	4,6. 5,6. 20,6. 37,9
	HUN	16,1. 28,1
	SHR	3d,7
	SOM	19,57. 25,55
	SFK	1,102. 3,70. 25,49;76. 27,7. 58,1. 76,2;
		5
	WIL	68,16
Robert (son of Wymarc/the sheriff)	ESS	24,1;36-39;54;57;59-60;63;65-66
	SFK	27,3-6;8-12
Robert son of Wymarc: *see also* Swein the		
sheriff/of Essex, father of		
Robert the bald	CAM	26,36;39
Robert the bursar	GLS	47. EvN13
	HUN	19,18
	LEC	19. C16
	LIN	38. CS,1;3;12;23-24;33-34;36. CN,22
	NTH	EH6
	WAR	23
	WIL	*4,4*
	WOR	2,13;19;49;67;73. 9,1d
Robert (the butler)	GLS	40,1
Robert the chamberlain	CAM	AppxP
Robert the cleric	SSX	3,3
Robert the clerk, brother of Gilbert	HAM	2,10
Robert the constable	SOM	*19,7;29*
Robert the corn-dealer	DOR	*55,37*
Robert the crossbowman	NFK	54. 1,66. *15,21*. 17,43. 26,5
	SFK	76,16
Robert the Englishman, of Fordham	CAM	AppxA
Robert the lascivious/Robert the perverted	ESS	6,12. 32,28
Robert the lorimer	NFK	1,61
Robert the Perverted: *see* Robert the Lascivious		
Robert the priest	CAM	*14,36*
Robert the priest, monk	LIN	7,55
Robert the usher	CAM	*39,3*
	LEC	20. 43,9
Robert Tilly	DOR	*47,4;10*
Robert Trublet	KEN	*M11*
Robert, William of Percy's man	LIN	22,12;34
Robert, William Peverel's man	NTT	10,2
Robert Wymarc: *see* Robert son of		
Robert's wife	LEC	13,37

Roc	SFK	25,91
Rodhere	HRT	4,5;23. Appx
Rodric: *see* Humphrey son of		
Roger	BDF	23,48. 24,17. 55,7
	BRK	21,2;4. 55,3-4
	BKM	4,5-8;10-12;15;17;19;26;28-29;31. 14, 8. 23,3-4;18;26. 39,1. 53,3;8
	CAM	32,24;27;29;31;40. 41,13-15. AppxC
	CHS	2,14. 24,3. FD2,5. R1,43;45. R3,1. R6, 4
	CON	5,26. *4,22*
	DBY	6,14;16;29;55;96
	DEV	2,20. 3,92. 16,4;18-20;168. 20,5. 34,3; 7;9;29-30;44;46;52;55-57. 48,7. 49,6
	DOR	*1,13.* 35,1
	ESS	1,19. 3,4;6-8;10. 4,5. 20,3;75. 23, 31-32. 24,38. 27,15. 30,6. 33,16-17. 36,3. 37,4;6;20. 39,2. 40,4;6-8. 51, 1-2. 90,10;46. B3a
	GLS	41,5
	HAM	45,7-9. Iow7,12;22
	HEF	8,1;6. 13,2
	HRT	5,1. 16,8. 22,2. 34,4;18;25. 36,2;5;16
	HUN	19,26
	KEN	9,14;16
	LEC	3,13. 13,31. 14,13;15;25;28;31-32. 15, 11;14;16. 17,18. 18,2. 21,1-2. 29,18. 43,2;5
	LIN	8,19. 24,57-58
	NFK	1,1;2. 8,41. 10,40;58. 14,14. 19,10;12. 21,4;10;32;35-36. 23,13. 34,5. 64,1
	NTH	4,31. 6a,2;20-21;28. 23,17. 26,7. 28,1. 31,1. 33,1
	OXF	2,1. 6,13. 7,9;17-18;25;28;34. 9,4;6. 19,1. 28,12;20-21;25-26. 35,15. 58,7. 59,7;10;21;29. EN2;7
	SHR	4,1,7-9. 4,3,48. 4,4,3. 4,11,8. 7,4
	SOM	1,28. 5,47;*53*-54;65. 8,31. 25,6;25-26; 39;48
	STS	8,10-11;27. 10,7. 12,11;21-22. ED3
	SFK	8,6. 25,11;56;63-64;78;80. 26,4. 39, 18. 40,2. 41,14;16. 53,2. EE6
	SRY	19,1;17;36
	SSX	9,120;130. 10,1;15;22;79. 11,54;64; 68. 12,32
	WAR	16,50;58. 17,10-11;59. 18,12-13. 25,1. 27,6. 28,5;9. 29,3. EG14-15
	WIL	5,1-3. 7,1;11. 26,16. 30,2-3. 41,8
	WOR	20,3. 23,9
	YKS	9W96;99
Roger, a man-at-arms	DEV	*48,10*
	KEN	*2,11*
	WOR	1,1c
another Roger	BRK	55,3
Roger Arundel	DOR	47. 9,1
	SOM	22. 6,19
Roger (Arundel)	DOR	8,1
Roger (Baskerville)	GLS	45,1-2;4-5
Roger Baynard?	NFK	*9,160*
Roger Bigot/the sheriff	ESS	43

	NTT	16. 20,7
	SFK	8. 1,1. 53,2 *note*
	YKS	30. 1L1
Roger of Raismes [Rames]	ESS	39. 1,27. 6,8. 43,1
	MDX	18
	NFK	43. 9,200. 15,25
	SFK	38. 7,64;68. 8,63. 25,56;59. 76,22
Ro(ger) of Rames	SFK	16,16
Roger of Rames, daughter of	SFK	38,9;11
Earl Roger (of Shrewsbury)	BRK	1,8. 47,1
	CAM	13
	CHS	G2
	GLS	27
	HAM	21. 55,2. 56,1. NF3. ESx
	HEF	E9
	HRT	18
	MDX	7
	SHR	4. C12. 3b,1. 3c,1;9. 3d,7. 3g,7
	STS	8. B4. ES1. EW1-4
	SRY	18. 29,1
	SSX	11. 13,15;57
	WAR	12
	WIL	21
	WOR	14. E8;30-32
Earl (Roger, of Shrewsbury)	SHR	C14. 3e,1
Earl Roger: *see also* Hugh son of		
Earl Roger's father (Earl William)	GLS	16,1
Earl Roger's father: *see also* William son of Osbern		
Roger of St Germain	SFK	25,47. 76,3
Roger of Sommery	CAM	*22,2;8*
	ESS	20,74-76
Roger of Stanton	SOM	*1,28*
Roger of Westerham	KEN	D9
Roger, Peter of Valogne's officer	HRT	28,1
Roger, Rainer of Brimeux's man	LIN	40,4
Roger Ralph(?)	DEV	*34,46*
Roger, Robert Malet's man	NFK	14,31
Roger, Robert of Tosny's man	LIN	18,12
Roger, Roger of Bully's man	NTT	9,3;44;62;69;90;107-108;120;122;129
Roger, Roger of Poitou's man	LIN	16,4;7;10;27;32
Roger son of Ansketel	KEN	5,158;225
Roger son of Arnold	SFK	8,7-8;17
Roger son of Corbet	SHR	4,4
Roger son of Morin	CAM	AppxN
Roger son of Nigel	SOM	*20,2-3*
Roger son of Payne	DEV	*16,155. 34,12*
Roger son of Rainard	NFK	50. 12,45. 27,2. *57,2*
Roger son of Ralph	DEV	*34,46 (but see note)*
	GLS	75
	SOM	*5,24*
Roger son of Siegfried/Sifrid	BRK	B9. 49,2-3
Roger son of Theodoric	BDF	23,41
Roger, the Abbot of Peterborough's man	LIN	8,19
Roger, the Bishop of Lincoln's man	LIN	7,21;23
Roger, the Bishop of London's man	ESS	1,27
Roger the Breton	SOM	10,2
Roger the bursar	SOM	*5,34*
Roger the marshal	ESS	62. 30,16

Roger the priest	BDF	23,55
	BRK	3,1
Roger the sheriff	MDX	3,3. 15,1
	NFK	9,86
Roger/the sheriff/of Gloucester: *see* Walter son of		
Roger the sheriff's father	NFK	73,1
Roger Whiting/Wythent	SOM	5,*4;23;35;41*;47
Roger's man-at-arms' wife	ESS	39,7
Roghard	SOM	6,9;13
Rogo	DEV	16,76-77;104-105;150;158;170
Rohais (fem.): *see* Ro(t)hais		
Roland	BDF	21,12
	NFK	24,2
	NTH	42,2-3
	SSX	11,17;81;100
Roland the archdeacon	CON	*2,10*
Rolf	DEV	16,6. 23,10-11
	LEC	35,2
	NFK	4,44. 65,1
	NTT	26,1
	OXF	24,3
	SFK	74,8
Rolf: *see also* Aelfric son of		
: *see also* Robert son of		
: *see also* Thurstan son of		
Rolf, a thane	LEC	15,7
Roric	SFK	14,59;79
Rosell	ESS	B3a
Roskell	NTT	9,101
Roskell: *see also* Rossketill		
Rossketill	YKS	1W11;14;16. 6N144;147. 9W24. 13W35
Rossketill: *see also* Roskell		
Ro(t)hais (fem.)	NTH	56,50
Ro(t)hais, wife of Richard son of Count Gilbert/of Clare/of Tonbridge	HRT	42a
	HUN	28
Rothais (fem.): *see* Ro(t)hais		
Rothmundr	YKS	29E16
Rothulfr	LIN	4,38;41;46;81. 7,17;24. 8,14;20;22. 12, 19. 27,10;20;30;33. 30,9;12;17. 44,5; 7-11;16
Rothulfr son of Skjaldvor	LIN	T5
Rotlesc, a royal Guard	GLS	1,59
Rotroc	OXF	8,1;4
Rozelin	DEV	34,24;32;*47*
	NTH	6a,18
	SSX	3,6
	YKS	13W6;10-12
Rozelin: *see also* Robert son of		
Rozelin, Earl Hugh's man	LIN	13,21
Rozo	WIL	24,39
Ruillic	HEF	9,16
Rumbald	GLS	73,2-3
Rumold	HRT	17,5;6;10
	SOM	44,2
Rumold of Coton	CAM	AppxK
Rumold the priest	WIL	1,12
Saefowl	ESS	B3a

Saegar	DEV	34,33
	ESS	18,40. B3a
Saegar: *see also* Segar		
Saegard	SFK	40,1
Saegeat	BDF	57,17
Saegeat, a thane	OXF	1,7b
Saegifu (fem.): *see* Saeva, Saevia, Saieva		
Saegrim	ESS	B3a(x2)
	NTH	18,95
	STS	13,6
Saegrim: *see also* Saegrimr, Segrim		
Saegrimr	LIN	12,7
Saegrimr: *see also* Saegrim		
Saegyth (fem.): *see* Saeith		
Saehild (fem.), Earl Leofwin's man	HRT	5,20
Saeith (fem.)	WAR	16,10
Saeith (fem.): *see also* Saegyth		
Saelufu (fem.): *see* Saloua		
Saeman	SRY	19,41. 36,2
Saemer	DEV	15,63. 19,43. 24,16. 34,45
	ESS	25,3. *30,41*
	HEF	1,10b. 10,59. 27,1. 28,2
	HUN	3,1
	NTH	EH1
	SHR	4,3,13
	SOM	24,26. *35,2.* 46,8-9
Saemer, Alnoth's man	HRT	5,7
Saemer, Edmer Ator's man	DEV	*15,20*
Saemer, Leofwin's man	BDF	24,25
Saemer the priest	HRT	37,21
Saemer the priest, Countess Gytha's man	BDF	22,2
	NTH	EB4
Saer	SFK	*14,63*
Saered	DOR	26,37
	SOM	37,12
Saered's brother	DOR	26,37
Saeric	DEV	34,36;42
	HEF	1,17. 10,53. 24,7
	LEC	17,33
	OXF	58,21-22
	SOM	1,6. *5,3;64.* 22,28. 24,8. *25,40.* 46,5
	WIL	67,95-96
Saeric: *see also* Gest brother of		
: *see also* Godmund son of		
Saeric, a thane	SOM	*5,3;64.* 22,28. *25,40*
Saeric, Earl Harold's thane	HEF	10,51
Saeric, father of Godmund	HEF	10,71
Saeric of Auberville	CAM	5,2
Saeric: *see also* Seric		
Saeva (fem.) [for Saieva, = Saegifu]	WIL	67,25;88
Saevia (fem.) [for Saieva, = Saegifu]	CAM	19,4
Saeward	BKM	12,31
	DEV	21,14. 26,1
	DOR	49,13. 54,14. 56,55
	ESS	B3a
	HAM	1,W7
	HRT	33,10
	KEN	5,152
	SHR	4,3,3. 5,2. 7,1

	SOM	*19*,72. 28,1
	WAR	22,21
	WIL	27,27. 67,97
	WOR	20,2
Saeward, a thane	SOM	*28,1*
Saeward, Azor son of Toti's man	BKM	14,29
Saeward, Earl Harold's man	BKM	12,11
Saeward of Harlton	CAM	AppxK
Saeward's mother	SOM	*19,72*
Saeware (fem.)	ESS	B3a
Saeware (fem.): *see* Saewaru		
Saewaru (fem.): *see* Saeware		
Saewata	NTH	18,85
Saewin [for Saewine]	BRK	41,5. 44,1. 65,13
	CON	5,5,6. 5,9,2. 5,11,2
	DEV	3,30;88;98. 15,25. 16,22;38;134. 17, 11-12. 35,26;29-30. 36,3-4. 39,3. 42,2; 4
	DOR	37,8. 55,39. 56,42-47
	GLS	34,13
	HAM	1,W9. 3,6;12. 69,33;54. NF9,3;10;23. IoW8,3
	NTH	2,5
	NTT	30,19-20;23-24
	SHR	4,27,1
	SOM	19,24. 22,20
	WIL	27,11
	WOR	2,11
Saewin, a thane	DEV	*17,12*
	DOR	55,45
	SOM	1,1. *19,24*
Saewin, Edmer Ator's man	DEV	*15,22*
Saewin the falconer	HUN	D8
Saewin the priest	ESS	30,15
Saewin the priest: *see also* Brictferth uncle of		
Saewin, the Queen's priest	DEV	13a,2
Saewin, the reeve of Bristol	GLS	75,1
Saewin Tuft, a thane	DEV	*16,7*
Saewin: *see also* Sawin, Sewin		
Saewold	KEN	5,148
	OXF	B10. 6,10;16. 45,1-3. 58,19;31-34
	WAR	28,8
	WIL	27,27
	WOR	16,2;4
Abbot Saewold (of St Peter's, Bath)	SOM	*7,1;5-7;9;13*
Saewold, Young Wulfward's man	BKM	17,31
Saewold's son	WOR	16,4
Saewold's wife	OXF	58,34
Saewold: *see also* Saswald		
Saewulf	BRK	34,3-4
	BKM	7,2. 19,1
	CON	5,2,29. 5,6,10. 5,19,1
	DBY	6,53
	DEV	15,48. 17,72. 39,11. 52,47-49
	DOR	56,8. 57,5
	ESS	30,9. B3a
	HAM	23,22. 69,17;51. NF3,11. 9,11;24-25; 40
	NFK	10,61
	NTH	2,4. 18,30;37

	SHR	4,11,1. 6,32
	SOM	2,11. *5,59;64*. 8,27. 21,93;96. *24,10.*
		26,8
	WAR	28,7;15
	WIL	24,18. 42,1. 67,84
	WOR	8,10a-10b;16
Saewulf: *see also* Alfwy son of		
Saewulf, a thane	HAM	19,1
	SOM	*5,59.* *24,10.* *26,28*
Saewulf, Alfwy's father	HAM	69,17
Saewulf, Earl Leofwin's man	BKM	51,1
Saewulf, Earl Ralph's man	BKM	51,3
Saewulf of Oxford	BRK	B1
Saewulf's father	WIL	67,84
Saewulf's wife	HAM	NF9,11
Saewy	OXF	B10
	WIL	25,16
Saewynn (fem.): *see* Sewen		
Saexfrith [for Seaxfrith]	YKS	2N26-30. 29N13. SN,Y6
Saexfrith the deacon	YKS	C31 *and note*; C1 *and note*; C35
Saexfrith: *see also* Sasfrid, Saxfrid, Seaxfrith		
Saieva (fem.): *see* Saegifu, Saeva, Saevia		
Saksulfr [MS. Saxulf(us)]	YKS	9W22. 28W30
Salecoc	LIN	22,38
Saleva (fem.): *see* Svala		
Saleva (fem.): *see also* Azor son of		
Salide	HAM	NF3,5
Salie's wife	SRY	19,4-5;34
Salo	WAR	14,4. 16,41
Salomon	YKS	23N4
Saloua (fem.)	CAM	*32,32*
Saloua (fem.): *see also* Saelufu		
Salvi	BRK	7,18
Samson	STS	7. 7,1;13
Bishop Samson (of Worcester)	GLS	EvK1
Samson the chaplain	SOM	*4,1*
Sandi	YKS	1W17 *and note*;18
Sasfrid	NTH	35,9-11
	RUT	EN12
Sasfrid: *see also* Saexfrith, Seaxfrith		
Sasgar	NTH	46,2
Sasselin	ESS	57
	SFK	59
Saswald [misprint for Saewald (= Saewold);	SOM	*2,11*
MS. Sawald]		
Saswalo	BRK	38,1-2
	DBY	6,47;49;98
	ESS	34,7
	NTH	25,2
	OXF	39,2-3
	SSX	9,119
	WAR	19,4
Saswalo, Henry of Ferrers' man	LIN	21,1
Saswalo, the Abbot of Peterborough's man	LIN	8,7
Saswalo: *see also* Saxwalo		
Sasward	SSX	9,14
Saul	DOR	1,19
	WIL	29,4
Sawin	CAM	32,28
Sawin: *see also* Saewin, Sewin		

Saxfrid	BRK	33,4
	LEC	25,5
	SHR	4,14,14-15
Saxfrid, William Peverel's man	NTT	10,22;51
Saxfrid: *see also* Saexfrith, Seaxfrith		
Saxi	BRK	1,17-18;46
	CAM	32,30
	ESS	45,1. 51,2. 58,1
	GLS	40,1
	HAM	1,25. 50,1. 61,1. 62,1
	HUN	14,1. 25,1-2. D13
	LEC	9,1-5. 44,8;10
	SHR	4,3,60. 6,21
	SFK	6,11. 7,64. 16,8;13;16;20-23;26;28;
		30-31;33. 34,12-13;17. 38,11;22. 75,5.
		77,2;4
	WAR	16,9;12;15;28;38-40;43. 44,2. EG12
Saxi, a royal Guard	HRT	22,2
Saxi, a royal thane	BKM	35,2
	CAM	24,1
Saxlef	SFK	74,13
Saxulfus *see* Saksulfr		
Saxwalo of Bouville	SFK	16,11 *note*. 32,31
Saxwalo of Bouville: *see* William of Bouville,		
son of		
Saxwalo: *see also* Saswalo		
Saxwin	SFK	31,35
Scaldward: *see* William son of		
Scalpi	ESS	32,40
	SFK	16,35. 36,8;16. EE3
Scalpi, a Guard of (Earl) Harold	ESS	30,16
Scalpi, Harold's thane	SFK	36,1-2
Scalpi: *see also* Skalp		
Scalpi's wife	ESS	30,16
Scolland	SSX	12,54
Scotel	NTH	18,82
Scova, Leofwin's man	HRT	5,10
Scroti	WAR	16,35-36. 37,7
Seaxfrith: *see* Saexfrith		
Segar	SFK	7,109
Segar: *see also* Saegar		
Segrim	OXF	B10
another Segrim	OXF	B10
Segrim: *see also* Saegrim		
Seisyll	HEF	24,8;11
Selakollr	YKS	C10
Selva	ESS	32,34
Selwin	WIL	37,6
Seric	BKM	23,17
	HAM	69,27
	NTT	15,5. 30,46
Seric, Count Eustace's man	HRT	Appx
Seric, Earl Leofwin's man	BKM	4,41-42
	HRT	15,11
Seric, Queen Edith's man	BKM	14,27
Seric, Sired's man	BKM	36,1
Seric son of Aelfeva	BKM	14,5
Seric the chamberlain	HAM	69,14
Seric: *see also* Saeric		
Serlo	DBY	7,2. 10,9

	DOR	3,11
	ESS	28,1;7-8;10;13. 34,1-4;13. 38,1
	LEC	13,42;63
	WIL	7,1
Serlo of Burcy	DOR	48
	SOM	37. 1,9;21. *6,9. 8,17;20-21;28;30.* 27,3
	WIL	E4;5
Serlo of Burcy's daughter	SOM	27,3. 37,7
Serlo of Rots	BDF	23,28-29. 25,4
Serlo's daughter	WIL	E5
Sessibert	GLS	W4
Sewen (fem.) [= Saewynn]	KEN	P1
Sewen [= Saewine] the canon	KEN	P1
Sewin [= Saewine]	SFK	7,102;111
Sewin: *see also* Saewin, Sawin		
Sharp	SOM	25,20
Shearman	SFK	7,77
Shed-butter	ESS	B3a
Sheerwold	CON	5,24,10
	DEV	42,18. 50,1
	DOR	26,14;54
	GLS	31,10
	SOM	5,54;*62;65.* 8,18;20. 19,1. 25,5
	WIL	24,20
Sheerwold, a thane	SOM	*5,62;65*
Sibbi	LIN	C23
	SOM	5,15
Sibbi: *see also* Sired son of		
Sibbi, a thane, Alric son of Goding's man	BKM	23,31
Sibert	CON	5,24,20
Sibold	NTH	51
Sictric	SFK	6,19. *21,16;47*
Sictric: *see also* Sihtric		
Sidred	DBY	17,7
Sidwin	DEV	16,98. 17,86. 35,5
Siegfried/Sifrid: *see* Ralph son of		
: *see* Roger son of		
Siferth	BKM	18,3
Sifred, the reeve of Wetherley Hundred	CAM	*32,16-17.* AppxK
Sifrith	SFK	7,77
Sigar	CAM	1,16. 35,1
	ESS	4,9
	KEN	M10-11;20. 13,1
	NFK	20,14
	SFK	74,13
	WIL	26,17
Sigar, Asgar the constable's steward/man	CAM	*22,23-4;8-10.* AppxH
Sigar, Earl Waltheof's man	CAM	38,5. 39,1
Sigar of Chocques	BDF	36. 3,6
	CAM	*32,25*
	GLS	72
	HRT	41. EC2
	NTH	49. B28
Sigar: *see also* Sigarr		
Sigarr	LIN	4,28;31
Sigarr: *see also* Sigar		
Sigar's father	KEN	M20
Sigeric	DEV	17,92
	HEF	25,1

	NFK	55,1
	SOM	*37,8. 45,7*
Sigeric, a thane	SOM	*37,8. 45,7*
Sigeric: *see also* Siric		
Sigerid (fem.)	CHS	9,15
Sigerid (fem.): *see also* Sigrithr		
Sigewine	LIN	CW,3
Sigfrothr	LIN	12,96
Sighvatr	LIN	24,81. 29,10. 57,55
Sighvatr/Godwine brother of Alnoth, Asketill and Fenkell	LIN	CN,30. CS,38
Sighvatr: *see also* Siwat		
Sighvatr's father	LIN	CS,38
Sigketill, brother of Agmundr	LIN	28,11-12
Sigmund	WOR	2,78
Sigmund, Earl Edwin's thane	WOR	19,6
Sigmund the Dane	WAR	22,24
Sigmund: *see also* Sigmundr, Simond		
Sigmundr, Heppo the crossbowman's man	LIN	61,4;7
Sigmundr: *see also* Sigmund, Simond		
Sigref	WOR	2,33
Sigref's daughter	WOR	2,33
Sigref's mother	WOR	2,33
Sigrithr (fem.)	YKS	6N126. 13E12
Sigrithr (fem.): *see also* Sigerid		
Sigsteinn	SHR	4,3,28
Sigvarthbarn	YKS	17W1
Sigvarthbarn: *see also* Siward Ba(i)rn		
Sihere	BDF	32,15
Sihere: *see also* Walter brother of		
Sihtric	CON	5,1,17
	NTH	56,39;51
Abbot Sihtric (of Tavistock)/a thane	CON	*3,1,7.* 5,1,7;*16*
	DEV	5,8;11;*14. 16,7*
Sihtric: *see also* Sictric		
Silac of Teversham	CAM	AppxE
Abbot Simeon/of Ely	CAM	5. B12. 1,11. 3,5. *6,1.* 7,11-12. 8,1. 9, 4. 13,11. 14,30;57;59. 17,2-3. 18,3;7; 9. 19,1. 25,9. 26,17-18;27;29-30;33; 48-57. 27,1. 28,2. 30,3. 31,1-2. 32,2;5; 21-22;27;29-33;35-37;39-41;43. 35,2. 39,3. 40,1. 43,1. 44,2. AppxE; L; M; P
	ESS	10. 18,36. 22,7-8. 25,3;12;20. 30,27; 41. 34,19;30. EHu
	HAM	2,16
	HRT	8. 4,15;21. Appx
	HUN	4. B3. D19. Appx
	LIN	C24
	NFK	15. 1,61. 4,15;16. 8,15;16;37;39-40;44; 89. 9,79;167. 10,43;93. 12,6;17. 13,1; 19. 19,24. 22,1. 23,9;16. 24,4. 29,7. 49,6. 50,10. 57,2. 65,13. 66,53

	SFK 21. 1,75. 2,1-2;16;20. 3,27;31;*32-33*; 34;36;*46*;57;62;86;89;92-95;97-103. 4, 1;3-4;6;10;42. 5,2. 6,11-12;14-15;17; 19-20;21-22 *note*; 23;25;28-30;32-37; 39;41;43-49;51-56;114;116-118; 148-149;*164-165*;239;247;251;258; 265;*271*. 7,15; 55-56;58;61;67;71-72; 77;79-122 *note*; 130;136-146;148;151. 8,1-2;4-6;8-10;12;17;20-*21*;25;27;46; 56-57;59;63;66;68;80-82. 12,2. 14,40. 16,3-4;5;6;8;13;20;22;27-34;38-39;48. 21,12;16-19;21-22;25-31;36-37;40; 45-46;49-52;64-65;75;79-80;82-85. 22, 2-3. *25,53*; 112. 26,1;3;5. 28,2;6. 29,9. 32,1;14;21-31 *note*. 34,4;12;15-16. 38, 3;22. 39,3;5;8;10;22. 41,18. 45,1-3. 46, 8;*10*. 47,2-3. 52,4;10. 53,1;7. 63,3-6;9; 11-12;15;22;29-30. 74,10. 77,4
Simon	NFK 8,33;37-38;55;108
Simond	ESS 22,10
Simond: *see also* Sigmund, Sigmundr	
Sindi	YKS 9W132
Sinoth	DOR 2,6. 3,1;10
	HRT 37,8
Sinoth, the Abbot of Chatteris' man	HRT 31,2
Sired	BKM 14,1. 36,1
	ESS 20,72
	HAM 21,9. 23,35
	HRT 37,14. Appx
	KEN M3;6;20;22. P1. 5,124;144;159-160; 174;214
	SOM 21,8
	SSX 11,115
Sired : *see also* Dering son of	
: *see also* Edeva wife of	
Sired, a royal thane	BKM 14,2
Sired, Earl Algar's man	CAM 26,31
Sired, Earl Harold's man	BKM 17,5-6
	HRT 37,8
Sired of Chilham	KEN D17. C6
Sired son of Aelfeva, a royal thane	BKM 14,3
Sired son of Sibbi	BKM 12,1
Sired the canon	KEN P1
	MDX 3,2. 15,1
Sired's father	KEN M6
Siric	ESS 18,22. 24,1;59;64. 37,2. B3a
	LIN 68,5;12-13
	SFK 1,51. 6,186;218-221. 7,121. 16,43. 38, 21. 53,2;4. 62,1
Siric, King Edward's man	SFK 8,6
Siric: *see also* Sigeric	
Siward	BRK 34,2. 38,4
	BKM 14,18. 35,3
	CAM 3,1. *32,22;35. 44,2*
	CHS 8,24;30
	CON 5,5,7
	DBY 6,5;14;17;54;57;66;69-70;79;100
	DEV 16,43;76;143-144;148;163. 39,1;21
	DOR 42,1

	HUN	B5. D14
	YKS	1N36 *note.* 4N1-3
Siward, Earl Harold's man	BKM	12,13. 51,1-2
	CAM	3,6
Siward, Earl Waltheof's man	CAM	43,1
Siward Falconer/the falconer	SOM	8,36 *note.* 47,10
Siward Guntram	SOM	*47,11*
Siward Hunter	HAM	6,16
	OXF	58,23
Siward of Hormead	HRT	Appx
Siward (of Maldon)	ESS	34,9-12;18-20;23;26;30-31;33;36
Siward of Maldon, a thane	SFK	12,5. 34,1-4
Siward Rufus	LIN	CW,14
Siward Sot	KEN	5,12
Siward the falconer: *see* Siward Falconer		
Siward the priest	ESS	B3a
	LIN	68,38;42;46. CN,16
Siward the priest: *see also* Norman son of		
Siward the priest, a lawman	LIN	C2-3;14
Siward the priest's wife	LIN	C14
Siwat	NTT	6,10
	OXF	33,2
Siwat: *see also* Sighvatr		
Siwold	SOM	47,12
	SFK	7,92;117
Siwulf	SSX	9,109
Sjundi	LIN	16,14
Skaife	HAM	69,20
Skaenkel: *see* Skammketill		
Skalp	NFK	24,6. 38,4
Skalp: *see also* Scalpi		
Skammketill [MS. Scanchel]	YKS	5N63
Skeet	NFK	21,36. 29,4. 34,14-15. 51,8
Skelfr	YKS	9W137
Skemundr	LIN	30,20
Skjaldfrithr (fem.)	YKS	23E18
Skjaldvor (fem.): *see* Rothulfr son of		
Skotakollr	YKS	5W11. 9W40
Skraema: *see* Strami, Stremius		
Skuli	LIN	4,80. 28,15
	NFK	19,1. 21,21. 24,6. 29,2-3. 66,100;106
	YKS	29E1
Skuli, a royal thane	SFK	4,10
Skuli, Harold's man	NFK	24,5
Skuli [erroneously indexed]: *see* Aswulf		
Slettan, a thane	YKS	2B8
Small	WIL	48,8;11
Smelt, King Edward's chaplain	KEN	M9
Smelt the priest	SSX	11,63-64
Smeri	SFK	16,41
Smert	SFK	6,193
Smewin	OXF	B10
	SOM	21,86;88
Snaebjorn	YKS	29W33
Snaring the priest	SFK	16,34
Snarri	LIN	28,37
	YKS	C3
Snelling	CAM	5,19. 26,55
Snerri, Edeva the fair's man	HRT	16,12
Snot	DEV	17,54

Snoterman	NTH	18,23
Snotta	DEV	25,26
Sol	HEF	1,64
Solomon	DEV	35,23
	GLS	E8
	HEF	15,1-2
Solomon: *see also* Gilbert son of		
Solomon the priest	BDF	28,2
Sorag	KEN	*7,1*
Sorcbes	SFK	6,216
Sotakollr	YKS	CW11 *and note*
Soti	WAR	31,7
Soting, Earl Tosti's man	BKM	43,3
Sotman	DEV	25,18
Sotr	LIN	50,1
Sparrowhawk	NTT	9,113-114;116
	SFK	3,95. 6,45
Sparrowhawk, Queen Edith's man	SFK	37,2
Sperri	STS	17,15
Sperri: *see also* Sperrir		
Sperrir	LIN	16,22. 45,2
Sperrir: *see also* Sperri		
Sperun	SFK	16,15
Spieta	SFK	36,14
Spillir	LIN	12,20
Spir(e)wic: *see* Eudo son of		
Spir(i)tes the priest/canon	HEF	7,4
	SHR	3d,7. 4,20,18. 9,1
	SOM	*8,30.* 13,1
	WIL	56,1-4
Spir(i)tes (the priest/canon)	HAM	63,1
	HEF	7,6;8-9
	KEN	M21
	SHR	9,2
Spirwic: *see* Spir(e)wic		
Spracheling	OXF	B10
Spretman	SFK	7,92
Sprot	ESS	32,29. B3a(x4)
	SFK	7,77
Sprot: *see also* Sprottr		
Sprottr	YKS	1E49. 1W9. 5E32. 6N26;46;155;158.
		13N8. 23N30. 29E30. CN4
Sprottr: *see also* Sprot		
Sprotwulf	SFK	1,18;55. *16,8*
Stable	SOM	46,8
Stan	ESS	B3a
Stanard	NFK	9,10;14-17;81;91;121;157-159. 66,84
Stanard: *see also* Stanhard		
Stanburg	ESS	B3a
Stanflaed (fem.): *see* Stanfled		
Stanfled (fem.)	SFK	7,93
Stanfled (fem.): *see also* Stanflaed		
Stanhard	CAM	*26,48*
	ESS	87. 11,7. B3a(x2)
	SFK	6,194;200. 7,1;15. *31,15.* 35,7. 67,11
Stanhard of Hauxton	CAM	AppxH
Stanhard of Silverley	CAM	AppxB
Stanhard son of Aethelwy	SFK	72
Stanhard the Englishman	NFK	9,81
Stanhard: *see also* Stanard		

Stankell	BRK	21,14
Stankell: *see also* Stanketel, Steinkell, Steinketill, Stenketel		
Stanketel	WAR	27,2
Stanketel: *see also* Stankell, Steinke(ti)ll, Stenketel		
Stanmer	SFK	7,76;87. 39,5
Stanwin	SFK	3,61. 6,17;98;172. 7,13
Stanwin, Edric's man	SFK	6,92
Staplewin	DBY	1,35
	NTT	10,4;16
Star	HAM	23,40
Starculf	NFK	62
Starker	ESS	41,9;12
	SFK	40,2
	SRY	19,10
Starker, a royal thane	BDF	1,1b
Starling	SFK	3,98. 45,2-3
Stein	SHR	4,3,4
	SFK	3,94
Stein: *see also* Steinn, Sten		
Steingrimr	LIN	12,3. 28,14. CW,10
Steinkell	NTH	18,82
Steinkell: *see also* Stankell, -ketel, Steinketill, Stenketel		
Steinketill	LIN	16,1-2. 68,44
Steinketill: *see also* Steinkell		
Steinn	LIN	4,7
	YKS	6N125. 30W25
Steinn: *see also* Stein, Sten		
Steinulf	DBY	5,1;3-5. 16,8. 17,9
	HEF	16,3
	NTT	9,70
	SHR	4,1,33
Steinulf: *see also* Steinulfr, Stenulf		
Steinulfr	YKS	6N130. 9W11;119;122;127;134-135; 139
Steinulfr: *see also* Steinulf		
Sten	CHS	1,16;20
Sten: *see also* Stein, Steinn		
Stenesnoc	HAM	23,36
Stenketel	CHS	14,3
Stenketel: *see also* Stanketel, Steinketill		
Stenulf	CHS	2,23. 14,13. 23,3. R1,5;25
	STS	11,33
Stenulf: *see also* Steinulf(r)		
Stephen	BDF	24,7
	BRK	22,4;6-7
	DEV	16,110;112;152. 17,78;106
	HEF	35. 1,29. 14,3
	NTH	2,9
	SOM	6,13
	WAR	36. 4,1;6
Stephen Carpenter: *see* Stephen the carpenter		
Stephen, Count Alan's man	LIN	12,56
Stephen son of Erhard	BRK	64
Stephen son of Fulcred	GLS	E27. WoB7
	WOR	2,42
Stephen son of Wulfwy	GLS	EvC41
Stephen the carpenter	WIL	66,6-7

Stori, Earl Tosti's man	BDF	44,1
Stoting	ESS	B3a
Strami [? for Scrami, for Anglo-Scand Skraema]	WIL	68,22
Strang the Dane	GLS	73,1
Strangwulf	SFK	25,67
Stremius [? for Scremi, for Anglo-Scand Skraema]	WIL	24,19. 68,22
Stric	HUN	19,2
Stric: see also Alstan Stric		
Strui	LIN	16,47
Stubhard	SFK	6,194
Stur: see William son of		
Sturmid of Cottenham	CAM	AppxO
Sturmid: see also Sturmy		
Sturmy	SHR	4,1,33
	SHR	4,6,1
Sturmy: see also Richard Sturmy		
Styrr	LIN	32,1;28
Suadus	ESS	35,6
Sualeva (fem.): see also Atsurr son of		
Sualeva (fem.): see Svala		
Sucga	CHS	27,2
Sucga: see also Sugga		
Sudan	YKS	6N156
Sugga	CAM	32,31
Sugga: see also Sucga		
Sumarfugl	YKS	23N13
Sumarlithi	LIN	3,20;48. 14,79. 26,11. 68,46. CS,15
	YKS	1N92
Sumarlithi: see also Summerled		
Summerled	DEV	48,12
	HUN	19,26. D9
	SFK	4,19
Summerled: see also Sumarlithi		
Sunegod	ESS	B3a
Suneman	CAM	35,2
	SFK	7,86
	YKS	1W33
Sunnifa (fem.)	YKS	C10
Sunnulfr	YKS	1E40. 5E38;56. CE27
Sunnulfr the priest	YKS	C3
Sunwin	SFK	38,11
Svafi	LIN	12,96
Svafi : see also Sveinn son of		
: see also Swafi		
Svala (fem.): see Atsurr son of Saleva, Sualeva		
Svala (fem.): see also Saleva, Sualeva		
Svartbrandr	LIN	68. 12,92. 29,26. CW,1
Svartbrandr: see also Ulfr father of		
Svartbrandr son of Ulfr, a lawman	LIN	C2-3;13. CK,18;29
Svartbrandr: see also Swartbrand		
Svartgeirr	YKS	14E32;53
Svarthofuth	YKS	5N64 and note
Svartkollr	YKS	1N77;81. 1W20. 25W15. 30W24;34
Svartr	YKS	C10
Svartr: see also Swart		
Sveinn	LIN	T4. 2,40. 3,33. 4,69. 7,8. 12,96. 14,1; 87. 16,10;28. 17,1. 26,36;46. 45,3. 67, 9;22. 68,27;30. CW,15

	YKS	5N1-8;10. 9W34;57;69;74;91;96; 105-107;114;117;120. 10W20;22-23; 25;29;32-33;39;42. 14E31;34;38; 50-51. 27W1-2. 29W5. CW14
Sveinn, Alfred of Lincoln's man	LIN	27,56
Sveinn of Adwick le Street	YKS	CW22
Sveinn son of Svafi	LIN	C9. T5
Sveinn, the Bishop of Bayeux's man	LIN	4,78
Sveinn: *see also* Swein		
Sveinn's two sons	LIN	2,40
Svertingr, a lawman	LIN	C3
Svertingr son of Grimbald, a lawman	LIN	C2
Svertingr son of Harthaknutr, a lawman	LIN	C3
Svertingr: *see also* Swarting		
Swafi	LEC	17,15
Swafi : *see also* Swein son of		
: *see also* Svafi		
Swart	NFK	26,3
Swart Hoga	SFK	6,109
Swart: *see also* Svartr		
Swartbrand	NTT	30,46
Swartbrand: *see also* Svartbrandr		
Swarti	NTT	9,54
Swarting	BRK	B1
	BKM	17,13. 21,2. 22,2. 23,27-28. 57,15-17
	ESS	B3a
	HAM	1,W8. NF3,4. IoW7,5. 9,13
	NFK	13,10
	SFK	6,106. 28,5. 67,19;24;28;32
Swarting, Asgar's man	BKM	21,7
Swarting, Asgar the constable's man	BKM	14,30
Swarting: *see also* Svertingr		
Swartling	ESS	B3a
	NTH	45,2
	SFK	7,37
Swartrik	SFK	6,191. 76,23
Sweet	DEV	15,51
	SOM	*19,14.* 21,55
Sweeting	BDF	53,25
	BKM	33,1
	ESS	22,2
	OXF	9,8
Sweeting: *see also* Sweting		
Sweetman	NFK	9,56
	NTH	45,3
	OXF	B10
	SFK	7,77;80
another Sweetman	OXF	B10
Sweetman the moneyer	OXF	B10
Sweetman, Wulfmer of Eaton's man	BDF	55,12
Swein	DBY	1,30. 6,3. 7,11. 16,3
	DOR	26,27. 56,28-29;53;58
	ESS	40,9. 74,1. B3a
	GLS	3,2. WoB16
	HAM	68,1
	HUN	6,15
	LEC	13,60;67
	NTH	50. 48,3-10;17
	NTT	9,31. 11,4;12;14;33. 12,18. 16,1;11. 18,1;3;5;7. 22,2. 30,1

OXF	20,1
SHR	4,3,17. 4,20,4-5;7;13-14. 4,27,10
SOM	19,64. 45,11
STS	1,48;60. 8,8;20;24. 11,20;30
SFK	6,159;177. 7,77. 41,5;14
SRY	6,4. 9,1
WAR	18,1. 28,12;16
WIL	24,30. 27,23. 67,94

Swein : *see also* Edward son of
    : *see also* Robert son of Wymarc, father of
    : *see also* Wulfsi (son of?)

Swein, a royal thane	BKM	50,1
Swein, a thane	SOM	*19,64*
Swein, Alwin Varus's man	BKM	4,6
Swein, Asgar the constable's man	BKM	21,3-4;6
Swein, brother of Leofwin	SRY	25,3
Swein Child: *see* Young Swein		
Swein, Earl Harold's man	BKM	26,11
	HRT	5,25. 34,5. 35,1-2
Swein of Essex: *see* Swein the sheriff		
Swein son of Azor	NTH	B29
Swein son of Swafi	DBY	S5
	NTT	S5
Swein Swart	ESS	36,5. 52,1
	SFK	71,1
Swein Swart: *see also* Swein Swarthy		
Swein Swarthy, Earl Edwin's man	BKM	14,25
Swein Swarthy: *see also* Swein Swart		
Swein the sheriff/of Essex	ESS	24. 1,2-3;27-28. 10,5
	HUN	16
	OXF	42
	SFK	27
Swein (the sheriff/of Essex)	ESS	1,13;25. 9,14. 18,14;18;23. 30,21. 90, 35. B3m,n

Swein the sheriff/of Essex: *see also* Robert son
  of Wymarc

Young Swein [= Swein Child]	DBY	8,1;3-6
	NTT	11,10
Swein: *see also* Sveinn		
Swein's father	DOR	56,28-29;53
	WIL	67,94
Swening, Earl Harold's man	BKM	30,1
Sweting	SFK	7,98
Sweting: *see also* Sweeting		
Taldus	HEF	1,60
Talk	SFK	6,98
Tancred: *see also* Norman son of		
Tancred of Sutton	CAM	AppxP
Tanio	STS	11,28
Tascelin the priest	ESS	1,10. 3,11
Tascelin: *see also* Tesselin		
Tate	ESS	B3a
Teher	ESS	18,9
Teher: *see also* Teri		
Teit	SFK	6,217
Tela (fem.)	SFK	36,11
Teos	CHS	R1,37
Tepekin	SFK	29,11;14. 40,4
Teri	SFK	41,11
Teri: *see also* Teher, Thyri		

Theodoric: *see also* Theodric
Theodric   WIL   8,12. 24,20
Theodric: *see also* Theodoric
Theodulf   SHR   4,27,5-6
Theodulf, a thane   SOM   *26,8*
Theodwald   BKM   4,18;20
Theodwald: *see also* William son of
Theogar   WIL   26,16
Theogar: *see also* Theodger
Tholf   DBY   17,4-5
    STS   11,1. 13,4
    WIL   25,23
Tholf: *see also* Tholfr
Tholfr   YKS   1E16
Tholfr: *see also* Tholf
Archbishop Thomas/of York   DBY   S5
    GLS   2. EvK1. EvM3-4
    HAM   4
    LEC   2. C7
    LIN   2. 30,22. 57,46. CS,27-29. CN,10-11;
                23. CK,16
    NTT   5
    OXF   7,58
    YKS   2. C1a *and note*; 1b;21-22;30;37.
                6N142. CE25;28;33. SN,Y1-3;5;7-8.
                SW,Sk1-2. SW, BA1-2. SW,Ag1.
                SW,An12;15;18. SW,Bu5;20;45-48.
                SW,H1-3. SN,Ma5;7-8;11-12;15;19;
                21-22. SN,B13-14;17-19;23-25.
                SN,Bi2. SE,Wel4-5. SE,C2;4.
                SE,How11. SE,Wei4-7. SE,Sn1;3-5;
                7-9. SE,Dr1. SE,Wa3-7. SE,P2-3;6-9.
                SE,Hu2;6. SE,Tu3-4;6;8. SE,Bt3-5;8.
                SE,Sc1;3;6. SE,Ac6;10. SE,Th1;4;6-7;
                10-14. SE,So1-2 *note*. SE,Mid1-3. SE,
                No1. SE,No2 *note*
Thor   NFK   19,9
    NTH   57,1-2
    WOR   8,2
Thor: *see also* Thorr
Thorald, William of Warenne's man   NFK   1,195
Thorald: *see also* Thoraldr
Thoraldr   LIN   14,62. 16,20
Thoraldr: *see also* Alfred nephew of
Thoraldr of Greetwell   LIN   C20
Abbot Thoraldr/of Peterborough   BDF   7
    DBY   S5
    HUN   8. 1,4. 7,5;8. 9,2. 19,8. D28
    LEC   5
    LIN   8. 1,9. C16;20-21. S1;10. T5. 30,32.
                51,3. 56,4. 67,21. CW,2;6;8;14
    NTH   6. 42,2. EB3. B4. ELc1-2
    NTT   8. S5
    RUT   EN9-10. ELc1;10;18
Thoraldr, Roger of Bully's man   LIN   17,1
Thoraldr the priest   LIN   16,50. 26,14
Thoraldr the sheriff   LIN   11,9
Thoraldr: *see also* Thorald
Thorarna (fem.)   YKS   11N4 *and note*
Thorbern   ESS   20,57. 28,2;5;12. 90,80. B3b

	NFK	4,18;32. 22,16 23,11. 56,34
	NTH	4,28. 18,11;48;58-60;68-70;72
	NTT	10,2
	STS	1,46
	SFK	6,22. 7,96;101
	SRY	19,4. 25,1
	WAR	16,3;18. 20,1
Thorbern, a royal thane	WOR	26,8
Thorbern, a thane	GLS	76,1
Thorbern, Edeva's man	HRT	16,6
Thorbern, King Edward's man	HRT	25,1
Thorbern of Orwell	CAM	AppxK. (cf 14,41)
Thorbern the priest	SFK	38,11
Thorbern White	CAM	5,29. *26,27*
Thorbern: *see also* Thorbjorn, Thurber		
Thorbert	BDF	53,26
	BKM	5,19. 18,3
	CAM	4,1
	DEV	9,1
	ESS	28,17-18
	KEN	M11
	NFK	4,33. 9,46. 34,4
	SFK	67,11
	WIL	68,13;25
Thorbert, Countess Goda's man	BKM	53,5
Thorbert, Earl Algar's man	BKM	39,1
Thorbert, Earl Harold's thane	GLS	1,60
Thorbert, Earl Leofwin's man	MDX	2,3. 14,2
Thorbert Hunter	HAM	NF9,4
Thorbert, King Edward's man	BDF	3,10
Thorbert the priest	CAM	*26,26*
	HRT	37,3
Thorbjorn	YKS	C31;33. 1W1-2;36-37. 9W92. 13W19; 34. 14E43;48. 29N12. 29W30-32
Thorbjorn: *see also* Thorbern, Thurber		
Thorbrandr	YKS	1N48. 1W30. 8N1;8-10;23-28. 8W1;3. 8E1;3-4;6. 13N12. 23N4
Thored	CHS	5,1. 9,5. 16,1. 20,1. 22,1. 27,3. FD7,1
	HUN	13,5
	NFK	31,1;31;43;45. 32,1. 34,1
	NTH	18,49
	NTT	9,80. 14,1
	SHR	4,3,14;20;26;30-31;69. 4,27,10
	SFK	3,54. 4,36. 13,5. 33,4;6-7;9-11
	WIL	13,21
Thored: *see also* Azor son of		
Thored, a thane	NFK	31,17
Thored: *see also* Thorthr		
Thored's two daughters	WIL	13,21
Thorferth	NTT	9,54;118. 14,2. 30,40
Thorferth: *see also* Thorfreth		
Thorfin	CHS	Y5
Thorfin: *see also* Thorfinnr		
Thorfinnr	YKS	C3;29. 1E18. 1L4. 5N33-34;67;71;70; 72. 6N7;11;18;38-40;44;47;49-51;58; 67;73;75-76;78;80;91;135-137;141. 30W7-8;35. SN,Y8
Thorfinnr: *see also* Thorfin		
Thorfreth	RUT	ELc9
Thorfreth: *see also* Thorferth, Thorfrothr		

Thorfrothr	LIN	3,36. 4,17;42;77-79. 12,51. 16,46. 27, 54. 40,1. 51,10. 53,1. 54,1. 55,3. 56, 7-8. 59,13-14. 61,4. 66,1-2. CK,39
	YKS	14E12;44;48. 29E4. CE44
Thorfrothr: *see also* Godric son of		
Thorfrothr, brother of Ketill	LIN	22,26
Thorfrothr son of Wulfrith	LIN	1,23
Thorfrothr: *see also* Thorferth, Thorfreth		
Thorfroth's father	LIN	22,26
Thorgar	DBY	11,2;5
	HEF	21,2
	NTH	56,30
	SHR	4,7,5
	SFK	1,51
	WOR	23,12
Thorgar, a royal thane	CAM	26,42
Thorgar, Earl Algar's man	CAM	26,6
Thorgautr	LIN	T5. 12,18. 14,59. 16,43. 18,3-4;6. 22, 10. 49,3. EN,3
	YKS	7E1-2. 14E21-22 (*but see note*). 24W9. CE50
Thorgautr Lagr	LIN	18,1;7;13;29. 59,6
	YKS	C36 *and note*
Thorgautr: *see also* Thorgot, Thurgot		
Thorgils	BDF	24,1-4;19
	BKM	12,19
	DBY	6,43. 17,2
	DEV	17,22;35;53-54;61-62;80-81;97-101
	ESS	25,2-3. 36,2
	HAM	IoW8,9
	KEN	D17. 5,40;74-75;141-142. 9,4;18
	LIN	14,1;17;30-31;37
	NFK	24,4. 34,3;11
	SOM	25,7;41;54
	SFK	35,3
	SRY	5,20. 8,27
	SSX	11,106
Thorgils: *see also* Hugh son of		
Thorgils, a royal thane	BDF	23,19
	BKM	4,31
Thorgils, Baldwin son of Herlwin's man	BDF	3,13
Thorgils the Englishman	BDF	57,16
Thorgot	ESS	11,3
	KEN	5,156-157
	NTT	21,3
	OXF	34,1-2. 40,1
	SHR	4,3,62. 4,11,10. 4,23,17. 4,25,7. 4,27, 34
	STS	12,15
	SSX	11,62. 12,54. 13,53
	WAR	45,1
	WIL	25,18
Thorgot, a royal thane	BKM	28,1
Thorgot, Earl Leofwin's man	BKM	28,3
Thorgot: *see also* Thorgautr, Thurgot		
Thorgot's father	BDF	57,16
Thorgot's mother	BDF	57,16
Thorgrim	NFK	8,115
Thorgrim: *see also* Thorgrimr		
Thorgrimr	YKS	1W37

Thorgrimr: *see also* Thorgrim		
Thori	BRK	3,2
	BKM	43,7
	DBY	6,39
	HAM	66,1
	HUN	19,3
	NTH	18,96. 30,14. 38,1
	NTT	11,2;4;6;8-9;11;18;20;22;24-25
	OXF	33,1
	SOM	17,5
	WAR	17,68
	WOR	18,4
Thori, a royal Guard/thane	BKM	14,35. 43,11
Thori, King Edward's man	BKM	41,7
Thori: *see also* Thorir, Thuri		
Thori's father	BRK	3,2
Thorild	SFK	7,103
Thorir	LIN	7,54. 18,24. 31,1;3;5;7. CK,55-56
	YKS	19W1 *and note.* 19W3
Thorir, Earl Leofwin's man	HRT	15,11
Thorir son of Roaldr	LIN	T5
Thorir: *see also* Thori, Thuri		
Thork	CAM	26,2
Thork: *see also* Thorkell		
Thorkell	BDF	53,21. 57,21
	BRK	21,8. 22,12
	BKM	36,2. 53,1
	CON	*4,22*
	DEV	3,5
	DOR	56,19
	ESS	14,3-7. 18,38. 24,9;58. 26,2. 30,5. 66, 1. B3a,h
	GLS	39,2. 63,1
	HAM	IoW6,9
	HRT	30,2. 33,5
	HEF	1,65. 10,25;32-34;37-38;44. 15,6-7. 29,12;16
	HUN	20,1-2. D26
	LEC	39,2. 40,26. 42,10
	NFK	4,45. 19,3-5;7;17. 21,2-3;6-7. 28,1. 50, 7. 66,22
	NTT	9,57;59;60. 15,9. 20,3;8
	NTH	10,3. 31,1. 41,10. 56,7-8;28;49
	OXF	57. 35,6
	SHR	4,3,66
	SOM	5,14;19;30
	STS	11,48. 12,26
	SFK	1,123f. 6,116;223;264. 7,36. 21,29-30; 62. 22,2. 26,12a. *39,10.* 74,13
	SSX	11,26;101
	WAR	EN1
	WIL	25,25. 67,63;85
	WOR	2,56. 3,1. 8,20
Thorkell: *see also* Alwin brother of		
: *see also* Godmund brother of		
: *see also* Ketelbern brother of		
Thorkell, a royal thane	BDF	23,18
Thorkell, a thane	BKM	14,45
	SFK	34,7
Thorkell, Asgar the constable's man	HRT	33,5;15

Thorkell Battock	WAR	28,1
Thorkell, father of Alwin the sheriff	WAR	17,15
Thorkell, father of Alwin (the sheriff)	WAR	17,6;32;62
Thorkell Hako	NFK	19,21-22
Thorkell, King Edward's man	BKM	44,3
Thorkell, King Edward's steersman	WOR	8,1
Thorkell of Digswell	HRT	Appx (cf 33,5)
Thorkell of Warwick	WAR	17. B2. 7,1. 28,2;12. 44,15
Thorkell of Wrentham, Edric's man	SFK	26,12d
Thorkell the Dane	HUN	2,8
	SOM	*44,2*
Thorkell the priest	HUN	B12. 19,9
Thorkell the reeve	ESS	86
Thorkell White	HEF	29,2;11;20
Thorkell, Wulfmer's man	HEF	15,9
Thorkell's father	WIL	67,85
Thorkell: *see also* Thorketel, -ketill, Thork, Thorkil		
Thorketel	NFK	13,1;3-7;12-17;19;23. 21,23. 34,17. 50, 1
	NTT	9,15
	SHR	4,14,17
	WIL	24,37. 27,21. 28,5
Thorketel: *see also* Thorkell, -ketill		
Thorketill	LIN	2,32-33. 12,90. 26,27;40. 27,15;40;51; 53. 67,12. CK,34
	YKS	C8;11;29. 1Y13. 1N8-9;64-65;85;87. 1E3;8;51. 1W58-59. 2N27. 5N56;63; 66. 5E1-2;5;23;25;29;32;34;36;45;47; 49;56. 5W19. 6N34;37;63;85;96;108; 113-114;120;134;140;160-161. 13W1; 12;38. 14E13;17;26-27;29-30. 21E11. 23N31. 23E9;18. 25W24;28;29-30 *note.* 29W12;19. 29E1;4. 29W29. CN5. CE9. CW3;5. SN,Y8
Thorketill: *see also* Thorkell, -ketel		
Thorkil, Earl Tosti's priest	CAM	41,9
Thorkil: *see also* Thorkell		
Thorlaug (fem.)	YKS	1N77
Thormar	SFK	16,16
Thormod	HEF	2,31
	SFK	1,75. 22,1;3
Thormod of Parham	SFK	1,93
Thormod: *see also* Thormoth, Thormothr		
Thormoth	NFK	29,6
Thormoth: *see also* Thormothr		
Thormothr	YKS	5N66
Thormothr: *see also* Thormoth, Thormod		
Thormund	DOR	5,1
	SOM	5,70
	NFK	9,9. 31,6-8;10
Thorn	YKS	5N67. 13N19. 25W29-30 *note.* CW4
	NFK	50,6
Thorodd		
Thorodd: *see also* Azor son of Thorold		
Thorold	BRK	11,1
	ESS	4,7. 18,37. 24,6-7. 30,4. 34,7;15;21-22; 33-34. 90,13;44-45
	HAM	21,3;5. IoW8,12
	HRT	33,4;11
	HUN	16,1

	LEC	44,1
	NFK	8,3;8-9;13;133-136. 9,30;60;62;72;106;
		141;177;228. 20,19;32. 50,6(?)
	OXF	20,10
	SHR	4,19. 3f,1
	SFK	7,97. 31,41. 34,15. EE4
	SRY	18,2-4
	SSX	11,11
	WIL	21,1-2. 68,12
	WOR	26,3

Thorold: *see also* Azor son of
     : *see also* Gilbert son of
     : *see also* Ilbert son of
     : *see also* Ralph son of
     : *see also* William son of

Thorold, a man-at-arms of the wife of Hugh	DOR	*55,32;35*
son of Grip		
Thorold of Rochester	ESS	9,1. 18,36;43;44 *note*
Thorold (of Rochester)	ESS	20,1

Thorold of Rochester: *see also* Ralph son of

Thorold of Rochester's son	KEN	5,31
Thorold, Roger of Bully's man	NTT	9,10;46;50;59;70
Thorold the priest	BRK	20,2
Thorold, Wigot's nephew	GLS	27,1

Thorold/Thorolf/Thorulf: *see* Richard son of
Thorolf: *see* Richard son of

Thorp	NFK	31,33
Thorr	LIN	3,51. 4,10. 14,72. 26,30. 28,19
	YKS	1N41;48;134. 1W9-10;55. 6N2;5-6;8;
		11-13;15;18-21;23-25;30;57;64;66;
		68-69;86;98;101;104;109;122;145-146;
		155. 14E13;17;40-41;48;52. 23N5.
		25W3;6 *note*;8. 29W4

Thorr: *see also* Frani son of
     : *see also* Thor

Thorr, the Bishop of Bayeux's man	LIN	4,79
Thorsteinn	YKS	1N87. 9W33;124. 11E2. 14E27. CN5.
		CE43
Thorsteinn, Drogo of Beuvrière's man	YKS	14E38
Thorsteinn, Erneis of Buron's man	LIN	34,3;8
	YKS	24W12
Thorsteinn, the Bishop of Durham's man	LIN	3,20;27;48

Thorsteinn: *see also* Thurstan, Thursten

Thorthr	YKS	11E2;4. 23E7. 29E26

Thorthr: *see also* Thored

Thorulf	CAM	AppxJ
	CHS	Y9
	HUN	D9
	NFK	11,4
Thorulf, Earl Leofwin's man	BKM	14,19

Thorulf: *see* Richard son of
Thorulf: *see also* Thorulfr, Thorwulf

Thorulfr	LIN	4,61. 14,92. 26,4;17. 32,12. CS,13
	YKS	1N20;87. 1E34. 1L8. CN5

Thorulfr: *see also* Thorulf, Thorwulf

Thorvold	SFK	7,123
Thorwulf	NTH	60,2

Thorwulf: *see also* Thorulf, Thorulfr

Thrasemund	DOR	40,1. 44,1
	WIL	48,7

Thrond	NTH	42,3
Thurber: *see* Alfwy son of		
Thurber: *see also* Thorbern		
Thurgot	SFK	16,46
Thurgot: *see also* Thorgautr, Thorgot		
Thuri	SFK	16,30. 25,67. 71,2
Thuri, a royal thane	SFK	25,61;63
Thuri of Kyluertestuna	SFK	6,110
Thuri: *see also* Thori, Thorir		
Thurs	DEV	22,1
Thurstan	BDF	3,12. 55,3
	BKM	4,32;43. 14,18;28-29. 19,7
	DEV	34,38
	DOR	*36,5*
	ESS	37,6. B3a
	GLS	48,3. 53,8. 56,1. 68,10
	HAM	2,5. 3,8
	HEF	10,73. 14,1. 17,2. 19,1;9
	HRT	5,11
	HUN	2,1;5
	KEN	5,145;199
	LEC	20,2-3. 43,10-11
	NFK	4,46. *8,89.* 9,1;74;153. 19,17. 66,16
	NTH	4,35. 35,14;25
	NTT	9,19;37;76;101
	OXF	28,15. EN6. ES2
	SHR	4,11,2. 4,14,10. 4,28,1. 6,14-15
	SOM	1,4;20. 16,9. 19,1;33
	STS	12,8;18;31
	SFK	1,107. 3,74-78. 41,4-5. 77,4
	SSX	11,20
	WAR	19,1
	WIL	6,1. 12,1;3. 26,21. 29,6. 68,18
Thurstan: *see also* Robert son of		
Thurstan, a man-at-arms	WIL	12,2
Thurstan, a royal thane	MDX	19,1
(another) Thurstan	NTT	9,19
Thurstan Mantle	BKM	36
Thurstan of Cormeilles	GLS	EvK116
Thurstan of Flanders	HEF	9,2
Thurstan of Giron/Gironde	BKM	4,27
	KEN	5,157
Abbot Thurstan (of Glastonbury)	SOM	*8,1;5;11;16-18;21;23-25;31*
	WIL	7,3
Thurstan of Thetford	NFK	66,76-77
Thurstan of Wigmore	SHR	6,3
Thurstan of Wigmore: *see also* Agnes wife of		
Thurstan Red	HAM	3,1
Thurstan Red: *see also* Thurstan the Red		
Thurstan Small	HAM	3,1
Thurstan son of Guy	NFK	9,83;85;135-138;150
	SFK	7,122;125;133. 76,15
Thurstan son of Richard	CAM	*21,1*
Thurstan son of Rolf	BRK	55. EW1
	BKM	35. 14,3
	DEV	37
	DOR	33
	GLS	67. W18. 3,1;7. 19,2. 35,2. E8. EvK400. WoB15;19
	HAM	38

	HEF	17
	SOM	36. *8,18*. 45,12. EDe1
	WIL	49,1a
	WOR	8,7
Thurstan (son of Rolf)	GLS	E36
Thurstan the chamberlain	BDF	47
	HAM	40. 23,16. S3
	WIL	68,26
Thurstan the engineer	HAM	S3
Thurstan the priest	BKM	23,21
Thurstan the red	ESS	5,8
Thurstan the red: *see also* Thurstan Red		
Thurstan the sheriff	CON	*5,4. 1,1. 4,22. 6,1*
Thurstan Tinel	KEN	5,196;210-212 *note*
Thurstan Tinel's wife	KEN	5,196
Thurstan Wishart	ESS	B3p
Thurstan (Wishart)	ESS	40,2
Thurstan: *see also* Thorsteinn, Thursten		
Thurstan's father	SOM	16,9
Thurwulf: *see also* Thorulf, Thorulfr		
Thyri	NFK	34,8
Thyri: *see also* Teri		
Tidbald	ESS	3,2
Tidwulf	SOM	5,28
Tigier	SFK	6,23;127;271
Tihel	SFK	16,1
Tihel of Helléan/the Breton	ESS	38. 18,21a
	NFK	37. *Notes to* 1,195. 2,11
	SFK	42. 16,9
Tihel, the Abbot of Ely's reeve	CAM	AppxL
Tihel the Breton: *see* Tihel of Helléan		
Tofa (fem.)	NFK	12,6
Tofi	LIN	28,1
Tofi: *see also* Tovi		
Toki	BKM	17,30
	CAM	18,3;5-7. 26,8
	CHS	1,4;6. 2,29. 5,2-3. 9,20
	DBY	6,27. 9,1;3-4;6. 17,17. B5. S5
	HRT	31,3
	KEN	5,23;211
	LEC	28,1-5
	LIN	29,18. 32,26. 64,1;15;18. 68,19
	NFK	1,89. 4,14. 8,7;21-22;30;47;62;68;
		98-100;103-105;107;110;116. 9,172.
		25,20. 31,16. 34,10;19
	NTH	44,1-4
	NTT	S5. 12,1;12;15-16;19;21
	OXF	16,1
	SHR	4,9,3-4. 4,27,1
	SOM	21,95
	STS	11,26
	SFK	7,80. 26,4;9-11. 35,3
	SRY	19,7;31
	SSX	10,69
	WAR	17,11
	WIL	28,8. 62,1
	YKS	5E17. 9W37. 10W2. 18W1;3. CW16;
		19

Toki: *see also* Alward son of
   : *see also* Godwin son of/Godwin Tokeson

Toki, a royal Guard	MDX	7,8
Toki, a royal thane	BKM	19,1
	CAM	18,1;8
Toki, a thane	SFK	26,9
Toki of Winterton	NFK	9,87
Toki son of Auti	LIN	C4. T5.
Toki son of Ottarr	YKS	C36
Toli	DBY	17,14-15
	DEV	22,2
	ESS	30,17
	KEN	5,24;105
	LIN	27,58. 42,9
	NFK	21,2;4-5;14
	OXF	35,13;29
	SOM	19,57
	SFK	6,106. 7,29;36. 27,11. 51,1
	WAR	18,5-6;12
	WIL	29,3. 32,16-17
	WOR	8,15
	YKS	1W64
Toli, Count Alan's man	LIN	12,58;88
Toli son of Alsige	LIN	T5
Toli the Dane	HAM	32,1-2
Toli (the Dane)	DEV	22,2
	DOR	34,2;5-6;8;12;14-15
Toli the sheriff (of Suffolk)	NFK	1,229. 14,35. 47,4
	SFK	4,15. 7,31;67. 31,53
Tonni	BRK	37,1
	LIN	22,17;19;23. 24,24;37;54;61;68;76. CS, 13;23;30-31;33
	NTH	46,1-6
	OXF	38,1
	WAR	2,2. 17,62
	YKS	25W2. 29W29
Topi	DEV	16,146
	ESS	32,34
	LIN	25,5
	SFK	32,30
Topi: *see also* Ulf(r) son of		
Topi, Aelmer's man	HRT	36,2
Tortwald	CON	5,4,1
Tosard	SSX	12,3
Tosti	ESS	6,7. 40,5
	HAM	31,1. S2
	HEF	10,4;29
	HUN	10,1
	LIN	4,17;69. EN,1
	NFK	10,83
	NTH	18,23. 41,2
	NTT	1,65. 9,97
	SFK	55,1
	SSX	13,37
	WAR	37,7
	YKS	1Y3;5
Tosti: *see also* Eric brother of		
Earl Tosti	BDF	23,47. 24,14. 44,1. 47,3. 49,2-3. 53,2; 16;20;29-30;32-33. 54,3. 57,2
	BRK	20,2
	BKM	2,1. 4,5. 6,1-2. 13,4. 14,4. 15,2. 17,7. 43,3

	CAM	38,2. 41,9
	CHS	Y2-4;7;13
	GLS	26,2. 55,1
	HAM	1,29-30;W10. 45,1. NF10,3. IoW1,1-3; 5. 9,2
	HRT	1,18
	HUN	20,5. D11
	NTH	25,1. 49,1
	NTT	B2. 1,9
	OXF	1,7b. 20,5. EBu1
	SOM	1,17
	SSX	11,39
	WIL	1,11. 31,1
	YKS	1L1-3;6. 5W8. 14E1. 30W37;40
Tosti of Sawtry	HUN	19,1. D27
Tosti's reeve	HAM	IoW7,22
Toti	BRK	26,1-3
	ESS	23,1
	NTT	7,6
	SSX	10,91
	WAR	37,7
	WIL	41,4
Toti: *see also* Azor son of		
Tovi	BRK	21,10. 27,1;3. 65,6
	DEV	17,62-63;65;67. 34,2;6. 39,15
	ESS	70,1. B3a
	GLS	11,14. 29,1. 31,1. 58,1-2. 67,1;6. 78,1. E11
	HAM	2,17. 23,39;66. 28,1-2;5;7-8. 59,1. IoW6,17;19;22. 9,15
	HUN	2,7. 19,13
	NFK	48. 9,8;117. 20,1. 53,1
	OXF	35,28
	SOM	17,6
	SRY	5,2. 10,1. 19,8. 35,1-2
	SSX	11,52
	WIL	M13. 8,7. 27,19. 42,7
Tovi, a free man	SFK	29,9
Tovi, a royal Guard	BDF	46,1. 53,12
Tovi, a royal thane	BKM	43,2. 48,1
Tovi, a thane	GLS	76,1
	SFK	29,12
Tovi, Alric son of Goding's man	BKM	14,33
Tovi the priest	BDF	2,4
Tovi the reeve	SRY	1,1c
Tovi the sheriff (of Somerset)	SOM	47,3. *Notes to* 1,28. 5,35. 22,25. 47,4-5; 8
Tovi Widenesci, Earl Harold's Guard	GLS	1,66
Tovi: *see also* Tofi		
Tovild (fem.)	ESS	90,72
	SFK	74,13
Toxus (the priest?)	DOR	34,8
Traswin(?)	DOR	26,51
Travers	HAM	IoW6,8
Trumwin	SFK	30,1. 36,9
Tual	CHS	FT2,11
Tubbi	BKM	17,6
	WAR	16,59
Tudur, a Welshman	SHR	4,1,13
Tuffa, Earl Waltheof's man	BDF	53,31

Tuini, a royal thane	WOR	24,1
Tuini: *see also* Tumi		
Tulf	SFK	7,148
Tumbi	SFK	1,122d
Tumbi: *see also* Tunbi		
Tumi	WAR	EBW5
	WOR	23,5. 26,7
	YKS	C12
Tumi: *see also* Tuini		
Tunbi	HAM	21,7
Tunbi: *see also* Tumbi		
Tuneman, a royal thane	SFK	16,40
Tunric	ESS	B3a
Turot	YKS	6N81 *and note*
Tutfled (fem.)	SFK	3,101
Ubbi	DBY	6,46
Udi	STS	17,2
Uglubarthr	YKS	1E57;59
Uhtbrand	CHS	19,3
	DBY	1,38. 6,93
	NTT	29,2
Uhtbrand: *see also* Uhtbrandr		
Uhtbrandr	LIN	59,1
Uhtbrandr: *see also* Uhtbrand		
Uhtred	CHS	3,11. 9,20. R1,2;7;13;16;22;26-28; 31-32;34;36;41
	CON	5,2,7
	DBY	6,3-4. 17,1
	DEV	16,59. 17,47. 19,20. 43,2
	HRT	37,9
	SOM	*25,40*
	STS	1,50
	SFK	3,96. 43,1;3
	YKS	C2 *and note*; 10. 1N96. 1E28. 5N9; 11-21;25-26;32;38-42;49-50;52. 5E32; 40-41. 6N3-4;56;59-60. 9W18. 29E10; 14;22. 29N8;10;12. 30W27;33
Uhtred, a thane	SOM	*25,40*
Ulf	BKM	4,1. 17,18;28. 22,2. E8
	CHS	3,2. Y1;11
	DBY	6,46;83. 16,8
	DEV	3,39;46;55. 16,36;44;70;152-153;169. 17,29-30;48. 19,13;*45*. 34,16. 35, 20-21. 39,10. 47,1-2. 52,40
	DOR	47,8
	GLS	46,1-3
	HUN	9,1-3. 21,1
	LEC	3,10. 13,5-6;36;39. 17,8. 29,2. 36,2. 40,9. 44,3
	NFK	1,85;147;186;208. 9,76;95-96;98;159; 161;163-164;184;186. 20,6;27. 30,1. 31,41. 35,5
	NTH	14,3;5-6. 18,15. 46,7. 56,32;47;64
	OXF	38,2. 58,13
	RUT	R15. ELc5
	SHR	4,11,15;18
	SOM	21,18;32. 25,44. 47,13.
	SFK	1,19;48;55. 3,93;98;103. 7,15;27;37; 136;141. 8,34;42. 32,5. 69,3
	SRY	8,27. 29,1

	SSX	3,6. 9,64
	WAR	16,52. 17,26. EN7
	WIL	67,64
	WOR	8,23
Ulf: *see also* Alwin son of		
Ulf, a royal Guard	BKM	18,1
	MDX	7,2
Ulf, a royal thane	BDF	27,1
	BKM	17,17;19;27. 22,1. E1
	CAM	20,1. 23,1;5-6
	ESS	20,12
	MDX	7,6
Ulf, a thane	NFK	4,52. 9,94
	SFK	19,2. 44,1-2
Ulf, Asgar the constable's man	BKM	14,45. 21,8
Ulf, Earl Harold's man	BKM	12,6
Ulf, Earl Waltheof's man	NTH	53,1
Ulf Fenman/Fenisc: *see* Ulf(r) Fenman/Fenisc		
Ulf of Mutford	SFK	7,41
Ulf son of Azor	NTH	2,2-3
Ulf son of Burgred	BKM	12,29
Ulf son of Manni	MDX	7,8
Ulf son of Manni Swart	SFK	6,109
Ulf son of Topi: *see* Ulf(r) son of Topi		
Ulf the priest	SFK	4,13
Ulf: *see also* Ulf(r), Ulfr, Wulfa		
Ulfarr: *see* ?Gulfer		
Ulfgrim, Earl Leofwin's man	BKM	26,10
Ulfgrim: *see also* Wulfgrim		
Ulfkel	CHS	3,6
Ulfkel: *see also* Ulfkell		
Ulfkell	DBY	6,7;36-37;52;56;60;90. 14,4
	NTT	9,11;32;40;41;51;128. 10,6;34. 29,1.
		30,2;6;9;25;30-31;36;45
Ulfkell: *see also* Ulfkel, -ketel, -ketill		
Ulfketel	CHS	3,4. 8,25
	DBY	6,38
	GLS	2,13
	HEF	8,2. 9,2. 31,5
	LEC	44,12-13
	NFK	58. 1,120. 4,47. 7,5;15. 8,63;85. 9,18;
		26-29;33-42;52-55;69-109;111. 21,29.
		35,16. 66,37;93-94
	NTH	14,2. 18,16. 30,12-13. 56,60
	NTT	9,66. 10,32. 15,4;6-7. 30,5;22;33
	SHR	4,4,19. 4,20,27. 4,23,9
	STS	2,22
	SFK	1,53. 4,19. 6,272;274-275. 7,25;27;41;
		119
	WAR	16,44. 17,38
	WOR	15,10. 20,4. 21,2
Ulfketel, a thane	SHR	4,16,2
Ulfketel, Harold's man	NFK	20,19
Ulfketel, Hermer's man	NFK	15,2
Ulfketel, the King's reeve	NFK	9,49-50. 66,106
	SFK	ENf4
Ulfketel: *see also* Ulfkel, -kell, -ketill		
Ulfketill	LIN	C12. 4,2-3;26. 12,4. 14,9. 16,20. 19,1.
		25,7. 26,10. 32,20;27. 34,11. 59,2.
		CW,9

	YKS	C10. 1N10-11;15;17;21;25;28;35;52; 109;133. 1E38-39;45. 1W32;64. 5N30; 35. 5E9. 5W9-10;20;25;29. 6N30;34; 45-46;133;138. 9W9;12;40;47-48;50; 68;111. 10W8;12-13;27. 13W25;35. 13E8;14. 14E31. 21W1;6. 29W1;9;13; 16;20;22. 29E15. 29W36;47. 30W15. CE29. CW12-13. CE35
another Ulfketill	YKS	10W12-13
Ulfketill of Asterby	LIN	CS,39
Abbot Ulfketill (of Crowland)	LIN	CK,48
Ulfketill son of Merewine	LIN	S3
Ulfketill Sveinnbrothir	YKS	CW37
Ulfketill, wife of	YKS	29W36
Ulfketill: *see also* Ulfkel, -kell, -ketel		
Ulf(r) Fenman/Fenisc	CAM	*23,1-6*
	DBY	13,1-2. S5
	HUN	B2
	LIN	T5. 24,1. 42,14-15. 63,25. CW,17. CK, 44
	NTT	S5
	YKS	C36 *and note*
Ulf(r Fenman/Fenisc)	NTT	17,1;4;9;12-16
Ulf(r) son of Topi	LIN	CK,10
	NTH	ELc4
	RUT	ELc19
Ulf(r): *see also* Ulf, Ulfr		
Ulfr	LIN	C7. T5. 2,42. 4,39. 6,1. 24,5;9-10; 12-13;17;20;22;25;36;78;80;82. 25,3. 30,6-8;20;32;36. 32,1;32;34. 34,4. 63, 12;21. CK,63
	YKS	1N40;44;59;100;136. 1E7;11;15;49. 1W52;70. 2B16-17. 2N2-4;6-15. 5E44. 6N1;3-4. 9W12;66. 11N22-23. 13W3;35. 14E11;23-25;31-32;36. 21W10. 29N11. 29W26;48. 30W4-5; 38. CN2. CE2. CW4. CE35
Ulfr: *see also* Arnketill son of		
: *see also* Northmann son of		
: *see also* Svartbrandr son of		
: *see also* Wulfbert brother of		
another Ulfr	YKS	14E31
Ulfr, brother of	YKS	CE35
Ulfr Child: *see* Ulfr Young		
Ulfr Fenman/Fenisc: *see* Ulf(r)		
Ulfr of Ormsby	LIN	CN,27
Ulfr son of Topi: *see* Ulf(r) son of Topi		
Ulfr, Svartbrandr's father	LIN	C2-3;13. CK,18;29
Ulfr the deacon	YKS	CE13. CW28
Ulfr (the deacon)	YKS	5E1
Ulfr Young [= Ulfr Child]	LIN	51,7
Ulfr: *see also* Ulf, Wulfa		
Uluuinchit: *see* Young Wulfwin, Wulfwin Child		
Ulvar	DBY	15,1
Unban	DBY	6,39
	NFK	*24,4*
Unfrid son of Robert	SFK	6,112-122 *and note*
Ungomar: *see* Oger son of		
Unnketill	YKS	9W21

Untan	STS	12,23
	WAR	17,13;69
Urfer	STS	11,14;51-52
	WAR	22,24
Urso	DOR	32,2. 40,4
	HEF	E5
	OXF	7,54. 11,1. EW1
	WAR	3,6. 37,2
	WIL	7,10-11. 25,19;22
	WOR	2,17-18;25-28;35;49;51-54;79. 3,2. 5,
		1. 8,2;4;7-8;9e;10b;11;16-18;27. 9,
		1b-1c;1e;4;5c;6c. 10,12. 11,1-2. 12,2.
		14,2. 15,9. 19,4
Urso of Abetot/the sheriff	GLS	65. 1,48
	HEF	30. 1,10c;13
	WAR	35
	WOR	26. 1,1b-c. 2,3;7-12;75. 8,15;22;24. 9,
		5b. E14;34
Urso (of Abetot/the sheriff)	GLS	E21-22;32;34. EvC25;27;42;106.
		WoB5;7
	HEF	1,38. E4
	WOR	2,8-12. 8,24
Urso of Berchères	BKM	45
Vagn: see Waga, Wagen		
Valhrafn	LIN	7,51. 33,2
Valhrafn, a lawman	LIN	C2-3
Valhrafn a lawman: see also Agmundr son of		
Valhrafn: see also Waleran, Walraven		
Veggi	LIN	34,24. 63,8. CW,18
	YKS	9W49
Veikr	YKS	14E31
Venning [rectius Wening]	SSX	9,11
Venning [rectius Wening], a man-at-arms	SSX	9,8
Venning [rectius Wening] the priest	SSX	9,6;14;26
Vestarr	YKS	9W135;139
Vestarr: see also Wester		
Vicking	BKM	23,9
Vicking: see also Viking, Vikingr, Wicking		
Vifli	YKS	1E5-6
Vigleikr	LIN	22,22. 38,8;10. CS,12;36
Vigleikr, brother of Aki, son of Siward	LIN	T5
Viking	DEV	19,8-9;22;26;38;45. 34,12;29-30;52;56
	SFK	7,108. 16,22;26
Viking, Earl Harold's man	CAM	14,75
Viking: see also Vicking, Vikingr, Wicking		
Vikingr: see Vicking, Viking, Wicking		
Vikings [an erroneous entry]	HAM	2,15
Vitalet	HAM	23,3
Vitalis	DEV	36,13. 42,9;13;24
	DOR	29,1
	ESS	28,9. 34,18;20
	HEF	29,13
	KEN	2,16;21. 5,43;139-140. 7,23
	OXF	6,9
	SOM	21,94-95. 33,2. 38,1
	STS	11,27
	WIL	42,2;8;10
Vitalis, a man-at-arms	ESS	23,3
Vitalis, Guy of Craon's man	LIN	57,15;33;48
Vitalis of Canterbury	KEN	C3. 2,14

Vitalis of Colyton	DEV	*16,129*
Vitalis the priest	HAM	1,44
	HUN	D1
	WIL	1,23b
Vitharr	LIN	12,53;57. 67,18-19
Vitharr: *see also* Wither		
Vondr: *see* W(igmu)nd		
W.	DEV	16,175
	ESS	4,8;21. 30,16. 37,1;14;19. 41,5;7
	NFK	8,91-92. 66,2
W. Corbun	ESS	32,11
Count W.	YKS	SW,An2 *and note*
W. de More	SFK	16,3
W. son of Gorham	SFK	67,7
W. the constable	SFK	4,32
Wace	BRK	B9
	CON	5,8,5
	OXF	EBe3
	SRY	3,1
Wacra	SFK	3,102
Wada	DBY	8,2
	DOR	55a,1
	HEF	16,1
	NTT	9,55. 17,3
Wada (son of Aethelgyth)	DOR	30,1
Wadard	BKM	E3
	DOR	4,1
	KEN	D8. P19. 1,3. 5,13-14;55;164-165. 7, 19-20
	LIN	4,9;53;81
	OXF	7,6;14-15;21;24;27;29;32;37-38;41-43; 46;48;65
	SRY	5,27
	WAR	4,3-4
	WIL	4,3
Wadard, the Bishop of Bayeux's man	LIN	4,2;7;23;28;31;39-40;59;74
Wadard's son	OXF	9,6. 29,16
Waddell	CON	5,1,18. 7,1
	DEV	*15,78.* 16,10. 34,3. 36,14
	SOM	9,8
Waddell: *see also* Wadilo		
Wadilo	DEV	*16,48;52;56.* 28,16
Wadilo: *see also* Waddell		
Wado	DEV	15,49-50;73;76;78. 16,48;52;56
	SOM	19,20
	WIL	67,81
Waerstan	HEF	1,52
Waga	STS	12,25
	WAR	22,1-2;4;6-7;9;23
Waga: *see also* Vagn, Wagen		
Wagen	NFK	13,24
Wagen: *see also* Vagn, Waga		
Wailolf	SFK	4,3. 7,67
Wala	NFK	1,61
Waland	NTT	10,1
	WOR	8,14
Walbert	STS	11,41. 12,7;17;23
Walbert, the Bishop of Durham's man	LIN	3,6-7;40
Walchelin, a man-at-arms	YKS	2B18
Walchelin, the Archbishop of York's man	LIN	2,34;36-37;40

Walchelin: *see also* Walkelin
Walcher: *see* Walcher(e)
Bishop Walcher(e)/of Durham   ESS   7,1 *note*
                                             YKS   C2
Walchere   ESS   33,3;11
Walchere: *see also* Walcher(e), Walkhere
Walcra   HRT   34,17
Waldin   DEV   17,7;68;95-96
                                             LIN   22,14. 46,3. 57,18;20. 68,37
                                             YKS   C6-7
Waldin, a thane   SOM   *45,7*
Waldin the artificer   LIN   47
Waldin the Breton   LIN   46. CK,32
Waldin, William of Percy's man   LIN   22,14
Waldwin   SFK   25,60. 29,7
Walefrid, Alfred of Lincoln's man   LIN   27,50
Waleran   DOR   2,6. 8,1
                                             ESS   1,27. 17,1. B6
                                             HAM   29,11. 69,22
                                             NFK   1,63. 8,120. 17,18
                                             SFK   32,16
                                             SRY   1,1f
                                             WAR   13,1
                                             WIL   7,15.
Waleran: *see also* John nephew of
       : *see also* John son of
Waleran, a certain priest   NFK   1,66
Waleran, a man-at-arms   WIL   2,1
Waleran, father of John   ESS   40,9
Waleran (father of John)   ESS   90,46-47
Waleran Hunter   DOR   40 *and note*
                                             HAM   45. 6,16. NF9,14
                                             WIL   37
Waleran: *see also* Valhrafn, Walraven
Walkelin   LEC   2,1-3
                                             NTH   4,5-11. 26,10
                                             NTT   11,24
                                             SHR   4,16
Walkelin: *see also* Robert son of
Bishop Walkelin/of Winchester   BRK   2. B2
                                             BKM   3
                                             CAM   2
                                             ESS   B6
                                             GLS   2,3
                                             HAM   2. 3. 1,16;21. 29,1;9. 41,1. NF2.
                                                   IoW2. ESr
                                             HRT   3
                                             OXF   3. B8. EBe1
                                             SOM   2. 1,27. 8,28. 19,40
                                             SRY   3. 19,12
                                             WIL   2
Bishop Walkelin: *see also* William nephew of
Walkelin, the Bishop of Winchester's nephew GLS   2,3
Walkelin, Walter of Aincourt's man   NTT   11,22
Walkelin: *see also* Walchelin
Walkhere   DOR   39,1
                                             OXF   6,9
Walkhere: *see also* Walcher(e)
Wallo   CON   5,2,30
                                             SOM   25,18

Wallo: *see also* Walo
Walo   SSX   9,18;60
Walo, Hugh son of Baldric's man   YKS   23N31
Walo, Jocelyn son of Lambert's man   LIN   28,5;19
Walo: *see also* Wallo
Walraven, Queen Edith's man   BDF   1,4
Walraven: *see also* Valhrafn, Waleran
W(alscin), brother of Raimer the clerk   SOM   24,35
Walscin of Douai: *see* Walter of Douai
Walter   BDF   18,2. 23,43;56. 25,5-6. 55,12
                                                     BKM   3a,2-5. 12,32;37. 17,5-6
                                                     CAM   14,59. 30,1. 32,36
                                                     CHS   1,22. R6,4
                                                     DEV   1,63. 5,4. 16,27;45-47;123;147. 24,5;
                                                            28-29. 35,25;28. 42,6;16
                                                     DOR   3,18. 37,6-8;9(?)-10. 55,24
                                                     ESS   4,8. 22,8. 24,2;14;28;46. 30,5;7-9;
                                                            22-23. 32,38a. 36,11. 37,13. 90,66.
                                                            B3a
                                                     GLS   75,3. EvO7
                                                     HAM   2,1;20. 3,1. 21,7. 23,9;11;21;29
                                                     HEF   1,18;30;54-55. 6,2. 10,18;43-44;60;66
                                                     HRT   31,5. 33,14
                                                     HUN   19,1
                                                     KEN   1,3
                                                     LEC   13,47;69-71. 15,8;11. 29,5
                                                     LIN   2,33
                                                     NFK   1,61. 7,4;8;12-13;15. 8,30;38;42-43;
                                                            105;118. 9,96;102. 12,5;34-35. 66,61
                                                     NTH   5,2-3. 6a,16. 18,82-83. 23,15. 30,8. 35,
                                                            24. 41,7. 56,49
                                                     OXF   15,4. 21,1
                                                     RUT   EN7-8
                                                     SHR   4,3,1. 4,14,11. 4,19,5
                                                     SOM   35,1;22. 37,5-6. 42,2-3
                                                     STS   8,9;26. 11,68. EW2
                                                     SFK   6,12;44-45;81;90;129;173;191;
                                                            202-204;305-306;308;311;314. 14,23;
                                                            87. 21,35. 33,2
                                                     SRY   33,1
                                                     SSX   2,1e. 8,13. 9,14;75-81;109. 10,1;4-5;
                                                            24;55;58;60;74. 12,18;32
                                                     WAR   12,9. 16,27;65. 18,16. 33,1. 37,8
                                                     WIL   3,2. 24,8-9. 37,2. 41,9
                                                     WOR   2,8-9. 15,11;13-14. 23,7. 26,3
                                                     YKS   6N31. 14E22

Walter: *see also* Osbern son of
       : *see also* R (...) son of
       : *see also* Ranulf son of
       : *see also* Robert son of
Walter, a man-at-arms   DOR   3,13
                                                     SHR   4,11,4. 4,20,8
                                                     WIL   14,1
                                                     WOR   1,1c
Walter, brother of Alfred of 'Spain'   SOM   *35,19*
Walter, brother of Sihere   BDF   33
Walter Canute   NFK   66,107
Walter (Cockerell)   GLS   53,7-8
Walter Cook/son of Gilbert   ESS   67. 1,11
Walter de Risboil/Risbou   SFK   6,28;284-285

Walter (Delamare)	GLS	52,5-6
Walter, Drogo of Beuvrière's man	LIN	30,30
	YKS	14E;42
Walter (Drogo of Beuvrière's man)	YKS	14E19 *note*
Walter, father of Roger of Lacy	HEF	10,3;37;66
Walter, Geoffrey Alselin's man	NTT	12,1
Walter Giffard	BDF	16
	BRK	20. B1;3;9. 1,11. 7,24
	BKM	14
	CAM	17. AppxC
	HAM	69,20
	HUN	12
	NFK	25. 1,19;52;55;57. 66,63
	OXF	20. B9. 28,16. EBe3
	SOM	23
	SFK	45
	WIL	31. E3
Walter Hackett	BKM	14,40
Walter, Hugh de Montfort's man	NFK	*23,9*
Walter Hussey	SOM	7,4;*10. 8,26*
	WIL	B5. *34,1*
Walter, Ivo Tallboys' man	LIN	14,63
Walter, Jocelyn son of Lambert's man	LIN	28,35;42
Walter, Kolsveinn's man	LIN	26,33
Walter, nephew of Durand of Gloucester	HEF	22,5-6
Walter, nephew of Peter the cleric	SFK	*14,87*
Walter of Abbeville, a man-at-arms	KEN	5,128
Walter of Aincourt	DBY	8. B16. S5
	LIN	31. 2,32. CK,14;55;57;59
	NTH	38
	NTT	11. S5
	YKS	19. SW,Sf12
Walter of Bainton	SOM	*24,17*
Walter of Beauchamp	GLS	WoC4;6
Walter of Bec	BKM	14,22
Walter of 'Burgh'	GLS	EvQ29
	WOR	2,69
Walter (of) Burgundy	DEV	*25,1;3-4*
Walter of Caen	NFK	7,3. 66,57
	SFK	4,15. 6,5;7;67 (*but see note*); 90;98-99;
		103;143;191;245;247;301;316. 25,61
Walter (of Caen)	ESS	44,4
W(alter) of Caen	SFK	6,93;162;165;168-170;264;265 *note*
Walter of Cambremer	KEN	*M10*
Walter of Clais	CAM	AppxF; N
Walter of Claville/of Glanville	CON	1,19
	DEV	24. 1,63 *note; 66*
	DOR	41
Walter of Claville: *see also* Gotshelm brother of		
Walter of Dol	NFK	6,1;5-6
	SFK	4,15. 6,212;215. 14,146. 16,34. 31,34
		note
Walter/Walscin of Douai	DEV	23
	DOR	39
	ESS	52
	KEN	5,32
	SOM	24. *8,7;11;34.* 21,4. 46,5
	SFK	31,34 (*but see note*)
	SRY	23
	WIL	36

	BKM	29
	HAM	46. 9,1
	MDX	11
	SRY	22. 1,2
Walter son of Poyntz	BRK	30
	GLS	55. 2,8. EvK230. EvM3
	OXF	45. 1,6
Walter son of Richard	GLS	EvK1
Walter son of Richere	SFK	6,94
Walter son of Roger/the sheriff/of Gloucester	GLS	56. 3,2. EvK1. EvL1. WoB16
	HAM	47
Walter, son of the wife of Ralph the chaplain	HEF	34,2
Walter, son-in-law of Gilbert son of Thorold	WOR	20,6
Walter son-in-law of Hugh son of Baldric: *see* Walter (of Rivers)		
Walter, the Bishop of Lincoln's man	LIN	7,39-40
Walter the bowman	GLS	58. W3;9
	SOM	*32,1*
Walter the butler	DEV	*16,123*
Walter the canon	MDX	3,29
Walter the crossbowman	SFK	6,191;238
Walter the deacon	DOR	24,5
	ESS	42. 1,27
	GLS	57
	NFK	1,64. 10,19
	SFK	41. *21,35*. 25,24
Walter the deacon: *see also* Theodoric brother of		
Walter the Fleming: *see* Walter of Flanders		
Walter the monk	BDF	55,8
	CAM	42,1. AppxJ
Walter the steward	DEV	*24,4;13*
Walter the vinedresser	SRY	21,3
Walter the wild	DEV	*24,9-10;31*
Walter Thunder	DOR	*55,16;42;44*
Walter (Thunder)	DOR	55,24
Walter Ti(r)rel(l)	ESS	23,38
	SOM	*3,1-2*
Waltheof	DBY	6,58
	WAR	16,35-37;45
	WIL	25,8
	YKS	C27 *and note.* 5N24;36;44-46;55;62;65; 72;75. 5E64-66. 5W38
Earl Waltheof	BDF	6,2. 23,17. 40,3. 53,31. E3
	BKM	5,10. 53,2
	CAM	1,6. 13,3;11-12. 21,7-9. 25,8. *26, 34-35.* 32,14;40. 36,1. 37,1-2. 38,3;5. 39,1-3. 40,1. 41,8;11-16. 43,1. *44,1*
	DBY	6,40
	ESS	55,1
	HRT	19,2
	HUN	2,8. 20,9. D3;11-12;18
	LEC	13,67. 14,16. 40,1-7
	LIN	T5. 56,11;13-14;17
	MDX	24,1
	NTH	56,1-6;20a-k;22;39
	RUT	R7;11-12. ELc11;13-14
	SRY	6,4
	YKS	10W41
Warenbold	NFK	13,15. 66,24

Warengar	DOR	40,1
	ESS	39,3. 43,1-2
	SFK	3,59. 7,63-65;66 *and note*; 67-68. 16,12;38-39. 38,5;21
War(engar)	SFK	16,16-17
Warengar: *see also* Warenger		
Warenger	NFK	9,199;202. 43,1-3
Warenger: *see also* Warengar		
Warhelm	KEN	5,164
Warin	BRK	7,11;41
	CHS	R1,43. R3,1
	DEV	17,31. 19,27;34;42;44
	ESS	34,9. 35,5
	LEC	17,11;28. 24,3
	LIN	18,31
	NFK	66,90
	SHR	4,14,18-20
	STS	11,55-56
	SFK	6,64;304. 14,15;66. 34,4
	SSX	11,40;45;53;65;87;94. 12,6
	WAR	7,1. 16,50. 17,61. 22,17
Warin: *see also* Gilbert son of		
: *see also* Robert son of		
Warin, a man-at-arms	CHS	R5,6
Warin Cook	NFK	*6,4.* 7,20
Warin, Earl Roger's man	SSX	6,1
Warin, Ilbert of Lacy's man	YKS	9W2
Warin of Soham	CAM	AppxA
Warin son of Burnin	SFK	4,20-29 *and note*. 6,296
Warin the bowman	WIL	68,30
Warin the priest	CAM	AppxL
Warin (the sheriff)	SHR	4,3,8;71
Warin: *see also* Warin(g), Waring		
Warin(g)	NFK	*6,4.* 32,2-7
Waring	NFK	6,7. 20,6
	SSX	8,11. 9,1-2;4
Waring: *see also* Warin		
Warmund	DOR	8,3
	SOM	1,35. 8,5. *10,2.* 19,71. 21,98. *22,19.* 25,4;56
Warmund Hunter	CHS	FT3,3
Warner	BDF	23,30
	DBY	7,5-6
	ESS	20,2. 23,2. 24,21;43;47
	HEF	19,1
	NTT	15,10
	SOM	26,7
	SFK	67,5-6;8
	SSX	10,115. 12,50
	WIL	32,11
Warner, Guy of Craon's man	LIN	57,11;13;19
Warner, Richard's man	ESS	90,77
Warner, William Peverel's man	NTT	10,25;35
Wastret	NFK	*1,130*
Waswic the reeve	GLS	W2
Waswic's son	GLS	W4
Watson: *see* Robert son of		
Waua	KEN	5,167
Wazelin	DBY	6,39
	LEC	14,14

	NFK	8,44
	WAR	19,3;5
Wazelin, Drogo of Beuvrière's man	YKS	14E40
Wazelin, Geoffrey of la Guerche's man	LIN	63,7
Wazelin, the Bishop of Bayeux's man	NTT	7,1
Weland	DEV	3,76
Weleret	YKS	C10
Wending [misprint for Weneling]	BDF	23,46
Wenelinc(g)	SFK	67,22
Weneling: see also Wending, Wenelincg		
Wenesi	WIL	51,1. 67,80
Wenesi's wife	WIL	67,80
Wenesi: see also Wynsi		
Wening: see Venning		
Wenric	OXF	9,3;5
	WAR	EG10
Wenric: see also Wynric		
Werno of Poix, a monk	SFK	14,68
Werun	SSX	13,18
Wesman, a man-at-arms	KEN	5,128
Wesman	SRY	25,2
Wester	NFK	50,9. 57,1;3
Wester: see also Vestarr		
White	SFK	7,117
Wibald	BKM	50,1
Wiberga	ESS	39,1
Wibert	BKM	17,23
	KEN	2,21. 5,205
	NTH	26,11
	SSX	9,3;5;17;34;48-51;123
	WAR	EBW3
	WIL	68,24
Wibert the clerk	HAM	2,20
Wibert the priest	BRK	38,6
Wibert: see also Wigbeorht, Wigbert		
Wicard	ESS	24,27;56
Wicga	BKM	17,11
	CHS	9,21
	ESS	B3a
	SHR	4,3,29. 4,11,7. 4,14,1;4;7;18
	YKS	29W1;10
Wicga, a royal thane	BKM	14,17
Wicga, King Edward's man	BKM	12,15
Wicga, Oswulf son of Fran's man	HRT	15,7
Wicga: see also Wiga		
Wicking	WAR	28,10. 44,5;9
Wicking: see also Vicking, Viking, Vikingr		
Wictric	BRK	31,6
	DBY	6,7
Wictric: see also Wihtric		
Widald, Guy of Craon's man	LIN	57,10
Widard	GLS	G4
	HEF	1,10b. 22,5;8. E9
	SHR	4,28,4. 7,3
	SFK	25,104
	SSX	12,14
Widard: see also Widhard		
Widder	BDF	55,9
Widegrip [for Wilgrip]	STS	11,32 and note

Widelard	ESS	23,10;42. 90,52;75
	NTH	55,4
Widhard	LEC	13,61
Widhard: *see also* Widard		
wife of Alwin	HUN	29,6
wife of Brian	MDX	3,3
wife of Engelbald	DEV	3,86-88
wife of Hervey	DEV	16,156
wife of Hervey of Helléan	DEV	44 *note*
wife of Richard of Tonbridge: *see* Rothais		
wife of Richard son of Gilbert: *see* Rohais		
Wiflet (fem.)	GLS	1,4
	WIL	49,1
Wiflet (fem.): *see also* Wigflaed		
Wig, a royal thane	BDF	35,1. 36,1
Wiga	GLS	68,12
Wiga: *see also* Wicga		
Wigar	BRK	65,11
Wigar: *see also* Wihtgar, Withgar		
Wigbeorht	YKS	13W27;35-36
Wigbeorht: *see also* Wibert, Wigbert		
Wigbert	CHS	R1,29
Wigbert: *see also* Wibert, Wigbeorht		
Wiger	SHR	3f,3
Wigflaed (fem.): *see* Wiflet		
Wighen Delamere	CAM	*14,61.* AppxB
Wiglaf	BKM	B10
Wiglaf, a thane	BKM	4,30
Wiglaf, Earl Leofwin's man	BKM	4,34-35
Wiglaf, Earl Leofwin's thane	BKM	4,37
Wigmer	SFK	26,10
Wigmer: *see also* Wimer, Wymer		
Wigmund	LIN	14,6;101
Wigmund, Count Alan's man	LIN	12,18;20;31
Wigmund, Ivo Tallboys' man	LIN	14,5;64-65
Wigmund, Roger of Poitou's man	LIN	16,2
Wigmund, the Bishop of Bayeux's man	LIN	4,38
Wigmund: *see also* Wimund		
W(igmu)nd	LIN	14,101 *and note*
W(igmu)nd: *see also* Vondr		
Wigot	BRK	33,9. 41,2
	BKM	12,1
	GLS	64;1;3
	HRT	6,1
	HRT	19,1
	MDX	7,3-5;7
	OXF	28,2. 35,1;18;31
	SHR	1,5
	SRY	29,2
	SSX	11,15. 12,21. 13,30
	WAR	11,1
	WIL	28,9;12
Wigot: *see also* Alfred nephew of		
: *see also* Thorold nephew of		
Wigot, King Edward's huntsman	BDF	52,2
Wigot of Wallingford	BKM	23,7;12;33
	HAM	69,40 *note*
Wigot the priest	DEV	*3,7*
Wigstan	ESS	B3a
Wigstan: *see also* Wistan		

Wigulf	NFK	8,132. 10,64
	SFK	7,67-68. 8,56. 38,4
Wigwin	NFK	4,30
Wihenoc	DEV	39,2;7-8
	GLS	32,9
	NFK	1,61. 8,29. 9,233. 21,1;5;7-8;12-15;32; 35. 66,44;49-50;52
Wihenoc, a man-at-arms	NFK	*15,14*
Wihenoc of Burley	NFK	66,36
Wihomarch	CON	1,1. 5,24,13-14
Wihomarch: *see also* Wiuhomarch, Wymarc		
Wihtbert	NTH	45,4
Wihtgar: *see* Wigar, Withgar		
Wihtlac	HAM	23,63;65. NF6,2. 9,12;16;31;33. IoW9, 16;23
Wihtmer	SFK	2,7. 7,84;106-107;108(x3);109-110; 112-114
Wihtnoth	DOR	35,1
Wihtnoth: *see also* Wisnoth		
Wihtred	NFK	1,130 *and note.* 65,14
Wihtred the priest	SFK	1,52
Wihtric	HAM	68,11
	SHR	4,3,27. 4,25,2
	STS	11,10
	SFK	1,102. 7,61;76;83;120. 16,20
Wihtric, Harold's man	SFK	7,119
Wihtric of Carlewuda	SFK	6,110
Wihtric: *see also* Wictric		
Wilard	SFK	25,84
Wilbert	WOR	23,1
Wilfred	BKM	57,14
	KEN	5,1
Wilgrim	LIN	12,7. CW,15
Wilgrip	SHR	4,3,4. 4,23,1
	STS	11,32;65
	SFK	29,4
Wilgrip: *see also* Widegrip		
Willa	NTH	23,8;11
William	BDF	42. E5
	BRK	1,7. 7,12;14;20. 18,1. 33,1-2;5. 36,1. 54,3. 65,18
	BKM	5,5;9;15. 12,5. 13,4. 14,20;24. 23, 24-25;31
	CAM	32,34. AppxD; L
	CHS	B4. A13-14;17-18. 1,22. 2,23. 3,3-5;7. 27,3. FT3,5. R1,43. R3,1
	DBY	6,90
	DEV	16,42;97-103;146. 17,6;8;19;50-52;79; 83-90;93;107. *24,22*(?). 34,33;35-37; 42. 39,9;11-13;16. 41,2. 51,3-5
	DOR	2,4. 3,11. 34,8;12. 55,2;8;15a.
	ESS	3,1-3. 4,9-10;12. 9,4. 30,14;20;36; 40-41. 32,34. 36,7. 37,18
	GLS	69,3-4;8. E11-12
	HAM	2,15;25. 3,1;6;8. 23,49. NF3,7. IoW7, 11. 8,5. 9,13
	HEF	1,62. 10,1;4;6;17;41;57;72
	HRT	4,6-8;20. 24,1-2. 25,1
	HUN	2,3;9
	KEN	9,28

LEC	13,62. 15,10-11;16. 29,13-14;18. 44,3
LIN	2,1;23. 13,20. 16,33. 22,31. 27,7;14; 28-29. 62,2
NFK	7,7. 9,88;98. 13,3. 34,1;17. 43,4. 49,6
NTH	60. 2,2-8;10;12. 4,1;20;33-34. 6a,11. 18,42-66;88-89. 30,10;13-14;17. 35, 25. 44,1. 56,36
NTT	1,64. 2,5. 30,47
OXF	B10. 6,10-12. 15,2. 29,14;19. 33,2. 35, 18;20-21;23. 58,10;14. EN4;5. EW2
RUT	EN20
SHR	4,1,22. 4,8,1-2. 4,23,17
SOM	5,14-15;18;26. 18,1-3. 19,76. 21,6; 33-34;48-49;51-52;54;65;67-68;83;90. 22,15-16. 23,1
STS	2,22. 8,20-22;28;30
SFK	3,57. 4,19. 6,250;265. 19,16. 29,7;9. 41,11. 53,2. 66,3
SRY	1,3. 3,1. 8,4
SSX	3,7. 9,6;14-16;32-33;84;113-114;124. 10,1-2;11;21-22;25;27;38;42;47;53;58; 64;68;78;80-81;83;89;99-101;109-110; 117. 11,2;16;35;43-44;77;81-83;91;98; 102-107;114. 12,36. 13,7;11
WAR	12,6. 16,47. 17,16;23;50. 18,9. 22,22. 28,14. 29,5. 30,2. 37,3;9
WIL	2,5. 8,6-8. 22,1;5. 24,12. 26,2. 32,13. 50,1;4. 68,4. E3
WOR	1,2. 2,25. 8,26c. 25,1. 26,4;8;12. 27,1
YKS	1W63-64;66-67
NFK	10,7;52. 15,9. 19,6

W(illiam)
William: *see also* Hugh son of
    : *see also* Ilbert brother of
    : *see also* Richard son of
    : *see also* Robert son of

William, a man-at-arms	DOR 3,13
	HEF 19,1
	SSX 3,2. 11,3. 13,6;9;42
	WIL 2,10
	WOR 1,1c
William, a soldier	YKS 13W36
(a third) William	HEF 19,1
William Alis	HAM 49
William, an Englishman	NFK 1,61
another William	HAM IoW8,5
(another) William	HEF 19,1
	SSX 11,102;105
William, Archbishop Stigand's man	CAM *32,8*
William Baderon	GLS G4
	HEF 1,8

William Baderon: *see also* William son of
  Baderon

William Basset	BDF 23,26
William Baynard, nephew of Ralph Baynard	SFK 33,10

William Baynard: *see also* William nephew of
  Ralph Baynard

William Beaufour	BRK 1,5
William Bellett	BRK 1,1
	DOR 1,*19*;30. 57,1;*3*;12-14;19
	HAM 52

William (Bellett)	DOR	34,1-3
William Bertram	HAM	31
William Black	DEV	*16,97*
William Black, the Bishop of Bayeux's man	HRT	42,11
William Blunt	LIN	49. 12,29. CS,15. CN,20
William Bold	ESS	4,3
William Bonvallet	BKM	5,6
	LEC	26
	WAR	29. B2. 17,69 *note*
William Brant	NFK	8,16
William Breakwolf	GLS	36. EvK116
William, brother of Bishop Gundulf	KEN	*2,11*
William, brother of Ilbert	HEF	8,7
William, brother of Jocelyn son of Azor	HAM	IoW1,7
William, brother of Ralph of Pomeroy	DEV	19 *note*
William, brother of Roger Bigot	NFK	9,88
William, brother of Roger of Auberville	HRT	29
William Cardon, Geoffrey de Mandeville's man	ESS	10,5. 20,71. 30,46. 90,34
William Cheever	CON	*5,10*
	DEV	19. 1,11. 5,8. *26,1*
William (Cheever)	DOR	*47,7*
William (Cheever): *see also* Beatrix sister of		
William Cheever's brother	DEV	*19,3*
William Chernet	DOR	*55,10;13-14*
William Cornelian	WIL	66,4. 68,32
William de Alno	SFK	36,1-7;16-17
William (de Alno)	ESS	32,40
	SFK	EE3
William de Mandeville	GLS	EvK1
William de Vere	MDX	3,5
William de Warenne: *see* William of Warenne		
William Delamere	CAM	AppxB
	HRT	28,3;8
	WIL	32,4
William (Devereux)	GLS	39,13-14
Earl William/William son of Osbern	BRK	44,4
	DOR	40,7
	GLS	G4. S1. W4;16;19. 1,6;8;13;16;19; 34-35;53-56;59-62. 2,10. 16,1. 35,2. 56,2. E2;5
	HAM	1,27. 2,17. 21,7. 69,12-13. IoW6,10. EW1
	HEF	1,3-5;39-40;44-46;61;65;72. 2,8. 8,1. 9,1-2. 10,1;41;50;66. 19,1. 25,9. 29,1; 18. 31,1;7. E2-4
	HUN	14,1
	OXF	59
	SHR	6,3
	SSX	12,9(?)
	WIL	1,3;20-21
	WOR	1,1b. 6,1. 11,2. 23,8. E1-2;4-6. EG1
William, Earl Hugh's man	LIN	13,17
William Follet	KEN	2,39;*40.* 3,22
William Froissart	BDF	23,20-21
William Gerald	SOM	*22,27*
William, Gilbert of Ghent's man	LIN	24,24
	NTT	17,3;7
William Goizenboded	GLS	34. EvK116. EvN14
	WAR	EG11
	WOR	25

William Goulafre	SFK	6,10-11;14;25;65-66;138-141;206
W(illiam) Goulafre	SFK	6,271;293
William Gross	BDF	25,8
	NFK	66,61
William Hard	WIL	26,22
William Hastings	GLS	EvN5
William, Hermer's man	NFK	1,61
William, Hervey de Vere's man	NFK	1,61
William, Hugh son of Baldric's man	YKS	23E9
William Hurant	SFK	25,7
William Hussey	SOM	*1,28. 5,43. 7,8. 37,6.* 45,7
William, Ilbert of Lacy's man	YKS	9W2
William (Ilbert of Lacy's man)	YKS	9W19 *note*; 37;39;95
King William	BDF	32,1;15. 46,1. 56,2-3
	BRK	41,6
	BKM	3a,1. 56,1
	DEV	C3. 1,1-2;*23*; 41. *5,5. 19,35*
	DOR	3,6
	ESS	1,25;27. 3,11. 5,6-7. 6,9;11. 8,8. 20,41; 52;56. 24,43;48;55;59;65-66. 30,16; 18. 42,7. 52,2. 66,1. 79,1. 83,1. 90, 64-65
	GLS	2,4. 78,9
	HAM	53,2. 67,1
	HRT	36,19
	KEN	D7
	NFK	1,2;4;120-121;144;230. 9,5;79. 10,67; 77. 14,16. 15,1. 17,18. 21,13-14. 52,3
	OXF	1,6. 28,24
	STS	11,37
	SFK	1,110. 8,51. 18,1. 25,1. 76,4;6
	WIL	25,23. 32,17
King William: *see* Richard son of		
William, Kolsveinn's man	LIN	26,35;47-48;53
William Leofric/son of Leofric	BRK	EW1
	ESS	59
	GLS	38
	OXF	46
	WIL	49,1a
W(illiam) Leofric/son of Leofric	ESS	90,82
William Leofric: *see also* William (son of) Leofric		
William Lovett	BDF	41
	BRK	26. B3
	LEC	27
	NTH	37
William Malbank	CHS	8. S1,7. FD3
	SHR	4,15. E1
William (Malbank)	DOR	27,2-11
William Malet/father of Robert Malet	LIN	14,29
	NFK	9,211. 20,29 *note*. 66,60-62
	SFK	3,94-95;98 *note*; 100;101 *note*. 4,42. 6, 11. 7,8;15-16;17 *note*; 36;138-140;143; 148. 16,6;15 *note*; 30. 19,16. 26,13. 28, 6. 31,20. 45,2. 51,2 *note*. 52,1. 67,2;4; 19-21;28;30. 75,4. 77,4
	NFK	1,197. 4,39. 30,2
	YKS	CN3-4. CE13;15;17;19-23;26;30. CW2-3;25-32
W(illiam) Malet	NFK	8,12. 17,52. 35,16. 66,62

	SFK	3,39-40. 6,93;159. 7,26;33;131;133. 8, 42. 18,1. 67,15-16;31
William (Malet)	SFK	3,99;144;146. 38,6. 67,29
William Mauduit	HAM	35. 27,1
William, nephew of Bishop Walkelin	SRY	19,12
William, nephew of Geoffrey de Mandeville	CAM	*22,1*
William, nephew of Ralph Baynard	SFK	33,10
William, Odo the crossbowman's man	LIN	48,6
William of Adisham	KEN	2,42. *3,8*
William of Aller	DEV	16,97-103
William of Anneville	HAM	21,4
William of Arques	KEN	2,21;*25*. 5,128
	SFK	47. 6,192. 31,20
William of Auberville/brother of Roger	HRT	29
	SFK	30. 29,8. 76,14
(William of Audley) son-in-law of Robert Blunt	WIL	60,1
William of Audrieu	DOR	*34,6*
	WIL	32,2-3
William of Beaufour	WIL	1,23i
William of Bosc	ESS	37,17
	SFK	7,115-116;134. 16,3 (*but see note*). 39,5
W(illiam) of Bosc	SFK	39,6-11
William of Bosc-le-hard	BKM	18,3
William of Bosc-le-Hard: *see also* Roger (brother of)		
William of Bourneville	NFK	9,131
	SFK	7,56-59;117;120-121. 76,15
W(illiam) of Bourneville	SFK	1,11. 7,118-119. 62,7
William of Boursigny	ESS	9,13
W(illiam) of Bouville	SFK	21,95. 32,13;15 *note*
William of Bouville, son of Saxwalo of Bouville	SFK	16,11. 32,1-2; 19;31
William of Braose/a man-at-arms	BRK	25
	DOR	37. 19,10
	HAM	33
	SRY	20
	SSX	13. 2,10. 3,2. 11,71. 12,20-21;23; 28-29;47
	WIL	33. 2,1
William of Caen	SFK	6,67 (*but see note*)
William of Cailli/Cailly	BRK	29
	CAM	*18,7*. AppxH
William (of Cailly)	NFK	8,18
William of Cairon	BDF	4,2;6-8. 21,5;8-9;17. 24,28
William of Cairon's father	BDF	4,2
William of Castellion	BKM	B11
Abbot W(illiam, of Cerne?)	DOR	*11,16*
William of Chernet	HAM	23,1-2 *note*; 3;53-54. NF10,1
William of Chippenham	CAM	AppxA
William of Cholsey	BKM	17,20
William of Colleville	YKS	13E1;13
William of Courseulles	SOM	*19,12*
William of Daumeray	DOR	*55,19-20*. 57,4;11
	SOM	*21,36-37*
William of Donnington	GLS	EvE25. EvO6
Bishop William/of Durham	BDF	5
	BRK	4
	ESS	7
	LIN	3. 1,9. 14,72. 29,6-8. CK13;39;52. CN21;25;29-30. CS9;15;19-22;32
	NTH	3

	LIN	22. 7,13. 27,10. 28,26. CS,7;26;30;32. CN,24. EN,3
	NTT	21,3
	YKS	13. C10. 3Y1;3. 4N1. 4E2 *note*. 30W2. CN1. CE25;27;29-30. CW25;31;33;35; 40. SW,Sk18. SW,BA3-4;12. SW,Sf6; 19;23;25-26;30. SW, An4-7;17. SW,Bu9;19-21;32-33;35-36;39-44. SN,L1;11;21-22;25. SN, D3;5-9;13. SN,B22. SN,Bi4-5. SE, Wei4-5;7. SE,Sn4-6;9-10. SE,Wa1. SE,P1-2;4;7. SE,Tu6-7
William of Percy's wife	HAM	25
William of Picquigny: *see* William son of Ansculf		
William of Poilley	DEV	21
William of Poitou	DEV	34,27-28;33 *note*; 35 *note*
	KEN	M15
W(illiam) of Say	GLS	EvK1
William of Seacourt	GLS	EvE10. EvO25
William of Sept-Meules	SSX	9,11;106
William of Thaon's son	KEN	5,90;171
Bishop William/of Thetford	NFK	10. 1,57;61;68;128
	SFK	18-19. 6,70-72;76-77;308;311;8,42. 31, 3;5-6
Bishop W(illiam/of Thetford)	SFK	14,101;121
William of Vatteville/Watteville	ESS	B3n
	SFK	54
	SRY	8,7-8;13;27
	SSX	12,15;23;35;39;48
W(illiam) of Vatteville/Watteville	ESS	22,7
(William of) Vatteville/Watteville	SFK	70,1
William of Vauville	DEV	1,15. 3,32
William of Verly	YKS	2W6
William of Warenne/de Warenne	BDF	17. E6
	BRK	B1
	BKM	15
	CAM	18
	ESS	22. 7,1. 9,10. 10,2. 40,3
	HAM	34
	HUN	13
	LIN	15. CK,38
	NFK	8. 1,11;195;215. 16,1. 19,8. 66,47;64; 67
	OXF	22. EBu1
	SHR	4,13
	SFK	26. 8,55. 76,18
	SSX	12. 10,118. 13,1-3;46
	YKS	12. CW7-10. SW,Sf1
W(illiam) of Warenne	NFK	1,1;57;211. 4,3. 15,1;7-8. 16,5. 31,29. 40,1
	SFK	7,25. 21,1
William of Warenne: *see also* Frederick brother of		
William of Warenne: *see also* Ranulf nephew of		
William of Watteville: *see* William of Vatteville		
William of Watteville's wife	SSX	12,37-38
William Pandolf	SHR	4,14
	STS	8,19. ES1
William (?Parler)	GLS	E21. EvC25. WoB5

William Peche/Petch	ESS	35,6. B3a
	SFK	25,6;91
W(illiam) Peche/Petch	ESS	23,4
	NFK	9,25
William Peret	SFK	25,89
William Peverel	BDF	22. 3,17. 32,5
	BRK	24
	BKM	16
	DBY	7. 1,29;32;35-36
	ESS	48. 18,32;34
	HAM	2,20
	LEC	25. 33,1. 44,2
	NTH	35. B15. 1,10. 2,1. 56,66. EB4
	NTT	10. B9;18
	OXF	23. B9. EN12
	RUT	EN12
William (Peverel)	BDF	42,1
William, Ralph of Buron's man	NTT	15,3;5
William, Ralph of Mortimer's man	LIN	36,3
William, Robert of Tosny's man	LIN	18,12
William, Roger of Bully's man	NTT	9,26;111
William Shield	SFK	6,63. 7,75
	WIL	1,16. 2,4. 68,20
William (Shield)	WIL	15,1-2
William son of Ansculf/of Picquigny	BRK	22
	BKM	17
	CAM	36
	HUN	23
	MDX	19
	NTH	36
	OXF	21. ES
	RUT	EN13
	STS	12. B8. EN3
	SRY	21. 19,43
	WAR	27. EBS2-3. EBW3-5. EN5-6
	WIL	24,19 *and note*. 68,22;23 *note*
	WOR	23. 1,1d
William son of Azor	HAM	IoW7. IoW1,5;7
William son of Azor's nephew	HAM	IoW7,7
William son of Baderon	GLS	32. G4. 1,13. 16,1. 19,2. E7;35. EvK1
	HAM	50
	HEF	15. 1,1;7;48
	WOR	8,9f
William son of Baderon: *see also* William Baderon		
William son of Bonnard	SSX	13,46;53
William son of Boselin	NTH	B16
William son of Brian	ESS	4,2
William son of Constantine	BKM	33
	ESS	74
William son of Corbucion	BRK	27
	OXF	ES1
	STS	12,30. EW5
	WAR	28. B2
	WOR	24. 8,14. E33
William son of Geoffrey	KEN	D8. M22
William son of Gross	ESS	1,2. 11,1. 27,2. 88,2. 90,15;18
	KEN	9,48
	SFK	31,50
William son of Guy	GLS	35

	SOM	28
	WIL	38
William son of Hermenfrid	KEN	*3,15*
William son of Leofric: *see* William Leofric		
William son of Mann: *see* William son of Magne/Manne		
William (son of) Leofric: *see also* William Leofric		
William son of Magne/Manne [mistaken for Mann or Manni]	BKM	34
	HAM	48
	SSX	13,14
	OXF	47
William son of Manni's wife	HAM	48
William son of Mauger	NTH	36,4
	WAR	EN6
William son of Nigel	BKM	12,14
	CHS	9. FD4
	LIN	13,10
William son of Norman/Northmann	GLS	37
	HEF	16. 1,1;4;10c;28;38;53-55;63
	SSX	13,19-21
William son of O(d)ger	BKM	4,16
	KEN	D8. M3. 5,33-34
William son of Odo	ESS	24,11
William son of Osbern: *see* Earl William		
William son of Osmund	BRK	B7
William son of Rainward	BDF	25,7
William son of Ranulf	SSX	13,22;26-27;29;54-55
William son of Reginald	BDF	25,2
	SFK	26,12b;15
	SSX	12,30-32;56
William son of Richard	BRK	28
	GLS	1,11. EvK10
	HEF	E1
	WOR	E35
William son of Robert	KEN	5,78
	SOM	*21,82*
William son of Scaldward	NTT	2,4
William son of Stur	HAM	51. S3. IoW6. IoW1,7;11
William son of Theodwald	KEN	D8. M19
William son of Thorold	SRY	29,1
William son of Wimund	DEV	*16,44*
William son of Wimund's wife	DEV	*16,44*
William Speke	BDF	25. 17,1. 56,2
William, steward of the Bishop of Coutances	BDF	3,5;9
	NTH	EB1
William Tallboys	LIN	66
William, the Abbot of Peterborough's man	LIN	8,31
William the archer	HAM	53
William the artificer	HUN	26. 19,15
	NTH	B17
William, the Archbishop of York's man	LIN	2,5;8-9;17;27
William the bald	GLS	G4
William, the Bishop of Durham's man	LIN	3,50;53
William, the Bishop of Lincoln's man	LIN	7,51
William the Breton	CAM	*19,1*
	HUN	28,1
William the bursar, a man-at-arms	KEN	*2,10*
William the chamberlain	BDF	40. 1,2b;3
	BKM	32
	CAM	1,18

	ESS	6,10
	GLS	33
	MDX	1,4. 3,8. 4,11. 9,1
	SFK	1,97-99
	SRY	21,1
	WAR	EG10
William the clerk/cleric	SHR	2,1
	SSX	3,5
William the deacon/the Bishop's nephew	BRK	1,9
	ESS	66. B3h *and note*
William the Englishman	NFK	1,61
William the falconer	KEN	12,2
William the forester	HAM	IoW7,20
William, the King's son	DOR	3,6
William the porter	DEV	51,1 *and note*
William the priest	LIN	56,23
	WOR	8,8
William the scribe	GLS	G4
William the usher	DEV	5,9. 51,2;3-4 *note*; 5-12
	NTT	29
William the usher: *see also* Robert son of		
William, Waldin the artificer's man	LIN	47,3-7
William, William of Percy's man	LIN	22,31
William: *see also* Wirelm		
Wimer	DOR	39,2
Wimer: *see also* Wigmer, Wymer		
Wimerus: *see* Wimer, Wymer		
Wimund	BDF	2,8. 23,24;33;38
	BRK	7,36;42
	ESS	28,16
	HRT	16,4;11
	NFK	31,11
	OXF	7,51. 40,1
Wimund: *see also* William son of		
Wimund of Tessel	BDF	23,37-38
Wimund: *see also* Wigmund		
Wine	CON	5,4,19
Winegot	WIL	24,26
Winegot the priest	SOM	8,12
Winemar	DEV	20,12. 25,13
	NTH	40. B20;34. 4,15-16. 39,16. 44,2. 48, 12. 56,54-57
Winemar of Hanslip/the Fleming	BKM	46
	NTH	56,51;65
Winemar: *see also* Winemer		
Winemer	ESS	B3a
	NFK	66,68
Winemer: *see also* Winemar		
Winge	ESS	60,1
Winman	SSX	11,101
Winstan	CHS	R1,8
	GLS	37,5
	SSX	9,17;123;128
Winstan: *see also* Wynstan		
Winterled	CAM	26,20
Winterled: *see also* Winterlet		
Winterlet	CHS	8,9
Winterlet: *see also* Winterled		
Wintrehard, Walter of Aincourt's man	LIN	31,18
Winulf	SOM	19,87

Wirelm [for Wilelm = William]	KEN	9,6
Wisnoth [for Wihtnoth]	GLS	43,2
Wisnoth: *see also* Wihtnoth		
Wistan	NFK	1,202
Wistan: *see also* Wigstan		
Withbert, a man-at-arms	SSX	9,1
Wither	NFK	8,1;3
Wither: *see also* Vitharr		
Withgar [error for Wihtgar]	CAM	26,8
	ESS	21,1. 23,2-3;6-15;30-32;34-35;37; 39-42. 90,63-64
	HRT	34,9-10. 37,6-7
	SFK	25,78-102. 7,121. 8,35;46-47;59;63; 66. 16,11;38. 25,2-17 *note*; 19;25; 27-35;37-38;40-49;52;55-56. 29,1. 32, 1. 43,4. 67,1. 72,1. 76,2-5
	WOR	23,7;13
Withgar [= Wihtgar]: *see also* Aelfric son of		
Withgar [= Wihtgar] father (and son) of Aelfric	SFK	25,1 *note*; 60
Withgar [= Wihtgar] of Orwell	HRT	Appx (cf 37,6)
Withgar [= Wihtgar] son (and father) of Aelfric	SFK	25,1;60
Wihtgar: *see also* Wigar, Wihtgar		
Withi	ESS	28,8
Withri	NFK	9,87;142-144;148-149
Withri, Harold's man	NFK	20,19
Wiuhomarch, Count Alan's man	YKS	6N57;100-101 *note*
Wiuhomarch: *see also* Wihomarch, Wymarc		
Wivar	SHR	4,17,3
	STS	11,43. 12,26
Wizo, Drogo of Beuvrière's man	LIN	30,22
	YKS	14E7
Wodi	DBY	6,56
	STS	1,52
Wonni	HEF	10,8
Woodbill	ESS	B3a
Woodbrown	SFK	6,271. 16,14;32
Woodman	CHS	2,19. 27,2
	DEV	24,18
	HAM	1,W8
	STS	11,39
Wordrou	DEV	24,17
Wulfa	ESS	26,4
Wulfa, a thane	SOM	*19,68*
Wulfa: *see also* Aelfric brother of		
: *see also* Ulf(r)		
Wulfbald	NTH	48,14
	SSX	8,3. 9,25;105
Wulfbald: *see also* Wulfbold		
Wulfbert	CHS	R1,18. FD2,4
	DBY	6,80
	ESS	22,9;12;14-15
	HUN	19,20
	LEC	13,48
	LIN	12,76
	MDX	9,3
	NTT	B11
	YKS	CW1;36
Wulfbert, a lawman	LIN	C2.
Wulfbert, Hugh son of Baldric's man	YKS	23N30
Wulfbert, Ulfr's brother, a lawman	LIN	C3

Wulfbold	SFK	7,65;79;111. 29,10
Wulfbold: *see also* Wulfbald		
: *see also* Wulfheah father of		
Wulfer: *see* ?Gulfer		
Wulfeva (fem.)	BDF	3,5
	BRK	52,1. 53,1
	CAM	19,2-3
	CHS	2,13. 8,43;45
	DEV	3,13-14;16;19;80-81;92. 10,2. 16,92.
		20,12. 28,1
	ESS	B3a(x2)
	HAM	1,8;39. 23,4. 35,9. 69,14;28. NF9,13
	SOM	5,16. 17,4;7
	SFK	3,102. 6,209;212-216;218;222-225;
		227-232. 7,3. 39,4
	SSX	10,100;109. 11,69. 12,49
	WIL	8,10. 24,7. 26,22
Wulfeva Bet(t)eslau	HAM	6,12
	WIL	68,24
Wulfeva (Bet(t)eslau)	DOR	58,1-3
Wulfeva, son of	SFK	6,212
Wulfeva, wife of Finn (the Dane)	ESS	84
Wulfeva (fem.): *see also* Wulfgifu		
Wulfflaed (fem.): *see also* Wulfled, Wulflet		
Wulfflaed, Wulfgeat's mother	LIN	CK,1
Wulffrith	DEV	3,27
Wulffrith: *see also* Wulfrith		
Wulfgar	BRK	17,11
	DOR	55,17
	GLS	37,4
	HAM	NF9,35
	LIN	14,27
	SHR	4,7,2. 4,15,1. 4,19,4;7. 4,26,6
	SOM	21,43;46
	STS	8,9
	SFK	25,48
	SSX	9,93
	WAR	16,33
	WIL	27,20. 29,6-7. 43,1-2
Wulfgar, a monk	SOM	8,26;35
Wulfgar, a royal thane	GLS	1,61
Wulfgar the priest, a thane	CHS	12,2
Wulfgar White	DOR	1,30 *(but see note)*
Wulfgeat	BKM	26,1-2
	CHS	1,11. 7,4. 8,18. 17,3;6-7;9; 11. 18,1-2.
		20,10. 26,4. 27,1
	CON	5,9,1
	DBY	6,7;35-36;43;83;98
	DEV	24,*14*;30. 25,12
	DOR	1,27. 8,6. 26,28;41. 33,5. 54,11. 56,34
	GLS	34,1
	HAM	1,W10. 69,29-31. NF9,8. IoW6,8
	HEF	1,46
	KEN	5,81-82;161
	LEC	3,16
	LIN	3,32;56. 27,37-38. 46,1;3-4. 59,17. 67,
		10-11. 68,27. CK,1;52
	NFK	1,51;88;206. 4,45
	NTH	48,12

	NTT	6,8;11. 9,55;73;102-104;107. 10,55; 64. 20,7. 30,1
	SHR	4,3,2;6;25;36. 4,4,7. 4,14,11;18. 4,19, 10. 4,23,4;6;10-11. 4,25,2. 4,26,4. 4, 27,29
	SOM	19,30
	STS	1,58;59;64. 11,2-3;17;19-22;28;33;36; 38. 17,10;19
	SFK	6,13;15;125. 16,35. 21,48. 35,7
	SSX	10,50
	WAR	40,2
	WIL	26,2;21. 67,79
	WOR	26,16. E6
	YKS	2E8;14-15. 11E2. 13E4
Wulfgeat : *see also* Aelfric son of		
: *see also* Alfgeat son of		
: *see also* Alwin son of		
: *see also* Arnbjorn a relative of		
: *see also* Wulfflaed mother of		
Wulfgeat, a royal thane	BDF	28,1
Wulfgeat, a thane	BKM	25,3
	SHR	4,16,2
Wulfgeat, Askell's man	BDF	23,24
Wulfgeat, father of Alwin	HAM	69,50
Wulfgeat, father of Cola Hunter	HAM	69,52
Wulfgeat Hunter	DOR	*56,16*
	HAM	69,36. IoW1,6;9
	WIL	67,77
Wulfgeat, King Edward's huntsman	WIL	1,5
Wulfgeat, King Edward's man	BDF	53,14
Wulfgeat the priest	LIN	C4;14
Wulfgeat's wife	LIN	3,32
Wulfgeat's wife's mother	LIN	3,32
Wulfgifu (fem.)	LIN	59,18
Wulfgifu (fem.): *see also* Wulfeva		
Wulfgith (fem.)	ESS	B3a
Wulfgrim	LIN	4,39;57. 57,7. CS,5
	YKS	13N19 *and note*
Wulfgrim: *see also* Ulfgrim		
Wulfhard	SFK	7,121
Wulfheah	CHS	1,2. 8,3;42. 15,1. FD8,1
	ESS	30,46. B3a
	GLS	32,8;12. 37,1
	HEF	1,62. 8,7
	HUN	15,1
	NTT	9,82;84;112
	SHR	4,3,2
	STS	1,43;56-57. 11,35;37. 13,2
	WOR	19,11
	YKS	9W68. 10W11-14;16
Wulfheah, a thane	GLS	32,7
Wulfheah, father of Wulfbold	SFK	7,76(x2);79;99-100
Wulfheah, King Edward's steersman	BDF	53,15
Wulfhelm	GLS	32,5. 39,3. 68,12
	STS	17,15
Wulfhere	STS	1,37
	SSX	10,10;66
Wulfhere, Godman's man	SFK	2,17
Wulfhun	SSX	10,31

Wulfled (fem.)

Wulfled (fem.): *see also* Wulfflaed, Wulflet
Wulflet (fem.)
Wulflet (fem.): *see also* Wulfflaed, Wulfled
Wulfmaer

Wulfmaer: *see also* Wulfmer
Wulfmer

Wulfmer, a royal thane
Wulfmer, a thane

Wulfmer, an Englishman
Wulfmer, Askell of Ware's man
Wulfmer Child: *see* Young Wulfmer
Wulfmer Cott
Wulfmer, father of
Wulfmer, Haldane's man
Wulfmer, Harold's thane
Wulfmer, King Edward's priest
Wulfmer of Eaton [Socon]/a royal thane

Wulfmer, Ordwy's man
Wulfmer, Robert son of Wymarc's man
Wulfmer the burgess
Wulfmer, the (King's) reeve
Wulfmer the priest

Young Wulfmer [= Wulfmer Child]

BRK	1,12
SFK	25,78
NFK	9,31
LIN	4,3;9;54-55. 7,19-21. 29,34. CW,9
YKS	9W11;90. CW14
BDF	55,4-5
BRK	22,4
CAM	*14,71.* AppxB
CHS	FD2,2
DEV	3,33;54. 5,9. 16,138;159. 21,8. 23,3. 25,22. 36,23
ESS	4,13. 18,42. 20,26. 22,19-20. 23,35. 25,4;11;13;15;18-19;25. 27,5;12. 46,1. 90,28
GLS	EvK1
HAM	1,37
HEF	23,1
NFK	1,129-130. 21,11. 31,12
NTH	18,7;98-99. 30,16;18
NTT	2,9;10. 9,12;15;33;37;125. 10,65. 30, 12;35;39
OXF	B10
SHR	4,21,8
SOM	1,28. 5,43. 8,15;23
STS	1,62-63. 8,25. 11,2;5. 13,3
SFK	73. 1,110. 2,11. 3,59;95(x2). 6,49;64; 211. 7,16;26;61;76-77;85;89;98. 8, 20-24. 13,3. 16,35. 21,58. 25,10;58;60; 77;84. 35,7-8. 67,2;12. 74,4
SRY	1,14
SSX	9,14;51;107;10,32;11,27
WAR	37,3
WIL	24,16. 25,22. 26,21;23. 48,3. 68,8
WOR	15,8;10-11. 21,1-3. X1
BDF	55,6
NTT	9,69
SFK	8,44;48;55
SOM	*47,13*
HRT	37,4
DEV	16,90
SFK	73,1
SFK	67,11
SFK	8,55
BDF	6,1
BDF	21,1;5-6;9-10;14-15;17. 45,1. 55,12-13
CAM	25,9. 32,10. 42,1
HRT	B3
BDF	53,27
CAM	26,39
BDF	56,4
SFK	73 *note.* 1,7. 74,4;7. 76,13-14
BDF	57,4
BKM	32,1
SFK	*6,110*
SSX	9,46
SSX	10,54

Wulfmer: *see also* Wulfmaer, Wulmer
Wulfnoth

BRK	33,3
CHS	12,1
CON	5,4,3;20. 5,8,3
DEV	3,67-71. 16,17;29. 17,73. 19,42. 21,5; 12. 30,3. 34,51. 39,5. 47,8
GLS	6,9. 31,3
HAM	1,W8;W13. 23,17. 55,2. 57,1. IoW7, 12. 8,8. 9,4;17;22
HEF	10,61. 34,1
KEN	5,49;155;158;167;195;225. 9,22;31;52
LEC	19,19. 44,2
LIN	4,50. 14,39
NFK	3,1. 30,4. 40,1
NTT	10,15;24
SOM	17,8. 19,8. 24,11
SFK	1,55;102. 2,6;9-10;13. 6,121. 7,71;76; 140. 53,6
SRY	19,12
SSX	10,40. 11,16;84
WAR	17,30
WIL	67,76;78

Wulfnoth, a thane   DOR   *55,34*
Wulfnoth Child: *see* Young Wulfnoth
Wulfnoth, Godric the sheriff's man   BDF   23,25
Wulfnoth the priest   SSX   10,14
Wulfnoth the priest, a lawman   LIN   C3;14
Young Wulfnoth [= Wulfnoth Child]   KEN   *2,31*
Wulfnoth, Wulfsi son of Burgred's man   BDF   25,5
Wulfnoth's father   WIL   67,78
Wulfraed: *see* Wulfred
Wulfred

DOR	26,69
HAM	64,2
OXF	43,1-2
SOM	8,20
SFK	8,55

Wulfred: *see also* Gulfered, Gulfer?
Wulfric

BDF	18,5. 55,3
BRK	1,12. 7,10. 44,3
CAM	32,15. AppxF
CHS	1,32. 2,27-28. 5,14. 8,26. 12,3. 13,1. 26,8;11
CON	5,5,8. 5,6,9. 5,24,8
DEV	1,29. 15,74. 16,16;64. 23,3;6;14
DOR	1,31
ESS	20,2;31;60. 22,3. 30,1;30;34. 33,3. 36, 7. 90,5;20;71;77. B3a(x13)
GLS	11,14. 39,15. 45,4. 78,1
HAM	2,4. 23,13;18. 69,18;35. NF9,34. IoW1,14. EW2
HEF	10,40;43
HRT	34,4x
HUN	19,21. 29,5
KEN	M5. *2,11*. 5,41;56;137
LEC	4,1. 10,2
LIN	30,30. 67,9;22
NFK	9,99. 15,12. 26,6. 33,1-2;4;6. 35,7. 66, 99
NTH	2,6. 18,57;66. 24,1

Wulfric Wilde	LIN	3,32. 67,10. CK,52
Wulfric Wilde's wife's mother	LIN	3,32
Young Wulfric [= Wulfric Child]	NTT	S5
Wulfric's brother, wife of	DOR	56,13
Wulfric's father	DOR	56,13;18
	HAM	69,18. EW2
	WIL	67,66-67;72
Wulfrith, a thane	GLS	76,1
Wulfrith: *see also* Thorfrothr son of		
: *see also* Wulffrith		
Wulfrun (fem.)	DEV	3,90. 24,11
	KEN	5,167
	NFK	51,1;3
Wulfrun, a free woman	DEV	28,3
Wulfsi	CHS	9,15. 21,1
	CON	5,24,1-2;7
	ESS	5,7. 27,18. 40,9. 41,7. 72,1-3. B3a(x2)
	HAM	IoW9,19
	KEN	5,140
	LEC	40,36
	NFK	21,26
	NTT	9,36;39;44;46;60;65. 10,29-30. 16,11. 30,31;55
	SOM	*5,59*
	SFK	1,16;19;23;36;46;60;111. 4,20-23. 7,6; 15;24;50;52. 31,33. 36,9. 50,1
	SRY	5,8
	SSX	9,79
	WAR	17,35;54;59
Wulfsi, a royal thane	WOR	26,5
Wulfsi, a thane	SOM	*5,59*
Wulfsi, brother of Wulfric	SFK	1,110
Wulfsi Child: *see* Young Wulfsi		
Wulfsi of Therfield	HRT	Appx
Wulfsi (son of?) Swein	NTT	10,39
Wulfsi son of Burgred	BDF	25,5
Wulfsi the prebendary	BDF	56,9
Wulfsi the priest	KEN	9,2
Wulfsi, two brothers of	SFK	7,24
Young Wulfsi [= Wulfsi Child]	NTT	10,3;16;35.
Wulfsi: *see also* Wulfsige		
Wulfsige	LIN	27,50. 59,12. 67,12
	YKS	5W26;30. 9W29. 29W6
Wulfsige: *see also* Wulfsi		
Wulfstan	DEV	25,27
	ESS	24,62. B3a(x4)
	HAM	2,10. 28,4. 47,2
	KEN	5,14;55
	LIN	4,59
	NFK	8,130. 9,87;144
	NTH	18,41
	NTT	9,31;55
	OXF	35,3;21-22
	STS	12,7;12;20
	SFK	3,81
	SRY	19,9
	SSX	10,41. 11,35
	WAR	17,41;45
	YKS	1E11. 5E32. 9W12;33. 10W27. 11W4. 13W2. 25W6 *note*. CW3

Wulfstan: *see also* Arnketill son of
     : *see also* Godwin son of
Wulfstan, a royal thane   BKM   26,4
Wulfstan, a thane   BKM   7,1
                                               DEV   25,27 *note*
Wulfstan Eadlac   ESS   B3a
Wulfstan of Wateringbury   KEN   D25
Bishop Wulfstan/of Worcester   GLS   3. E19;21-23;26;29. EvC22;38;41.
                                                      EvK80. EvM8. WoA;B;C
                                               OXF   EW1
                                               WAR   3. 36,2. 44,12
                                               WOR   2
Wulfstan son of Wulfwin   KEN   M16
Wulfstan son of Wulfwin's father   KEN   M16
Wulfstan the priest   YKS   CW29
Wulfstan (the priest)   YKS   25W3;6
Wulfwara, a widow   NTH   4,16
Wulfwara (fem.): *see also* Wulfwaru
Wulfward   BRK   59,1
                                               CON   1,1. 5,24,6
                                               DEV   15,24. 16,68. 21,2. 24,13. 28,5-8. 34,
                                                      34
                                               DOR   6,1. 26,14. 34,4. 57,1
                                               ESS   60,3. B3a(x4),t
                                               GLS   1,6;57. 22,1. 34,1. 53,3. 63,2-4. 68,1
                                               HAM   1,3. 3,8. 18,1-2. 23,18;20. 35,3. NF3,
                                                      13. IoW9,9
                                               HEF   1,24. 10,14. 26,1
                                               KEN   5,215
                                               MDX   7,8
                                               NFK   1,153
                                               NTH   4,30-31;33-34
                                               OXF   EN1;2;4;5
                                               SHR   6,20. 7,1
                                               SOM   *1,28*. 2,9. 9,3;6. 21,71. 22,23. 32,7-8.
                                                      47,1
                                               SFK   7,98;118. 8,47. 14,12;19;*20*;39. 29,5.
                                                      39,5. 42,1
                                               SRY   8,15;24. 19,3;30. 21,3
                                               SSX   9,15. 10,103;117. 11,58. 12,15;50. 13,
                                                      12;33
                                               WAR   16,11
                                               WIL   5,5. 25,15. 37,2. 40,1. 63,1. 67,73. 68,
                                                      20
Wulfward: *see also* Edeva wife of
Wulfward (?): *see also* Edward son of
Wulfward, a royal thane   BKM   42,1
Wulfward, a thane   BKM   57,7
                                               SOM   *9,3*
Abbot Wulfward [error for Wulfwold]   SOM   7,10;*14-15*
Wulfward, Asgar the constable's man   HRT   17,11. 24,2. 42,6
Wulfward Child: *see* Young Wulfward
Wulfward Leofed   BDF   20,1
Wulfward, Queen Edith's man   BKM   14,6. 56,2
Wulfward son of Edeva   BKM   B3. 12,31
Wulfward, the King's purveyor   WIL   67,74
Wulfward the priest   ESS   34,37. B3a
                                               HEF   10,64
                                               SSX   9,14
Wulfward Tumbi   SOM   *44,3*

Wulfward White, a royal thane	DOR	8,5. 35,1 (cf 1,30 *note*)
	GLS	60,2
	HAM	10,1
	KEN	D25. 5,114
	MDX	8,5. 10,1-2. 15,2
	OXF	40,3
	SOM	*1,28*;32-35
	WIL	3,1
Wulfward (White, a royal thane)	BRK	50,1
Wulfward White's wife	SOM	*1,28*
Wulfward Wight [error for White]	MDX	8,5. 10,1-2. 15,2
Young Wulfward [= Wulfward Child]	BKM	5,5. 17,31
Wulfward: *see also* Wulfweard		
Wulfwaru (fem.)	SFK	5,8. 35,7
Wulfwaru (fem.): *see also* Wulfwara		
Wulfweard	LIN	57,38
	YKS	6N125
Wulfweard White	LIN	T5
Wulfweard: *see also* Wulfward		
Wulfwen (fem.) [= Wulfwynn]	BRK	65,1
	BKM	24,3. 43,4
	DEV	3,61. 42,15
	DOR	31,1-2
	GLS	E14
	HRT	32,1
	SOM	40,1
	WIL	24,24;27;41
Wulfwen, King Edward's man (fem.)	BKM	24,1
	MDX	20,1
Wulfwen of Creslow	BKM	24,2
Wulfwig: *see* Wulfwige, Wulfwy		
Bishop Wulfwige: *see* Bishop Wulfwy		
Wulfwige [erroneous form] *see* Wulfwig, Wulfwy		
Wulfwin [= Wulfwine]	BRK	7,22;41. 17,12
	BKM	5,19
	CAM	1,15. 29,11
	CON	5,24,7
	DEV	51,10. 52,36
	DOR	56,5
	ESS	4,6-7. 18,26;31. 22,14. 23,34. 30,6;12; 29. 32,23;26;42. 34,21. 35,1-2;4-6; 8-12. 36,9;11. 57,1. 90,3;47. B3a(x12)
	GLS	66,2
	HAM	54,1
	HEF	27,1. 29,14
	KEN	5,43;54;106-107. 9,41
	NTH	17,3. 18,19. 36,4
	SHR	4,3,7. 4,9,2. 4,27,2
	SOM	21,51;68;82. 22,22
	STS	11,47. 16,1. 17,10-11
	SFK	6,211;216;227. 7,92;96. 8,55. 16,41. 25,103. 35,5-6. 62,2. 67,10;13. 74,13. 76,1(x2);21. EE4-EE5
	SRY	5,19. 8,28
	SSX	9,129. 11,28
	WAR	12,1-2;6. 17,1;39;61. 22,8. 27,5. 41,2. EBW3. EN6
	WIL	27,8
Wulfwin: *see also* Wulstan son of	WOR	2,9. 14,1. 23,1;3;11

Wulfwin, a royal thane	CAM	29,1-3;5;7-10
	SFK	35,1. 68,5 *and note*
Wulfwin, Asgar the constable's man	HRT	38,2
Wulfwin Child: *see* Young Wulfwin		
Wulfwin, Earl Edwin's thane	WOR	1,1d
Wulfwin, Earl Harold's man	HRT	34,13
Wulfwin, Earl Harold's thane	HRT	34,24
Wulfwin, Edric of Laxfield's man	SFK	2,17
Wulfwin Hapra	ESS	62,3
Wulfwin, King Edward's huntsman	CAM	4,1
Wulfwin, King Edward's man	BDF	53,34
Wulfwin of Eastwick	HRT	34,24
Wulfwin of Whaddon	BKM	26,6
Wulfwin the canon	BRK	4,1
Wulfwin the mead-keeper, the Abbot of Ely's man	CAM	*3,5.* 17,3
Wulfwin the monk	WAR	9,1
Wulfwin the priest	SFK	1,122d. 6,124;181. 46,7
Wulfwin the summoner	ESS	B3a
Young Wulfwin [for Uluuinchit, = Wulfwin Child]	CHS	9,4
Young Wulfwin [= Wulfwin Child], of Weston	HUN	D10;17-18 (cf 25,1)
Wulfwin: *see also* Wulfwine		
Wulfwin's son	WOR	23,1
Wulfwin's two sisters	ESS	23,34
Wulfwin's wife	WOR	23,1
Wulfwine	LIN	2,34. 62,2
	YKS	13W23
Wulfwine: *see also* Wulfwin		
Wulfwold	SOM	25,39
Abbot Wulfwold (of Bath & Chertsey)	SOM	7,10;*14-15*
	SRY	19,27
Abbot Wulfwold: *see also* Oswald brother of		
Wulfwold the priest	SOM	*5,43*
Wulfwy	BRK	7,22
	CHS	2,15-16;24
	DEV	24,14
	ESS	34,32
	GLS	19,2. 31,9. 39,5. 67,2
	HAM	NF3,10
	HEF	8,9. 15,8
	KEN	5,150;219
	NFK	19,7
	SOM	5,9. 8,24. 19,12
	SFK	7,121. 16,18
	SRY	16,1
	WAR	17,53
	WIL	24,31. 25,19-20
Wulfwy: *see also* Stephen son of		
Wulfwy, a man-at-arms of St Edmunds	SFK	14,69
Wulfwy, a thane	DEV	*24,14*
	SOM	*5,9*
Wulfwy, Asgar the constable's man	HRT	4,20
Wulfwy Child: *see* Wulfwy Young		
Wulfwy, Edeva's man	CAM	14,64
Wulfwy, Godwin of Benfield's man	HRT	4,19
Wulfwy Hunter	SRY	36,10
Bishop Wulfwy/of Dorchester	BDF	1,1c. 16,4. 24,23. 28,2. 34,2
	BKM	B2. 3a,1;6. 14,43;48-49. 26,1. 43,6. 53, 7-8

CAM	3,2. 14,58
HUN	2,7
LIN	12,29. CS,5. CK,65
SRY	36,10

Bishop Wulfwy: *see also* Alwin brother of
       : *see also* Godric brother of

Wulfwy of Hatfield	HRT	B7
Wulfwy of Hatley St George/Wulfwy of Doesse	CAM	AppxL
Wulfwy, Radfrid's man	NFK	19,2
Wulfwy the fisherman	OXF	B10
Wulfwy Wilde	KEN	9,9
Wulfwy Young [= Wulfwy Child]	HEF	29,1

Wulfwy: *see also* Wulfwig, Wulfwige
Wulfwynn (fem.): *see* Wulfwen
Wulmer: *see also* Wulfmer

Wymarc	NFK	4,26;38
	SHR	3d,6

Wymarc: *see also* Robert son of
       : *see also* Swein of Essex

Wymarc, Count Alan's steward	CAM	*14,68;71;79-80*
	SFK	*EC2*

Wymarc: *see also* Wihomarch, Wiuhomarch

Wymer	NFK	1,66. 8,6;62-64;69;95

Wymer: *see also* Wimer, Wimerus

Wyngeat	SHR	4,4,17
Wynning	SFK	67,30
Wynric	BRK	7,34
	GLS	33,1
	HEF	10,65

Wynric: *see also* Wenric

Wynsi [= Wynsige]	BRK	31,2
	CAM	*31,1*
	HAM	23,47. 33,1
	SHR	4,3,21
	SRY	28,1
Wynsi the chamberlain	BDF	1,1b
	BKM	31,1

Wynsi: *see also* Wenesi

Wynstan	CAM	*31,2*
	SFK	6,193

Wynstan: *see also* Winstan

Ylfing	NFK	9,152 *and note*

Ylfing: *see also* Ilving

Yric	SFK	4,4. 25,59

Yric: *see also* Eirikr, Eric

PART TWO

Titles

Titles

Alfwold (of Holme)	NFK	8,128. 10,87
Alfwy/Aethelwig (of Evesham)	WOR	11,2. 26,15-16
Alnoth	KEN	2,31
Alnoth (of Glastonbury)	SOM	*8,3;5-6;11;16-18;20-21;23-25;28-30;*
		33. 19,9
Alwin (of Buckfast)	DEV	*6,1;7-12*
Alwin (of Ramsey)	HUN	D4
Baldwin (of Bury St Edmunds)	BDF	6,1
	GLS	19,2
	SFK	14,*5-6;21;26;106-107*;117;*137-139*;
		151;167. 18,4
Benedict (of Selby)	LEC	23,2;4
	NTH	41,3. ELe2
Brandr (of Peterborough)	LIN	CW,16
Edmund (of Pershore)	WOR	9,4
E(dward (of Cerne)	DOR	*11,10*
Geoffrey (of Tavistock)	CON	3,7
	DEV	*5,7*
	DOR	*16*
Godwin Young (of Westminster)	BKM	12,12
Leofric (of Peterborough)	DBY	3,2
	LIN	56,4
	NTH	ELc2
	RUT	ELc10
Leofsi, of Ely	CAM	*28,2. 35,2*
Leofstan (of St Edmunds)	SFK	25,1. 68,5
Leofward (of Muchelney)	SOM	9,3
R. [= Rhiwallon, of New Minster]	BRK	B9 *and note*
Robert (of Evesham)	GLS	EvE10. EvO26
Saewold (of St Peter's, Bath)	SOM	*7,1;5-7;9;13*
Sihtric (of Tavistock)	CON	*3,1;7. 5,1,7;16*
	DEV	*5,8;11;14. 16,7*
Simeon (of Ely)	CAM	*28,2. 35,2*
	HUN	Appx
Thoraldr (of Peterborough)	LIN	8,13-14;17;34. 67,21. CW,14
Thurstan (of Glastonbury)	SOM	*8,1;5;11;16-18;21;23-25;31*
	WIL	7,3
Ulfketill (of Crowland)	LIN	CK,48
Walter (of Evesham)	GLS	E34. EvE25. EvN1. EvO5-10
	WOR	10,12. 26,16
W(illiam?, of Cerne)	DOR	*11,16*
Wulfric (of Ely)	SFK	31,60
Wulfward [mistake for Wulfwold]	SOM	*7,10;14-15*
Wulfwold (of Bath & Chertsey)	SOM	*7,10;14-15*
	SRY	19,27
Abbot/Abbey: *see*		
Abbotsbury (St Peter's)	DOR	13. 23,1. 55,3
Abingdon (St Mary's)	BRK	7. B2;8
	GLS	13. 56,2
	OXF	9. B8. EBe2
	WAR	7. 17,67-68
Angers (St Nicholas of)	BDF	24,29
	WAR	31,1
Athelney (St Peter's)	DOR	15. E1
	SOM	10. 19,86. 21,98. 32,5
Bath (St Peter's)	GLS	7. 1,56
	SOM	7
Battle (St Martin's)	BRK	15
	DEV	9. 1,34;52
	ESS	13

Cluny (SS Peter & Paul)	CAM	18,2
	NFK	8,21
Cormeilles (St Mary's)	GLS	16. 1,11;60. 16,1. EvK10
	HAM	61,1. S3
	HEF	3. 1,1;3;6-9;39;47. 10,50. E1
	WOR	6. E1;7;35
Coventry (St Mary's)	GLS	15
	LEC	6. C9
	NTH	12. B6
	WAR	6. B2. 14,2. 44,7. EG7
	WOR	5
Cranborne (St Mary's)	DEV	8
	DOR	10. 55,47
	WIL	11
Crowland (St Guthlac's)	CAM	9. 26,49. 32,42
	HUN	5
	LEC	7. C10
	LIN	11. T5. 42,13. CK48-49
	NTH	11. EH2
Dives (St-Pierre-sur)	BRK	13
	NTH	46,6
Ely (St Ethelreda's)	CAM	5. B12. 1,11. 3,5. *6,1*; 7,11-12. 8,1. 9,
		4. 13,11. 14,30;57;59. 17,2-3. 18,3;7;
		9. 19,1. 25,9. 26,17-18;27;29-30;33;
		48-57. 27,1. 28,2. 30,3. 31,1-2. 32,2;5;
		21-22;27;39-33;35-37;39-41;43. 39,3.
		40,1. 43,1. 44,2. AppxEL;MP
	ESS	10. 18,36. 22,7-8. 25,3;12;20. 30,27;
		41. 34,19;30. EHu
	HAM	2,16
	HRT	8. 4,15;21. Appx
	HUN	4. B3. D19
	LIN	C24
	NFK	15. 1,61. 4,*15*;16. 8,15;*16*;37;39-40;44;
		89. 9,79;167. 10,43;93. 12,6;*17*. 13,1;
		19. 19,24. 22,*1*. 23,9;*16*. 24,4. 29,7.
		49,6. 50,10. 57,2. 65,13. 66,53
	SFK	21. 1,75. 2,1-2;16;20. 3,27;31;*32-33*;
		34;36;*46*;57;62;86;89;92-95;97-103. 4,
		1;3-4; ;6;42. 5,2. 6,11-12;14-15;17;
		19-20;23;25;28-30;32-37;39;41;43-49;
		51-56;114;116-118;148-149;*164-165*;
		239;247;251;258;265;*271*. 7,15;55-56;
		58;61;67;71-72;122;130;136-146;148;
		151. 8,1-2;4-6;8-10;12;17;20;*21*;25;27;
		46;56-57;59;63;66;68;80-82. 12,2. 14,
		40. 16,3-4;5;6;8;13;20;22;27-34;38-39;
		48. 21,12;16-19;21-22;25-31;36-37;40;
		45-46;49-52;64-65;75;79-80;82-85. 22,
		2-3. *25,53*;59;112. 26,1;3;5. 28,2;6. 29,
		9. 31,8-13;15-19;40. 32,1;14;26;29-30.
		31. 34,4;12;15-16. 38,3;22. 39,3;5;8;
		10;22. 41,18. 45,1-3. 46,8;*10*. 47,2-3.
		52,4;10. 53,1;7. 63,3-6;9;11-12;15;22;
		29-30. 74,10. 77,4
Evesham (St Mary's)	GLS	12. E29;34. EvC41. EvE10;25. EvK1;
		116;133-135. EvM65-67. EvN1. EvO5;
		25. WoB7
	NTH	13. B7
	WAR	11. EG5-6. EW6-7

	WOR	10. 2,44;74-75. 9,5c; 7. 11,1-2. 26, 15-17
Evreux (St Taurin's)	WOR	15,9
Eynsham (St Mary's)	GLS	18
	OXF	B8. 6,14
	WOR	E15
Fécamp	MDX	8,1
	SSX	5
Fontenay (St Stephen's)	WIL	48,5
Ghent (St Peter's)	KEN	8
Glastonbury (St Mary's)	BRK	8
	DEV	4
	DOR	8
	GLS	8
	HAM	11
	SOM	8. 5,12;43;50. 19,9-10. 25,7-8. 37,9
	WIL	7. 24,42. 41,8
Gloucester (St Peter's)	GLS	10. 2,4;8;10. EvK1;103;116;230. EvM3-4. E30
	HAM	7
	HEF	5. 1,61. 15,1
	WOR	7
Grestain (St Mary's)	CAM	12,1
	HAM	13
	NTH	14
	SOM	19,50
	SFK	2,9-10
	SSX	10,14;39-41;44-45
	WIL	20,1
Horton (St Wolfrida's)	CON	3,2
	DEV	7
	DOR	14
Jumièges (St Peter's)	HAM	10
	SOM	1,29
	WIL	1,17
Lewes (St Pancras)	SSX	10,22. 12,3;7
Lyre (St Mary's)	GLS	17. 1,56. E1
	HAM	1,25. W4. S3. IoW1,5;7. IoW4
	HEF	4. 1,40;43;45;46;62
	WOR	E2;5;6
Malmesbury (St Mary's)	GLS	9. 1,64. E12-13. EvM32
	WAR	9. B2
	WIL	8. 30,2. 41,4
Marmoutier	DOR	26,20
Milton (St Peter's)	DOR	12. 37,1
	HAM	12
Mont St Michel	BRK	1,7
	DEV	11. 1,33 *and note.* 10,1 *and note*
	HAM	5a
	WIL	1,15
Montebourg (St Mary's)	SOM	13
	WIL	56,4
Mortain	SSX	10,1
Muchelney (St Peter's)	SOM	9. 21,54(?)-55
Much Wenlock (St Milburga's)	SHR	3c. C13. 4,1,32
Paris (St Denis)	GLS	20. EvK 153-154. EvM 80
	OXF	13
	WAR	EG 9
	WOR	4
Pershore (St Mary's)	GLS	14. 35,2. EvK1

	HEF	E5
	WAR	EBW2
	WOR	9
Peterborough (St Peter's)	BDF	7
	DBY	S5
	HUN	8. 1,4. 7,5;8. 9,2. 19,8. D28
	LEC	5
	LIN	8. 1,9. C16;20-21. S1;10. T5. 30,32. 51,3. 56,4. CW2;6;8. CK2;6-7;45
	NTH	6. 42,2. EB3. B4. ELc1-2
	NTT	8. S5
	RUT	EN9-10. ELc1;10;18
Préaux (St Peter's)	BRK	19,1
	OXF	12. 16,2
	WAR	16,56
Ramsey (St Benedict's)	BDF	8. 19,1. 34,3
	CAM	7. 17,1. 26,2;41;48. 32,1;23;28. 41,4. AppxLM
	ESS	EHu
	HRT	11. 17,1. 37,7;13
	HUN	6. B1;9;13;21. 2,2. 7,8. 22,2. D4;7-8; 27
	LIN	10. T5. 12,59 CK32;43;65
	NFK	16. 1,134. 8,16-20. 9,8; ?88. 12,?4. 20, 3. 21,3. 66,4;8;46;54
	NTH	9. 55,1. B5. EH3
	SFK	17. 36,4
Reading (Holy Trinity)	BRK	15,2
Rheims (St Remy's)	NTH	16
	SHR	3a
	STS	5. EN1-2
Rouen (Holy Trinity)	MDX	5
Rouen (St Ouen's)	ESS	17
Rumburgh (St Michael's)	SFK	3,105
St Alban's	BDF	23,12. 53,25
	BRK	12. B6;9
	BKM	8. 12,17-18;22
	HRT	10. 1,17. 2,3. 5,2. 32,1. 33,1. 34,2
	OXF	EBe3
St Benet of Holme	NFK	17. 1,59;61;194;201;209. 4,26;37;40; 42;51. 8,8;10-12;128. 9,13;16;20;?88; 91;159;180. 10,43;82-84;90. 12,6;32; ?44. 13,7. 14,3. 19,24. 20,31-33. 21, 32. 25,25-28. 26,5. 31,2-4;6;28. 35,11. 36,2. 48,3;8. 65,13;15. 66,16;78
St Évroul	CAM	13,6-7
	GLS	22
	STS	8,5;8-9
	SSX	11,3
	WAR	18,1
St Leofroy (Holy Cross)	SRY	10
St Neot's	HUN	28,1
St Severus	SOM	18,4
St Valéry	ESS	14
St Victor (en-Caux)	HAM	29,2
St Wandrille	CAM	10. 5,2
	DOR	18. B3
	NTH	56,61
	SRY	9
	WIL	1,9;23g

Saumur (St Florent)	GLS	E35
	HEF	1,48
Sées (St Martin's)	SSX	11,2;39;76;93
Selby (St Germain's)	LEC	23,2;4
	LIN	63,15
	NTH	B8
	YKS	2B1
Sherborne (St Mary's)	DOR	3
Shrewsbury (St Peter's)	SHR	3b. 4,1,1;3-6;17;30. 4,3,8. 6,5
Stow (St Mary's)	LIN	7,10-11;55. CN27. CW9-11
Swavesey (St Andrew's)	CAM	14,60
Tavistock (SS Mary & Rumon)	CON	3
	DEV	5
	DOR	16
Tewkesbury (St Mary's)	GLS	1,26-33
Thorney (St Mary's)	BDF	10
	CAM	8
	HUN	7. 1,2. 20,1. D1;26
	NTH	10
	WAR	EN1
Tréport	SSX	9,13
Troarn (St Martin's)	GLS	24
	HAM	21,8
	SSX	11,111-112
Wenlock: *see* Much Wenlock		
Westminster (St Peter's)	BDF	9
	BRK	9
	BKM	7
	ESS	6. 90,17;19. B3k
	GLS	19. E31. EvM79
	HAM	8
	HRT	9. 2,1-2. 16,1. 28,1
	LIN	9. 65,5. CK27
	MDX	4
	NTH	7
	OXF	1,3
	STS	3
	SRY	6. 19,40
	SSX	4
	WAR	EG8
	WIL	9
	WOR	8. 9,7. C4
Winchecombe (St Mary's)	GLS	11. EvK116
	OXF	11. 24,7
	WAR	10. EG4
Winchester (St Peter's)	BRK	10
	DOR	9
	HAM	6. IoW7,13
	SRY	7
	SSX	7. 11,8
	WIL	10. 25,6
Winchester (St Swithin's)	SOM	2,9;11. 19,7
	SSX	10,116
Abbot/Abbey: *see also* Monks of; Bishop of		
Aelfeth: *see* Godwin	MDX	7,7
Albert: *see* Burnt	SFK	8,15
Albus/White: *see* Alwin	HAM	69,40
	MDX	25,2
Alfrith: *see* Edwin	LEC	19,14
Alis: *see* William	HAM	49

almsmen: *see*

BDF	57
BKM	57L
DOR	24
NTH	17
SFK	70
WAR	43

Alselin: *see* Geoffrey

DBY	9. 6,27;81. B5
LEC	28
LIN	64. C4;20
NTH	44. B25
NTT	12. B13
YKS	18. CW16;19;33-34. SW,Sf21. SW, An9

arblaster: *see* Godfrey

KEN	*2,21*

Archbishop of: *see*
   Canterbury

BRK	B3
HRT	2. 16,1
KEN	2. D19. C1;8. P15. 5,38;128. 13,1
MDX	2
OXF	2. B8
SRY	2
SSX	2

   York

DBY	S5
GLS	EvK1
LEC	2. C7
LIN	2. 57,46
YKS	2. C1a;1b;21-22;30;37. 6N142. CE25; 28. SN,Y1-3;5;7-8. SW,Sk1-2. SW, BA1-2. SW,Ag1. SW, An12;15;18. SW,Bu5;20;45-48. SW,H1-3. SN,Ma5; 7-8;11-12;15;19;21-22. SN, B13-14; 17-19;23-25. SN,Bi2. SE,Wel4-5. SE, C2;4. SE,How11. SE,Wei4-7. SE,Sn1; 3-5;7-9. SE,Dr1. SE,Wa3-7. SE,P2-3; 6-9. SE,Hu2;6. SE,Tu3-4;6;8. SE, Bt3-5;8. SE,Sc1;3;6. SE,Ac6;10. SE, Th1;4;6-7;10-14. SE,So1-2 *note*. SE, Mid1-3. SE, No1

Archbishop: *see*
   Aldred (of York)

DEV	5,12-13 *and notes*
GLS	1,2. 2,4;8;10. 32,6. 41,1. E20. EvM6; 99. WoB5
LIN	CK,10
NTH	ELc4
RUT	ELc19
WAR	3,4
WOR	2,20;24;32;63
YKS	2B3-7;9-11;13;18. 2W4;6-7. 2E2;12. CE33. CW22;39

   Edsi
   Lanfranc

KEN	*2,39*
BRK	B9
BKM	2
CAM	4,1
KEN	C8. *2,5*
MDX	2,1-2
OXF	EBe3
SFK	15
SRY	2,1
SSX	2

Stigand

BDF	16,5. 39,1;3. 51,1-3
BRK	2,2-3
BKM	3,1. 4,3;15;17. 12,5;20-21;23. 17,3-4. 29,1. 33,1
CAM	1,11. 2,3-4. *13,8-10*. 15,2. 26,21;23;26; 41. 28,2. 31,7. 32,8;10;13-14;21;23. 34,1
DOR	28,2
GLS	1,56. 2,1;5;9. 31,6. 39,11. 56,2. EvM100
HAM	1,16. 2,16;18. 14,6
HRT	1,10. 2,1;3;5. 4,4;6;11;17. 5,8;10; 12-19;21;23;26. 7,2-4. 10,10-11. 16,8. 17,5. 23,1-3. 34,14. 37,3;5-6;10;16. 38, 2. 41,1-2. 42a, 1. 43,1
KEN	M14. 5,138
MDX	2,1. 18,1
NFK	1,105;121;216-217. 8,120. 9,6;139. 12, 1
NTH	18,32
OXF	3,1. 15,2. 29,16
SOM	2,1;10;1-2
SFK	1,107-119. 6,93. 15,1;3. 18,4. 19,15. 32,16. 69,1
SRY	1,1b

Thomas (of York)

GLS	2. EvM3-4
HAM	4
LIN	30,22. CS,27-29. CN,10-11;23. CK,16
NTT	5
OXF	7,58
YKS	2B3-7;9-11;13;18. 2W4;6-7. CE33

archdeacon: *see*
   Alric

GLS	E20. EvC24. WoB5
WOR	2,20;24;57

   Ansketel
   Benzelin
   Gunfrid
   Roland

KEN	M14
SOM	*6,14*
NFK	10,16
CON	*2,10*

archer: *see*
   Reginald
   William

OXF	58,2
HAM	53

archer: *see also*
   Bolest
   bowman
   crossbowman
artificer: *see*
   Richard

BKM	42. E6
HUN	D24
NTH	B21
OXF	58,1

   Waldin
   William

LIN	47
HUN	26. 19,15
NTH	B17

Arundel: *see* Roger

DOR	47. 9,1
SOM	22. 6,19

Ator: *see* Edmer

BKM	12,3
DEV	15,*12*;13. *14-30*;31;*32-33*
HRT	15,12. 19,1
MDX	8,6
SOM	*8,31*. 19,44;46. 37,5;12. 47,10

Baderon: *see* William	GLS	G4
	HEF	1,8
Baderon: *see also* son of		
Bainard: *see* Baynard		
Ba(i)rn: *see* Barn		
baker: *see*		
Erchenger	CAM	44. *32,22*
Osmund	DOR	57,17
Reginald	HAM	IoW6,10
bald: *see*		
Alfwold	SOM	*36,7*
Edric	BDF	55,8
Leofwin	SFK	57,1
Richard	SFK	*14,54*
Robert	CAM	26,39
R(obert)	CAM	26,36
William	GLS	G4
Balehorn: *see* Brictmer	HUN	D5
Balliol: *see* Reginald	STS	14
Balliol: *see also* of Balliol		
Banks: *see* Ralph	CAM	B1. *14,17. 31,5-6. 32,3;18-21.* AppxK
Banks: *see also* of Barrington/Banks		
barber: *see* Durand	HAM	65
Barn: *see*		
Arnketill	LIN	16,49
Asketill	LIN	12,8
Siward	DBY	S5
	GLS	59,1
	LIN	T5. 21,1. 63,7. CW,17
	NFK	1,149. 19,18-19
	NTT	S5
	WAR	19,1
Baron: *see* Robert	NFK	1,61
Basset(t): *see*		
Ralph	BKM	19,4
	HRT	19,1
Richard	BDF	28,1
William	BDF	23,26
Bastard: *see* Robert	DEV	29
Battock: *see* Thorkell	WAR	28,1
Baynard: *see*		
Geoffrey	ESS	68,2
	NFK	31,1-2
Ralph	ESS	33. 1,2;27. 2,9. 5,10. 6,7. 20,46. 34,
		36. 90,39. B3r
	HRT	24. B9. Appx
	NFK	31. 1,1. 20,13
	SFK	33
R(alph)	SFK	4,36
(Ralph)	ESS	1,17a;27. 28,9
	NFK	9,232
William	SFK	33,10
Baynard?: *see* Roger	NFK	*9,160*
Baynard: *see also* Baynard the sheriff		
beadle: *see*		
Aelfric	BDF	57,3v
Aelmer	DOR	*56,63*
Alwin Cock	CAM	*1,20*
Alwin Maimcock	CAM	1,20
Brictmer	SFK	74,4

Godwin	BKM	57,18
Leofmer	BDF	57,3v
beadle: *see also*	BDF	57
Beard: *see*		
Alfsi	CAM	*31,2*
Bernard	HEF	1,10b
Brunman	SFK	7,36
Hugh	HAM	68,1
Beard: *see also*		
de Montfort		
with the beard		
Beauchamp: *see* Hugh	BDF	17,6. 21,6
Beauchamp: *see also* of Beauchamp		
Beaufour: *see* William	BRK	1,5
Beaufour: *see also* of Beaufour		
Bedruel: *see* Hervey	SFK	*21,51;56;58;63;87;96-100*
Bedruel: *see also* Hervey of Berry/of Bourges		
Bellett: *see* William	BRK	1,1
	DOR	1,*19*;30. *34,2.* 57,1;*3*;12;*19*
	HAM	52
Bellrope: *see* Alfward	BDF	25,1
Benfield: *see* Godwin	HRT	4,14. 20,11
Benfield: *see also* of Benfield		
Benne: *see* Leofwin	SFK	35,7
Bent: *see* Osmund	DBY	17,13
Bereson: *see* Aelsi	CAM	*31,2*
Berlang?: *see* Ralph	NFK	9,100 *and note*
Bernwin: *see* Jocelyn	DEV	*16,118*
Bertram: *see* William	HAM	31
Bet(t)eslau: *see* Wulfeva	HAM	6,12
	WIL	68,24
Big: *see*		
Aelfric	ESS	20,41
Alfred	KEN	*2,16.* 5,124
Esbern	KEN	D17. C5-6. 5,37;57;86-87;168. 7,6. 9,
		16
Bigot: *see*		
Roger	ESS	43
	NFK	9. 1,1;57;61;63;66;215;220. 2,1;7;12.
		4,39;56. 6,6. 12,34;38. 14,14;21;25.
		15,10;22. 16,5-6. 22,13. 48,5-6. 49,5.
		66,1;12;58;71;78-84;86
	SFK	7. 1,1;6;103;105;122a. 3,57;59. 4,9. 6,
		46;73. 16,*5*;12-14;16-17;*20*;23;*28-29*;
		30;*31-33*;34;40;48. 21,17;*18*;44-45;49;
		52. 22,2. 25,52. 39,3. 73,1. 74,7. 76,
		13. ENf4.
Ro(ger)	SFK	14,117. 16,3-4;6;8;15;35;37;46
R(oger)	NFK	1,70;106;111;223;229. 4,55. 12,42. 15,
		13
	SFK	1,17;30;60. 2,17. 4,15;32;42. 6,69;91;
		177;*271.* 16,2;23;27. 21,83
Bishop of: *see*		
Bayeux	BDF	2. 40,3
	BRK	41,3. 44,2;5. 65,19
	BKM	4. B11. E2
	CAM	28,2. 37,1. 43,1
	DOR	4
	ESS	18. 1,27. 4,9-10. 9,1. 20,1. 36,9. 48,2
	GLS	1,22-23;65. 41,5. E29;34

	HAM	23,56. NF10,2. EL
	HRT	5. 10,9. 31,8. 37,19. 42,11
	KEN	5. D7-8;10. M1;13-14. C3;5;8. P19. *1, 3. 2,5;30*. 3,3. 4,16. 7,5-6;10. 9,1;42. 13,1
	LEC	1,10
	LIN	4. 27,11. 30,14. 40,24. CN13;15-16. CS1-2;24;28
	NFK	2. 1,111;120-122. 4,44. 66,82
	NTH	2. B16;30
	NTT	7
	OXF	7. B8. 1,6
	SOM	4
	SFK	16. 75,5. 77,1;4. Also folio 372a
	SRY	5. 1,1c-d;5;11;13. 6,1. 8,29. 14,1. 36,1
	SSX	1,2
	WAR	4. 20,1
	WIL	4. M2. 13,21
	WOR	11. 2,44. 10,12
Chester	CHS	B. 2,1-2;5. S1,7. R4
	DBY	2. S5
	HRT	7
	NTT	S5
	SHR	1. C13
	STS	2. B2. EW5
	WAR	2. B2. 28,19. EBS1. EBW3
	WOR	23,1
Chichester	SSX	3. 1,1. 10,1. 11,8
Coutances	BDF	3. 31,1
	BRK	6
	BKM	5. B3. 40,1
	DEV	3. 1,1;11
	DOR	5
	GLS	6. W13. E9
	HAM	S3
	HUN	3. B13
	LEC	4
	LIN	6
	MDX	21,1
	NFK	*15,22*
	NTH	4. B2. 41,5. EB1-2. EH1
	OXF	B8. EN1-4
	SOM	5. 1,7;28. 8,2;25;38. 20,1. 44,2. EBe, 1-3. EBu1-2
	SFK	*21,17*. 29,9
	WAR	5. B2
	WIL	5. 7,10
	YKS	C9;16
Dorchester	HUN	2,7
Dorchester: *see also* Lincoln		
Durham		
	BDF	5
	BRK	4
	ESS	7
	LIN	3. 1,9. 14,72. 29,6-8. CK13;39;52. CN21;25;29-30. CS9;15;19-22;32
	NTH	3
	RUT	EN6
	SOM	2,9
	YKS	C2;37. 3Y11;13;15
Evreux	SFK	22

Exeter	BRK	5
	CON	2
	DEV	2
	DOR	35,1
	GLS	5
	OXF	5
	SRY	4
Hereford	ESS	19
	GLS	4. 1,55. EvK116. E5-6
	HEF	2. C9. 1,10c. 10,5;37;48;75
	OXF	B8
	SHR	2. 4,1,4. 4,14,12. 7,4
	WOR	3. 2,16. E9;21-26
Lichfield	WOR	23,1
Lincoln	BKM	3a. 1,1
	CAM	3
	HUN	2. B4. D29
	LEC	3
	LIN	7. C17;20. T4-5. 1,65. 12,59 *and note.* CN,15. CS4
	NTH	5
	NTT	6
	OXF	6. B8
	RUT	EN7-8
Lincoln: *see also* Dorchester		
Lisieux	BKM	4,5;14;41-42
	DOR	6. 1,31
	GLS	30. E9
	HRT	6
	KEN	5,29
	MDX	3,7
	OXF	8
	SRY	1,5. 5,10;13. 6,1
	WIL	6
London	DOR	7
	ESS	3-4. 20,4. 48,2
	HRT	4. 33,18. Appx
	MDX	3. 15,1. 16,1
Rochester	CAM	4
	ESS	EKt
	KEN	4. 1,1;2. 5,58
	SFK	20
Saintes	HAM	69,53
St Lô	SFK	21,17. 29,9
St Lô: *see also* Coutances		
Salisbury	BRK	3
	DOR	2. 3,1-18
	LEC	14,23
	OXF	4
	SOM	3. EDo1
	WIL	3. 32,2
Thetford	SFK	18-19. 6,70-72;76-77;308;311. 8,42. 31,3;5-6. 44,2. 64,3. *Also folio 372a*
Wells	SOM	6. 22,20
Winchester	BRK	2
	BKM	3
	CAM	2
	GLS	2,3
	HAM	2. 3. 29,1;9. 41,1. NF2. ESr
	HRT	3

	OXF	3. B8
	SOM	2
	SRY	3
	WIL	2
Worcester	GLS	3. E19-29. EvC22;38;41. EvK80. EvM8. WoA. WoB. WoC
	OXF	EW1
	WAR	3. B2. EW1
	WOR	2

Bishop of: *see also* Canons of; Monks of
Bishop: *see*

A(e)lmer (of Elmham)	NFK	1,28;61;68. 8,12. 9,20;30-31;178. 10, 2-5;8;11;16-17;19-21;28;35;42-43; 45-47;60;63;65-68;73-75;80;87-91
	SKF	2,3-5. 3,96. 6,311. 7,4. 8,42. 18,1;4;6. 19,11;14-16;18;20. 64,3. 75,4
A(elmer, of Elmham)	NFK	10,13;23;26
Aethelstan (of Hereford)	HEF	13,1
Alfwold (of Sherborne)	DOR	2,6. 27,9-10
	SOM	EDo1
Alric (of Selsey)	SSX	9,11;60
Alwine (of Durham)	YKS	3Y9-10;16-18
Brictheah/Beorhtheah (of Worcester)	GLS	E20. WoB5
	WOR	2,24
Brictheah [erroneously Brictric]	HEF	1,45
Erfast (of Thetford)	NFK	1,59;69. 10,21;27;43;53;69;78;81
	SFK	1,119. 18,1. 25,60. 75,3
Geoffrey (of Coutances)	BRK	6
	GLS	6. W13. 1,21. E10
	HAM	S3
	HUN	B13
	LIN	6
	NTH	35,1j. 41,5. 56,65
	SOM	*1,7*
	WIL	7,5
Gilbert (of Evreux)	SFK	22
Gilbert (of Lisieux)	BKM	4,14
Giso (of Wells)	SOM	6. 1,2;21. 22,20
Herman (of Salisbury)	BRK	3,2-3
	WIL	3,1
(Herman, of Salisbury)	WIL	67,11
Leofing (of Worcester)	HEF	1,44
	WOR	E4
Leofric (of Exeter)	CON	2,2;15
	DEV	*2,7-8;14;16-23*
	OXF	5,1
Leofwin (of Lichfield)	STS	11,12
Maurice (of London)	DOR	7. 1,31
	SOM	15. 1,19;21. 8,37
Odo (of Bayeux)	GLS	EvN1
	KEN	M3
	LIN	CS,13
Osbern (of Exeter)	BRK	5
	CON	5,1,3
	DEV	*2,2*
	GLS	5. G3-4. 1,56
	HAM	5
	NFK	L11
	SRY	4

	SSX	6
	WIL	1,5;23f
Osbert [for Osbern of Exeter]	NFK	L11 *see note*
Osmund (of Salisbury)	BRK	3. B6. 1,34
	LEC	14,23
	LIN	5. CK,62
	SOM	3
	WIL	3. 1,23h. 25,2. 67,11
Peter (of Lichfield & Chester)	BRK	B4. 1,9;11;42
	SOM	16,7;14. 47,1
Remigius (of Lincoln)	BDF	4. B. 1,1c. E5
	BRK	B4;9
	BKM	3a. B2
	CAM	3. B1
	LIN	C4;11. 2,37. 3,35. 14,21. 16,9. 28,4.
		56,5. CS, 5. CN,27. CW,7;13. CK, 13;
		33;45;65;67
	NTT	20,4
	OXF	6,4. EBe3
R(emigius, of Lincoln)	LIN	51,12
Robert (of Chester)	HRT	7
Robert (of Hereford)	GLS	4,1
	HEF	2,1;57
	OXF	5,1
R(obert, of Hereford)	ESS	1,24
	SHR	4,4,23
Samson (of Worcester)	GLS	EvK1
Walcher(e, of Durham)	ESS	7,1 *note*
	YKS	C2
Walkelin (of Winchester)	BRK	2. B2
	BKM	3
	CAM	2
	ESS	B6
	HAM	1,16;21. IoW2,1
	HRT	3
	OXF	EBe1
	SOM	2. 1,27. 8,28. 19,40
	SRY	19,12
	WIL	2
Walter (of Hereford)	GLS	E5
	HAM	5a,1
	HEF	2,1-3;8;12;26;31-33;37;50;56-57
	WOR	2,16. 3,2-3
William (of Durham)	YKS	3. C2. 5E15. 6N142-143. CE12;16-17;
		24. SW,H4-5. SN,Bi1;4;7. SN, A3;6.
		SE,Wel1-2. SE,C3-5;10. SE,How1-6;
		10. SE,Sn4;8-9
William (of London)	ESS	3,2;7;11-13
	HRT	4. 33,18
	MDX	3,3;9;11
W(illiam, of London)	ESS	3,7-8
William (of Thetford)	NFK	10. 1,61;128
	SFK	18
W(illiam, of Thetford)	NFK	1,57;68
	SFK	14,101;121
Wulfstan (of Worcester)	GLS	3,4-7
	WAR	3,4. 36,2. 44,12
Wulfwige/Wulfwy (of Dorchester)	BDF	1,1c. 16,4. 24,3. 28,2. 34,2
	BKM	B2. 3a,1;6. 14,43;48-49. 26,1. 43,6. 53,
		7-8

brother of Aelfric: *see*
Aethelstan	LIN	26,45
Alsige	LIN	26,45
Edmer	SOM	2,7
Edric	SFK	76,3
Guthfrithr	LIN	CS,21
Harold	LIN	CS,21
Ordric	KEN	5,110

brother of Aelfwin: *see* Goda   SFK   7,37
brother of Aelmer: *see* Ansgot   HAM   18,3
brother of Aethelstan: *see*
Aelfric	LIN	26,45
Alsige	LIN	26,45

brother of Agmundr: *see* Sigketill   LIN   28,11
brother of Aiulf the chamberlain: *see*   HAM   S3
   Humphrey
brother of Aki: *see* Vigleikr   LIN   T5
brother of Alfred of 'Spain': *see* Walter   SOM   *35,19*
brother of Alfsi: *see* Leofwin   BKM   17,1
brother of Alfward: *see* Godwin   KEN   5,33
brother of ?Alfward: *see* Algar   ESS   34,22
brother of ?Algar: *see* Alfward   ESS   34,22
brother of Alli: *see* Alfsi   BDF   47,1
brother of Alnoth: *see*
Asketill	LIN	CN,30. CS,38
Fenkell	LIN	CN,30. CS,38
Sighvatr/Godwine	LIN	CN,30. CS,38

brother of Alric: *see* Bondi   ESS   30,20
brother of Alsige: *see*
Aelfric	LIN	26,45
Aethelstan	LIN	26,45

brother of Ansculf: *see* Giles
	BRK	34
	BKM	51
	NTH	43. B26
	OXF	37

brother of Ansgot: *see* Aelmer   HAM   18,3
brother of Arnulf of Hesdin: *see* Ilbod   OXF   48L
brother of Asketill: *see*
Alnoth	LIN	CS,38. CN,30
Brandr the monk	LIN	CW,16
Fenkell	LIN	CS,30. CN,38
Sighvatr	LIN	CS,30. CN,38

brother of Baldwin: *see* Edwin   KEN   *M23*
brother of Bishop Brictric/Beorhtheah: *see*   HEF   1,45
   Aethelric   WOR   E5
brother of Bishop Gundulf: *see* William   KEN   *2,11*
brother of Bishop Osbern: *see* Earl William   GLS   1,56
brother of Bishop Wulfwy: *see*
Alwin	BDF	16,4
	BKM	41,2
Godric	BKM	3a,2

brother of Bondi: *see* Alric   ESS   30,20
brother of Brandr the monk: *see* Asketill   LIN   CW,16
brother of Brictric: *see* Alfwy   WIL   67,10
brother of Brictric: *see also* brother of Bishop
   Brictric
brother of Burghard: *see* Peter   SFK   *14,17*
brother of Durand: *see* Roger (of Pîtres)   GLS   2,10
   HEF   1,61
brother of Earl Ralph: *see* Hardwin   SFK   7,67

brother of Earl William: *see* Bishop Osbern	GLS	1,56
brother of Edric: *see*		
Aelfric	SFK	76,3
Godric	GLS	53,10
brother of Fenkell: *see*		
Alnoth	LIN	CN,30. CS,38
Asketill	LIN	CN,30. CS,38
Sighvatr	LIN	CN,30. CS,38
brother of Gilbert: *see* Robert the clerk	HAM	2,10
brother of Goda: *see* Aelfwin	SFK	7,37
brother of Godric: *see* E(a)dric	GLS	53,10
	LIN	CS,6
brother of Godwin the priest: *see* Aelfric	CAM	*31,1*
brother of Guthmund: *see* Abbot Wulfric	SFK	31,60
brother of Harold: *see* Gyrth	SFK	1,102
brother of Harold and Guthfrithr: *see* Aelfric	LIN	CS,21
brother of Hubert the Breton: *see* Reginald	SFK	*14,68*
brother of Ilbert: *see* William	HEF	8,7
brother of Ilger: *see*		
Ranulf	BDF	29. 53,30
	CAM	34
	ESS	37. 1,1;27. 7,1
	HRT	25
	HUN	24
	MDX	22
	NFK	36. 1,192. 66,103
	SFK	39
R(anulf)	SFK	67,15
brother of Jocelyn son of Azor: *see* William	HAM	IoW1,7
brother of Ketill: *see* Thorfrothr	LIN	22,26
brother of Leofing: *see* Ordric	SOM	*45,1*
brother of Leofwin: *see*		
Alwin	WAR	44,11
Swein	SRY	25,3
brother of Odo: *see* Aldred	HAM	6,16. 53,2. 69,45
	WIL	*67,38*
brother of Ordric: *see* Leofing	SOM	*45,1*
brother of Picot the sheriff: *see* Roger	CAM	*32,35*
brother of Raimer the clerk: *see* W(alscin)	SOM	24,35
brother of Ralph of Pomeroy: *see* William	DEV	*19 and note*
brother of Ranulf: *see* brother of Ilger		
brother of Robert Blunt: *see* Ralph	SFK	66,10
brother of Robert the clerk: *see* Gilbert	HAM	2,10
brother of Roger Bigot: *see* William	NFK	9,88
brother of Roger of Auberville: *see* William of Auberville	SFK	30
brother of Roger of Berkeley: *see* Ralph	GLS	42-43
	SOM	*45,8*
brother of Roger (of Pîtres): *see* Durand	GLS	2,10
	HEF	1,61
brother of Saeric: *see* Gest	WIL	67,96
brother of Sighvatr: *see*		
Alnoth	LIN	CN30. CS38
Asketill	LIN	CN30. CS38
Fenkell	LIN	CN30. CS38
brother of Sihere: *see* Walter	BDF	33
brother of Siward: *see* Atsurr	LIN	51,12
brother of Stigand: *see* A(e)lmer	NFK	10,30
brother of Swein: *see* Leofwin	SRY	25,3
brother of Thorfrothr: *see* Ketill	LIN	22,26

brother of Thorkell: *see* Godmund	WAR	17,7
brother of Tosti: *see* Eric	HUN	D27
brother of Ulfr: *see* Wulfbert	LIN	C3
brother of Walter of Douai: *see* Raimer the clerk	SOM	*24,35*
brother of Walter the deacon: *see* Theodoric	ESS	42,1
	SFK	41,10
brother of William of Bosc-le-Hard: *see* Roger	BKM	18,3
brother of William (of Warenne): *see* Frederick	CAM	18,7
brother of William: *see* Ilbert	HEF	8,7
brother of Wulfa: *see* Aelfric	SOM	*19,68*
brother of Wulfric: *see* Wulfsi	SFK	1,110
brother: *see*		
Aelmer's	LIN	CK19
Aelmer of Bennington's	HRT	36,16
Alfward's	SOM	47,14
Alfwold's	HUN	19,15;17. D21
Arnketill's	YKS	CW2
Atsurr's	LIN	7,34
Brictric's	WIL	67,5;10
Browning's	HAM	IoW6,2
Ebrard's	LIN	26,25
Edric's	HAM	23,44
Elaf's	GLS	52,3
Frani's	YKS	CE45
Fulcric's	LIN	12,4
Gamall's	YKS	29E20
Godric, Eadric's	LIN	CS,6
Godric's	DEV	*40,6*
Halfdan's	LIN	31,17
Herbert's	LEC	42,3 (*see note*)
Hunning's	SHR	4,19,9
Ilbert's	HEF	8,7
Ingimundr's	LIN	12,31. CN26
Ketilbjorn's	YKS	1E60
Ketill's	YKS	CW3
Leofnoth's	DBY	10,16
Ranulf of Vaubadon's	KEN	5,223
Reinbald's	GLS	10,12
Roger Corbet's	SHR	4,1,15
Saered's	DOR	26,37
Saewulf's	BKM	51,1
Seric's	NTH	15,5
Ulfr's	YKS	CE35
William Cheever's	DEV	*19,3*
Wulfric's	DOR	56,13
brother's wife: *see* Wulfric	DOR	56,13
brothers: *see*		
Alfward's	SOM	47,14
Godric's	LIN	3,41
Wulfsi's	SFK	7,24
Brownson: *see* Alric	CAM	*44,2*
Brownson: *see also* son of Brown		
Brutin: *see* Robert	KEN	*2,12*
Bubba: *see* Brictmer	SFK	6,226
Burdel: *see* Robert	LEC	13,41 (*but see note*)
Burdet: *see*		
Hugh	LEC	40,12;24

Robert	LEC	13,41 *and note*; 53. 17,29
Burdet: *see also*		
Robert's son		
Robert's wife		
burgess: *see*		
Aelfric son of Rolf	SFK	74,8
Culling	SFK	1,122d
Godric	ESS	B3a
Godwin	BDF	56,2
Ordwy	BDF	56,3
Peter	HRT	42,7
Wulfmer	BDF	56,4
burgess: *see also*	BDF	56
	ESS	B3a
burgess: *see also* Ordwy of Bedford		
Burgundy: *see* Walter	DEV	25,3-4
Burgundy: *see also* of Burgundy		
Burnt: *see* Burnt Albert	SFK	8,15
bursar: *see*		
Azor	BRK	41,6
Robert	GLS	47. EvN13
	HUN	19,18
	LEC	19. C16
	LIN	38. CS,1;3;12;23-24;33-34;36. CN,22
	NTH	EH6
	WAR	23
	WIL	*4,4*
	WOR	2,13;19;49;67;73. 9,1d
Roger	SOM	*5,34*
William	KEN	*2,10*
Bush: *see* Aelfric	HRT	34,6
Bushell: *see* Roger	DOR	*11,6. 55,3*
	SOM	22,23
Buss: *see* Siward	LIN	CS,9
Butler: *see*		
Hugh	BDF	35
	CAM	*2,3*
Richard	CHS	6
	SHR	4,1,5
Robert	SHR	4,6
butler: *see*		
Alfred	DEV	*15,16-19;32-33;55*
	DOR	*15,1. E1*
	SOM	*19,39;80;86*
Walter	DEV	*16,123*
Buxton: *see* Alwin	LEC	13,21
Cabe/Cappe: *see* Algar	CAM	5,37 *and note*
Canon: *see*		
Ansfrid	BDF	13,2
Durand	MDX	3,15
Engelbert	MDX	3,6
Estan	HEF	6,2
Geoffrey	SSX	9,126
Godric	KEN	P1
Gotshelm	DEV	*25,28*
Gyrth	MDX	3,16
Osmund	BDF	13,1
Ralph	MDX	3,19
Sewen	KEN	P1
Sired	KEN	P1

	MDX	3,2. 15,1
Spirtes	SHR	3d,7
Walter	MDX	3,29
Wulfwin	BRK	4,1
Canons of: *see*		
Arundel (St Nicholas)	SSX	11,2;6
Bayeux	CAM	16
	SRY	5,6-7
?Berkeley (St Mary's)	GLS	1,63
Bedford (St Peter's)	BDF	13. 53,32;35
Beverley (St John's)	YKS	C37. 2E1-2. 2E3;15-17;22;33. CE11; 24;33. CW39. SE,Sn10. SEHoll2
Bodmin (St Petroc's)	CON	1,15;18. 4,3-22. 5,6,6
	DEV	51,15-16
Bosham	HAM	5,1
	SSX	6,1-5
Boxgrove	SSX	11,102
Bromfield (St Mary's)	SHR	3d,4;6-7. 4,20,21
Chester (St John's)	CHS	B10;12
Chester (St Werburgh's)	CHS	A. 1,35. 2,21
	STS	10,7
Chichester (Holy Trinity)	SSX	3,10
Cirencester (St Mary's)	GLS	25. 1,7. 39,8
Clare (St John's)	SFK	25,1
Coutances	DOR	22
Dover (St Martin's)	KEN	6. D1. 9,9
Exeter (SS Peter & Mary)	DEV	2,2;8;22 *and notes.* 16,89-92 *and notes*
Gloucester (St Oswald's)	GLS	2,5(?);11;12(?)
Hartland (St Nectan's)	DEV	45,3
Hereford (St Albert's)	HEF	2,13
Hereford (St Guthlac's)	HEF	6. 7,1;5;7. 14,2. 19,8
	WOR	12
Hereford (St Peter's)	GLS	E6
	HEF	2. C9
	WOR	E9;21-26
Launceston (St Stephen's)	CON	1,7. 4,2
Lichfield (St Chad's)	CHS	B6;13. 2,1. 16,2. 27,3
Lincoln (St Mary's)	HUN	2,8
	LEC	3,3
	LIN	7,8;57
	OXF	6,5
Lisieux	WIL	19
London (St Martin's)	BDF	12. 57,8. E2
	ESS	12. 6,1. 20,34;60
	HRT	17,14
London (St Paul's)	ESS	5. 3,5;11. 20,67. 33,22. 57,5
	HRT	13
	MDX	3,2;14-30. 9,4. 15,1
	SRY	13. 2,3
Malling (St Michael's)	SSX	2,1f;3
Oxford (St Frideswide's)	BKM	10
	OXF	14. B10
Plympton (St Peter's)	DEV	1,17. 29,10
Ripon (St Wilfrid's)	YKS	C37. 2W7 *and note.* SW,Bu45
Rouen (St Mary's)	DEV	10. 1,11
St Achebran	CON	4,23
St Buryan	CON	4,27
St Carantoc	CON	4,25
St Constantine	CON	4,29
St German	CON	2,6;12-14

St Kew	CON	5,24,14
St Michael's	CON	4,1. 5,25,5
St Neot's	CON	4,28
St Piran	CON	4,26. 5,8,10
St Probus	CON	4,24
?Shrewsbury (St Alkmund's)	SHR	3g. C13. 4,20,19. 9,1
Shrewsbury (St Chad's)	SHR	3f. C13. 1,4. 4,26,3
	STS	2,5;10;15. 11,13
(Shrewsbury), St Juliana	SHR	3h. C13
(Shrewsbury), St Mary's	SHR	3d,1-3;5. C13
(Shrewsbury), St Michael's	SHR	3e
	NTT	5,3;13
Stafford (St Mary's)	STS	6. B10
Sudbury (St Gregory's)	SFK	1,97
Tettenhall	STS	7,5
Twynham (Holy Trinity)	HAM	17
Waltham (Holy Cross)	BDF	5,1-2
	BRK	4,1
	ESS	8. 7,1
	HRT	14. 34,13
	SRY	17,1;4
Warwick (All SS in castle)	WAR	17,63
Wells (St Andrew's)	SOM	6,1;16-17
Wolverhampton	STS	7. 12,1
	WOR	13
York (St Peter's)	YKS	C1a *and note*; 2;21-23;25;30-31;35;37. 2B4-8;12;15-17;19. 2N1-6;14-15; 19-30. 2W1-3;5;7;13. 4N1. 8N1;2-5 *and note*. CN2. SN,D20-21 *and note*. SN,Ma1 *and note*; 13-14 *and note*. SN, B2 *and note*
Canons of: *see also* Bishop of		
Canute: *see*		
Reginald	WIL	62. *28,9*
Walter	NFK	66,107
Cappe/Cabe: *see* Algar	CAM	*5,37 and note*
Cardon: *see* William	ESS	10,5. 20,71. 30,46. 90,34
carpenter: *see*		
Durand	DOR	*55,48.* 57,20
Landric	YKS	C20
Rabel	NFK	66,101-102
Rayner	HEF	32,1
Stephen	WIL	66,6
Catchpoll: *see* Aelfric	MDX	3,9
Catenase: *see* Earnwine	YKS	CW32
Cave: *see*		
Leofwin	BKM	57,8
Wulfric	ESS	25,6. 30,28
Chafersbeard: *see* Alfwy	BRK	65,22
chamberlain: *see*		
Aelfric	BKM	34,1
Aethelwold	KEN	5,66;*99-100;134*
Aethelwulf	BDF	40,3
Aiulf	DOR	49
	HAM	S3
Alfwold	BRK	1,43. 65,15
Aubrey	BRK	65,16
	HAM	68,9
	WIL	68,27-28
Bernard	HAM	NF9,13

Ipswich (St Augustine's)	SFK	1,122d. 31,56
Ipswich (St George's)	SFK	38,3
Ipswich (St Julian's)	SFK	74,9
Ipswich (St Laurence's)	SFK	1,122f
Ipswich (St Mary's)	SFK	1,122d
Ipswich (St Michael's)	SFK	1,122d
Ipswich (St Peter's)	SFK	1,122f. 25,52;54 *note*; 60;62
Ipswich (St Stephen's)	SFK	1,122f
Kilmersdon	SOM	16,14
Lambeth (St Mary's)	GLS	21
	SRY	14
Leighton Buzzard	BDF	4,9
Lewes (St John's)	SSX	10,44;63
Lincoln (All Saints')	LIN	CW2
Lincoln (St Lawrence's)	LIN	C20
?Lincoln (St Michael's)	LIN	68,47
Lincoln (St Peter's)	LIN	1,6
Luton	BDF	1,2b
(Manchester), St Mary's	CHS	R5,2
Milbourne Port (St John's)	SOM	1,10
Milverton	SOM	16,4
(Morville), St Gregory's	SHR	4,1,5
Netheravon	WIL	56,3
North Curry	SOM	1,9
North Petherton (St Mary's)	SOM	16,7
Norwich (All Saints')	NFK	1,61
Norwich (Holy Trinity)	NFK	1,61
Norwich (St Laurence)	NFK	1,61
Norwich (St Martin's)	NFK	1,61
Norwich (St Michael's)	NFK	1,61
Norwich (SS Simon & Jude)	NFK	1,61
Oakham	RUT	R17;21
Oxford (St Mary's)	OXF	B6
Oxford (St Michael's)	OXF	B10
Oxford (St Peter's)	OXF	2,8;28
Ramsbury	WIL	3,3
Rome (St Peter's)	SOM	11
Ropsley (St Peter's)	LIN	CK56
St Everilda's	YKS	25W14
St James's	DEV	52,50
St Michael's (?Lower Gwent)	GLS	W6
Shrewsbury (St Mary's)	SHR	3d,1-3;5
?Shrewsbury (St Withburga's)	SHR	3c,14
Singleton	SSX	11,3
Stamford (All Saints')	NTH	1,5
	RUT	EN5
Stamford (St Peter's)	LIN	S13
	NTH	1,5
	RUT	R21. ELa3. EN5
Stogumber (St Mary's)	SOM	16,2
Stoke on Trent	STS	11,36
Stonham	SFK	64,2
Stow on the Wolds (St Edward's)	GLS	12,1. EvO10
Stowmarket	SFK	2,8. 34,6
Tangmere	SSX	2,6
Thetford (St Helen's)	NFK	1,210
Threekingham (St Peter's)	LIN	3,55. 48,7. 67,11
Thurleston (St Botolph's)	SFK	1,122e
Tuddenham	SFK	38,15
(Warrington), St Elfin's	CHS	R3,1

?Whalley (St Mary's)	CHS	R4,1
Wigmore (St Mary's)	SHR	6,19
(Winwick), St Oswald's	CHS	R2,1
Yealmpton	DEV	1,18
York (Christ Church)	YKS	C37. 11W2 *and note.* 22W1-3;5. SW, An1;8;13-14;16

York (Holy Trinity): *see* Christ Church
Cild: *see* Child
Cilt: *see* Child

Clack: *see* Godwin	WIL	67,47
Clamahoc: *see* Eudo	NFK	66,94

Clamahoc: *see also* son of Clamahoc
cleric: *see* clerk
clerk: *see*

Alan	KEN	M13
Albert	BRK	1,1
	LIN	ER,1
	RUT	7. R21
	SRY	34L
	WAR	1,8
Albold	SFK	14,13
Alfred	OXF	29,17
Alfward	SSX	3,3
Ansfrid Male	KEN	5,*146-151;162;189-190;197;201. 7,18; 24*
Ansger	NTH	15,1
Boia	CON	*1,6*
Durand	SFK	*14,119*
Edward	DOR	6,2
Eustace	SSX	9,72
Geoffrey	SSX	9,11
Godfrey	SSX	10,71
Hugh	SSX	3,3
Hugh's	GLS	62,6
Osbern	LIN	7,29
	SSX	6,2
Peter	SFK	14,13;87
Raimer	SOM	24,35
	SSX	3,3
	SRY	1,1b
Ralph	DOR	*26,9*
Ranulf	LIN	2,42
Richere	HAM	3,15-16
Robert	HAM	2,10
	SSX	3,3
Roger	SSX	9,11. 10,2;72
Sampson	STS	7
Theobald	SFK	*14,14*
Wibert	HAM	2,20
William	SHR	2,1
	SSX	3,5

clerk: *see also*	NTH	17L
	OXF	14
	STS	7

clerk: *see also* Albert of Lorraine

Clock: *see* Godric	GLS	E31
	WOR	8,9b
Cobbe: *see* Leofric	SFK	7,36
Cobbold: *see* Alwin	NTH	4,14
Cock: *see* Alwin	CAM	1,20

Colling: *see*
    Aelfric   DEV   *19,40*
    Al(f)ward   DOR *1,23*
                        WIL   67,14
    Algar?   SHR   4,7, 5
commissioner: *see*
    Hervey   BKM 48L
    Hugolin   SOM 1,31
    Richard   GLS   49
commissioner: *see also* Hugolin the interpreter
concubine: *see* Harold's   KEN   C4
constable:
    see Alnoth/Ednoth   BRK   7,7
                        SOM *39,1.*
    Asgar   BDF   1,5
                        BKM 2,3. 14,29-30;45. 21,2-6;8. 28,2
                        CAM 14,29. 15,4. 21,5. 22,*1*;2;6-8. 26,21;
                                    28. 32,11;*16*;17;23
                        HRT B8. 4,7;12-13;15;20;25. 5,11. 17,6-7;
                                    11-12;14-15. 20,10;12. 24,2. 33,1;5;
                                    8-9;11;13-15;17-18. 34,11 38,1-2. 42,6
                      MDX 9,4-9
                      NFK 4,49. 31,5
                      SFK   25,73. 66,10
                      WAR 30,1
    Boding   BKM 27,1-2
    Bondi   BDF   57,4
                      BKM 12,29. 17,9
    Earl Ralph   SFK   1,101
    Geoffrey   CAM AppxP
    Harold   LIN   T5
    Ralph   CON 5,1,6
                      LIN   T5. 1,8. 12,21;43;47-49;60;91. CK,23;
                                    51;66
                      NFK 1,202-204. 4,24;37. 8,8;10;124. 10,66.
                                    17,21;24;33;37. 20,31. 48,4
                      SFK   3,15;61;98-100. 4,14. 14,101. 31,53.
                                    46,7
    R(alph)   NFK 1,94;96;98-99. 10,80. 55,2
                      SFK   3,10;17-18. 13,6. 32,10
    Richard   KEN   *2,34-35*
    Robert   SOM *19,7;29*
    W.   SFK   4,32
constable: *see also*
    Earl Ralph (the constable)
    Ednoth the steward
    Robert son of Wymarc
consul: *see*
    Alan   CAM *14,44*
    Eustace   ESS   12,1
    Waltheof   CAM *13,11*
consul: *see also* Count
Cook/with the beard: *see* Baldwin   CAM AppxE
Cook: *see*
    Albold   HAM 1,8
    Alric   BKM 55
    Ansger   ESS   75
                      SOM 1,27. 46,16
                      WIL   66,3
    Baldwin   CAM AppxE

Gilbert	NTH	57
Gotshelm	DOR	8,1
Hugh	BRK	7,9
Humphrey	GLS	71
	WIL	*68,16*
Leofric	SFK	6,107
Mannasseh	DOR	*3,6*
	SOM	46,24
Ralph	SHR	4,27,1
Robert	CHS	4
	KEN	9,33
	SSX	9,4;14
Tesselin	SRY	36,7
Walter	ESS	67 *and note*
Warin	NFK	*6,4.* 7,20
cook: *see*		
Asketill	LIN	22,26
Corbet: *see* Roger	SHR	4,1,15;36
Corbet: *see also* son of Corbet		
Corbun: *see* W.	ESS	32,11
corn-dealer: *see* Robert	DOR	*55,37*
Cornelian: *see* William	WIL	66,4. 68,32
Cott: *see* Wulfmer	DEV	16,90
Count of: *see*		
Eu	ESS	31
	HUN	10
	KEN	*C8.* 2,25;32. 5,67;175
	SSX	9. 8,4;7;13;15
(Eu)	SSX	7,14
Evreux	BRK	17. B5
	HAM	S3
	OXF	17. B9. 7,51
Meulan	LEC	9. 44
	NTH	19
	WAR	16. B2;5. 17,60. EN2
Mortain	BRK	19
	BKM	12
	CAM	12. B1
	CON	5. 1,1;4;6-7. 2,2;6;14. 3,7. 4,1-2;*3*;7; *21*;26
	DEV	15. 1,11;23;25;50. 2,10. 7,4. 34,2. 35, 10
	DOR	26. 19,14. 56,36. E1
	GLS	29
	HAM	19. 1,47. S3
	HRT	15. 10,6;9. 39,1
	MDX	8
	NFK	3
	NTH	18. B9
	NTT	4
	OXF	16. B9
	SOM	19. 1,4-5;9;*11*;12;19-20. 2,8. 8,30-31; 39. 10,1;6. 21,92. 46,4
	SFK	21,1. 31,48. 76,16
	SRY	17. 1,4. 6,1
	SSX	10. 2,1a. 8,6. 12,2;10-11
	WIL	20. 16,5

	YKS	5. C3;27. SW,Sk18-20. SW,BA3. SW, Sf21;23-24;26;28-34. SW,O2. SW, St8-9. SW,An5. SW, Bu8;44. SW, H8-9. SN,L5-10;12;15-18;20-26;28; 38-39;41-44. SN,D3;14-15;17. SN, Ma2;4;6;14-15;17-19;21;23-24. SN, B2-16;26-27. SN,Bi6;8. SN,A8-9. SE, He2;4;7;9-10. SE,Wel6. SE,C2;5-9. SE, How7-9. SE,Wei2;4-5;7. SE, Sn1-7;10. SE, Dr4-5. SE,Wa2. SE,P3. SE,Hu1-7. SE,Tu5;7-8. SE,Bt4-7;9. SE,Sc1;4;7;9-10. SE,Ac4-5;7-11. SE, Th1-3;5-7
(Mortain)	CON	4,8-14;19-20;23;25;27-29

Count: *see*

Alan	CAM	14. B1-2;12. 29,10. 35,1. ESf
	DBY	7,13
	DOR	25
	ESS	21. 1,13
	HAM	18
	HRT	16. B2. 37,19
	LIN	12. 1,33. 67,18. CS,4;18. CN,7;18; 21-22;25-26. CK,38;65-69;71
	NFK	4. 1,11;57;197;215. 9,49. 10,19. 12, 35. 32,1. 66,63
	NTH	20
	NTT	2
	SFK	3. 1,122f. 4,13. 13,3. 26,12a; 12d;15. *46,10*. 76,17. EC2. ENf2;4
	YKS	6. SN,CtA. C24;28;30;32-33. CW42. SN, Y4-7. SW,An3;18. SN, B6;10; 16-18;27. SE, Wa7-8. SE,P4-6
A(lan)	NFK	10,59
(Alan)	CAM	AppxF
Brian	SFK	2,5-6;9
Eustace	BDF	15
	CAM	15. AppxK
	ESS	20. 1,24. 3,2. 12,1. 28,9. B1;3g
	HAM	20
	HRT	17. 24,2. Appx
	HUN	9
	KEN	10
	NFK	5. 8,31. 66,86
	OXF	19
	SOM	17. 1,28
	SFK	5
	SRY	15. 5,28. 25,2
E(ustace)	ESS	1,3;24;27. 17,2
Robert of Mortain	SFK	2
	YKS	6L
Robert (of Mortain)	CON	*4,7*
	NTT	4,3
	SFK	1,1. 2,8
	YKS	CE6. CW37
W	YKS	SW,An2

Count: *see also*
Robert of Beaumont
son of Count Gilbert
William of Eu

Count Gilbert: *see*
    Richard of Clare
    Richard son of
    Richard of Tonbridge

Countess of:

Aumale	ESS	54
	SFK	46
Boulogne (Ida)	DOR	58
	SRY	16

Countess: *see*

Aelfeva	DBY	S5
	ESS	B3j
	LEC	12
	NTT	S5
Edeva	SFK	4,17
Goda	BKM	37,1. 38,1. 53,5
	DBY	3,2
	DOR	1,30-31
	GLS	21,1. 23,2. 72,1
	MDX	13,1
	SRY	14,1. 32,1
	SSX	5,3. 9,34;37;40;44-45;49-50;52;66-68; 70;72-73;82;99;122. 11,77
Godiva	DBY	S5
	LEC	11
	NTT	S5. 6,1;13;15
	SHR	4,1,31. 4,7,1. 4,11,11. 4,19,2;8
	STS	4,2. 12,5;21-22
	WAR	15
	WOR	26,13
Gytha	BDF	22,2
	BKM	16,9-10
	BRK	10,1
	DBY	S5
	DEV	11,1
	HAM	1,19;W14
	NTT	S5. 10,5. 23,1
	SOM	*1,22-23*
	SSX	11,4;6-7;33;41. 12,41. 13,22
Ida of Boulogne	SOM	17,7
Judith	BDF	53. 21,1. 54,3
	BKM	53
	CAM	41. *37,2*
	ESS	55
	HUN	20. B5;14. 19,27
	LEC	40. C17. 14,16
	LIN	56. C10;20. S8. 34,12. CK,2;19;25
	MDX	24
	NTH	56. B11;16;34;38. 2,2-3. 9,6. 18,1. 40, 2. 53,1. ELc2-3
	OXF	53
	RUT	2. R7-8;11-13. EN16-20. ELc10-18
	YKS	10W41. SW,Sf35

Countess: *see also*
    Edeva Puella
    mother of Earl Harold
    mother of Earl Morcar
    sister of King Edward
    wife of Earl Godwin
    wife of Earl Leofric

wife of Earl Ralph		
wife of Earl Waltheof		
cramped: *see* Ansgar/Ansger	DEV	*1,23-24*
Crassus: *see* Norman	LIN	33. C3;21. CW,3-4;17
Cratel: *see* Godric	BKM	57,13
cripple: *see* Edric	DEV	1,11
Crispin: *see* Miles	BDF	19. 53,7
	BRK	33. B1
	BKM	23
	GLS	64. 1,2. E15
	OXF	35. B9
	SRY	29
	WIL	28. 30,5. 68,25
Crist: *see* Leofwin	ESS	B3a
Croc: *see*		
Alfward	SOM	*6,1*
Leofwin	ESS	46,2
	SFK	8,49
Reginald	HAM	59
Croc: *see also* Reginald son of Croc		
Crook: *see* Esbern	NTT	21,1-2
Crooked Hands: *see* Ralph	SOM	*6,9. 8,2;20;30*
crossbowman: *see*		
Berner	NFK	51. 1,3. *15,18*
	SFK	21,11
Gilbert	NFK	52. 1,61
	SFK	68
Heppo	LIN	61. CK,41
Odo	LIN	48. 1,36
	YKS	26. C17. CE32. SE,P8. SE,Bt2;7. SE, Ac3;6-8;11-12
Ralph	NFK	53. 1,61
	SFK	69
Robert	NFK	54. 1,66. *15,21*. 17,43. 26,5
	SFK	76,16
Walter	SFK	6,191;238
crossbowman: *see also*		
archer		
Bolest		
bowman		
d'Abernon: *see* of Abernon		
dane: *see*		
Aki	CAM	*17,5*
Anand	ESS	18,39
Fin(n)	BKM	19,5. 57,16
	ESS	23,38;43
Gunni	SOM	*29,1*
John	SOM	6,14. *44,1*
Odin	ESS	18,37
Osmund	NTH	43,7
Sigmund	WAR	22,24
Strang	GLS	73,1
Thorkell	HUN	2,8
	SOM	*44,2*
Toli	HAM	32,1
Daniel: *see* Roger	SSX	9,14
daughter of Alfred of Marlborough: *see* Agnes	HEF	19,10
daughter of Earl Godwin: *see* Gunhilda	SOM	*1,24*
daughter of the King: *see* Matilda	HAM	67,1

daughter: *see*

Aelfric's	SRY	19,35
Alfred of Marlborough's	HEF	19,6
Baldwin the sheriff's	DEV	*16,44*
Edric's	SRY	1,13
Geoffrey de Mandeville's	SRY	25,2
Godric the sheriff's	BKM	19,3
Guy's	HAM	44,4
Hugh Donkey's	WIL	50,5
Hugh son of Baldric's	HAM	44,4
Payne's	NFK	46,1
Ralph Tallboys	HRT	44
Roger of Rames'	SFK	38,9;11
Serlo of Burcy's	SOM	27,3. 37,7
Serlo's	WIL	E5
Sigref's	WOR	2,33
Thored's	WIL	13,21
Walter of Lacy's	BRK	14,1
William Bellet's	HAM	52
William of Falaise's	DOR	35,1
Wulfward's	BKM	56,2

deacon: *see*

Aelfric	SFK	38,22
Algar	LIN	CK,31
Alsige	LIN	CK,14
Edric	SFK	76,20
Godric	CAM	*29,6*
	KEN	2,42
	LIN	68,31;35
Godwin	ESS	88,1. 30,11
Leofric	SFK	7,31
Oddi	YKS	25W14. CE52
Rainer	LIN	CN,9;11;13;18;23
Saexfrith	YKS	C31;35
Ulfr	YKS	CE13. CW28
Walter	DOR	24,5
	ESS	42. 1,27
	GLS	57
	NFK	1,64. 10,19
	SFK	41. *21,35*. 25,24
William	BRK	1,9
	ESS	66. B3h
Wulfric	SFK	7,36

de Alno: *see* William	SFK	36,1;16
de Arches: *see* of Arques/de Arches		
de Belefol: *see* Miles	SFK	38,25
de Busli: *see* of Bully/de Busli		

de l'Isle: *see*

Humphrey	WIL	27. M9
Ralph	BDF	51

de Mandeville: *see*

Geoffrey	BRK	38. 1,14
	BKM	21. 38,1
	CAM	22. AppxA
	ESS	30. 5,2. 8,9. 90,20;28;34. B3l. ESf2
	GLS	G4
	HRT	33. B8. 9,3;10
	MDX	9. 2,3. 25,2
	NTH	45
	OXF	39

	SFK	32. 8,4. 61,1. 67,11
	SRY	25
	WAR	30. B2
G(eoffrey)	ESS	1,3. 10,5. 20,71. 25,16. 34,7. 52,1. 77, 1
	SFK	6,112. 21,58;95
Hugh	KEN	9,31
William	GLS	EvK1
de Margella: *see* Roger	DOR	*47,1*
de Montfort: *see*		
Hugh	ESS	27. 1,4;17;27. 24,24. 34,36. 90,15. B3e
	KEN	9. *C8.* 2,22;41. 5,122;130;163;166;169; 182;185-186;192;204. 6,1. 12,1
	NFK	23. 10,53. 15,1. *23,9;16.* 34,6. 66,95
	SFK	31. 1,1. 2,6. 29,1. 36,6. 41,11
(Hugh)	SFK	1,17
de Montfort: *see also* Hugh Beard		
de More: *see* W.	SFK	16,3
de Nemore: *see* of Bosc		
de Risboil/Risbou: *see* Walter	SFK	6,28;284
de Silva: *see* of Bosc		
de Vere: *see*		
Aubrey	CAM	29. 1,16. 26,9. AppxB
	ESS	35. 21,3;8. 90,36;38. B3t. EHu
	HUN	22. 6,18. D7
	MDX	21
	SFK	35. 1,105. 6,216;227. 68,5. 76,21. EE5
Bodin	NFK	25,15
Hervey	NFK	1,61. 25,15
William	MDX	3,5
de Villana: *see* Hugh	SOM	*2,6*
Dear: *see* Godwy	BDF	57,14
Delamere: *see*		
Wighen	CAM	*14,61*
William	CAM	AppxB
	HRT	28,3;8
	WIL	32,4
Delamere: *see also* of Delamere		
Dese: *see* Aelfhild	BRK	31,3
Devil: *see* Alwin	BDF	4,2;6-8. E9
	HUN	19,30. D16
Ditcher: *see* Gerard	SOM	*8,15;17. 21,38*
ditcher: *see* Hereberd	NFK	1,61
doctor: *see*		
Aelfric	HAM	NF9,12
Nigel	GLS	1,2
	HAM	63. S3
	HEF	7
	KEN	M21
	SHR	9. 3d,6
	SOM	*8,30.* 13,1
	WIL	56. 1,18
	WOR	12,1
Theobald	WIL	*68,16*
Dod: *see* Alwin	HRT	36,4
Doda: *see*		
Aelfric	DOR	7,1
Leofwin	WAR	37,2
Dodson: *see* Alwin	HRT	36,4. 42,6

	WIL	23. 67,61
	YKS	SW,Sf13;15
Aubrey: *see also* Aubrey of Coucy		
'Edgar'	CAM	EE1
	ESS	1,9 *(but see note)*
Edwin	BKM	14,25. 17,7
	CHS	1,1;8;13;22;24-26;34. 2,1-6;21. 14,1. 17,2. S1,1. FD1,1-2. FD6,1. FT1,1. FT3,1
	DBY	6,25;59
	DOR	1,2 *(but see note)*
	HEF	1,40;47
	LIN	1,38
	OXF	1,7a;7b;12
	SHR	3b,3. 4,1,16;19;21-22;25-27;30. 4,6,5. 4,7,4. 4,11,6. 4,18,3. 4,19,1;3
	STS	8,5. 11,6;67-68
	WAR	1,1;6-7. 16,44. 17,60;63. 26,1. 27,1;3. 42,1. EBW1
	WOR	C1. 1,1a;1c-1d;3b. 19,6. 23,10. 26,4. E2;7
	YKS	1Y2. 1W73. 5W14. 6N1;52. 6W1. 9W1. 10W1
Godwin	DOR	*1,2*
	GLS	1,63. E4
	HAM	1,13;19;W12;W14. 18,2. 20,2. 21,6-7; 10. 23,32. 28,2;7. 66,1. 69,1. IoW7,1. ESx
	HEF	1,74. 19,8
	KEN	D1. *2,41;43*. 4,16. 5,40;64-65;79; 84-85;89;93;109;128;142;178. 7,10. 9, 4;10. 10,1-2
	SRY	5,28. 24,1
	SSX	1,1-2. 8,3. 9,1;104;106-108;121. 10,27; 31;39-41;43;45-46;61;93;115. 11,3;5; 8-10;13-14;16;30;36-37;41;45;65; 75-76;95-98;105. 12,9-10;13;28;30;33; 36;42;48. 13,6;13;17-18;20;31;35;42; 46-47;51;53
	WIL	48,12
	WOR	19,12
Gyrth	BDF	53,5. 54,1
	CAM	*14,18*. 25,4;6-7. 26,13;18. 32,10. 41, 5-7
	HRT	24,1. 26,1. 37,11
	NFK	14,16-*17*. 66,16
	SFK	1,23;101-102;122a. 3,55
	SSX	13,9
Harold	BDF	23,4. 35,2. 50,1. 53,7;9. E1;8
	BRK	1,19. 4,1. 7,34. 15,1. 18,2. 49,1
	BKM	1,3-5. 3a,3-5. 4,13;15. 12,2;6-7;11;13; 24;37. 17,2;5-6. 23,5;10. 26,11. 30,1. 37,1-2. 43,11. 45,1. 51,1-2
	CAM	1,17. 3,1;6. 12,1. *14,75*. 17,1;5-6. 21, 1. 26,4;*5*;7;18. 32,5. 41,1;3-4
	CHS	8,21;41
	CON	1,13. 4,2;21. 5,1,5. 5,2,17. 5,4,17
	DEV	1,36. 3,6. 11,2-3
	DOR	1,7;14;30. 17,2. 19,14. 27,2. 48,1. 54,6
	ESS	B3k

GLS	B1. 1,5;14;54;60;62-63;66. 5,1. 6,4. 28,4. 39,2. 45,3. 50,3. 53,5. 60,1. 68, 2. E5
HAM	1,1;20;40;W11;W15. 20,1. 21,2;9. 23, 35. 28,6. 29,14. 30,1
HEF	C11-12. 1,7-8;56;65;67. 2,8;12;26; 31-33;37;50. 8,3;6. 10,25;28;30;32;34; 44;51;56. 14,7. 15,6-8. 17,2. 19,2-5; 7-10. 21,7. 22,1. 23,2. 24,6. 25,5;9. 29, 17-18. 31,1-2
HRT	B6. 1,1-15;17. 5,5;23;25. 15,1. 17,2-3; 8-9;13. 20,13. 23,4. 24,3. 30,1. 33,17. 34,5;12-13;24. 35,1-2. 36,11. 37,8;11; 14;22. 44,1
HUN	13,1. D10;14;17
KEN	5,29;108
LEC	43,1;5-6
LIN	C8. T5. 13,1;10;17;28;34;38-39. 15,1. CK,38
MDX	5,1-2. 8,3-4. 11,3. 18,2
NFK	3,2
OXF	1,6;9. 10,1. 15,4. 58,29
RUT	R16. ELc4
SHR	4,13,1. E1-2
SOM	1,12-13;15;19;21;25. 5,51. 6,9. 19,35. 35,11
STS	1,12
SFK	68,1
SRY	1,4-5;11. 2,3. 5,17;20. 6,1. 20,1-2. 26, 1. 36,5
SSX	9,18;21;42-43;59;74. 10,59;63;83;86. 11,93. 12,4-5. 13,33;41
WIL	B5. 1,8;12;14;18-19. 18,2. 23,7. 24,4. 28,2;11. 30,7. 41,1. 47,2. 68,15
WOR	3,3
YKS	C36. 4E1-2. 12W1

(Henry), of Warwick	GLS	EvQ29
Hugh (of Chester)	BRK	18. B4;9. 7,7
	BKM	13. B4
	CHS	1. FD1. FT1
	DBY	4. B9. S5
	DEV	14
	DOR	27
	GLS	28. 2,10. EvK1;159. EvM4;108;112
	HAM	22
	HUN	11
	LEC	43. C8
	LIN	13. C8;20. 36,4. CS,2;6;12;14-16;24; 35. CK,17
	NFK	6. 66,97
	NTH	22. B10
	NTT	3. S5
	OXF	15. B9. EBe3
	RUT	6. R16. ELc4
	SHR	4,2
	SOM	18
	SFK	4. 6,19-20. 16,34. 31,2;34. 67,3
	WAR	13
	WIL	22

	YKS	4. C2;10. CN1. SN,L1-5;10;12-13; 19-24;33-37. SE,P4. SE, Hu1;8
H(ugh)	SFK	1,110
Leofric	SHR	3b,2. 4,28,4
	STS	EW3
	WAR	3,4. 8,1. 12,10. 29,3. 43,1
Leofwin	BKM	B11. 2,2. 4,3;5;7-10;13-14;19-20;22; 27;33-35;37;40-42. 12,12. 14,19. 26, 10. 28,3. 43,4. 51,1
	DEV	1,51 *and note*
	HRT	B6. 5,1;9;20. 6,1. 15,2;10-11. 34,1;7. 42,14
	KEN	5,48;52-53;58-59;67;71;106-107
	MDX	2,2-3. 9,6. 14,2. 18,1. 25,2-3
	SOM	4,1
	SRY	5,11;19
	SSX	9,27-29
Morcar	BKM	23,2
	CHS	2,21. 8,16. 20,11
	HEF	1,6
	HRT	5,24
	LEC	1,2
	LIN	C6. T5. 1,1;4-5;26;65. 2,37;39. 30,1; 22;26;28. 35,13. 42,1. CK, 34;40
	NTH	1,4. 32,1
	NTT	1,58
	RUT	EN4
	SHR	4,1,17;24. 4,3,16. 4,4,6;20. 4,9,1. 4,11, 4. 4,23,16
	STS	10,3
Oda	HEF	1,44. 10,39. 23,6
Ralph (of E. Anglia)	WOR	E4
	BRK	24,1
	BKM	51,3
	ESS	1,30
	HRT	16,2. 35,3
	LIN	T5. 12,76. CK,68
	NFK	1,7;10;57;64;66;71;81;139;147;185; 197;209;211;213. 4,*15-16*;28;30; 44-45. 8,10;56-57. 9,88. 10,8. 14,32. 17,50. 32,1. 34,17. 47,1-2. 51,5-7
	SFK	1,61-62;73;122f. 3,56. 20,1. 77,4
R(alph, of E. Anglia)	ESS	21,9
	NFK	1,63-64;75;95;106;111;131;149;152; 172;201-202;216. 4,1;26;52;56. 8,5. 9, 4;13;30;49;160. 10,59;69;71. 12,1;42. 15,18;17,1;30. 19,25. 21,14. 26,5. 38, 2-3. 51,9. 52,3. 65,8;17. 66,42;80-81; 83-84
	SFK	1,10. 3,1;40-41. 4,32. 6,169. 7,19;44; 133. 16,3. 46,8. 74,8-9. 76,13;17. ENf4
Ralph (of Hereford)	GLS	61,1-2
	LEC	5,2. 13,1;15. 17,19. 37,1
	NTH	41,2
	WAR	29,1. 38,1. 44,6
Ralph: *see also* Harold son of		
Ralph the Constable	SFK	1,101
Ralph the Elder	NFK	1,151;153
Roger (of Hereford)	GLS	S1. W19. 1,53;56;58. 16,1. E13

	HAM	1,25. IoW1,6
	HEF	1,47
	WOR	E7
Roger (of Shrewsbury)	BRK	1,8. 47,1
	CAM	13
	CHS	G2
	GLS	27
	HAM	21. 55,2. 56,1. NF3. ESx
	HEF	E9
	HRT	18
	MDX	7
	SHR	4. C12. 3b,1. 3c,1;9. 3d, 7. 3g,7
	STS	8. B4. ES1. EW1-4
	SRY	18. 29,1
	SSX	11. 13,15;57
	WAR	12
	WIL	21
	WOR	14. E8;30-32
(Roger, of Shrewsbury)	SHR	C14. 3e,1
Siward	BDF	E8
	DBY	4,1
	HUN	B5. D14
	YKS	4N1-3
Tosti	BDF	23,47. 24,14. 44,1. 47,3. 49,2-3. 53,2; 16;20;29-30;32-33. 54,3. 57,2
	BRK	20,2
	BKM	2,1. 4,5. 6,1-2. 13,4. 14,4. 15,2. 17,7. 43,3
	CAM	38,2. 41,9
	CHS	Y2-4;7;13
	GLS	26,2. 55,1
	HAM	1,29-30;W10. 45,1. NF10,3. IoW1,1-3; 5. 9,2
	HRT	1,18
	HUN	20,5. D11
	NTH	25,1. 49,1
	NTT	B2. 1;9
	OXF	1,7b. 20,5. EBu1
	SOM	1,17
	SSX	11,39
	WIL	1,11. 31,1
	YKS	1L1-3;6. 5W8. 14E1. 30W37;40
Waltheof	BDF	6,2. 23,17. 40,3. 53,31. E3
	BKM	5,10. 53,2
	CAM	1,6. 13,3;11-12. 21,7-9. 25,8. *26, 34-35*. 32,14;40. 36,1. 37,1-2. 38,3;5. 39,1-3. 40,1. 41,8;11-16. 43,1. *44,1*
	DBY	6,40
	ESS	55,1
	HRT	19,2
	HUN	2,8. 20,9. D3;12;18
	LEC	13,67. 14,16. 40,7
	LIN	T5. 56,11;13-14;17
	MDX	24,1
	NTH	56,6;20k;22;39
	RUT	R7;11-12. ELc11;13-14
	SRY	6,4
	YKS	10W41
William (of Hereford)	BRK	44,4
	DOR	40,7

	GLS	G4. S1. W4;16;19. 1,6;8;13;16;19; 34-35;53-56;59-62. 2,10. 35,2. 56,2. E2;5
	HAM	1,27. 2,17. 21,7. 69,12-13. IoW6,10. EW1
	HEF	1,3-5;39-40;44-46;61;65;72. 2,8. 8,1. 9,1-2. 10,1;41;50;66. 19,1. 25,9. 29,1; 18. 31,1;7. E2-4
	HUN	14,1
	OXF	59
	SHR	6,3
	SSX	12,9
	WIL	1,3;21
	WOR	1,1b. 6,1. 11,2. E1-2;4-6. EG1
William (of Warenne)	SSX	12,9
Earl: *see also*		
Ralph the constable		
Ralph Wader		
William son of Osbern		
Eastry: *see* Aelmer	DEV	*15,47*
engineer: *see*		
Rabel	NFK	55
Thurstan	HAM	S3
englishman: *see*		
Alfred	NFK	9,78
Alstan	NFK	9,75
Brictmer	SOM	*47,17*
Brungar	SOM	*5,28*
Cola	BRK	41,5
Colgrim	SOM	*7,11*
Godwin	ESS	76,1
	SOM	*16,10. 47,15*
Godwy	BDF	15,3
Odo (son of Edric)	DEV	*52,22-25*
Robert of Fordham	CAM	AppxA
Stanhard	NFK	9,81
Thorgils	BDF	3,13
William	NFK	1,61
Wulfmer	SOM	*47,13*
englishwoman: Alfith	ESS	24,35
Fafiton: *see*		
Robert	BDF	30
	CAM	38. *12,2-3. 32,15*
	HUN	25
	MDX	15
(Robert)	HUN	D13
Fafiton: *see also* son of Fafiton		
fair: *see*		
Edeva	BKM	13,1. 17,9. 44,2;5
	CAM	1,12. *13,8-10.* 14,1-2;*7;9;11*;13;*14-16;* *19-20;22;24;27;31;33-36;*37;*38;41;*44; *46;48;56-57;61;*74. 19,4. 26,*16;*38. 29, 10. 31,3;7. 32,*8;32;*44
	HRT	4,22;25. 16,1-2;7;10;12. 35,3. 37,19
	SFK	1,67;73. 3,67. 46,4. EC1
Edith	CAM	*14,45*
fair: *see also*		
Countess Edeva		
puella		
rich		

father: *see*

Aelfric's	ESS	20,44
	HAM	NF9,41;44
	LIN	CS21
Aelmer's	BDF	56,6
Agenwulf's	WIL	19,4
Alfred's	KEN	M8
Alfsi's	HAM	6,16
Alfward's	SOM	47,14
Alfward the goldsmith's	BRK	65,5
Alnoth's	LIN	CS38
Alric's	HAM	69,38
Alwin the priest's	BRK	7,29
Ansfrid Male's	KEN	5,149
Asketill's	LIN	CS28
Brictric's	WIL	67,6-9
Brictward the priest's	WIL	1,23j
Cola's	WIL	67,42
Earl Roger's	GLS	16,1
Edgar's	WIL	1,11
Edmund's	HAM	69,20
Edward's	BDF	56,5
	WIL	67,54
Edwulf's	HAM	69,25
Ernwin the priest's	BDF	14,1
Fenkell's	LIN	CS38
Gamel's	CHS	26,9-10
Godfrey Scullion's	DOR	57,22
Godric's	WIL	67,46
Godric Malf's	HAM	69,39. NF9,36-39
Guthfrithr's	LIN	CS21
Harold's	LIN	CS21
Ketel's	LIN	22,26
Ketel Hunter's	SRY	36,9
Oirant's	HAM	IoW9,7
Ordgar's	OXF	35,25
Osmer's	SOM	47,25
Osward's	WIL	67,91
Otho's	WIL	67,92
Roger of Courseulles'	SOM	8,41
Roger of Lacy's	HEF	10,3;37
Roger the sheriff's	NFK	73,1
Saewulf's	WIL	67,84
Sigar's	KEN	M20
Sighvatr's	LIN	CS,38
Sired's	KEN	M6
Swein's	DOR	56,28-29;53
	ESS	24,20
	WIL	67,94
the beadle's	BDF	57,17
Thorfrothr's	LIN	22,26
Thorgot's	BDF	57,16
Thori's	BRK	3,2
Thorkell's	WIL	67,85
Thurstan's	SOM	16,9
William of Cairon's	BDF	4,2
Wulfmer's	SFK	73,1
Wulfnoth's	WIL	67,78
Wulfric Hunter's	DOR	56,30
	HAM	69,47

guard, royal: *see*
Aki	MDX	17,1
Alli	BKM	53,4
Anand	HRT	34,15
Azor	MDX	11,1
Azor son of Toti	BKM	49,1
Brand	HRT	27,1
Burghard	BKM	13,2
Godnir	BKM	12,36
Haldane	BKM	46,1
Rotlesc	GLS	1,59
Saxi	HRT	22,2
Stergar	NFK	49,7
Thori	BKM	14,35. 43,11
Toki	MDX	7,8
Tovi	BDF	46,1. 53,12
Ulf	BKM	18,1
	MDX	7,2

gunner: *see* under bowman
Guntram: *see* Siward	SOM	*47,11*
Hackett: *see* Walter	BKM	14,40

Hagni: *see*
Cock	NFK	9,83-84
Wulfric	SFK	53,6
Hako: *see* Thorkell	NFK	19,21
Haldane: *see* Godwin	NFK	61. 1,216
Halden [indexing error for Haldane]	NFK	1,216
Halebold: *see* R.	WAR	17,60
half man of Brunmer: *see* Brunman Beard	SFK	7,36

half man of Edric: *see*
Aelfric Stickstag	SFK	7,77
Durand	SFK	67,17
Wulfheah	SFK	7,79

half man of Manulf: *see*
Alfheah	SFK	4,15
Leofric	SFK	4,15
half man of Norman: *see* Brunman Beard	SFK	7,36
Hapra: *see* Wulfwin	ESS	62,3
Hard: *see* William	WIL	26,22
harper: *see* Alwy	CAM	17,2
Hastings: *see* William	GLS	EvN5

Hastings: *see also*
of Hastings
son of Ralph
haunted: *see* Ralph	ESS	36,8;12
Herecom: *see* Robert	SOM	*21,8*
Hiles: *see* Alfwy Hiles	GLS	69,6
Hobbeson: *see* Leofric	SFK	7,59. 29,7. 30,3
Hoga: *see* Swart Hoga	SFK	6,109

Holdfast: *see*
Aelmer	ESS	61,2
(Aelmer)	ESS	22,3
Horn(e): *see* Alwin	BDF	30,1
	HRT	42,1-2;5
	KEN	D25
	MDX	4,11
Houerel: *see* Richard	SFK	*14,151*
Hubald: *see* Hugh	BDF	44,1-3
	CAM	*24,1*

Hunter: *see*
Aelfric	DOR	*56,6;52;57;60*
	WIL	13,2
Aelmer	SRY	4,2
Alfward	SOM	*19,51*
Alfwy	ESS	90,70
Alwin	HRT	6,1. 33,4
	NTH	60,1
Cola son of Wulfgeat	HAM	69,32;52
Colman	SRY	19,39
Croc	HAM	60
Edward	DOR	56,66
Edwin	DOR	*56,31-33*
	HAM	69,41
Gilbert	CHS	18
Godric	DOR	*56,4*
	WIL	67,45
Godwin	DOR	56,24;27
Jocelyn	HEF	1,40
	WOR	E2
Ketel	SRY	36,9
Ralph	CHS	21. FD8
Richard	WAR	B2. 44,7-8
Robert	WAR	21,1. 22,10
Roger	SHR	4,26. 4,1,2. 4,3,15. 4,26,7
	WOR	14,1
Siward	HAM	6,16
	OXF	58,23
Thorbert	HAM	NF9,4
Waleran	DOR	40L *and note*
	HAM	45. 6,16. NF9,14
	WIL	37
Warmund	CHS	FT3,3
Wulfgeat	DOR	*56,16*
	HAM	69,36. IoW1,6;9
	WIL	67,77
Wulfric	DOR	56,*13;18*;30
	HAM	69,47
	WIL	*67,65;70*
Wulfwy	SRY	36,10

Hunter: *see also* forester
huntsman: *see*
Judicael	CAM	12,2-3
Wigot	BDF	52,2
Wulfgeat	WIL	1,5
Wulfwin	CAM	4,1

Hurant: *see* William
	SFK	25,7

husband: *see*
Alfhild's	WIL	67,87
Ealdhild's	WIL	67,90
Godiva's	SOM	8,25
Leofgeat's [rectius Leofgyth]	WIL	67,86

Hussey: *see*
Walter	SOM	7,4;10. 8,26
	WIL	B5. 34,1
William	SOM	1,28. 5,43. 7,8. 37,6. 47,5

Illing: *see* Alfsi
	DBY	S5
	NTT	S5

in Kyluertestuna: *see* Ordgar
	SFK	6,110

interpreter: *see*
Ansgot	SRY	36,8
David	DOR	54,7
Hugh	SOM	1,31 *and note.* 7,11
Hugolin	SOM	*1,31 and note.* 45,9
Richard	SOM	*5,54. 45,14*

interpreter: *see also*
  commissioner
  Latimer
Iuvenis, Juvenis: *see* A young man; The young
  man

Ivry: *see* Hugh	NTH	24,1

Ivry: *see also* of Ivry
jester: *see*
Adelina (fem.)	HAM	1,25
Berdic	GLS	W4
Karlson: *see* Godric	KEN	D17

Karlson: *see also* Godric son of Karl
keeper of the granaries: *see* Gundwin	WIL	68,29

Kemp: *see*
Aelfric	CAM	*21,2*;3. 25,*1*;2;*3*
	ESS	32,38. 33,16. 39,5;7
	SFK	16,41. 28,7. 38,2. 76,4
Wulfric	BRK	5,1
kentishman: *see* Alnoth	BKM	4,36. 17,25

King: *see*
Aethelred	GLS	12,1
Canute	CHS	2,1. B13
	ESS	3,9
	SHR	3c,2
	WIL	2,1
Caradoc	GLS	W2
Edmund	SFK	14,167
Edward	CHS	B7
	DEV	2,2
	DOR	34,8
	ESS	24,23;25;29;35
	HAM	6,10
	HEF	1,41
	HRT	17,15
	KEN	*5,149*
	SHR	3d,7. 4,26,3
	SFK	33,15. 34,5. 40,2
	WIL	1,3
Gruffydd	CHS	B7. FT3,7
	GLS	W4
	HEF	1,49
Maredudd	HEF	29,1. 31,1;7
William	BDF	32,1;15. 46,1. 56,2-3
	BRK	41,6
	BKM	3a,1. 56,1
	DEV	C3. 1,1-2;*23*;41. *5,5. 19,35*
	DOR	3,6
	ESS	1,25;27. 3,11. 5,6-7. 6,9;11. 8,8. 20,41;
		52;56. 24,43;48;55;59;65-66. 30,16;
		18. 42,7. 52,2. 66,1. 79,1. 83,1. 90,
		64-65
	GLS	2,4. 78,9
	HAM	6,12. 53,2. 67,1
	HRT	36,19

	KEN	D7
	NFK	1,2;4;120-121;144;230. 9,5;79. 10,67; 77. 14,16. 15,1. 17,18. 21,13-14. 52,3
	NTH	8,4
	OXF	1,6. 28,24
	STS	11,37
	SFK	1,110. 8,51. 18,1. 25,1. 76,4;6
	WIL	25,23. 32,17
kinsman of King Edward: *see* Siward	HEF	1,41
Krakr: *see* Grimbald	LIN	12,9;13
Lacy: *see* Roger	HEF	24,11
	SHR	4,8,3
	WOR	2,78
Lacy: *see also* of Lacy		
Lagr: *see* Thorgautr	LIN	18,1;7;13;29. 59,6
	YKS	C36 *and note*
La Guerche: *see* of La Guerche		
Lang: *see* Edric	GLS	1,62
Lang?: *see* Radbod	NFK	*9,100*
Lang: *see also* Long		
larderer: *see* Odilard	HUN	19,22
lascivious/perverted: *see* Robert	ESS	6,12. 32,28
Latimer: *see*		
Godric	KEN	*M24*
Hugh	HAM	NF10,3
Leofwin	HEF	1,10c;36
Ralph	CAM	*5,37*
	ESS	90,42
Robert	KEN	2,4. 5,19;49;84;89;102;209. 7,2
Latimer: *see also* interpreter		
lawman: *see*		
Agmundr son of Valhrafn	LIN	C3
Alwold	LIN	C2-3
Beorhtric	LIN	C2
Burgwald son of Leofwine	LIN	C3
Godric son of Eadgifu	LIN	C2-3
Godwine son of Beorhtric	LIN	C3
Guthrothr	LIN	C2-3
Halfdan the priest	LIN	C2-3
Harthaknutr	LIN	C2
Leodwine son of Rafn	LIN	C3
Leofwine the priest	LIN	C2
Norman Crassus	LIN	C3
Peter of Valognes	LIN	C3
Siward the priest	LIN	C2-3
Svartbrandr son of Ulfr	LIN	C2-3
Svertingr	LIN	C3
Svertingr son of Grimbald	LIN	C2
Svertingr son of Harthaknutr	LIN	C3
Valhrafn	LIN	C2-3
Wulfbert	LIN	C2
Wulfbert brother of Ulfr	LIN	C3
Wulfnoth the priest	LIN	C3;14
Leofed: *see* Wulfward	BDF	20,1
Leofric: *see*		
William	BRK	EW1
	ESS	59
	GLS	38
	OXF	46
	WIL	49,1a

	SFK	1,10;14. 2,17-18;20. 3,28;41. 7,6;13; 17;21;26;30;33;36;75;79. 8,8. 16,26. 21,48;65;74;88;*92;94*. 32,28. 34,15. 52,1. 53,6. 67,5;15. 77,4
(Robert)	NFK	20,29 *and note*
	SFK	3,98-102. 6,177. 7,144. 16,25;33;38
William	LIN	14,29
	NFK	9,211. 66,60
	SFK	3,94-95;100. 4,42. 6,11. 7,8;15-16;36; 138-140;143;148. 16,6;30. 19,16. 26, 13. 28,6. 31,20. 45,2. 52,1. 67,2;4; 19-21;28;30. 75,4. 77,4
	YKS	CN3-4. CE13;15;17;19-23;26;30. CW2-3;25;27-30;32
W(illiam)	NFK	8,12. 17,52. 35,16. 66,1-2
	SFK	3,39-40. 6,93;159. 7,26;33;131;133. 8, 42. 18,1. 67,15-16;31
(William)	NFK	20,29 *and note*. 30,2
	SFK	7,17. 16,15. 55,2
	YKS	CE29
(Malet): *see*		
R(obert)	NFK	66,60
William	SFK	3,99. 7,144;146. 38,6. 67,29
	YKS	CW31
Malet: *see also*		
father of Robert Malet		
father of (Robert) Malet		
son of William Malet		
Malf: *see* Godric	HAM	69,39. NF9,36-37
Mallory: *see* Geoffrey	DOR	*36,1*
Malregard: *see* Geoffrey	SOM	*5,46*
Malsor: *see* Fulchere	RUT	R18
Maltravers: *see* Hugh	SOM	*26,5*
Maminot: *see*		
Gilbert	BRK	1,1
	BKM	4,33
	GLS	30. E11
	KEN	5,36
	YKS	C14. SE,Ac2
Hugh	GLS	30,1
Maminot: *see also* Bishop of Lisieux		
man-at-arms: *see*		
Aelfric	DOR	3,17
Aethelhard	CHS	9,17
Alfred	KEN	5,128
	SSX	9,1
	WOR	1,1c
Alfred the butler	SOM	19,86
Alfred the steward	KEN	5,128
Ansfrid	SSX	3,3
Ansgot	WIL	2,1
Ansketel of Rots	KEN	*2,11*
Arnold	HEF	19,1
Aubrey	WIL	12,2
Baldric	KEN	5,128
Bernard of St Ouen	KEN	5,128
Bretel	SOM	19,86
Brictsi	DOR	49,12
Drogo	SOM	19,86
Duncan	SOM	19,86

Edward	WIL	14,1
Edward the sheriff	WIL	12,2
Engelbert	DOR	2,6 (cf 3,1)
Eudo	KEN	5,128
Farman	KEN	*2,10*
Gamel	CHS	R5,6
Geoffrey	CHS	9,17. R5,6
	NTH	6a,6
	SHR	4,4,20
	SSX	11,3
Geoffrey of Rots	KEN	*2,10*
Gerald	SSX	9,1
Gerard	NFK	*8,37;44*
	SSX	9,6;8
Gilbert	HEF	19,1
	SSX	13,9
Gislold	SHR	4,20,8
Godfrey	DOR	3,17
Grento	DEV	*5,13*
	SHR	4,4,20
Gunfrid	WIL	12,2
Harold	SSX	3,3
	WIL	2,10
Hugh	DOR	*55,32-33*
	HUN	6,1
	SSX	9,8
Hugh son of Mauger	ESS	27,17
Hugh son of William	KEN	5,128
Humphrey	CHS	9,17
Ingelrann	SSX	9,1
Leofwin	SSX	13,9
Lovell	SSX	3,3
Ludo	DEV	*23,20. 42,16*
Murdoch	SSX	3,3
Nigel	CHS	R5,6
Norman	SSX	9,8
Odard	CHS	9,17
Odbold	DOR	2,6 (cf 3,1)
Osbern	SSX	9,1;8
Osmer	DOR	3,17
Payne	SSX	11,3
Picot	SHR	4,4,20. 4,20,8
Rainfrid	SHR	4,4,20
Ralph	CAM	*26,24*
	DEV	*19,33. 23,16*
	DOR	2,6 (cf 3,1). *55,43*
	KEN	*2,11*
	SOM	*25,30*
	STS	10,10
	SSX	9,6;8. 13,9
	WIL	2,1
	WOR	15,10
Ralph Banks	CAM	*14,17*
Ralph the Breton	CAM	*14,17*
Ranulf	KEN	5,138
Reinbert	SSX	9,1
Richard	HEF	19,1
	HUN	6,1
	KEN	5,128

Robert	CAM	*26,24*
	SSX	9,1. 13,42
Robert son of Watson	KEN	*3,18*
Robert Vessey	SHR	4,11,4
Roger	DEV	*48,10*
	KEN	*2,11*
	WOR	1,1c
Sinoth	DOR	2,6 (cf 3,1)
Thorold	DOR	*55,32;35*
Thurstan	WIL	12,2
Venning	SSX	9,8
Vitalis	ESS	23,3
Walchelin	YKS	2B18
Waleran	DOR	2,6 (cf 3,1)
	WIL	2,1
Walter	DOR	3,13
	SHR	4,11,4. 4,20,8
	WIL	14,1
	WOR	1,1c
Walter of Abbeville	KEN	5,128
Walter son of Engelbert	KEN	5,128
Warin	CHS	R5,6
Waring	SSX	9,1
Wesman	KEN	5,128
Wihenoc	NFK	*15,14*
William	DOR	3,13
	HEF	*19,1*
	KEN	*2,11*
	SSX	3,2. 11,3. 13,6;9;42
	WIL	2,10
	WOR	1,1c
	YKS	13W36
William of Braose	WIL	2,1
William the bursar	KEN	*2,10*
Withbert	SSX	9,1
Wulfwy	SFK	14,69
man-at-arms: *see also*	DEV	22. 26-27. 31-33. 40-41. 43. 45-46
	HRT	*37.* 4,1-21
	KEN	2,28-40
man of Abbot of Abingdon: *see*		
Azelin	BRK	7,27
Gilbert	BRK	7,36;42
Godfrey	BRK	7,12
Reginald	BRK	7,27
William	BRK	7,12
Wimund	BRK	7,36;42
man of Abbot of Chatteris: *see* Sinoth	HRT	31,2
man of Abbot of Chertsey: *see*		
Aelfric	MDX	8,2
Corbelin	SRY	8,22
Odin	SRY	8,22
man of Abbot of Ely: *see*		
Albert	CAM	32,39
Edward	CAM	*13,11*
Edwy	CAM	27,1
Godwin	CAM	*5,2.* 26,50
Godwin the priest	CAM	*30,3*
Gold	CAM	*32,27*
Munulf the priest	SFK	26,5
Oswy	CAM	40,1

Wulfwin	CAM	3,5. 17,3
man of Abbot of Fécamp: *see* Robert of Hastings	SSX	5,1
man of Abbot of Glastonbury: *see*		
Alwin	BRK	8,1
Edward	BRK	8,1
Robert d'Oilly	BRK	8,1
man of Abbot of Holme: *see* Aski the priest	NFK	65,13
man of Abbot of Peterborough: *see*		
Asketill	LIN	8,8
Gilbert	LIN	8,9;22
Godfrey	LIN	8,36
Ralph	LIN	8,20;23;27
Richard	LIN	8,15
Roger	LIN	8,19
Saswalo	LIN	8,7
William	LIN	8,31
man of Abbot of Peterborough: *see also*	NTH	6a
man of Abbot of Ramsey: *see*		
Alric the monk	CAM	17,1. 32,1
Everard	HUN	6,7
Ingelrann	HUN	6,7
Leofric	BDF	34,3
Maynard	NFK	1,61
Ordmer	HRT	37,13
Pleines	HUN	6,7
man of Abbess of Romsey: *see* Hundger	HAM	15,1
man of Abbot of St Albans: *see*		
Black	HRT	10,17
Edward	BDF	53,25
Gladwin	BKM	12,18
Leofing	BKM	12,22
man of Abbot of St Benedict: *see* Maynard	NFK	1,61
man of Abbot of St Edmunds: *see*		
Berard	SFK	40,5
Berengar	SFK	76,19
Henry	SFK	*21,4*
Peter	NFK	1,61
Theobald	NFK	1,61
man of Abbot of Winchester (St Peter's): *see*		
Burghelm	HAM	6,3
Fulcred	HAM	6,3
man of Abbot of Winchester (St Swithin's): *see*		
Chipping	HAM	3,1
Hugh Mason	HAM	3,1
Osbern	HAM	3,1
Thurstan Red	HAM	3,1
Thurstan Small	HAM	3,1
William	HAM	3,1
man of Abbot Thorald: *see* Asfrothr	LIN	8,34
man of Aelfric: *see* Aelmer	HRT	2,2
man of Aelfric Little: *see* Alwin Dod	HRT	36,4
man of Aelfric of Flitwick: *see* Aelmer	BDF	25,2
man of Aelfric Small: *see* Aelfric	BDF	25,3
man of Aelfric son of Goding: *see*		
Aelmer	BKM	12,32
Gunni	BKM	57,17
man of Aelfric the priest: *see* Godwin	SFK	2,17
man of Aelmer: *see* Topi	HRT	36,2

man of Aelmer of Bennington: *see*		
Aelfric	HRT	20,4. 36,17
Alfward	HRT	38,2
Alstan	HRT	36,1
Alwin	HRT	36,5
Godric	HRT	20,8
Godwin	HRT	20,5
Leofrun	HRT	36,8
man of Aldeva: *see* Siward	BKM	12,4
man of Alfred of Lincoln: *see*		
Bernard	LIN	27,3;5;61
Boso	LIN	27,37
Doda	LIN	27,60
Doding	LIN	27,51;53
Gleu	LIN	27,12;14;47-48
	RUT	ELc6-7
Jocelyn	LIN	27,20;22;25;57-59
Ralph	LIN	27,1-2;40;44
Ranulf	LIN	27,23-24
Sveinn	LIN	27,56
Walefrid	LIN	27,50
man of Alfwy Hiles: *see* Harold	GLS	69,6
man of Algar: *see* Godric	CAM	*32*,7
man of Alli: *see*		
Alfsi	BDF	47,1
Hunman	BKM	53,3
man of Alnoth: *see* Saemer	HRT	5,7
man of Alnoth the Kentishman: *see* Athelstan	BKM	17,25
man of Alric: *see* Oswy	BKM	14,47. 29,4
man of Alric son of Goding: *see*		
Alfward	BDF	24,6
Fuglo	BDF	24,2;7
Godwin	BKM	23,31
Leofwin	BKM	12,28
Oswy	BKM	14,46
Sibbi	BKM	23,31
Tovi	BKM	14,33
Wulfric	BKM	14,28
man of Alstan: *see*		
Alwin	BDF	18,7
Godmer	BDF	18,3
Godwin	BDF	18,2
man of Alstan of Boscombe: *see*		
Alfgeat	HRT	28,3
Alfward	HRT	28,5
man of Alwin of Gotton: *see* Siward	HRT	42,12
man of Alwin son of Goding: *see* Alric	BKM	12,27
man of Alwin Varus: *see*		
Alwin	BKM	21,8
Swein	BKM	4,6
man of Archbishop of Canterbury: *see*		
Aethelwold	KEN	*2,16*
Alfward	KEN	*2,16*
Arnold	KEN	*2,21*
Geoffrey the arblaster	KEN	*2,21*
Godfrey the steward	KEN	*2,16*
Heringod	KEN	*2,21*
Mauger	ESS	6,8
Osbern Paisforiere	KEN	*2,21*
Ralph	SRY	2,1

Restald	SRY	2,1
Richard	KEN	2,34
Robert of Hardres	KEN	*2,16;26*
Robert son of Watson	KEN	*2,26*
Vitalis	KEN	*2,16;21*
Wibert	KEN	*2,21*
William	KEN	3,8

man of Archbishop of York: *see*

Auti	LIN	CK16
Geoffrey	YKS	2A,3
Gilbert	LIN	2,3;21
Herbert	LIN	2,6;11;18
Hugh	LIN	2,29
Osbern	LIN	2,38
Walchelin	LIN	2,34;36-37;40
William	LIN	2,5;8-9;17;27

man of Archbishop Stigand: *see*

Aelfric	HRT	2,3
Aelfric Black	HRT	2,5
Aldred	BKM	29,1
Alfled	CAM	*26,21*
Alfward	HRT	4,4;17
Algar	CAM	26,23
Alnoth	HRT	5,17;26
Alnoth Grut	HRT	5,14
Alric	HRT	16,8. 17,5
Alwin	HRT	1,10
Ansgot	CAM	32,13
	HRT	41,2
Baldwin	BKM	17,3-4
Edeva Puella	HRT	5,16
Godric	HRT	10,11
Godwin	CAM	*32,8*
Ledmer	HRT	7,3. 23,1-2
Leofrun	HRT	34,14
Leofwy	OXF	29,16
Osgot	CAM	*32,8*
Siward	HRT	4,11
Thorbert the priest	CAM	*26,26*
William	CAM	32,8
Wulfric	BKM	33,1

man of Asgar (the constable): *see*

Alfred	HRT	33,10
Burgi	HRT	33,12
Edred	HRT	33,6
Godith	HRT	17,10
Swarting	BKM	21,7

man of Asgar the constable: *see*

Aelmer	HRT	5,11
Alfred	HRT	4,13. 20,10
Alric	HRT	34,11
Azor	MDX	9,5
Danemund	CAM	26,28
Doding	BKM	21,2
Edric	HRT	4,7
Edwin	BDF	1,5
Godith	HRT	17,6-7;14. 33,13;18
Godric	BKM	28,2
Leofwy	CAM	14,29
Oswy	HRT	33,14

Sigar	CAM	22,8
Swarting	BKM	14,30
Swein	BKM	21,3-4;6
Thorkell	HRT	33,5;15
Ulf	BKM	14,45. 21,8
Wulfric	HRT	33,8
Wulfward	HRT	17,11. 24,2. 42,6
Wulfwin	HRT	38,2
Wulfwy	HRT	4,20
man of Askell: *see*		
Aelfeva	BDF	18,5
Aelmer	BDF	23,42
Augi	BDF	17,4
Godwin	BDF	23,13
Wulfgeat	BDF	23,24
man of Askell of Ware: *see* Wulfmer	HRT	37,4
man of Augi: *see* Black	BDF	17,6
man of Azor: *see*		
Edwin	BKM	12,26
Leofric	BKM	41,5
man of Azor son of Toti: *see* Saeward	BKM	14,29
man of Baldwin son of Herlwin: *see* Thorgils	BKM	4,31
man of Berengar of Tosny: *see* Ralph	NTT	21,1
man of Bishop Erfast: *see* Bondi	NFK	10,53
man of Bishop of Bayeux: *see*		
Baldric	LIN	4,76
Erneis	LIN	4,23
Gilbert	ESS	18,34. 48,2
Hugh nephew of Herbert	NTT	7,6
Ilbert	LIN	4,3-4;10-16;42-43;46;54;56-57;67;72
Kolsveinn	LIN	4,2
Losoard	LIN	4,8;41;61
	NTT	7,2-3;5
Ralph	LIN	4,50
Sveinn	LIN	4,78
Thorr	LIN	4,79
Wadard	LIN	4,2;7;23;28;31;39-40;59;74
Wazelin	NTT	7,1
Wigmund	LIN	4,38
William Black	HRT	42,11
man of Bishop of Chichester: *see*		
Geoffrey	SSX	3,7
Gilbert	SSX	3,6
Herbert	SSX	3,8
Ralph	SSX	3,8
Rozelin	SSX	3,6
Ulf	SSX	3,6
William	SSX	3,7
man of Bishop of Coutances: *see* Colswein	DEV	25,3
man of Bishop of Durham: *see*		
Alnoth	LIN	3,35;37
Jocelyn	LIN	3,3
Kolsveinn	LIN	3,36
Lambert	LIN	3,31
Nigel	LIN	3,5;8;39;51
Thorsteinn	LIN	3,20;27;48
Walbert	LIN	3,6-7;40
William	LIN	3,50;53
man of Bishop of Hereford: *see* Askell	HEF	28,1

man of Bishop of Lincoln: *see*

Adam	LIN	7,32;52
Alwin Devil	BDF	4,2
Alwin Sack	BDF	4,5
Erchenold	LIN	7,14;38
Hugh	LIN	7,54
Jocelyn	LIN	7,19;28
Leofric	BDF	4,4
Mauger	LIN	7,16;34
Nigel	NTT	6,13;15
Ralph	LIN	7,30;53
Ranulf	LIN	7,18;22;27
Roger	LIN	7,21;23
Walter	LIN	7,39-40
William	LIN	7,51

man of Bishop of London: *see*

Ansketel	ESS	48,2
Roger	ESS	1,27

man of Bishop of Thetford: *see* Ralph   NFK   10,48

man of Bishop of Winchester: *see*

Alfsi	HAM	IoW2,1
Herpolf	HAM	IoW2,1
Robert	HAM	IoW2,1
Wace	SRY	3,1
William	SRY	3,1

man of Bishop Wulfwy: *see*

Aelfric	BKM	53,7
Alfward	BDF	24,23
Alfwold	BDF	34,2
Alric	BKM	53,8
Alwin	BDF	28,2
Godwin	BKM	14,48-49
Raven	BKM	43,6

man of Bisi: *see* Grimbald   BKM   17,21
man of Bondi the constable: *see* Aelmer   BKM   17,9
man of Brictmer: *see* Brictmer son of Asmoth   SFK   4,15

man of Brictric: *see*

Aelmer	BKM	23,18;22
Alwin	BKM	17,8
Colman	BKM	23,6
Herch	BKM	23,23
Leofmer	BKM	23,21
Leofric	BDF	19,3
Leofsi	BKM	23,26-28
Odo	BKM	26,5
Oepi	BKM	36,3
Ordmer	BKM	12,9
Oswulf	BKM	23,25
Oswy	BKM	17,14
Wulfric	BKM	23,6

man of Brictric son of Algar: *see* Ebbi   GLS   6,1

man of Burgred: *see*

Aelfric	BDF	3,15;17
	NTH	EB2
Alwin	BDF	3,9;13
	NTH	EB1
Azor	BDF	2,4
Godwin	BDF	54,4
Leofric	BDF	25,6
Leofwin	BKM	41,3

Wulfric	BKM	5,16
man of Count Alan: *see*		
Aelmer	CAM	*14,82*
Algar	LIN	CK,66
Edric	NFK	1,197. 4,51
Eudo	LIN	12,40;80;82;85;93;96
Geoffrey (of) Tournai	LIN	12,89
Godric	LIN	12,53;57
Gyrthr	LIN	12,90. CK,69
Hervey	NTT	2,4
	LIN	12,51
Kolgrimr	LIN	12,52;55;91-92
Landric	LIN	12,7;37
	YKS	6N36;53
Odo	YKS	6N56
Picot	LIN	12,14
	YKS	6N58
Robert	LIN	12,4
	YKS	6N147;151
Robert of Moutiers	NTT	2,9
Stephen	LIN	12,56
Toli	LIN	12,58;88
Wigmund	LIN	12,18;20;31
Wiuhomarch	YKS	6N57
man of Count Eustace: *see*		
Berengar	ESS	90,87
Seric	HRT	Appx
man of Count of Eu: *see*		
Alfwold	SSX	9,130
Alwin	SSX	9,59
Ansketel	SSX	9,130
Ednoth	SSX	9,109
Geoffrey	SSX	9,109
Hugh	SSX	9,130
Osbern	SSX	9,130
Remir	SSX	9,109
Roger	SSX	9,130
Theobold the priest	SSX	9,109
Walter	SSX	9,109
man of Count of Mortain: *see*		
Alfred	NTT	4,5;7
	SSX	10,2
Alwin	SSX	10,27
Ansgot	SSX	10,27
Gilbert	SSX	10,3;22;27
Godfrey	SSX	10,3
Godfrey the priest	SSX	10,27
Jocelyn	SXX	10,22;27
	SFK	21,1
Osbern	SSX	10,27
Roger	SSX	10,22
Roger the clerk	SSX	10,2
William	SSX	10,2;27
man of Countess Goda: *see* Thorbert	BKM	53,5
man of Countess Gytha: *see* Saemer the priest	BDF	22,2
	NTH	EB4
man of Countess Judith: *see*		
Herbert	LIN	56,18
	RUT	ELc15

Hugh	LIN	56,13
	RUT	ELc12-13
Nigel	LIN	56,6
Theodbald	BDF	21,1
man of Drogo of Beuvrière: *see*		
Albert	YKS	14E45
Baldwin	YKS	14E48
Earnwulf	LIN	30,28
Franco	YKS	14E33;37;47;51
Frank	NFK	8,137
Frumold	YKS	14E44
Fulco	YKS	14E53
Geoffrey	LIN	30,17-20
Gerbodo	YKS	14E36
Ingelrann	LIN	30,28
Jocelyn	LIN	30,3
Kolgrimr	LIN	30,25
Kolsveinn	LIN	30,36
Lanbert	YKS	14E46
Rainer	LIN	30,6
	YKS	14E30;39
Ralph	YKS	14E50
Robert	LIN	30,7;9;12;33
	YKS	14E32
Roger	YKS	14E52
Theobald	YKS	14E43
Theodbald	LIN	30,5
Thorsteinn	YKS	14E38
Walter	LIN	30,30
	YKS	14E42
Wazelin	YKS	14E40
Wizo	LIN	30,22
	YKS	14E7
man of Durand Malet: *see*		
Alfred	LIN	44,2
Richard	LIN	44,8
man of Earl Algar: *see*		
Alfgeat	CAM	14,47
Alfward	HRT	4,10. 37,2;20
Alwin	CAM	*32,8*
Edric	HRT	35,3. 37,18
Goda	CAM	*13,1*
Godman	CAM	*32,8*
Sired	CAM	26,31
Thorbert	BKM	39,1
Thorgar	CAM	26,6
man of Earl Edwin: *see*		
Leofric	BKM	17,7
Swein Swarthy	BKM	14,25
man of Earl Gyrth: *see*		
Aelmer	HRT	24,1
Godwin	BDF	54,1
Leofmer	CAM	*41,5*
man of Earl Harold: *see*		
Abo	HRT	1,10
Aelmer	BKM	12,24
Aki	CAM	17,5-6
Alfward	HRT	17,2;4;8-9
Alfwy	GLS	5,1
Algar	MDX	18,2

man of Edric: *see*
Aelfric	SFK	26,13
Blackman	SFK	6,93
Durand	SFK	67,12
Harold	SFK	7,13
Stanwin	SFK	6,92
Thorkell of Wrentham	SFK	26,12d

man of Edric of Laxfield: *see*
Blackman	SFK	7,36
Edric	NFK	4,39
Osmund	SFK	7,36
Wulfwin	SFK	2,17

man of Edric son of Ingold: *see*
Cynric	SFK	4,15
Grim	SFK	4,15

man of Edric the Bald: *see* Goding   BDF   55,8

man of Edwin: *see*
Leofric	BKM	5,4
Leofwin	BKM	23,30

man of Engelric: *see* Godwin   HRT   15,5
man of Erneis de Burun: *see* Erneis of Buron
man of Erneis of Buron: *see*
Humphrey	YKS	24E2
John	LIN	34,24
	YKS	23W18
Ralph	YKS	24W4
Ranulf	LIN	34,9
Thorsteinn	LIN	34,3;8
Wulfric	LIN	34,4-6

man of Estan: *see* Alwin   BKM   4,43
man of Eudo son of Spirewic: *see* Ivo   LIN   29,27
man of Eustace the sheriff: *see*
Herbert	HUN	19,13
	NTH	EH4
Roger	HUN	19,7

man of Frodo: *see*
Anselm	SFK	*14,139*
Jocelyn	SFK	*14,137-138*

man of G. of Laxfield: *see* Edric   NFK   4,41
man of Geoffrey Alselin: *see*
Walter	NTT	12,1

man of G(eoffrey) de Mandeville: *see* William   ESS   10,5
Cardon
man of Geoffrey of la Guerche: *see*
Rainald	LIN	63,2
Ranulf	NTT	19,1
Robert	LIN	63,1
Wazelin	LIN	63,7

man of Gilbert of Ghent: *see*
Azelin	LIN	24,86
Ecbeorht	LIN	24,22;76
Fulbert	LIN	24,84
Geoffrey	LIN	24,36;80;83
	RUT	5,15. ELc5
Ivo	LIN	24,27;73
Kolsveinn	LIN	24,2
Rademer	LIN	24,61
Ralph	LIN	24,41;74
Ravemer	LIN	24,66;68

Robert	LIN	24,10;12;92
	NTT	17,16
Roger	LIN	24,54;72;81
William	LIN	24,24
	NTT	17,3;7
man of Gilbert of Tison: *see*		
Asketill	LIN	23,1
Fulco	YKS	21E4
Geoffrey	YKS	21E9
Humphrey	YKS	21E11
Richard	YKS	21E7
man of Godfrey of Cambrai: *see*		
Euremar	LIN	51,6
Gleu	LIN	51,10
	RUT	ELc9
man of Goding: *see* Alfward	BKM	17,20
man of Godith: *see* Edsi	HRT	4,23
man of Godiva: *see* Brictric	DEV	*52,52*
man of Godman: *see*		
Brictric	SFK	2,17
Godric	SFK	2,17
Wulfhere	SFK	2,17
man of Godric: *see* Leofwin	BKM	12,10
man of Godric Ross: *see* Godric	NFK	66,91
man of Godric the sheriff: *see*		
Aelfric	BKM	44,1
Wulfnoth	BDF	23,25
man of Godric the steward: *see*		
Ralph	NFK	9,42
Robert Farthing	SFK	14,146
man of Godwin of Benfield: *see*		
Alwin	HRT	4,18
Leofwin	HRT	20,12
Wulfwy	HRT	4,19
man of Godwin son of Algar: *see* Wulfric the	SFK	7,36
deacon		
man of Godwin son of Wulfstan: *see* Aelfric	HRT	20,9
man of Guy of Craon: *see*		
Aethelstan of Frampton	LIN	CK,66
Alfred	LIN	57,1;5-7
Godwine	LIN	57,18;55
Ranulf	LIN	57,22;24
Vitalis	LIN	57,15;33;48
Warner	LIN	57,11;13;19
Widald	LIN	57,10
man of Haldane: *see* Wulfmer	SFK	67,11
man of Hamo: *see* Richard	ESS	89,3
man of Hardwin of Scales: *see* Alfred	CAM	*13,2*
man of Harold: *see*		
Aelfric	NFK	4,26
Alnoth	SFK	7,102
Edric	SFK	6,92
Godric	BKM	17,22
Godwin the priest	SFK	7,122
Skuli	NFK	24,5
Ulfketel	NFK	20,19
Wihtric	SFK	7,119
Withri	NFK	20,19
man of Henry of Ferrers: *see*		
Cola	DBY	6,2

Saswalo	LIN	21,1
man of Heppo the crossbowman: *see* Sigmundr	LIN	61,4;7
man of Hermer: *see*		
Englishman	NFK	9,227
Ulfketel	NFK	15,2
William	NFK	1,61
man of Hervey de Vere: *see* William	NFK	1,61
man of Hugh de Montfort: *see*		
Durand	NFK	*23,9*
Walter	NFK	*23,9*
man of Hugh of Beauchamp: *see* Rhiwallon	BDF	25,7
man of Hugh son of Baldric: *see*		
Geoffrey	YKS	23E14
Gerard	YKS	23N9-11;13;15-16
Gilbert	LIN	25,13
Hamelin	LIN	25,6;11
Hugh	YKS	23E6
Ralph	LIN	25,2
	YKS	23N28
Walo	YKS	23N31
William	YKS	23E9
Wulfbert	YKS	23N30
man of Ilbert de Lacy		
Warin	YKS	9W2
William	YKS	9W2
man of Ivo Tallboys: *see*		
Atsurr	LIN	14,95
Geoffrey	LIN	14,11;13;84. CN19
Hermer	LIN	14,3
Hugh	LIN	14,9
Jocelyn	LIN	14,25;40
Nigel	LIN	14,16;32;38;45
Odo	LIN	14;12;14-15;31;34;43-44;59-59;87;93
Peter	LIN	14,20;41
Rainfrid	LIN	14,17
Roger	LIN	14,30;33;39
Walter	LIN	14,63
Wigmund	LIN	14,5;64-65
man of Jocelyn son of Azor: *see*		
Donald	HAM	IoW8,5
Geoffrey	HAM	IoW8,5
William	HAM	IoW8,5
man of Jocelyn son of Lambert: *see*		
Asketill	LIN	28,7
Baldric	LIN	28,16;33
Eurold	LIN	28,32
Godard	LIN	28,20
Herman	LIN	28,29
Kolsveinn	LIN	28,3
Lambert	LIN	28,38
Rainer	LIN	28,25;37;43
Walo	LIN	28,5;19
Walter	LIN	28,35;42
man of King Edward: *see*		
Alfward	CAM	*32,8*
Alfwold	BDF	15,7
Algar	MDX	23,1
Alnoth	CAM	*32,8*
Alric	BKM	14,31
Alric Wintermilk	BDF	57,8

Alwin	BDF	53,17-18
	MDX	14,1
Alwin Devil	BDF	4,6-7
Alwin of Gotton	HRT	44,1
Alwin Stickhare	ESS	76,1 *note*
	MDX	16,1
Blackwin	CAM	3,2
Blackwin the sheriff	CAM	32,43
Boti	SFK	7,33
Branting	BDF	57,3iv
Edric	BDF	53,28
Edward son of Swein	MDX	25,1
Edwin	MDX	22,1
Gode	HRT	17,4
Godmund	BDF	3,8
Godric	CAM	29,6
Godwin	BDF	53,19
	BKM	44,3
Grim	MDX	9,3
Grimbald	BDF	41,1
Heming	CAM	14,40
Huscarl	CAM	14,64
Leofeva	BDF	53,8
Leofgar	BDF	53,23
Leofing	BKM	17,13
Leofnoth	BKM	43,1
Ordric	CAM	*32*,7
Ordwy	BDF	57,10;12
Osgeat	BDF	23,56
Oswulf	BKM	5,20
Siric	SFK	8,6
Thorbern	HRT	25,1
Thorbert	BDF	3,10
Thori	BKM	41,7
Thorkell	BKM	44,3
Wicga	BKM	12,15
Wulfgeat	BDF	53,14
Wulfric	BDF	53,36
Wulfwen	BKM	24,1
	MDX	20,1
Wulfwin	BDF	53,34
man of Kolgrimr: *see*		
Frithgestr	LIN	67,20
Roaldr	LIN	67,1
man of Kolsveinn: *see*		
Aethelhelm	LIN	26,22
Alfred	LIN	26,17
Asketill	LIN	26,11;30
Brunel	LIN	26,36-37
Conded	LIN	26,27;30;38
Matthew	LIN	26,20;46
Rainald	LIN	26,43
Ralph	LIN	26,40
Roger	LIN	26,11
Walter	LIN	26,33
William	LIN	26,35;47-48;53
man of Leofnoth: *see*		
Golderon	BDF	24,20
Lank	BDF	32,6
Ordric	BDF	32,9

man of Leofnoth son of Osmund: *see* Kentish	BKM	12,38
man of Leofwin: *see*		
Saemer	BDF	24,25
Scova	HRT	5,10
man of Manulf: *see* Brunwin	SFK	4,15
man of Nigel of Aubigny: *see* Herfast	BDF	16,3
man of Norman: *see* Godric the priest	SFK	7,114
man of Norman of Arcy: *see*		
Berewold	LIN	32,3
Gamall	LIN	32,7;27
Geoffrey	LIN	32,4;6;8
Herbert	LIN	32,12;28;31
Odo	LIN	32,9
Robert	LIN	32,15
Roger	LIN	32,11
man of Norman the sheriff: *see* Alnoth	SFK	7,36
man of Odo the crossbowman: *see*		
Alfred	LIN	48,2
Herbert	LIN	48,9;11
Kolgrimr	LIN	48,13
William	LIN	48,6
man of Ordgar: *see* Alstan	CAM	*14,75*
man of Ordric: *see* Ansketel	CAM	*32,7*
man of Ordwy: *see* Wulfmer	BDF	53,27
man of Osbern of Arques: *see*		
Alfred	LIN	41,1
Ermenfrid	YKS	25W13;16
Fulco	YKS	25W6;29-30
Hugh	YKS	25W20
John	YKS	25W24
Osbern	YKS	25W19
man of Osbern the monk: *see* Goding	HRT	10,12
man of Oswulf: *see*		
Alric	BKM	18,3
Leofric	HRT	15,5
man of Oswulf son of Fran: *see* Wicga	HRT	15,7
man of Oswy: *see* Godric	BKM	17,29
man of Queen Edith: *see*		
Aelfric	BKM	43,11
Alfgeat	BKM	14,40
Alfsi	BDF	2,1. 23,29
Alfsi of Bromham	BDF	23,28
Algar	BDF	49,4
Alwin	BKM	4,11. 16,2. 25,1
Alwin Hunter	HRT	33,4
Azor son of Toti	BKM	41,1
Brictric	BKM	23,14;20. 26,3
	HRT	15,5
Gode	HRT	42,7
Ketelbert	BDF	57,6
Moding	BDF	23,32
Seric	BKM	14,27
Sparrowhawk	SFK	37,2
Walraven	BDF	1,4
Wulfward	BKM	14,6. 56,2
man of Radfrid: *see* Wulfwy	NFK	19,2
man of Rainer of Brimeux: *see*		
Baldwin	LIN	40,6
Gerard	LIN	40,7
Kolsveinn	LIN	40,2

Roger	LIN	40,4
man of Ralph: *see* Drogo	LIN	64,2
man of Ralph of Buron: *see*		
Jocelyn	NTT	15,9
Osmund	NTT	15,4;7
William	NTT	15,3;5
man of Ralph of Limsey: *see* Manfred	NTT	14,7
man of Ralph of Mortimer: *see*		
Odo	LIN	36,2
Richard	LIN	36,1
William	LIN	36,3
man Ralph of Pagnel: *see*		
Hakon	LIN	35,11
Hubert	YKS	16W3
Odger	LIN	35,13
man of Richard: *see* Warner	ESS	90,77
man of Robert Blunt: *see* Richard	SFK	75,2
man of Robert Gernon: *see* Robert the perverted	ESS	6,12
man of Robert Malet: *see*		
Aelfric	SFK	26,13
Drogo	NFK	66,59
Roger	NFK	14,31
man of Robert of Stafford: *see*		
Baswin	LIN	59,9;11
Brian	LIN	59,14-15
Edelo	LIN	59,12
Ehelo	LIN	59,19
Geoffrey	LIN	59,4-5;7
Godwine	LIN	59,20
Gulfered	LIN	59,16-17
Hugh	LIN	59,2
Kolgrimr	LIN	59,18
man of Robert of Tosny: *see*		
Gunfrid	LIN	18,17;20
Ivo	LIN	18,15;24;32
Roger	LIN	18,12
William	LIN	18,12
man of Robert son of Wymarc: *see*		
Aelmer	CAM	25,5
Alfward	CAM	32,24
Ordnoth	CAM	30,1
Wulfmer	CAM	26,39
man of Roger Bigot: *see* Reynold	NFK	1,61
man of R(oger) Bigot: *see* Aitard	NFK	1,106;111
man of Roger of Bully: *see*		
Bernard	NTT	9,57
Ernulf	NTT	9,89
Fulk	DBY	16,1
	NTT	9,18;20;55;64;70;126-127
Geoffrey	NTT	9,6;33;36;116;118-119
Gilbert	NTT	9,52
Ingran	NTT	9,45
Ralph	NTT	9,110
Richard	NTT	9,37
Robert	NTT	9,2;22;70
Roger	NTT	9,3;44;62;69;90;107-108;120;122;129
Thoraldr	LIN	17,1
Thorold	NTT	9,10;46;50;59;70
William	NTT	9,26;111

man of Roger of Poitou: *see*

Albert	LIN	16,14
Asketill	LIN	16,43;45
Blancard	LIN	16,28;35;44
Earnwine	LIN	16,1;33;47
Geoffrey	LIN	16,9
Gerard	LIN	16,39
Hakon	LIN	16,12
Mainard	LIN	16,3
Roger	LIN	16,4;7;10;27;32
Wigmund	LIN	16,2

man of Sired: *see* Seric	BKM	36,1
man of Sired son of Sibbi: *see* Alwin	BKM	12,1
man of Stori: *see* Alwin	BDF	44,2;4

man of Swein: *see*

Aelfric Bush	HRT	34,6
Odo	ESS	9,14

man of the sheriff: *see* Godric	BDF	17,7

man of Thorkell: *see*

Arkell	WAR	17,16
Ceolred	WAR	17,16

man of Thorold: *see* Godric	SRY	18,2
man of Toli: *see* Osferth	SFK	6,106
man of Toli the sheriff: *see* Asmoth	SFK	4,15
man of Tovi: *see* Alfward	BKM	43,2

man of Ulf: *see*

Aelfric son of Bondi	SFK	7,37
Aelfwin	SFK	7,37
Askell	SFK	7,37
Bondi the smith	SFK	7,37
Goda	SFK	7,37
Godwin	BKM	17,28

man of Ulf son of Manni: *see* Alwin	MDX	7,8
man of W. the constable: *see* Ralph	SFK	4,32
man of Waldin the artificer: *see* William	LIN	47,3-7
man of Waldin the Breton: *see* Godwine	LIN	46,1
man of Walkelin: *see* Hardwin	NTH	4,7
man of Walter Giffard: *see* Germund	NFK	66,63

man of Walter of Aincourt: *see*

Alwige	LIN	31,2
Odo	LIN	31,8
Rainald	LIN	31,3;5
Reginald	NTT	11,25
Walkelin	NTT	11,22
Wintrehard	LIN	31,18

man of Wigot: *see*

Alwin	MDX	7,3
Godwin Aelfeth	MDX	7,7

man of Wigot of Wallingford: *see* Ordwy	BKM	23,33
man of William of Écouis: *see* Hugh	NFK	1,61
man of William (of Écouis): *see* Hugh	SFK	9,2

man of William of Percy: *see*

Aethelwulf	LIN	22,32
Eburhard	YKS	1W53. SW,Bu49
Evrard	LIN	22,35-36
Fulco	LIN	22,25;28;33
Norman	LIN	22,3;8;13
Osbern	LIN	22,10;29
Robert	LIN	22,12;34
Waldin	LIN	22,14

William	LIN	22,31
man of William of Warenne: *see*		
Aldelin	LIN	15,1
Alfward	SSX	12,6
Gilbert	SSX	12,6
Richard	SSX	12,6
Thorald	NFK	1,195
Warin	SSX	12,6
man of W(illiam) of Warenne: *see* Humphrey	SFK	21,1
man of William Peverel: *see*		
Ambrose	NTT	10,39
Payne	NTT	10,51
Robert	NTT	10,2
Saxfrid	NTT	10,22;51
Warner	NTT	10,25;35
man of William son of Ansculf: *see* Hugh	SRY	21,7
man of Withgar: *see*		
Aelfric	SFK	76,3
Algar	HRT	34,9-10
man of Wulfmer: *see*		
Aelmer	BDF	55,4
Thorkell	HEF	15,9
man of Wulfmer of Eaton: *see*		
Raven	BDF	21,14-15
Sweetman	BDF	55,12
man of Wulfsi son of Burgred: *see* Wulfnoth	BDF	25,5
man of Wulfward Wight: *see* Aelmer	MDX	15,2
man of Wulfwin of Eastwick: *see* Bettica	HRT	34,23
man of Young Aelfric: *see* Edric	CAM	32,3
man of Young Edward: *see* Algar	BKM	14,45
man of Young Wulfward: *see* Saewold	BKM	17,31
man of: *see also*	LEC	44
Mantle: *see* Thurstan	BKM	36
Mapson: *see*		
Aelfric	HEF	E6
	WOR	18,6
Godric	HEF	1,60
Maredudd, King: *see* Gruffydd son of	HEF	31. 29,1
Marlborough: *see* Alfred	SOM	17,1
Marlborough: *see also* of Marlborough		
marshall: *see*		
Alfred	CON	5,1,3
Ansketell of Rots	KEN	*7,13*
Geoffrey	HAM	62. 56,3
	WIL	M12. *68,21*
Gerald	SFK	65
Robert	WIL	59
Roger	ESS	62. 30,16
marshall: *see also* Ansketell of Rots		
Mart: *see* Alward	DEV	*24,23-24;28.* 52,30
Martel: *see*		
Geoffrey	ESS	30,3
(Geoffrey)	ESS	30,24;31;35;43
Mason: *see* Hugh	HAM	3,1
Mauditt/Mawditt: *see*		
Gunfrid	WIL	53
William	HAM	35. 27,1
mead-keeper: *see* Wulfwin	CAM	*3,5*
Milk: *see* Aelmer	ESS	B3r
Molay: *see* Miles	BRK	B8

Molbec: *see* Hugh	BRK	B5 *(but see note)*
Molbec: *see also*		
Bolbec		
of Bolbec		
of Molbec		
moneyer: *see* Sweetman	OXF	B10
monk: *see*		
Abel	KEN	*3,5*
Aelmer	WOR	2,27
Aethelhard	DEV	*34,53*
Alfgeat	WOR	26,16
Alfsi	WIL	2,3
Algot	WOR	8,6
Alnoth	SOM	8,20
Alric	CAM	17,1. 32,1
Brandr	LIN	CW16
Columban	OXF	6,6
Doda	DOR	57,8
Godric son of Garwine	LIN	C16
Ingulf	SRY	9,1
Leofric	BRK	33,5
Leofwine	LIN	C3
Lindbald	BRK	7,25
Osbern	HRT	10,12
Robert the priest	LIN	7,55
Walter	BDF	55,8
	CAM	42,1. AppxJ
Werno of Poix	SFK	14,68
Wulfgar	SOM	8,26;35
Wulfwin	WAR	9,1
Monks of: *see*		
?Abbotsbury	DOR	13,1;4
Angers (St Nicholas of)	BKM	12,8
Bath (St Peter's)	GLS	1,56
Battle (St Martin's)	DEV	1,4
Bec (St Mary's)	OXF	35,33
Bodmin	DEV	51,15-16
Burton	DBY	3,6
(Bury) St Edmunds	SFK	14,163;167
Canterbury Holy Trinity	ESS	90,79
	SFK	15
Chester (St Chad's)	CHS	B6;13. 2,1. 16,2. 27,3
Chester (St John's)	CHS	B10;12
Chester (St Peter's)	CHS	C25
Chester (St Werburgh's)	CHS	A. 1,35. 2,21
Cluny	HUN	18,1
Durham	LIN	3,4
Ely (St Ethelreda's)	CAM	5,26. 17,2. 26,30;56
	ESS	1,2. 27,14. 79,1
?Eynsham (St Mary's)	GLS	EvQ29
Gloucester (St Peter's)	GLS	10,14. EvQ29
Grestain (St Mary's)	BKM	12,6;29
La Couture (St Peter's of)	BKM	14,37
Lewes (St Pancras of)	SSX	12,3
Lyre (St Mary's)	HAM	IoW1,7
	HEF	1,44
	WOR	E4
?Milton (St Peter's)	DOR	12,14
Mont St Michel	DEV	16,93
Mortain	SSX	10,1;60 *note*

nun: *see*

Aelfeva	WOR	2,54
Alswith	LIN	1,9
Cwenhild	GLS	78,8
Cwenthryth	LIN	67,27
Edeva	HRT	15,4
Edith	SOM	16,12
	WOR	2,67
Estrild	MDX	17,1
Leofeva	WAR	B2. 43,1

Nuns of: *see*

Chatteris	CAM	11,2
Caen (Holy Trinity)	DOR	21
	GLS	23
Chester (St Mary's)	CHS	B11
Elstow (St Mary's)	BDF	53,1;3-4
Hereford	HEF	2,17

Nuns of: *see also* Abbess/Abbey

Odson: *see* Aelfwin	CAM	AppxJ
of Abbeville: *see* Walter	KEN	5,128
of Abernon: *see* Roger	SFK	25,76
	SRY	19,31
of Abetot: *see* Urso	GLS	65
	HEF	30. 1,10c;13
	WAR	35
	WOR	26. E34

of Abetot: *see also*
   Urso of Worcester
   Urso the sheriff

of Adisham: *see* William	KEN	2,42. *3,8*
of Adwick le Street: *see* Sveinn	YKS	CW22
of Aincourt: *see* Walter	DBY	8. B16. S5
	LIN	31. 2,32. CK,14;55;57;59
	NTH	38
	NTT	11. S5
	YKS	19. SW,Sf12
of Alderford: *see* Aelfric	ESS	90,49
of Alençon: *see* Bernard	SFK	67,15;29
of Aller: *see* William	DEV	*16,97*

of Alno: *see* de Alno

of Anjou: *see*

Guy	CAM	*15,2*
	NFK	1,1. 5,1
Osmund	ESS	1,3

of Anneville: *see*

Humphrey	CAM	*24,7. 31,3.* AppxJ
	HRT	B5
William	HAM	21,4
of Arcy: *see* Norman	LIN	32. 3,7. CS,30. CW,20
of Ardres: *see* Arnulf	BDF	15,1;4-6
	CAM	15,3
of Argenton: *see* David	BDF	50
	CAM	39
of Armentières: *see* Robert	BRK	B9
	OXF	EBe3

of Arques/de Arches: *see*

Haimeric	DEV	*50,1-2;5*
Osbern	LIN	41. CK,26

	YKS	25. C16. CW1;24;26;28;32;36;38;41. SW,BA4;8;13. SW,An4-15. SW,Bu1-2; 6-7;10;18
William	KEN	2,21;25. 5,128
	SFK	47. 6,192. 31,20
of Asholt: *see* Edith	KEN	D25
of Asterby: *see* Ulfketill	LIN	CS,39
of Auberville: *see*		
Robert	SOM	1,2. *8,17*. 24,8. 46,1;*2-5*
Roger	ESS	26. 90,86
	SFK	29. 1,1. 21,14;19;26
Saeric	CAM	5,2
William	HRT	29
	SFK	30. 29,8. 76,14
of Aubigny: *see* Nigel	BDF	24. 8,2. 16,3
	BRK	12,1
	BKM	39
	LEC	39
	WAR	41
of Audrieu: *see* William	DOR	*34,6*
	WIL	32,2
of Aumale: *see* Robert	DEV	28
of Auvers: *see* Robert	NTH	B22
of Aylesbury: *see* Alfgeat	BKM	12,16
of Bacton: *see* Leofwin	SFK	6,212;217. 41,10 (cf 41,7)
of Badlingham: *see* Ordmer	CAM	*14,67*. AppxA
of Bainton: *see* Walter	SOM	*24,17*
of Balliol: *see* Reginald	STS	14,1
of Balliol: *see also* Balliol		
of Ballon: *see* Hamelin	GLS	EvK1
of Balsham: *see*		
David	CAM	AppxD
Pinna	CAM	AppxD
of Bapaume: *see* Ralph	LIN	C20
of Barbes: *see* Robert	KEN	5,193
of Barre: *see* Richard	SOM	*29,1*
of Barrington: *see* Ralph	CAM	AppxH. Cf 32,18
of Barrington/Banks: *see also* Banks		
of Barthetona: *see* ...	SFK	41,11
of Barton: *see* Brictgeat	CAM	AppxK
of Basing: *see* Cola	HAM	69,13
of Bayeux: *see* Bishop of		
of Beauchamp: *see*		
Geoffrey	YKS	CE9. SE,Ac2
Hugh	BDF	23. 4,2. 17,2;4;6. 21,10. 25,7. 54,2. 55, 9
	BKM	25
	HRT	27. 44,1
Walter	GLS	WoC4;6
of Beauchamp: *see also* Beauchamp		
of Beaufour: *see*		
Ralph	NFK	20. 1,11;66;215;239;241. 15,19;*20*. 19, 40. 22,11. 48,5. 65,16. 66,90-91
	SFK	11
R(alph)	NFK	1,218. 6,7. 48,6. 50,13
William	WIL	1,23i
of Beaufour: *see also* William Beaufour		
of Beaumont: *see*		
Robert	DEV	*16,40;65;67-68;137*
Roger	DOR	28 *and note*

of **Borley:** *see* Aelmer ESS 90,49
of **Bosc-le-hard:** *see* William BKM 18,3
of **Bosc (de Nemore, de Silva):** *see*
  William ESS 37,17
  SFK 7,115;134. 16,3 (*but see note*). 39,5
  (William) SFK 39,11
of **Bosc:** *see also* Silvester
of **Boscherbert:** *see* Hugh DOR 53. *36,3. 55,17;46*
of **Boscombe:** *see* Alstan BDF 18,1;4;6
  GLS 58,4
  HRT 28,1-3;5;7-8
  SOM *19,61*
  WIL 32,2;14
(of **Boscombe**): *see* Alstan BDF 18,2-3;7
  DOR 34,1
  GLS 31,4;7;10-11
  HAM 1,32. 32,4
  HRT 28,4;6
  WIL 8,12. 32,11

of **Boscombe:** *see also* Boscombe
of **Bottisham:** *see* Leofwin CAM AppxC
of **Bouillé:** *see* Gilbert WAR B2
of **Bourges:** *see* Hervey SFK 67. 8,59. 21,*36;66-68*;96
of **Bourges:** *see also* Hervey Bedruel/of Berry
of **Bourn:** *see* Aelmer CAM *14,23-24;47;49*
of **Bourn:** *see also* son of Colswein
of **Bourneville:** *see*
  William NFK 9,131
  SFK 7,56;117;121. 76,15
  W(illiam) SFK 1,11. 7,119. 62,7
of **Boursigny:** *see* William ESS 9,13
of **Bouville:** *see*
  Humphrey HEF 28
  Saxwallo SFK 32,31
  William SFK 16,11. 32,1;19
  W(illiam) SFK 21,95
of **Braose:** *see*
  ?Robert WIL *33,1* (*but see note*)
  William BRK 25
  DOR 37. 19,10
  HAM 33
  SRY 20
  SSX 13. 2,10. 3,2. 11,71. 12,20-21;23;
  28-29;47
  WIL 33. 2,1
of **Bray:** *see* Alnoth DEV *52,36*
of **Bréboeuf:** *see* Hugh KEN 5,98
of **Breteuil/Bretteville:** *see* Gilbert BRK 36
  HAM 43. 11,1. S3
  OXF 59,1
  WIL 29. 68,23
of **Breuil:** *see*
  Osbern BDF 23,31
  Osbert BDF 23,27
of **Brimeux:** *see* Rainer LIN 40. CS,9;14;25;29. CN,10;23
of **Bromham:** *see* Alfsi BDF 23,28 (cf 23,29)
of **Brundon:** *see* Wulfric ESS 90,49
of **Brus:** *see* Robert YKS 31
of **Bruyère:** *see* Ralph DEV *16,12;35;48-49;153;163*
of **Bucy:** *see* Robert LEC 17. 13,27. 40,15

	NTH	30. B17
	STS	15,1-2
of Bully/de Busli: *see* Roger	CHS	R4,2
	DBY	16
	DEV	27
	GLS	1,37
	LEC	18. 43,8
	LIN	17. C9. T4
	NTT	9. B8. 2,10
	WAR	EG2
	YKS	10. CW7;15;19. SW,Sf2-4;6-10;14; 18-20;22-23;27-29;34;36. SW,O1-3
of Burcy: *see* Serlo	DOR	48
	SOM	37. 1,9;21. *6,9. 8,17;20-21;28;30. 27,3*
	WIL	E4;5
of Burgh: *see*		
Aethelric	SFK	8,6;9. 32,23;28. 67,23 (cf 26,16)
Brunman	SFK	6,110
of 'Burgh': *see* Walter	GLS	EvQ29
	WOR	2,69
of Burgundy: *see* Walter	DEV	*25,1;3-4*
of Burgundy: *see also* Burgundy		
of Burley: *see* Wihenoc	NFK	66,36
of Buron/Burun: *see*		
Erneis	LIN	34. CS,24;26. CW,18
	YKS	24. C13. SE,An2-3. SW,Bu3-5;7-14; 25-26;28;31;35;40-44. SE,C9. SE,Sn2. SE,Wa7
Ralph	DBY	11
	NTT	15. B10
of Burwell: *see* Alan	CAM	AppxA (cf 14,69)
of Butterleigh: *see* Edwin	DEV	*52,38-39*
of Caen: *see*		
Morin	DEV	*16,173-174. 51,14*
Walter	ESS	44,4
	NFK	7,3. 66,57
	SFK	4,15. 6,5;7;67 (*but see note*); 90;98-99; 103;143;191;245;247;301;316. 25,61
W(alter)	SFK	6,93;162;165;264;265
William	SFK	6,67 (*but see note*)
of Caerwent: *see* Belward	GLS	W7
of Cahagnes/Keynes: *see* William	BKM	21,8
	CAM	37
	NTH	34
	SSX	2,1g. 10,1;7;17-18
of Cailli/Cailly: *see* William	BRK	29
	CAM	*18*,7. AppxH
	NFK	8,18
of Cairon: *see* William	BDF	4,2;6-7. 21,5;8-9;17. 24,28
of Calverleigh: *see* Godric	DEV	*52,21*
of Cambrai: *see* Godfrey	LEC	30
	LIN	51
	RUT	ELc9
of Cambremer: *see* Walter	KEN	*M10*
of Cambridge: *see* Picot	CAM	32
of Cambridge: *see also* Picot the sheriff		
of Candos: *see* Roger	SFK	31,3;20;53;56;60
of Canterbury: *see*		
Alnoth	NTH	2,6
Vitalis	KEN	*C3. 2,14*

of **Carlewuda:** *see* Wihtric	SFK	6,110
of **Carteret:** *see*		
Humphrey	DOR	*3,10*
Mauger	DEV	*15,57*
	SOM	*10,1. 19,16;68.* 46,21
of **Castellion:** *see* William	BKM	B11
of **Chartres:** *see* Ralph	LEC	10,15
of **Chaworth:** *see* Patrick	GLS	EvK1
of **Chelsfield:** *see* Esbern	KEN	D25
of **Cherbourg:** *see*		
Ansketel	DOR	*54,8*
Osbern	GLS	71,1
of **Cherbourg:** *see also* son of Amelina		
of **Chernet:** *see* William	HAM	23,3. NF10,1
of **Cherry Hinton:** *see* Robert	CAM	AppxE (cf 14,4)
of **Chesfield:** *see* Geoffrey	HRT	Appx
of **Chester:** *see* Earl Hugh	BKM	13L
of **Chester:** *see also* Earl Hugh		
of **Chesterton:** *see* Bruning	CAM	AppxO
of **Cheveley:** *see* Karl	CAM	AppxB
of **Childerley:** *see*		
Ernwy	CAM	AppxO
Roger	CAM	AppxO (cf 3,6)
of **Chilham:** *see* Sired	KEN	D17. C6
of **Chippenham:** *see* William	CAM	AppxA
of **Chittlehampton:** *see* Godwin	DEV	*52,17;19* (cf 52,10)
	SOM	47,7
of **Chocques:** *see*		
Gunfrid	BDF	37
	BKM	50
	LEC	31
	LIN	52. S7. CK,3
	NTH	48. B27. 1,10
Sigar	BDF	36. 3,6
	GLS	72
	HRT	41. EC2
	NTH	49. B28
of **Cholsey:** *see* William	BKM	17,20
of **Cirencester:** *see* Reinbald	BRK	61
of **Cirencester:** *see*		
Reinbald the chancellor		
Reinbald the priest		
of **Clais:** *see* Walter	CAM	AppxFN
of **Clare:** *see* Richard	SFK	67,1. 76,7 (cf 25,1)
of **Clare:** *see also*		
of Tonbridge		
son of Count Gilbert		
son of Gilbert		
of **Claville/Glanville:** *see* Walter	CON	1,19
	DEV	24. *1,66*
	DOR	41
of **Claville:** *see*		
Robert	SFK	6,46
R(obert)	SFK	6,110
of **Cluny:** *see* Ralph	CAM	AppxD
of **Cokenach:** *see* Algar	HRT	B3 (cf 34,10)
of **Colcarr:** *see* Modgeva	SFK	6,110
of **Colchester:** *see*		
A(i)lwy	NFK	17,22
Godric	ESS	20,42

of Coleville/Colleville: *see*
    Gilbert   SFK   6,127;180;236;272
    William   YKS   13E1;13
of Colombières: *see* Ranulf   KEN   D8-9. *C3.* P19. 5,48;95;101;123;133;
                                        219. 7,19

of Colyton: *see* Vitalis   DEV   *16,129*
of Conteville: *see* Ralph   SOM   *8,33. 24,11;36-37*
of Corbon: *see* Hugh   NFK   9,48. 66,83
                               SFK   7,18;37;75

of Cormeilles: *see*
    Ansfrid   GLS   68. 1,59
                                 HEF   21. 1,1
    Jocelyn   HAM   61
    Thurstan   GLS   EvK116
of Coton: *see* Rumold   CAM   AppxK
of Cottenham: *see*
    Aelmer   CAM   AppxO
    Sturmid   CAM   AppxO
of Coucy: *see* Aubrey   BRK   3,1
                               YKS   27

of Coucy: *see also* Earl Aubrey/of Coucy
of Courbépine: *see* Ralph   KEN   D8. C4. P19. 5,57;86;132;*133*;137;
                                        166-168;191;215;217;220;222. 6,1. 7,
                                      22. 9,16
                               SFK   16,10
of Courcy: *see* Richard   OXF   32. B9. 1,2
of Courseulles: *see*
    Roger   DEV   *34,52*
                             DOR   29
                             SHR   4,7
                             SOM   21. 1,4. 8,*2;4-5;8;11-14;18;20;23-24;*
                                      *27-28;33;*41. 10,2;6. 25,55
                           WIL   44
    William   SOM   *19,12*
of Courseulles: *see also* Roger Whiting
of Courson: *see*
    Robert   NFK   9,29;100;178
                             SFK   7,6-7;23;51. 76,17
    R(obert)   SFK   4,14. 7,8
of Coutances: *see*
    Bishop Geoffrey
    Bishop of Coutances
    Bishop of St Lô
of Cranborne: *see* Ralph   DOR   54,10
of Craon: *see* Guy   LEC   24
                             LIN   57. 2,42. 24,61;81. 46,2. CW,15. CK,
                                      49;53;58;60;66;69
of Creslow: *see* Wulfwen   BKM   24,2
of Criel: *see* Robert   SSX   9,7;11
of Croxton: *see* Godric   CAM   AppxL
of Culey: *see* Humphrey   NFK   9,5;84
of Curry: *see* Doda   SOM   *47,12*
of Daumeray: *see* William   DOR   *55,19.* 57,4;11
                             SOM   *21,36*
of Delamere: *see* Hugh   CHS   10
of Delamere: *see also* Delamere
of Digswell: *see* Thorkell   HRT   Appx (cf 33,5)
of Ditton: *see* Fulk   CAM   AppxE (omitted: cf ICC 25)
of Dives: *see* Boselin   CAM   43
of Doese: *see* Wulfwy of Hatley St George   CAM   AppxL

of Dol: *see*
    Hugh   DEV   *20*,7
    Walter   NFK   6,1;5-6
                       SFK   4,15. 6,212;215. 14,146. 16,34. 31,34
                                    (see note)

of Donnington: *see* William   GLS   EvE25. EvO6
of Douai: *see* Walter/Walscin   DEV   23
                       DOR   39
                       ESS   52
                       KEN   5,32
                       SOM   24. *8,7;11;34*. 21,4. 46,5
                       SFK   31,34 *(but see note)*
                       SRY   23
                       WIL   36

of Douai: *see also* Walter of Flanders
of Downham: *see* Reginald   CAM   AppxP
of Dreux: *see*
    Amalric   WIL   26,19. 28,10. 66,2
    Herman   HEF   27
                       WIL   66,1

of Dry Drayton: *see*
    Giffard   CAM   AppxO
    Ledmer   CAM   AppxO
of Dullingham: *see* Algar   CAM   AppxD
of Duxford: *see* Leofwy   CAM   AppxG
of Easthorpe: *see* Edric   ESS   37,20 (cf 20,40)
of Eastwick: *see* Wulfwin   HRT   34,23 (cf 34,24)
of Eaton (Socon): *see* Wulfmer BDF   21,1;5-6;9;14-15;17. 45,1. 55,12-13
                       CAM   25,9. 32,10. 42,1
                       HRT   B3

of Écouis: *see*
    William   DOR   38
                       ESS   45
                       GLS   E36
                       HEF   14. 1,23;38
                       NFK   19. 1,61. 15,11. 16,5. 66,56
                       SFK   9. 21,21
    W(illiam)   NFK   1,1
                       SFK   21,27

of Elsham: *see* Edric   KEN   5,185;210
of Eltham: *see* Aethelwold KEN   D25
of Ely: *see* Huna   CAM   AppxP
of Émalleville: *see* William SFK   6,30;33
of Essex: *see*
    Peter the sheriff   CAM   33,1
    Swein   ESS   24
                       HUN   16
                       SFK   27

of Essex: *see also* Swein the sheriff
of Eu: *see*
    Osbern   HAM   ESr
                       SRY   1,9. 3,1
    William   BDF   18
                       BRK   23
                       DEV   22. 1,4
                       DOR   34
                       GLS   31. W8;16. 1,64
                       HAM   32. 54,2. NF4
                       HRT   28

| | SOM | 26 |
| | WIL | 32. M8. 8,12. 25,23 |

of Eu: *see also* Count of
of Evreux: *see*

| Roger | NFK | 19,39 |
| R(oger) | NFK | 19,9 |

of Exeter: *see*

Baldwin	DOR	42L
	SOM	20
Gotshelm	DEV	25,28

of Exeter: *see also* Baldwin the sheriff
of Exning: *see* Hugh
of Falaise: *see* William

	CAM	AppxA
	DEV	20
	DOR	35
	SOM	27
	WIL	35

of Falkenham: *see* Leofstan

| | SFK | 6,110 |

of Faringdon: *see* Alfsi

	BRK	65,7 (cf 1,34)
	GLS	1,66. 11,14. 78,1
	OXF	1,9

of Fécamp: *see* William

| | HAM | 3,5 |

of Felbrigg: *see* Aelward

| | NFK | 9,158 |

of Ferrers: *see*

Henry	BRK	21. B4. 1,25-26;32;37;42
	BKM	27
	DBY	6. 1,27. 8,2
	ESS	29. 90,81
	GLS	59. 31,2
	HEF	13
	LEC	14. C16. 19,6;9
	LIN	21. CW,17
	NTH	25. B13
	NTT	24. S5
	OXF	24. B9. 1,6
	STS	10. B9. 8,23
	WAR	19. B2
	WIL	39. 1,2. E1-2
Hermer	NFK	13L. 66,1
	SFK	10
Robert	GLS	EvK116

of Feugères/Fougères: *see*

Ralph	BRK	65,18
	BKM	37
	CAM	AppxM
	DEV	33
	NFK	41. 66,83
	SFK	50
	SRY	32
William	BKM	31

of Flanders: *see*

Hugh	BDF	34
Odo	SOM	45,6
Roger	DEV	*35,7-8*
Thurstan	HEF	9,2
Walter	BDF	32. 31,1
	BKM	30
	DEV	*23,9*

of Flanders: *see also* fleming
of Flitwick: *see* Aelfric

| | BDF | 25,2 |

of Flocques: *see* Geoffrey

| | SSX | 9,105 |

of Fordham: *see* Robert	CAM	AppxA
of Fougères: *see* Feugères		
of Fourneaux: *see* Ansketel	CAM	*14,8*
of Fowlmere: *see* Godric	CAM	AppxH
of Frampton: *see* Aethelstan	LIN	CK,66
of Fulbourn/Nabson: *see* Godwin	CAM	AppxE
of Gatemore: *see* Robert	SOM	*22,11*
of Ghent: *see* Gilbert	BDF	27
	BRK	37. B3
	BKM	22. E1
	CAM	23. AppxM
	DBY	13. 9,5. 16,1
	HUN	21. B2
	LEC	33
	LIN	24. C7. 4,1. 8,9. 18,19. 25,19. 42,8. 57,40. CS,13;18-19;23;30;33;36-37. CN, 1. CW,6;11;17-18. CK,6;35-36;44
	NTH	46
	NTT	17
	OXF	38
	RUT	5. R15. EN14-15. ELc5
	WAR	32. B2. EN7
	YKS	20. CW4. SE,Tu1-2
of Gimingham: *see* Rathi	NFK	8,128
of Giron/Gironde: *see* Thurstan	BKM	4,27
	KEN	5,157
of Girton: *see*		
Godmer	CAM	AppxN
Wulfric	CAM	AppxN
of Glanville/Claville: *see* Walter	CON	1,19
	DEV	24. *1,66*
	DOR	41
of Glanville: *see*		
Robert	NFK	17,51
	SFK	6,3;5;51;54;157;291;308-309
R(obert)	SFK	6,124;160;179;181. 26,16;19
of Gloucester: *see*		
Durand	GLS	53. E15
	HAM	37. S3
	HEF	22
	WIL	30. M7. 26,19
Walter	GLS	EvK1
of Gloucester: *see also*		
Durand the sheriff		
Roger of Pîtres		
son of Roger		
Walter the sheriff		
of Gotton: *see* Alwin	HRT	25,2. 33,17
of Gotton: *see also* Gotton		
of Gournai: *see*		
Hugh	ESS	47
Nigel	SOM	*5,30;32;38;44-45*
of Gouville: *see* Hugh	LEC	C12
	NTH	B35. ELe1
of Grand-Court: *see* Walter	CAM	18,1;4. AppxD
of Grandmesnil: *see* Hugh	BDF	29,1. 54,1;4
	GLS	62
	HAM	S3
	HRT	26. 5,26. 43,1
	LEC	13. C5;11. 40,8;22. 43,4

	STS	11,34
	WIL	25. M16. 3,1. 10,3. 32,17
of Hill Row: *see* Bernard	CAM	AppxP
of Hinton Hall: *see* Aelfwin	CAM	AppxP
of Hinxton: *see* Leofmer	CAM	AppxG
of Histon: *see* Gilbert	CAM	AppxO
of Holderness: *see* Drogo	YKS	14L
of Holderness: *see also* of Beuvrière		
of Hoo: *see* Aelmer	BDF	23,48
of Hopewella: *see* Aelfric	SFK	6,110
of Hormead: *see*		
Godwin	HRT	Appx (cf 38,2)
Siward	HRT	Appx
of Horseheath: *see* Aelfric	CAM	AppxF
of Horton: *see* Ording	KEN	D25
of Hotot: *see*		
Hugh	RUT	R11
Ralph	CAM	AppxB
of Houdain: *see*		
...	SFK	7,2
Hugh	ESS	43,6
	NFK	9,182
	SFK	7,60;62;103. 30,3. 76,14
H(ugh)	SFK	1,60
of Huntingdon: *see* Eustace	CAM	30. 39,2
	LIN	S4
	NTH	55L
of Huntingdon: *see also* Eustace the sheriff		
of Ivry: *see*		
Acard	BDF	23,17
Hugh	DOR	54,1
	NTH	24
	OXF	26
Roger	BRK	44. 2,1
	BKM	41. B6. 4,31
	GLS	41. W1. B1. 1,5;60. 2,9. 44,2. 53,4
	HUN	17
	NTH	23,16
	OXF	29. B9. 6,14. 9,10. 59,12. EN8-9
	WAR	20. B2
of Ivry: *see also* Ivry		
of Jort: *see* Robert	LEC	42,5
of Kennett: *see* Nicholas	CAM	*18,8*. AppxA
of Kent: *see* Alnoth	OXF	7,4
of Keynes/Cahagnes: *see* William	BKM	21,8
	CAM	37
	NTH	34
	SSX	2,1g. 10,1;7;17
of Kinsbourne: *see* Humphrey	HRT	Appx
of Kirtling: *see* Frawin	CAM	AppxB
of Kyluertestuna: *see* Thuri	SFK	6,110
of l'Isle: *see* de l'Isle		
of la Beuvrière *see* of Beuvrière		
of la Guerche: *see* Geoffrey	LEC	29. C14
	LIN	63. CW,17
	NTH	47. B24
	NTT	19
	WAR	31. B2. 14,6
	YKS	17. SW,St2

of Lacy: *see*		
Hugh	GLS	EvK1;116. EvN11
Ilbert	BRK	B9
	BKM	4,38. E2
	LIN	20. 40,24. CS,11
	NTT	20
	OXF	1,6. 7,5. EBe3
	SRY	5,19
	YKS	9. SW,BA5-11. SW,Sf37. SW,O2-14; 16. SW,St1;3-8;10-16. SW, Ag1-8;13; 15-16. SW,M1-10
Robert	GLS	EvK116
Roger	BRK	45. B5-6;8. EW1
	GLS	39. G4. W17. 1,64. 17,1. 28,3. 54,1. E33. EvC108
	HEF	10. 1,3;5;8;10b-c; 15;38;58;61. 2,12. 6, 8. 30,1. E6
	OXF	59,11;15;23;27
	SHR	7. 4,8. 2,2
	WIL	49,1a
	WOR	18. 2,4;21;34;70. 8,9g
Walter	BRK	14,1
	GLS	1,56. 68,13
	HEF	1,5;40. 2,58. 5,2. 10,1;5;48;50;75
	WOR	E2
of Lacy: *see also* Lacy		
of l'Aigle/son of Richere: *see* Gilbert	NFK	42
	SFK	ENf5
	SRY	24
of Lanquetot: *see* Ralph	BDF	16,5;9
	SFK	45,1;3
of Laxfield: *see*		
Edric	NFK	1,203;205. 4,38-39;51. 9,88;105. 35,16
	SFK	1,31. 3,34;39;41. 6,28;58;62;79-80; 83-84;110;114;128-129;135;148;260; 264;272-273;295;303. 7,23;36. 8,29. 14,68. 16,6;15;25. 19,16. 31,20;27. 64, 3. 67,28-29;33 (cf 6,305)
E(dric)	SFK	67,15
G.	NFK	4,41
of le Marais: *see*		
Clarenbold	BKM	19,1
Richard	KEN	5,145
of le Vast: *see* Nigel	BDF	24,9-10;22-23
	BKM	39,2
of les Andelys: *see* Richere	HAM	S3
	SOM	*16,2*
of les Roches: *see* John	BDF	8,2. 24,12
of Lessness: *see* Azor	KEN	D25
of Lestre: *see* William	DEV	*15,56*
	DOR	*26,45*
	SOM	*19,27*
of Letchworth: *see*		
Godwin	HRT	34,7
William	HRT	Appx (cf 20,7)
of Levington: *see* Gleman	SFK	6,110
of Limésy: *see* Ralph	DEV	31
	DOR	34,6
	ESS	49. 1,3
	GLS	S1. W16. 1,56. 31,2;4;9-10

of Mardley: *see* Alfward	HRT	42,13. Appx
of Marlborough: *see* Alfred	HAM	36
	HEF	19. 1,8;56
	SOM	34
	SRY	33
	WIL	26. M11
	WOR	8,26a
of Marlborough: *see also*		
Alfred the sheriff		
Marlborough		
of Marlow: *see* Edric	BKM	7,2
of Melksham: *see* Aelfric	WIL	67,15
of Mendlesham: *see*		
Alwin	SFK	31,51 (cf 1,77)
Burghard	SFK	1,152 (cf 1,76)
of Mentmore: *see* Leofwin	BKM	43,4
of Merri: *see* Richard	SOM	*35,3;17*
of Merriot: *see* Harding	SOM	*47,3* (cf 47,6)
of Merriot: *see also* Harding son of Alnoth		
of Meulles: *see* Roger	DEV	16,9-*10;59;139*
of Mohun: *see* William	DEV	18. 23,5
	DOR	36. 55,17
	SOM	25. 1,*13;17*;31. 21,90
	WIL	34
of Molbec: *see* Hugh	BKM	14,1
	BRK	B3
of Molbec: *see also*		
Bolbec		
Molbec		
of Bolbec		
of Monceaux: *see* William	SOM	*5,1;3;25;42-43;63-64*
of Mont-Canisy: *see* Hubert	SFK	57. 6,190;260
	YKS	C19
of Montacute: *see*		
Ansger	DEV	40,1
	SOM	45,18
Drogo	SOM	45,12
of Montacute: *see also*		
Ansger of Senarponte		
Ansger the Breton		
of Montbegon: *see* Robert	ESS	89,2
of Montfort: *see* de Montfort		
of Montgomery: *see* Hugh	STS	9
of Mortagne: *see* Matthew	BRK	59
	DOR	46
	ESS	53
	GLS	73
	SOM	44
	WIL	63
of Mortain: *see*		
Count of		
Count Robert of		
of Mortemer/Mortimer: *see* Ralph	BRK	46. EH1
	HAM	29. 3,1;9. 23,44. NF5. S2;3
	HEF	9. 1,5;10b-c; 19;38. 31,7
	LEC	21
	LIN	36. 30,14. CN,14. CW,11
	OXF	30
	SHR	6. 4,11. C13. 3d,3
	SOM	29

	WAR	25
	WIL	41. M6
	WOR	16
	YKS	15. CE14. SN,Ma16. SE,He1;3-8;10. SE, Wel6. SE,C6-7;10. SE,Sc2-4;8. SE, Th3;5

of Moutiers: *see*		
Lisois	CAM	25,9
Robert	NTT	2,9
William	DOR	*11,2. 34,6. 55,15;22*
of Mucedent: *see* Walter	MDX	11,3-4
of Munden: *see* Alfward	HRT	Appx
of Muneville: *see* Nigel	YKS	C4
of Mussegros(s): *see* Roger	HEF	11
	HRT	16,2
of Mutford: *see* Ulf	SFK	7,41
of Neville: *see*		
Ralph	LIN	CW,14
Richard	DEV	*16,57*
of Newnham [?error for Nuneham]: *see* Leofwin	WAR	37,9
of Newton: *see* Alward	NFK	1,64
of Noron: *see* Ralph	NFK	66,85
of Norton: *see* Osward	KEN	D25
of Norwich: *see* Jocelyn	NFK	65,15
of Nosterfield End: *see* Norman	CAM	AppxF
of Noyers: *see*		
Howard	HRT	Appx
Robert	BKM	4,42. 6,1
William	CAM	1,11
	NFK	1,61. 10,23;26;60;62-63
	SFK	1,107-119. 19,17
W(illiam)	NFK	1,63;79;209. 9,167. 10,13;31-32;42;56; 64;68;73-74;77. 16,5
of Nuneham: *see*		
Alwin	BKM	12,25
Leofwin	BKM	57. B13. 40,1
	OXF	EW2
	WAR	37,9 [error]
of Offton: *see* Durand	SFK	67,23
of Oilly: *see* d'Oilly		
of Olney: *see* Roger	BKM	53,6
of Omonville: *see* Walter	DEV	*35,3;5-6*
of Orange: *see* William	BKM	25,3
of Orbec: *see* Roger	SFK	25,56. 76,2
of Ormsby: *see* Ulfr	LIN	CN,27
of Orwell: *see*		
Thorbern	CAM	AppxK (cf 14,41)
Withgar	HRT	Appx (cf 37,6)
of Oxford: *see*		
Saewulf	BRK	B1
Wulfric	KEN	M13
of Pagnell: *see* Paynel		
of Palluel: *see* Peter	SFK	67,18
of Parham: *see* Thormod	SFK	1,93
of Paris: *see* Fulchere	BDF	16,7. 24,25. 53,17
of Parthenay: *see* W(illiam)	NFK	66,88
	SFK	76,8-12
of Paynel: *see* Paynel		
of Percy: *see* William	HAM	25

	LIN	22. 7,13. 27,10. 28,26. CS, 7;26;30; 32. CN,24. EN,3
	NTT	21,3
	YKS	13. C10. 3Y1;3. 4N1. 4E2 *note*. 30W2. CN1. CE25;27;29-30. CW25;31;33;35; 40. SW,Sk18. SW,BA3-4;12. SW,Sf6; 19;23;25-26;30. SW,An4-7;17. SW, Bu9;19-21;32-33;35-36;39-44. SN, L1; 11;21-22;25. SN,D3;5-9;13. SN,B22. SN,Bi4-5. SE, Wei4-5;7. SE,Sn4-6; 9-10. SE, Wa1. SE,P1-2;4;7. SE,Tu6-7
of Peronne: *see* Robert	BRK	65,19
of Peyton: *see* Godric	SFK	6,238 (cf 27,13)
of Picquigny: *see*		
Ansculf	BKM	17,2
William	WIL	24,19
of Picquigny: *see also* son of Ansculf		
of Pierrepont: *see*		
Godfrey	SFK	26,12c;14
Raynold	NFK	10,93
Robert	SFK	26,12a
of Pirton: *see* Edward	HRT	1,10
of Pîtres: *see* Roger	GLS	E2
	HEF	1,72. 22,8
of Pîtres: *see also*		
Roger brother of Durand		
Roger the sheriff		
son of Roger of Pîtres		
of Poilley: *see* William	DEV	21
of Poitou: *see*		
Roger		
	CHS	Y2;11-13
	DBY	5
	ESS	46. 1,19. 32,24. 47,3. B3f
	HAM	1,46
	LIN	16. 22,5. 68,31. CS,25
	NFK	26. 1,61;231
	NTT	16. 20,7
	SFK	8. 1,1. 53,2 *note*
	YKS	30. 1L1
William	DEV	*34,27-28*
	KEN	M15
of Poix: *see* Werno	SFK	14,68
of Pomeroy: *see* Ralph	DEV	34. *1,11. 15,66.* 16,7;*51-52;63;114; 120. 17,20;23;25;44.* 19,33. 35,4
	SOM	30
of Pont Audemer: *see* Herbrand	HAM	58L
of Pont-Chardon: *see* Robert	DEV	1,5. *16,69;72;74*
	HRT	20,28
of Port: *see*		
Hubert		
	ESS	32,29. 83,2
	HAM	24
Hugh	SFK	16,34. 77,4
	BRK	52. 10,1-2
	CAM	28
	DOR	51
	HAM	23. 1,27;29. 2,23. 3,9. 4,1. 6,4;6;13; 16. 9,2. 43,6. 47,1. 53,2. NF6. NF10, 1. S3
	KEN	1,1;3. 5,1;7;45;70;115;143;153;174; *185-188*

of Snailwell: *see* Aelfric	CAM	AppxA
of Soham: *see* Warin	CAM	AppxA
of Sollers: *see* Richard	GLS	EvK116
of Sommery: *see* Roger	CAM	22,2;8
	ESS	20,74
of Soulbury: *see* Godwin	HRT	20,7
of Sourdeval: *see* Richard	YKS	C8. 5N9. CE6;31. CW6
of 'Spain': *see*		
Alfred	DEV	38
	DOR	45. *8,2*
	GLS	W19
	HEF	20
	SOM	35. 1,1;6. *2,8. 8,5*
	WIL	54. 1,1
Hervey	ESS	21,9 (cf 21,2)
Hugh	SOM	*35,8*
Walter	SOM	*35,1*
of Stafford: *see*		
Nigel	DBY	14
	STS	ED5
Robert	BRK	42
	LIN	59. CK,12;16;20;23;51;64
	NTH	27
	OXF	27
	STS	11. B6
	WAR	22. B2. EN4
	WOR	17
of Stanton: *see*		
Godwin	GLS	1,67
Roger	SOM	*1,28*
of Stevington: *see* Alfwold	BDF	2,8 (cf 15,2)
of Stone: *see* Edward	KEN	D25
of Stowey: *see* Aelfric	SOM	*6,13*
of Stratford: *see* Robert	SFK	71
of Stretham: *see* Osmund	CAM	AppxP
of Stringston: *see* Ranulf	SOM	*35,4*
of 'Struostuna': *see* Goda	SFK	6,110
of Sutton: *see*		
Alnoth	CAM	AppxP
Godwin	SFK	6,169 (cf 6,165)
Ketill	LIN	CK,70
Leofnoth	KEN	D25
Tancred	CAM	AppxP
of Swaffham: *see* Huscarl	CAM	AppxC (cf 14,64)
of Tessel: *see* Wimund	BDF	23,37
of Tetbury: *see* Azelin	GLS	EvK1
of Teversham: *see*		
Hugh	SOM	*35,9*
Silac	CAM	AppxE
Wulfric	CAM	AppxE
of Tewin: *see* Haldane	HRT	Appx (cf 36,19)
of Thame: *see* Alfred	BKM	51,3
of Thaon: *see*		
Robert	BKM	4,36
William	KEN	5,90;171
of Thatcham: *see* Aelfric	BRK	1,38
of Therfield: *see* Wulfsi	HRT	Appx

of Thetford: *see*		
Aethelwy/A(i)lwin/A(i)lwy	NFK	1,239. 9,14;25;29;60;100 *and note*; 104. 65,10
	SFK	7,1
Thurstan	NFK	66,76
of Thorndon: *see* Leofric	NFK	7,14
of Thriplow: *see* Aelfric	CAM	AppxH
of Tilly: *see* Ralph	DEV	*5,1*
of Tilly: *see also* Tilly		
of Tonbridge: *see* Richard	HAM	1,8
	KEN	2,*3*-4;9-10;28-29. 3,2;4. 4,2. 5,6-7;26; 40;56;60;62;93;103;106. 11,1
	SRY	19. 1,6;13. 36,4
of Tonbridge: *see also*		
of Clare		
son of Count Gilbert		
son of Gilbert		
of Tosny: *see*		
Berengar	LIN	19. T2. 32,9. CN,29. EN,3
	NTT	21
	OXF	34. B9
	YKS	8. C15. 7E1-2. 30W3. SW,Bu27;33. SN, L6. SN,D7;10;13;16;20-21. SN, Ma1;6;9-13;15;20. SN,B1-2;5-6;8. SE, Sc4-6;10. SE,Ac1-3. SE,Th2;8-9
Ralph	BRK	47
	ESS	51
	GLS	45. EvN12
	HAM	S3
	HEF	8. 1,21;38;62
	HRT	22
	NFK	22. 1,211. 21,15. *22,1.* 66,69
	WOR	15
Robert	BDF	26. E4
	BKM	18
	CAM	20
	ESS	50
	GLS	46
	HRT	22
	LEC	15. 1,4. 40,20
	LIN	18. CW,11. CK,9;19-20;22;46
	NTH	26. B12;33
	RUT	EN11
	SFK	44. 7,19
	YKS	7. SE,Wa1-2
of Totnes: *see* Iudhael	CON	6
	DEV	17
of Tourleville: *see* Ralph	NFK	9,8
	SFK	7,73;86;98
[of] Tournai: *see* Tournai		
of Trelly: *see* Geoffrey	BDF	3,4;10
	DEV	*3,97*
	SOM	EBe2
	SSX	9,105
of Ulcombe: *see* Robert		
of Valognes: *see*		
Hamo	SFK	3,15;87
Peter	CAM	33. 1,17
	ESS	36. 5,2. ESf1
	HRT	36. B7. 1,9;12. 28,1
	LIN	60. C3;15;20

of Warenne: *see*
   William

	BDF	17. E6
	BRK	B1
	BKM	15
	CAM	18
	ESS	22. 7,1. 9,10. 10,2. 40,3
	HAM	34
	HUN	13
	LIN	15. CK,38
	NFK	8. 1,11;57;195;215. 16,1. 19,8. 66,47; 64;67
	OXF	2. EBu1
	SHR	4,13
	SFK	26. 8,55. 76,18
	SSX	12. 10,118. 13,1-2;46
	YKS	12. CW7-9. CW10. SW,Sf1
W(illiam)	NFK	8. 1,1;57;211. 4,3. 15,1;7-8. 16,5. 31, 29. 40,1
	SFK	7,25. 21,1

of Warwick: *see* Thorkell   WAR   17
of Wateringbury: *see*
   Leofric   KEN   D25
   Wulfstan   KEN   D25
of Watteville: *see* Vatteville
of Weinhou/Wenhou: *see* Aelfric   SFK   39,17. 46,3
of Wenhou/Weinhou: *see* Aelfric   SFK   39,17. 46,3
of West Wratting: *see* Grim   CAM   AppxD
of Westbrook: *see* Geoffrey   HRT   Appx
of Westerham: *see* Roger   KEN   D9
of Weston: *see*
   Aelmer   HRT   Appx
   Godwin   HUN   D13 (cf 19,28)
   Young Wulfwin   HUN   D10
of Weston Colville: *see* Adestan/Alestan   CAM   AppxD
of Whaddon: *see* Wulfwin   BKM   26,6
of Whittlesford: *see* Ledmer   CAM   AppxG
of Wick: *see* Alfred   SOM   *47,18* MIand note
of Wigmore: *see* Thurstan   HEF   19,10
                       SHR   6,3
of Wilbraham: *see* Aelfric   CAM   AppxC
of Wilton: *see*
   Gerald   WIL   18. 1,19
   Hervey   WIL   68,1 (cf B1)
of Wilton: *see also* Hervey the chamberlain
of Winchester: *see* Odo
	BRK	65. 10,1
	HAM	69L. 21,1. 69,7. S2
	SSX	14L
	WIL	67,1

of Windsor: *see* Odin   HAM   3,8
of Wing: *see* Alfred   BKM   12,12
of Winterton: *see* Toki   NFK   9,87
of Wissant: *see* Gilbert   SFK   6,30;143;239;281;286
of Witcham: *see* Osmund   CAM   AppxP
of Witchford: *see* Ledmer   CAM   AppxP
of Withern: *see* Arnketill   LIN   CS,39
of Wootton: *see* Aelmer   BKM   23,33
of Worcester: *see* Urso   GLS   65,1
of Worcester: *see also*
   Urso of Abetot
   Urso the sheriff

	BKM	16
	DBY	7. 1,29;32;35-36
	ESS	48. 18,32;34
	HAM	2,20
	LEC	25. 33,1. 44,2
	NTH	35. B15. 1,10. 2,1. 56,66. EB4
	NTT	10. B9;18
	OXF	23. B9. EN12
	RUT	EN12
Piercehedge: *see* Ralph	BRK	B6
Pig: *see* Aelfric	DEV	*34,10*
Pigman: *see* Norman	HEF	1,4
Pike: *see*		
Aelfric	DEV	28,13
Alwin	SOM	8,7
Pinel: *see* Ralph	ESS	77. B3a
	SFK	61. 39,3. 73,1
Pippin: *see* Ralph	LEC	17,33
Poinc: *see* Godric	ESS	22,18
Pointel: *see*		
Theodoric	ESS	71. 1,2;6;14;16;27. 33,21. 90,4-9
(Theodoric)	ESS	18,7;19. 33,4
Ponther: *see* Walter	GLS	19,2
	HEF	E5
	WOR	2,5;49;58;77. 8,8;10d;19;22. 9,6c
porter: *see*		
Miles	HAM	68,7
William	DEV	51,1 *and note*
Poynant: *see* Richard	BDF	39
	BRK	43. 1,7
	HAM	42. S3
	NFK	1,217. 9,167
	OXF	33
	WIL	58. 13,9
Poyntz: *see* Walter	OXF	45L. 45,1
Poyntz: *see also* Walter son of		
prebendary: *see* Wulfsi	BDF	56,9
predecessors of:		
Abbot of St Edmunds: *see* Wulfric	SFK	15,4
Aelmer: *see* Aelmer	SRY	19,28
Aitard of Vaux: *see* Alfred	NFK	1,120-121
Alfwy son of Thurber: *see* Alwin the rat	HAM	69,16
Archbishop Thomas: *see*		
Aelmer	LIN	CS,29
Godwine	LIN	CS,27
Aubrey de Vere: *see* Wulfwin	CAM	29,1;11
	ESS	B3t
	SFK	6,216;227. 35,2. 76,21
Bishop Remigius: *see*		
Halfdan	LIN	CK,67
Wulfwige	LIN	CK,65
Count Alan: *see* Edeva the fair	CAM	*14,35*
Count Brian: *see* Wulfnoth	SFK	2,9
Count Eustace: *see* Engelric	SFK	5,4
Count Robert (of Mortain) *see*		
Count Brian	SFK	2,5-6
Drogo of Beuvrière: *see* Rada	SFK	48,1
Durand: *see*		
Alric	HAM	2,1
Edward	HAM	2,1

Eudo son of Spirewic: *see*		
Heinfrid	NFK	29,8
	SFK	53,1
Herfrith	NFK	29,7
Wulfric	SFK	6,210
Eudo the steward: *see*		
Aelfric Kemp	SFK	16,41
Herfrith	NFK	29,7
Lisois (of Moutiers)	NFK	24,6. 66,100
	SFK	28,2
Frank: *see* Humphrey	NFK	8,137
Frodo, brother of the Abbot: *see* Ordgar	ESS	90,85
Geoffrey: *see* Alric	HAM	2,10
Geoffrey de Mandeville: *see*		
Asgar	SFK	32,1
Haldane	SFK	6,112. 8,4. 67,11
G(eoffrey) de Mandeville: *see* Haldane	SFK	6,112. 8,4
Geoffrey of Bec: *see* Ilbert	HRT	1,9
Gilbert: *see* Wulfstan	HAM	2,10
Gilbert of Ghent: *see*		
Aelfric	LIN	CK,36
Ulfr Fenman	LIN	CK,44;63
Gilbert Tison: *see* Alwine	YKS	CE14
Godric the steward: *see* Edwin	NFK	9,30. 12,17. 35,8
Guy of Craon: *see* Wilgrim	LIN	CW,15
Hamo the steward: *see* Thorbern	ESS	B3b
Henry of Ferrers: *see* Godric the sheriff	BRK	1,37. 21,13
Hugh de Montfort: *see*		
Bondi	NFK	10,53
Godmund	NFK	*23,16*
Godric	ESS	B3e
Guthmund	SFK	29,1. 31,43;45-46. 41,11
Hugh Donkey: *see* Thorkell	HEF	1,65
Hugh of Beauchamp: *see* Askell	BDF	17,4. 23,2
Ivo: *see* Atsurr	LIN	CK,63
Ivo Tallboys: *see* Siward	LIN	CS,27
Norman: *see* Godric	LIN	CW,5
Norman Crassus: *see* Guthrothr	LIN	C21
Oder: *see* Ralph of Beaufour	NFK	19,40
Osbern de Arches: *see* Wulfbert	YKS	CW1;36
Peter of Valognes: *see* Anand	NFK	10,20
Pico: *see* Aelmer	SRY	19,28
R(alph) Baynard: *see* Thored	SFK	4,36
R(alph) of Beaufour: *see*		
Eudo Clamahoc	NFK	1,218
Eudo (Clamahoc)	NFK	20,1;31
Osmund	NFK	6,7
Ralph of Limésy: *see* Norman	SFK	8,46
R(alph) of Savenay: *see* Saxi	SFK	16,8
Ralph Pagnell: *see* Merlesveinn	LIN	CK,31
Ranulf Peverel: *see*		
Saxi	SFK	6,11. 7,64. 16,20-23;26;30;33. 38,11. 77,2
Siward	SFK	34,3
Reginald the sheriff: *see* Warin	SHR	4,3,8;71
Richard of Clare: *see* Withgar	SFK	67,1
Richard son of Count Gilbert: *see*		
Finn	SFK	25,51;75
Withgar	ESS	23,30. 90,64
	SFK	25,25;35;37;78

Richard (son of Count Gilbert): *see*		
Finn	SFK	8,59
Withgar	SFK	8,35;47;63. 29,1. 76,2;4-5
Robert: *see* Wulfric Chipp	HAM	2,1
Robert Blunt: *see* Aki	SFK	6,57
Robert d'Oilly: *see* Wigot	HRT	19,1
Robert Gernon: *see* Aelfric	SFK	36,5
Robert Malet: *see*		
Atsurr	LIN	CK,36
Durand	SFK	39,12
Edric of Laxfield	NFK	1,205. 35,16
	SFK	6,79. 16,25
Edric (of Laxfield)	NFK	4,39;53. 7,4;9. 44,1
	SFK	3,95. 4,15. 6,3;82;92;97. 7,13;58;79. 8,
		8. 16,14;16;26;29;33;38. 26,12d;13.
		38,6. 51,1. 54,1. 67,2;5;15. 77,4
E(dric of Laxfield)	SFK	52,1. 67,10
Leofric	SFK	75,5
Robert Malet's mother: *see* Leofric	SFK	6,8
Robert of Stafford: *see* Leofsige	LIN	CK,16
Robert of Tosny: *see*		
Manni	SFK	7,19
Oswulf son of Fran	HRT	21,1
Ulf	CAM	20,1
(Robert son of) Fafiton: *see* Saxi	HUN	D13
Robert the bursar: *see*		
Aki	LIN	CS,34
Vigleikr	LIN	CS,36
Robert the clerk: *see* Alnoth	HAM	2,10
Roger Bigot: *see*		
A(i)lwin/A(i)lwy	NFK	9,15-16;183;228. 66,84
Brown	SFK	7,65-66
Godman	SFK	2,17
Leofwin	SFK	7,56
Leofwin Hobbeson	SFK	7,59
Wigulf	SFK	7,67
R(oger) Bigot: *see*		
Godman	SFK	2,17
Wulfsi	SFK	7,24
Roger of Poitou: *see*		
Aelfled	ESS	B3f
	SFK	8,55
Klakkr	LIN	CS,25
Ulf	SFK	8,42
Wulfmer	SFK	8,55
R(oger) of Poitou: *see* Raymond Gerald	NFK	1,226
Swein: *see* Godric	SFK	6,159;177
Tihel: *see* Leofstan	NFK	1,195
Uhtred: *see* Edgar	SFK	43,1
Walter: *see* Osbern	HAM	2,1
Walter Giffard: *see* Bodin	NFK	1,57. 25,25
Walter of Aincourt: *see* Stori	DBY	B16
Walter the deacon: *see* Theodric	SFK	41,11
Wihenoc: *see* Herman	NFK	21,8
William Goizenboded: *see* Young Richard	GLS	34,8
William Malet: *see* Edric (of Laxfield)	SFK	26,13
William of Auberville: *see* Godric of Ringshall	SFK	29,8
William of Eu: *see* Ralph of Limésy	GLS	31,2
William of Warenne: *see*		

Earl Harold	LIN	CK,38
Toki	CAM	*18,6*
W(illiam) of Warenne: *see* Ulfketel	SFK	7,25
William son of Baderon: *see*		
Wihenoc	GLS	32,9
William	GLS	34,8
priest: *see*		
Abraham	GLS	W4
Acard	SSX	11,81
Aelfric	CAM	19,1
	ESS	24,3;5. B3a
	HAM	3,5;7
	HRT	37,7
	LEC	8,5
	SOM	*5,64. 16,3*
	SFK	2,17. 3,64;74. 16,30. 74,14
Aelmer	BRK	B7
	CAM	26,29. *31,1*
	DEV	25,19
	SFK	1,56
Aelmer, another	BRK	B7
Aethelwold	SFK	3,31
Agmundr	LIN	68,47
Ailbold	SFK	14,39
Aitard	NTT	B13
Aldred	SSX	3,5
Aldwy	NFK	9,82
Alfgar	ESS	B3a
Alfgeat	CAM	5,40
	SOM	16,5
Alfheah	ESS	B3a
Alfred	HAM	64
	NFK	2,12
Alfsi	HAM	17,3. 23,51
	WIL	56,6
Alfward	BRK	7,8
	WIL	1,23e. 19,2
Algar	DEV	13a,3. *34,17*
	SFK	8,75
Alnoth	HAM	17,2
	LIN	CS,19
Alric	BDF	23,25
	CAM	14,16
	DEV	*34,50. 42,14;23*
	STS	7,13
Alwin	BDF	57,19
	BRK	7,29
	HUN	D6
	KEN	9,39
	OXF	B10
	SFK	1,13. 16,30
	WIL	67,22
Alwold	SFK	16,22
Alwulf	SFK	1,122d
Ansfrid	LIN	62,2
Ansgot	WAR	31,8
Ansketel	BDF	23,39
	KEN	4,4
	SFK	7,36
Anund	SFK	67,11

	ESS	82
	HUN	20,5-6
	SFK	32,4
	SRY	6,1
Goda	DEV	*45,2*
Godbold	SHR	3g,3
Godfrey	SSX	10,27
Godman	DEV	*16,51;129*
Godric	CON	5,14,2
	DOR	*56,48*
	HAM	23,64. IoW9,1
	HUN	19,31. D12
	SFK	6,128. 7,114
Godwin	BKM	12,20. 17,22. 57,5
	CAM	*30,3. 31,1.* AppxM
	DBY	B12
	DEV	*15,7*
	ESS	68,8
	HAM	5,1
	LEC	8,1
	NTH	B32. 17,2-3;5
	NTT	10,27;56
	SOM	*8,33*
	SFK	7,122. 38,11
	SSX	6,4. 12,33;42
Guy	HRT	34,21
	SOM	5,34
Halfdan	LIN	C2-3. 68,28
Harold's	ESS	1,24
Judicael	NFK	44
	SFK	64. 75,3
Ketill	YKS	C6
Lambert	BRK	B7
Ledman	CAM	AppxP
Ledmer	ESS	20,77. 23,4
	SFK	25,1
Leofgeat	BDF	13,1
Leofing	HRT	16,5
	YKS	C3
Leofnoth	WOR	8,13
Leofric	SOM	*9,3*
	WIL	1,13
Leofstan	SFK	1,122d. 7,40
Leofwin	CAM	*31,1*
	NTH	17,1
Leofwine	LIN	C2
Morcar	BDF	1,2b. 40,1-2
Munulf	SFK	26,5
Norman	NTT	9,1
Oddi	YKS	CE49
Ordmer	SSX	10,1
Osbern	LIN	53. 54,1. 2,16
	WIL	57. 1,6. 19,3
Osmer	DBY	B11
Osmund	OXF	14,3
Oswy Wild	KEN	*M24*
Radfred	HAM	1,7
Ralph	BRK	1,24
	CAM	*14,29*
	HAM	2,9

	SFK	1,122a-122b. 6,112
	WIL	19,1
Emma	HAM	10,1
Matilda	BKM	52
	CON	1,13
	DEV	1,57. *13a,2.* 27,1
	DOR	1,15. 17,1
	GLS	1,47;50
	HAM	1,8
	NTH	8,4
	WAR	3,4
	WIL	17,1
(Matilda)	DOR	54,8. 56,19
	ESS	1,11-12;23. 60,3. 82,1. B3j
	GLS	1,24;37;42;44. 69,7
	HAM	6,12. 53,2
	LIN	68,30
	SRY	1,8. 31,1
	WAR	EG2-3
Ralph(?): *see* Roger	DEV	*34,46*
rat: *see* Alwin	HAM	69,16
Reckless/Sturmid: *see* Sturmy		
Red: *see* Thurstan	ESS	5,8
red: *see* Thurstan	HAM	3,1
red: *see also*		
Roote		
Rufus		
reeve: *see*		
Aelfric	CAM	AppxL
	SOM	*8,33*
	SFK	1,17;103. 14,152
Aelmer	ESS	90,78
	SFK	8,60
Aethelward	SFK	7,18;36
A(i)lwy of Colchester	NFK	17,22
Alfred	ESS	90,74
Alfwy	SOM	35,1 *and note*
Alnoth	SOM	*24,24. 25,29*
Alric	SFK	1,60 (*but see note*)
Alstan	KEN	1,1
Alward	DOR	*56,62*
Alwin	BDF	*57,3iii-v*
	CAM	*31,2*
Ansketel	NFK	10,58
Baldwin	NFK	10,71
Bleio	GLS	W2
Brictmer	SFK	4,15
Brictric	SFK	62,5
Brictwin	DOR	*56,9-11;17;35-38*
Brown	NFK	1,2
	SFK	7,63
Brunman	KEN	C8
Cave	HAM	4,1
Colwin	DEV	*42,3. 52,4*
Durand	NTH	B33
(Earl) Harold's	ESS	1,24
Eccha	DEV	1,4
Edric	DOR	*56,43*
	SFK	6,217
Edwold	ESS	18,11

Scrope: *see* Richard	HEF	12,1. 24,7
	WOR	19,1
Scullion: *see* Godfrey	DOR	57,22
Sech: *see* Godwin	ESS	90,28
servant: *see* Hugh	LIN	CS,40
servant of the Count: *see*		
Nigel	SFK	2,8
Ranulf	HRT	15,1
servant, royal: *see*		
Ansger	DEV	*51,13*
Baldwin	HRT	42,8
servant: *see also*	DEV	53L
	DOR	57
	HAM	68L
	LEC	42
	SOM	46L
	SRY	36L
	WAR	44L
	WIL	66. 68
Shed-butter	ESS	B3a
sheriff of: *see*		
Staffordshire	WOR	1,5
Surrey	ESS	1,23
sheriff: *see*		
Aelfric	HUN	B10. D20
Aelfric Godricson	CAM	B14
Aiulf the chamberlain	DOR	48L. *49*
Aiulf (the chamberlain)	BRK	57
	WIL	55
Alfred	DOR	49,15
Alfwy	OXF	58,27
Alwin	GLS	1,2;13. 34,8;12
	HEF	10,66
	HUN	19,25
	WAR	6,9. 14,2. 17,15. 23,4
Ansculf	BKM	17,20
	SRY	21,3
Baldwin of Exeter	CON	Exon. fo. 72 [omitted]
	DOR	42,1
	SOM	20
Baldwin (of Exeter)	DEV	16. *1,5;30;36-37. 2,24.* 52,33
B(aldwin of Exeter)	DEV	*C2. 1,38;40*
Blackwin	CAM	32,34-35;38;43
Durand of Gloucester	GLS	53
Durand (of Gloucester)	GLS	G4. W8;15. B1. 2,10. 3,7. 35,2. E16.
		EvM4. WoB19
	HEF	1,31;38
Edric	GLS	E16
	WIL	45,2
Edsi	HAM	6,10. 47,1
Edward of Salisbury	HRT	32
	WIL	24p. 24
Edward (of Salisbury)	HAM	12,1
	OXF	B9
	SOM	*1,31.* EW1
	WIL	M5. B4. 12,2. 67,100. 68,14;23
Edwin	OXF	24,5
	WAR	4,3. 17,10
Eustace (of Huntingdon)	HUN	19. D20
	NTH	EH4

Froger	BRK	1,10
Gilbert	HEF	8,1
	SSX	10,1
Godric	BDF	?17,7. 23,25
	BRK	1,26-27;32;37;42. 21,15;17;22
	BKM	4,5. 19,3. 44,1
	WIL	E1
Hamo	KEN	12. C1. 1,1-3. 2,16;31. 5,30;42;126
	SRY	30. 8,15;23
Heca	DEV	*17,38*
Hugh	HAM	30,1
	YKS	C10
Hugh son of Baldric	NTT	B3
Hugh (son of Grip)	DOR	B1;2;3-4
Ilbert	HRT	1,6;8-9;12-13
	HEF	1,1
Ivo	LIN	CW,4
John	HEF	10,19
Merlesveinn	LIN	CW,12
Norman	SFK	63. 6,91;290. 7,36
Ordgar	CAM	22,6. 28,1
Osward	KEN	1,1
Peter of Valognes	CAM	33,1
	HRT	1,9. 36,9;13
Peter (of Valognes)	ESS	1,2;4. 49,3
	HRT	B11. 1,13;19. 9,10. 37,19
Picot (of Cambridge)	CAM	21,9. 29,12. AppxAK;L
	ESS	1,9
(Ralph) Baynard	ESS	1,2;27
Ralph of Bernay	HEF	1,70
Ralph Tallboys	BDF	54,2. 57,1;3vi
Ralph (Tallboys)	BDF	21,6
Ranulf	SRY	1,1c. 5,28
Reginald	SHR	4,3
Robert Blunt	NFK	1,66
Robert Malet	SFK	1,105
R(obert) son of Wymarc	ESS	83,1
Roger	MDX	3,3. 15,1
Roger Bigot	SFK	1,105
Roger (Bigot)	NFK	9,86
	SFK	1,7,122. 25,52. 39,3. 73,1. 74,7
R(oger Bigot)	NFK	9,80
Roger (of Pîtres)	GLS	56,2. EvK1;116
Swein (of Essex)	ESS	1,2-3;27-28. 10,5
	OXF	42
Thoraldr	LIN	11,9
Thurstan	CON	*5,4. 1,1. 4,22. 6,1*
Toli	NFK	1,229. 14,35. 47,4
	SFK	4,15. 7,31;67. 31,53
Tovi	SOM	*47,3*
Urso (of Abetot)	HEF	E4
	WOR	1,1b-1c. 2,3;7;75. 8,15;22. 9,5b. E14
Walter	GLS	EvL1
William Malet	YKS	CW35
William (of Mohun)	SOM	1,2;*21-25*
Shield: *see*		
Godwin	CAM	*41,14*
William	SFK	6,63. 7,75
	WIL	1,16. 2,4. 68,20

Silvester: *see* Hugh   DOR   54,2
Silvester: *see also* of Bosc
sister of Earl Harold: *see* Aelfeva   BKM   4,21
sister of Earl Oda: *see* Edith   HEF   18,1
sister of King Edward: *see* (Countess) Goda   GLS   24,1
                                                               SRY   14,1
sister of Ralph of Pomeroy: *see* Beatrix   SOM   *30,1*
sister of William (Cheever): *see* Beatrix   DEV   *19,40;46*
sister: *see*
   Aki's   STF   11,8
   Alfwold's   WIL   38,1
   Alric Grangemere's   BKM   4,20
   Eric's   HNT   D27
   Ordwulf's   DEV   15,41
   Stigand's   NFK   1,61
   Wulfgeat's   LIN   CK1
   Wulfwin's   ESS   23,34
Skipper: *see* Godric   ESS   22,16
Small: *see*
   Aelfric   BDF   24,16. 25,3
                                                               HAM   69,53. NF20;21
                                                               WIL   67,18
   Thurstan   HAM   3,1
Small: *see also*
   Little
   little
smith: *see*
   Bondi   SFK   7,37
   Edwin   SFK   6,110
   Godric   SFK   7,76
Snipe: *see*
   Edric   CAM   21,5. 31,*1*;2
   Leofric   SFK   7,143
Snook: *see* Edward   KEN   5,139
Sock: *see* Leofwin   DEV   *51,7*
soldier: *see* man-at-arms
(son of?) Aelfeth: *see* Godwin   MDX   7,7
son of Aelfeva: *see*
   Seric   BKM   14,5
   Sired   BKM   14,3
son of Aelfric: *see*
   Edric   SHR   3c,8
   Withgar   SFK   25,1;60
son of Aethelwy: *see* Stanhard   SFK   72
son of Agmundr: *see* Godric   LIN   68,45
son of Aiulf: *see* Edmund   WIL   67,58
son of Alan: *see* Richard   NFK   10,43
son of Alfhere: *see* Godwin   SFK   6,1;112
son of Alfred: *see* Robert   GLS   EvO10
son of Alfsi of Faringdon   BRK   B1
son of Algar: *see*
   Brictric   DEV   *24,21*
                                                               GLS   1,39;47. *6,1. 31,5. 69,7*
                                                               WOR   2,30;37
   Godwin   SFK   7,36
son of Algot: *see* Edmund   ESS   61
                                                               MDX   3,10
son of Almund: *see* Alward   SHR   4,27,17
son of Alnoth : *see* Harding   SOM   47,3
son of Alnoth: *see also* Harding of Merriot

son of Alsi: *see* Godwin	SFK	6,26
son of Alsige: *see* Toli	LIN	T5
son of Alwin(e): *see* Leofwin(e)	DBY	S5
	LIN	T5
	NTT	S5
son of Amelina: *see* Ansketel	DOR	54,8
son of Amelina: *see also* of Cherbourg		
son of Ansculf: *see* William (of Picquigny)	BRK	22
	BKM	17
	CAM	36
	HUN	23
	MDX	19
	NTH	36
	OXF	21. ES
	RUT	EN13
	STS	12. B8. EN3
	SRY	21. 19,43
	WAR	27. EBS2-3. EBW3-5. EN5-6
	WIL	68,22
	WOR	23. 1,1d
son of Ansculf: *see also* of Picquigny		
son of Ansger: *see* Hervey	DOR	*12,14*
son of Ansketel: *see* Roger	KEN	5,158;225
son of Arcold: *see* Walter	GLS	39,21
son of Arnfastr: *see* Richard	YKS	23. C18. SW,An1;8;13-14;16
son of Arnold: *see* Roger	SFK	8,7;17
son of Arnulf	SFK	8,8 (*but see note*)
son of Asgautr: *see* Arnold	LIN	57,12
son of Asmoth: *see* Brictmer	SFK	4,15
son of Asmundr: *see* Gamall	YKS	CW2
son of Atsurr/Azor: *see*		
Auti	LIN	T5
Henry	BDF	43
Jocelyn	HAM	IoW8. IoW1,7
Swein	NTH	B29
Ulf	NTH	2,2-3
William	HAM	IoW7. IoW1,5;7
son of Aubrey: *see*		
Humphrey	NFK	39. ESf7
	SFK	56. 34,9
Walter	CAM	17,4;*6*
	SFK	6,2;32;80;183;292
W(alter)	SFK	6,189
son of Auti: *see* Toki	LIN	C4. T5
son of Azor: *see* son of Atsurr/Azor		
son of Baderon: *see* William	GLS	32. G4. 1,13. 16,1. 19,2. E7;35. EvK1
	HAM	50
	HEF	15. 1,1;7;48
	WOR	8,9f
son of Baderon: *see also* Baderon		
son of Baldric: *see*		
Hugh	BRK	51
	HAM	44
	LEC	1,2
	LIN	25. C20;25. CN,8;24
	NTH	1,4
	NTT	22. B3
	RUT	EN4
	WIL	51

	YKS	23. C11;26. SW,An1. SW,Bu1. SN, L14;41. SE,He4. SE,Wel3;7. SE,C2-3. SE,How9. SE, Sn5. SE, Dr4-5. SE, Wa7-8. SE,P4-6. SE,Sc1-7. SE,Ac7;12. SE,Th1-2;8
H(ugh)	LIN	24,66

son of Baldric: *see also* son-in-law of Hugh

| **son of Banna:** *see* Al(f)wy?Alwin | SOM | *1,27. 6,9. 8,5. 35,13-14;16;24* |
| **son of Bell:** *see* Aethelward | SFK | 25,20 |

son of Beorhtric/Brictric: *see*

Aelfric	SOM	47,21
Godwine	LIN	C3
Wulfric	SFK	55,1

son of Berner: *see* Theobald	DEV	36
son of Bishop Peter: *see* Reinbald	BRK	1,42
son of Bloc: *see* Walter	NFK	*4,16*
son of Bondi: *see* Aelfric	SFK	7,37
son of Bonnard: *see* William	SSX	13,46;53
son of Bose: *see* Leofric	NFK	20,23
son of Boselin: *see* William	NTH	B16
son of Boso: *see* Osbern	YKS	C3

son of Brian: *see*

Evrard	CAM	*29,1.* AppxB
Ralph	ESS	3,5. 4,15;18. 34,26;30. 90,12
	SFK	34,8
William	ESS	4,2

| **son of Brictmer:** *see* Alwin | MDX | 3,11 |

son of Brictric: *see* son of Beohrtric/Brictric

| **son of Brictsi:** *see* Alfsi | HAM | 6,13. 69,9;21. IoW9,2 |

son of Brown: *see*

| Aelfric | SFK | 16,11 |
| Leofwin | SFK | 6,110 |

son of Brown: *see also* Brownson

| **son of Burg:** *see* Atsurr | LIN | T5 |

son of Burgred: *see*

Edwin	BKM	5,9;20
	NTH	4,32;36
	OXF	EN3;7
Ulf	BKM	12,29
Wulfsi	BDF	25,5

| **son of Burnin:** *see* Warin | SFK | 4,20;29 *and note.* 6,296 |

son of Camm: *see*

| Brictric | DEV | *3,32. 19,12* |
| Brictwy | DEV | *17,13* |

| **son of Chipping:** *see* Alwin | BRK | 65,6 |
| **son of Clamahoc:** *see* Eudo | NFK | 1,11. *20,18.* 22,11 |

son of Clamahoc: *see also* Clamahoc

| **son of Colswein:** *see* Aelmer | CAM | *14,23-24.* AppxJ |

son of Colswein: *see also* of Bourn

son of Constantine: *see*

Hugh	WAR	18,15
William	BKM	33
	ESS	74

son of Corbet: *see*

| Robert | SHR | 4,5 |
| Roger | SHR | 4,4 |

son of Corbet: *see also* Corbet

son of Corbucion: *see*

| Robert | ESS | 41. 1,4 |

	NFK 35. 1,229. 31,11;44
	SFK 40
R(obert)	NFK 31,12;17
William	BRK 27
	OXF ES1
	STS 12,30. EW5
	WAR 28. B2
	WOR 24. 8,14. E33
son of Count Eustace: *see* Geoffrey	SRY 25,2
son of Count Gilbert: *see* Richard	BDF 38
	CAM 19
	DEV 26
	ESS 23. 1,11;13;27. 30,23. 90,49;75
	HRT 42a
	HUN 28
	KEN 11. *C8.* 5,209
	MDX 13
	SFK 25. 8,63. 16,15. 21,44. 33,1. 76,1. EE2
	SRY 19
	SSX E1
	WIL 40
son of Count Gilbert: *see also*	
of Clare	
of Tonbridge	
son of Gilbert	
son of Countess Gytha: *see* (Earl) Gyrth	NTT 10,1
son of Croc: *see* Reginald	HAM 59. S3. IoW1,6
son of Doda: *see* Brictric	WOR 2,63
son of Dudeman: *see* Godwin	ESS EKt
	KEN 5,104
son of Durand Malzor: *see* Adam	ESS 63
son of Eadgifu: *see* Godric	LIN *C2-3*
son of Eadric/Edric: *see*	
Edward	DEV 1,11
Godwine	YKS *CW27*
Odo	DEV *52,22-25*
son of Earl Godwin: *see* (Earl) Harold	HEF 19,8
son of Earl Ralph: *see* Harold	GLS 61
	MDX 9,1
	WAR 38
	WOR 22
son of (Earl) Ralph the constable: *see* Ralph	NFK 10,21
	SFK 31,53
son of Earl Roger: *see* Hugh	STS B5
son of Earl William: *see* Earl Roger	HEF S1. W19. 1,53
son of Edeva: *see* Wulfward	BKM B3. 12,31
son of Ednoth: *see* son of Alnoth	
son of Edric: *see* son of Eadric/Edric	
son of (?Edwin): *see* Aelfric	SFK 6,110
son of Edwy: *see* Alwin	HEF 10,15
son of Edwy Young: *see* Alwin	HEF 10,70
son of Engelbert: *see* Walter	KEN 5,128
son of Erchenbald: *see* Reginald	SRY *33L* (cf 33,1)
son of Erhard: *see* Stephen	BRK 64
son of Ernucion: *see* John	ESS 40,1
son of Estan: *see* Leofwin	BKM 12,31
son of Everbold: *see* (Odo)	DOR 54,13
son of Everbold: *see* Odo	DOR 54,11
son of Everwacer: *see* Aelfric	SOM *8,33*
son of Fafiton: *see* Robert	HUN 25,1

son of Fafiton: *see also* Fafiton
son of Fran: *see* Oswulf

	BDF	26,1. E4
	BKM	18,2
	HRT	15,7. 17,1. 19,1. 21,1-2
son of Fulbert: *see* Hugh	KEN	5,159
son of Fulcred: *see*		
Robert	SFK	6,46
Stephen	GLS	E27. WoB7
	WOR	2,42
	DEV	42
son of Gamelin: *see* Odo	SOM	38. *21,65*
	LIN	C16
son of Garwine: *see* Godric		
son of Geoffrey: *see*		
Osbern	SSX	9,52;70
William	KEN	D8. M22
son of Gerald: *see* Robert	BRK	40
	DOR	30
	HAM	28
	SOM	33. 1,9
	WIL	42
son of Gilbert: *see*		
Richard	SFK	76,2
Robert	SOM	*25,5*
Walter	ESS	1,11 *and note*
son of Gilbert: *see also*		
son of Count Gilbert		
Walter Cook		
son of Gobert: *see* Robert	ESS	78
son of Goda: *see* Alwin	SOM	*24,34*
son of Goding: *see*		
Aelfric	BKM	12,32. 57,17
Aelmer	CAM	*13,12. 25,8*
Alric	BDF	24,2;6-7
	BKM	12,28;31;33-35. 14,7-8;10;26;28-29;33; 37;41;44;46. 23,31. 53,6
Alwin	BKM	12,27
son of Goding: *see also* Godingson		
son of Godram: *see* Aethelstan	LIN	T5. CK,66
son of Godric: *see* Godricsson		
son of Godwin: *see* A(e)lmer	NFK	65,2
son of Gold: *see* Hugh	SFK	26,8
son of Gorham: *see* W.	SFK	67,7
son of Gozhere: *see* Hugh	BKM	57,7
son of Grim: *see* Leofric	CAM	AppxG
son of Grimbald: *see* Svertingr	LIN	C2
son of Grip: *see*		
Hugh	DOR	55. 1,22. 2,6. *11,5.* 13,*1*;4. 19,11. 23, 1. *36,3.* 37,13. 56,36
Walter	SFK	6,132;308;311;317
son of Grip: *see also* wife of		
son of Gross: *see* William	ESS	1,2. 11,1. 27,2. 88,2. 90,15;18
	KEN	9,48
	SFK	31,50
son of Gross: *see also* Gross, William		
son of Gunfrid: *see* Ralph	SSX	10,9
son of Guy of Raimbeaucourt: *see* Ingelrann	LIN	39,4
	OXF	36,1

son of Guy: *see*		
Thurstan	NFK	9,83;85;135;150
	SFK	7,122;125;133. 76,15
William	GLS	35
	SOM	28
	WIL	38
son of Hagni: *see* Ralph	NFK	57. 50,9
son of Hamo: *see*		
Geoffrey	SFK	25,86
Robert	GLS	EvK1;116
son of Harold: *see* Godwin	SOM	1,14;16
son of Harthaknutr: *see* Svertingr	LIN	C3
son of Herebold: *see* Godric	SFK	6,108
son of Herlwin: *see*		
Baldwin	BKM	4,31
	GLS	1,22
Ralph	NFK	9,8-9;12;73;231. 19,8. 66,75
son of H(erlwin): *see*		
Ralph	NFK	9,118
R(alph)	NFK	9,120
son of Hermenfrid: *see* William	KEN	*3,15*
son of Hubert: *see*		
Adam	KEN	5,6;24;71;93;125;130. 13,1
	OXF	7,45
	SRY	5,8;18
Eudo	BDF	21
	BRK	32
	CAM	25
	HAM	30
	HRT	31
	HUN	15
	NTH	42
Ralph	DBY	10. 2,1. 6,99. B6
	LEC	22
	LIN	62
	NTT	13. B12
	STS	15
	WOR	23,8
son of Hubert: *see also* Eudo the steward		
son of Hugh: *see*		
Robert	CHS	2. B13
Wulfric	SFK	*28,6*
son of Ilger: *see* Ranulf	SFK	*39,10 (but see note)*
son of Ilger: *see also* brother of Ilger		
son of Ingold: *see* Edric	SFK	4,15
son of Ivo: *see*		
Herbert	BDF	2,6-7
	HRT	10,9
	KEN	D10. P19. 5,54;138;156. 9,35
Herlwin	NFK	66,51
Reynold	NFK	21. 1,3;57;61-62. 8,29. 15,14. 66,44
Robert	DEV	*15,10;14*
	DOR	*26,7 note; 24*
	SOM	*19,13-14;35;66;85*
son of Karl: *see*		
Godric	KEN	5,25
Godwin	KEN	5,105
son of Karl: *see also* Karlson		
son of Kaskin: *see* Alfsi	DBY	S5
	NTT	S5

son of Ketel: *see* Edric
son of King William: *see* Richard
son of Lambert: *see*
   Jocelyn
   Modbert
   Walter
son of Ledhard: *see* Osbern/Osbert

son of Leofmer: *see* Brictwold
son of Leofric: *see* Osmund
son of Leofric: *see also* Leofric
son of Leofsi: *see* Azor
son of Leofwin(e): *see*
   Burgwald
   Godwin
   Leofric
son of Maelcolumban: *see* Northmann
son of Magne/Manne: *see* William

son of Malleterre: *see* Geoffrey
son of Mann: *see* son of Magne/Manne
son of Manne: *see* son of Magne
son of Manni: *see* Ulf
son of Manni Swart: *see* Ulf
son of Maredudd: *see* Gruffydd
son of Mauger: *see*
   Drogo
   Hugh
   William

son of Merewine: *see*
   Norman
   Ulfketill
son of Mergeat: *see*
   Aelfric
   Alric

son of Modbert: *see* Geoffrey
son of Morin: *see* Roger
son of Murdoch: *see* Robert

son of Nigel: *see*
   Eudo
   Robert
   Roger
   William

son of Norman/Northmann: *see*
   Hugh

   William

son of Northmann: *see* son of Norman
son of O(d)ger: *see* William

GLS	78,5;16
HRT	36,19
LIN	28. 3,4. 24,53. CS,3. CN, 17;19. CW,3
DEV	*16,50*
SSX	9,18;60;74;122;125
KEN	2,38. 5,135;200 *and note*; 205-206;216; 218. 7,19
SFK	*14,5-6;21;28;65;106*
NTH	18,1
NTH	18,67
LIN	C3
BDF	24,9
LEC	29,3;18
YKS	CE23. CW26
BKM	34
HAM	48
OXF	47
SSX	13,14
KEN	5,124
MDX	7,8
SFK	6,109
HEF	31. 29,1
DEV	*3,9;13-14;16*
ESS	27,16-17
NTH	36,4
WAR	EN6
LIN	CK,21
LIN	S3
LIN	T5. CK,27
LEC	16,9
WAR	24,1
KEN	*D8*
CAM	AppxN
HAM	68,10
OXF	50
SFK	2,16
BDF	29,1
SOM	*20,2-3*
BKM	12,14
CHS	9. FD4
LIN	13,10
CHS	11. FD5,3. FT3,1-2
SFK	4,6;35;39
YKS	4N3. 4E1
GLS	37
HEF	16. 1,1;4;10c;28;38;53;63
SSX	13,19
BKM	4,16
KEN	D8. M3. 5,33

son of Odin: *see* Hundger	DOR	57,15
son of Odo: *see* William	ESS	24,11
son of Oger: *see* son of O(d)ger		
son of Osbern: *see*		
Hugh	CHS	12. 16. FD5
William	WOR	23,8
son of Osbern: *see also* Earl William		
son of Osbert: *see* Gamall	YKS	C36
son of Osmund: *see*		
Ansketel	HAM	68,3. S3
Hugh	HAM	68,2. NF9,1
Leofnoth	BKM	12,38
Leofric	BDF	22,1
Ralph	HUN	27. 6,17. 22,2. D8
William	BRK	B7
son of Ospak: *see*		
Ansketel	NFK	66,99
Ralph	KEN	2,29
son of Othere: *see* Walter	BRK	31. B3. 1,1
	BKM	29
	HAM	46. 9,1
	MDX	11
	SRY	22. 1,2
son of Ottarr: *see* Toki	YKS	C36
son of Payne: *see*		
Edmund	HAM	69,51
	NFK	46
	SOM	46,21
Ralph	DEV	*19,43*
Roger	DEV	*16,155. 34,12*
son of Poyntz: *see*		
Drogo	GLS	54
	HEF	23. 1,29;38
	WIL	49. M14
	WOR	21. 8,9d
Walter	BRK	30
	GLS	55. 2,8. EvK230. EvM3
	OXF	45. 1,6
son of Poyntz: *see also* Poyntz		
son of Queen (Matilda): *see* Richard	DOR	*52,1*
son of Queen (Matilda): *see also* son of King		
William		
son of R.: *see* Humphrey	SFK	6,172
son of Rafn: *see* Leodwine	LIN	C3
son of Rainard: *see* Roger	NFK	50. 12,45. 27,2. 57,2
son of Rainward: *see* William	BDF	25,7
son of Ralph: *see*		
Robert	OXF	58,8
	WIL	68,8
Roger	DEV	*34,46 (but see note)*
	GLS	75
	SOM	*5,24*
son of Ralph of Hastings: *see* Robert	ESS	B7
son of Ralph of Hastings: *see also*		
Hastings		
of Hastings		
son of Ralph the chaplain's wife: *see* Walter		
son of Ranulf: *see*		
Hugh	SSX	6,1. 12,42
William	SSX	13,22;26;29;54

	SOM	36. *8,18*. 45,12. EDe1
	WIL	49,1a
	WOR	8,7
son of Rozelin: *see* Robert	BDF	15,7
	ESS	76
	HRT	17,2
	MDX	16
	SOM	*31,5*
son of Saeric: *see* Godmund	HEF	10,71
son of Saewulf: *see* Alfwy	HAM	69,17
son of Saleva: *see* Azor	DBY	S5
	NTT	S5
son of Saxwalo of Bouville: *see* William	SFK	32,31
son of Saxwallo (of Bouville): *see* W(illiam)	SFK	32,13
son of Scaldward: *see* William	NTT	2,4
son of Sibbi: *see* Sired	BKM	12,1
son of Siegfried/Sifrid: *see*		
Ralph	BRK	49. B3
	HAM	3,5;10
Roger	BRK	B9. 49,2
son of Sired: *see* Dering	KEN	M19
son of Siward: *see* Aki	LIN	T5
son of Siward the priest: *see* Norman	LIN	C14
son of Skjaldvor: *see* Rothulfr	LIN	T5
son of Solomon: *see* Gilbert	BDF	48. 29,1
	ESS	73. 15,1
	HRT	40
son of Spirewic: *see* Eudo	LIN	29. CS,21. CN,30
	NFK	29. 1,221. 9,100
	SFK	53. 6,210
son of Stigand: *see* Robert	LIN	CS,30
son of Stur: *see* William	HAM	51. S3. IoW6. IoW1,7;11
son of Svafi/Swafi: *see* Sveinn, Swein	DBY	S5
	LIN	C9. T5
	NTT	S5
son of Svala: *see* Atsurr	LIN	T5
son of Swafi: *see* son of Svafi		
son of Swein: *see* Edward	ESS	85,1
	MDX	25,1
(son of?) Swein: *see* Swein		
son of Tancred: *see* Norman	SFK	8,35;46-47;49
son of Tezzo: *see* Osbern	CHS	24. FD5,3. FD6
son of the chamberlain: *see* Odo	DOR	36,8
son of the Earl: *see* Ralph	BRK	48
son of the King: *see* William	DOR	3,6
son of Theobald: *see* Robert	SHR	4,9
	SSX	11,2;8
son of Theodoric: *see*		
Ralph	SSX	13,45
Roger	BDF	23,41
son of Theodwald: *see* William	KEN	D8. M19
son of Thored: *see* Azor	BKM	1,7
son of Thorfrothr: *see* Godric	LIN	T5
son of Thorgils: *see* Hugh	SHR	4,22
son of Thorold: *see*		
Azor	SOM	*6,2*
Gilbert	CAM	24
	ESS	58
	GLS	52. 3,1. 19,2. WoB15
	HEF	25. 1,51

	SOM	42. 1,21
	WAR	33. EW3
	WOR	20. 2,47. 8,10c;23;25. 11,2
Ilbert	HEF	26. 1,3;5
William	SRY	29,1
son of Thorold (of Rochester): *see*		
Ralph	ESS	1,27. 18,20;36
	KEN	2,33. 5,3;*31*;44;51-52;61;97;103;108
(Ralph)	ESS	18,1;4-5;8;10;34
son of Thorold/Thorolf/Thorulf: *see* Richard	CON	*2,5. 5,3,1*
	DEV	*15,42. 16,115.* 30,1 *and note*
son of Thorr: *see* Frani	YKS	CE41
son of Thurber: *see* Alfwy	HAM	69,16;29
	WIL	67,26
son of Thurstan: *see* Robert	OXF	58,4
son of Toki: *see*		
Alward	DEV	19,*16;19*;35;*39. 34,14*
Godwin	NFK	29,9
	SFK	7,22;47
son of Toki: *see also* Tokeson		
[son of] Topi: *see* Topi		
son of Topi: *see* Ulf(r)	LIN	CK10
	NTH	ELc4
	RUT	ELc19
son of Toti: *see* Azor	BKM	B5;9. 4,25. 14,29. 19,6-7. 41,1;4;6. 47,
		1. 49,1
son of Ulf(r): *see*		
Alwin	NTH	41,5
Arnketill	YKS	CW25
Northmann	YKS	CE13
Svartbrandr	LIN	C2-3;13. CK,18;29
son of Ungomar: *see* Oger	RUT	R14
son of Valhrafn: *see* Agmundr	LIN	C3
son of Waleran: *see* John	CAM	35
	ESS	40. 1,4. B1;3p
	SFK	55. EE6
son of Walkelin: *see* Robert	OXF	6,12
son of Walter: *see*		
Osbern	BDF	45
R(...)	LEC	3,15
Ranulf	NFK	1,64. 9,6;11;24;32;45;80;82;197. 66,71
	SFK	7,20;124
R(anulf)	SFK	7,21
Robert	BKM	19,3
	SOM	*19,37*
son of Warin: *see*		
Gilbert	ESS	1,13
Robert	CAM	AppxM
son of Watson: *see* Robert	KEN	*2,26. 3,18*
son of William: *see*		
Hugh	KEN	5,128
Richard	KEN	5,119
Robert	DBY	15
	NTT	28. 3,1
son of William Malet: *see*		
Robert Malet	SFK	7,16. 67,2
Robert (Malet)	SFK	7,138. 75,4
son of William of Thaon	KEN	5,90;171
son of William the usher: *see* Robert	LEC	43,9
son of Wimund: *see* William	DEV	*16,44*

Talbot: *see*

Geoffrey	ESS	47,1
Richard	BDF	16,2

Tallboys: *see*

Ivo	BDF	1,1a;2a;3. 4,5
	LIN	14. C10. 1,80. CS,20;27;35. CN,3; 19-20;28. CK, 22
	NFK	27. 1,131. 4,44;51
	SFK	1,123f
Ralph	BDF	1,1b;4-5. 4,2. 13,1-2. 17,2;5. 23,7;12; 16;41-42;55. 24,14. 46,1. 54,2. 57,1; 3vi;4
	BKM	17,2. 38,1
	CAM	42
	HRT	1,9;12. 25,2
	NFK	1,52
	SFK	35,3
William	LIN	66

thane: *see*

Acwulf	SFK	12,1. 59,1
Aefic	DBY	6,42
Aelfeva wife of Harold	BKM	17,22
Aelfric	BKM	43,11
	DEV	17,13. *25,25*
	DOR	55,44 (cf 55,48 *note*)
	ESS	20,6
	SOM	1,1. *5,59. 19,68. 21,65. 24,10. 37,11*
	SFK	4,11. 9,1
Aelfric the priest	SOM	*5,64*
Aelmer	BKM	14,35
	SOM	*21,73. 37,8*
	SFK	4,42
Aelmer Eastry	DEV	*15,47*
Aethelstan	SFK	4,1
Aldeva	SOM	*28,1*
Aldred	DOR	*41,3*
Aldwulf	DEV	17,13
Alfgeat	SOM	*5,47*
Alfheah	DBY	6,42
Alfhild	SOM	*37,8*
Alfsi	BKM	14,45
Alfward	BKM	14,20
	DOR	*36,2*
	NTT	9,69
	SOM	1,21. *5,65. 8,4. 21,6;54. 27,3. 35,12*
	WIL	3,1
Alfwold	DEV	*35,9*
	HAM	1,W1
Alfwy	SHR	4,16,2
	SOM	*37,11*
Algar	DEV	*17,94*
	DOR	55,46 (cf *55,48 note*)
	SOM	*5,47*
Alnoth	SOM	*5,61*
Alric	BKM	14,45. 23,1
	GLS	37,3
	HAM	1,W1
	NFK	29,10
	SHR	4,3,10
	SOM	*5,9. 37,11*

Fridebert	ESS	30,4
Gamel	CHS	R5,3
Geoffrey of Rots	KEN	*2,4*
G(erald)	DEV	*45,1*
Godman	SFK	59,2
Godric	BKM	4,30. 5,21. 17,22
	DEV	*3,12. 19,4. 23,3. 40,6. 43,1. 51,2*
	DOR	*36,5*
	GLS	26,3. 37,3
	HAM	19,1
	HEF	19,2
	NTT	9,26
	SOM	*5,3. 21,85. 22,28*
Godwin	BKM	14,49. 43,11
	DEV	*2,15. 16,7*
	HAM	1,W1
	KEN	5,207
	NFK	1,198
	SOM	*19,29*
	SFK	33,3
Godwin the priest	BKM	17,22
Grimketill	LIN	25,1
Guthmund	SFK	31,41
Hagni	NFK	1,182
Halfdan	LIN	25,1
Hamo	KEN	*2,4*
Harold	BKM	17,22-23
	HAM	1,W1
Ingold	NFK	48,3
Ingvar	ESS	18,2
	SFK	19,16
Justan	NTT	9,69
Ketel	SFK	37,6
Kipping	DEV	*15,11. 16,79*
Leofing	SOM	*19,64. 21,54*
Leofric	BKM	25,3
	LEC	15,7
	SFK	5,1
Leofric the priest	SOM	*9,3*
Leofsi	DBY	6,42
Leofwin	DEV	*35,9*
	GLS	68,9
	HAM	19,1
	SOM	*19,32*
	SFK	41,15
Leofwold	NFK	13,24
Lodi	BKM	14,45
Manni Swart	SFK	3,1
Merdo	LIN	25,1
Norman	SFK	7,18
Odincar	DBY	13,2
Ording	NFK	20,34
Ordric	SHR	4,16,2
	SOM	1,21
Ordwold	SOM	*5,62*
Ordwulf	DEV	*15,11*
	SOM	1,21
Ordwy	SHR	4,16,2
Osbern	NFK	50,11-12
	SOM	*21,85*

Oslac	DEV	*28,2*
	SHR	4,1,35-36
	SFK	31,3
Osmund	LEC	15,7
	WIL	21,2
Osward	SOM	*35,12*
Oswulf	BKM	14,45
	DEV	*3,11*
	LEC	15,7
Othere	SHR	4,3,10
Raven	BKM	57,7
Rewruin	DEV	*19,4*
Robert Latimer	KEN	*2,4*
Rolf	LEC	15,7
Saegeat	OXF	1,7b
Saeric	SOM	*5,3;64. 22,28. 25,40*
Saeward	SOM	*28,1*
Saewin	DEV	*17,12*
	DOR	55,45 (cf 55,54 *note*)
	SOM	1,1. *19,24*
Saewin Tuft	DEV	*16,7*
Saewulf	HAM	19,1
	SOM	*5,59. 24,10. 26,28*
Sheerwold	SOM	*5,62;65*
Sibbi	BKM	23,31
Sigeric	SOM	*37,8. 45,7*
Abbot Sihtric	DEV	*16,7*
Siward	SHR	4,1,35-36
	SOM	*5,64*
	WIL	28,10
	WOR	E3
Siward of Maldon	SFK	34,2
Slettan	YKS	2B8
Swein	SOM	*19,64*
Theodulf	SOM	*26,8*
Thorbern	GLS	76,1
Thored	NFK	31,17
Thori	BKM	43,11
Thorkell	BKM	14,45
	SFK	34,7
Toki	SFK	26,9
Tovi	GLS	76,1
	SFK	29,12
Uhtred	SOM	*25,40*
Ulf	BKM	14,45
	NFK	4,52. 9,94
	SFK	19,2. 44,1
Ulfketel	SHR	4,16,2
Waldin	SOM	*45,7*
Wiglaf	BKM	4,30
Wulfa	SOM	*19,68*
Wulfgar the priest	CHS	12,1
Wulfgeat	BKM	25,3
	SHR	4,16,2
Wulfheah	GLS	32,7
Wulfmer	NTT	9,69
	SFK	8,44;48;55
Wulfnoth	DOR	*55,34*
Wulfric	BKM	5,17;21. 7,2

	SOM	*5,61*
	SFK	8,36;55
Wulfrith	GLS	76,1
Wulfsi	SOM	*5,59*
Wulfstan	BKM	7,1
	DEV	*25,27*
Wulfward	BKM	57,7
	SOM	*9,3*
Wulfward White	WIL	3,1
Wulfwy	DEV	*24,14*
	SOM	*5,9*
thane: *see also*	BRK	B9
	GLS	1,39
	SOM	*31. 32. 49*
thane of Archbishop Stigand: *see* Alnoth	HRT	38,2
thane of (Archbishop) Stigand: *see*		
Algar	NFK	6,4
Ketel	NFK	32,2
Offa	NFK	9,168
Osmund	NFK	6,7
thane of Earl Algar: *see*		
Aethelward	WOR	15,2
Edmer	SFK	8,33
Godric	WOR	15,4
Ludric	HEF	10,58
thane of Earl Edwin: *see*		
Alfwold	WOR	1,1c
Alwin	WOR	1,1c
Brictred	WOR	1,1c
Erngeat	WOR	1,1c
Fran	WOR	1,1c
Sigmund	WOR	19,6
Wulfwin	WOR	1,1d
thane of Earl Harold: *see*		
Aki	HRT	20,13. 37,22
Alfward	HRT	17,3
Alwin	HRT	24,3
Arkell	HEF	10,28
Edmer	HRT	15,1
Edric Lang	GLS	1,62
Ernwy	HEF	22,1
Gauti	HRT	17,13
Saeric	HEF	10,51
Thorbert	GLS	1,60
Wulfwin	HRT	34,24
thane of (Earl) Harold: *see*		
Aelfric	NFK	51,5
Alfhere	NFK	26,5
Alstan	NFK	9,104
Orthi	SFK	20,1
Scalpi	SFK	36,1
thane of Earl Leofwin: *see* Wiglaf	BKM	4,37
thane of Earl Oda: *see*		
Alfward	HEF	23,6
Merwin	HEF	10,39
thane of Queen Edith: *see*		
Brictric	WOR	19,5
Godwin son of Alsi	SFK	6,26
thane of Robert (Gernon): *see* Ordgar	ESS	32,7

thane, royal: *see*

Aelfric	BDF	24,15
	BKM	43,5;10
	CAM	13,11
	SFK	3,88
Aelfric Small	BDF	24,16
Aellic	BKM	5,18
Aelmer	BDF	53,6
	BKM	29,3
	CAM	33,1
	ESS	12,1. 34,6
Aelmer of Bennington	HRT	34,16;18
Aki	BDF	23,15;38
	CAM	17,4
	HRT	22,1
Aldred	HRT	4,3;5. 31,5-7
Alfsi	CAM	15,1
Al(f)si	CAM	15,1
	NFK	1,175
Alfward	GLS	6,5
Al(f)ward	GLS	6,5
Al(f)wold	BDF	15,2;4-6. 53,1
Algar	SFK	7,71
Alli	BDF	53,11. 57,6
Alnoth	BKM	4,38
Alnoth the Kentishman	BKM	4,36
Alric	BDF	16,1
	BKM	14,9;31-32;34
	ESS	24,2
	STS	12,10
Alric son of Goding	BKM	14,7
Alstan	BDF	18,2
	HRT	28,4
Alstan of Boscombe	BDF	18,1
	HRT	28,8
Alwin	BDF	41,2
	BKM	16,1;3-7
	ESS	24,1
	HRT	9,9. 15,3
Alwin Horne	HRT	42,1-2;5
	MDX	4,11
Ansketill	LIN	CK,11
Askell	BDF	23,1;3;5-6;11-12;22;33
	HRT	31,1
Avelin	BKM	4,2;4;23
Azor son of Thored	BKM	1,7
Azor son of Toti	BKM	47,1
Bisi	BKM	23,32. 26,8
Brictmer	ESS	20,1
	WOR	20,6
Brictric	BDF	19,1
	BKM	19,4. 23,29. 35,1
	GLS	39,6
Brictwin	BKM	12,24
Burghard	BKM	13,3
Burgred	BDF	3,16
Cynwy Chelle	GLS	1,58
Dena	GLS	42,1
Edmer Ator	BKM	12,3
	MDX	8,6

Edmund	BKM	20,1
Edric Snipe	CAM	*21,5*. 31,2
Edward	BKM	14,36. 15,1
Edwin	BKM	5,3
	MDX	21,1
	NFK	12,16
Edwin son of Burgred	BKM	5,9
Elaf	HRT	34,16
Fathir	NFK	20,2
Fridebern	SFK	32,6
Godric	BDF	4,1;3
	ESS	24,16;25
	GLS	39,16
	WOR	9,1e. 23,9
Godwin	BDF	29,1
	ESS	24,10. 25,5
	HRT	34,21
	SFK	28,1
Godwin Frambold	BDF	46,2. 47,2
Godwin of Soulbury	HRT	20,7
Guthmund	ESS	27,2
Haldane of Tewin	HRT	36,19
Haming	BKM	23,3-4
Horwulf	CAM	15,3
Ingvar	CAM	34,1
Kenward	GLS	39,7
Ketel	SFK	34,6
Leith	BKM	4,32
Leofcild	ESS	24,15
Leofmer	BDF	25,12
Leofnoth	BDF	32,1;3;5-6;8. 33,1-2
	WOR	23,8
Leofric son of Bose	NFK	20,23
Leofric son of Osmund	BDF	22,1
Leofwin	BDF	32,10;12-13;15
	BKM	14,42
	HRT	29,1. 33,2. 40,1
	SFK	8,32. 41,15
Leofwin of Bacton	SFK	41,10
Oswulf	BDF	26,2
	BKM	18,3
Oswulf son of Fran	BDF	26,1
	BKM	18,2
	HRT	21,1
Saxi	BKM	35,2
	CAM	24,1
Sired	BKM	14,2
Sired son of Aelfeva	BKM	14,3
Siward	ESS	34,9
	HEF	1,41
Skuli	SFK	4,10
Starker	BDF	1,1b
Swein	BKM	50,1
Thorbern	WOR	26,8
Thorgar	CAM	26,42
Thorgils	BDF	23,19
Thorgot	BKM	28,1
Thori	BKM	43,7
Thorkell	BDF	23,18
Thuri	SFK	25,61;63

Thurstan	MDX	19,1
Toki	BKM	19,1
	CAM	18,1;8
Tovi	BKM	43,2. 48,1
Tuini	WOR	24,1
Tuneman	SFK	16,40
Ulf	BDF	27,1
	BKM	17,17;19;27. 22,1. E1
	CAM	20,1. 23,1;5-6
	ESS	20,12
	MDX	7,6
Wicga	BKM	14,17
Wig	BDF	35,1. 36,1
Wulfgar	GLS	1,61
Wulfgeat	BDF	28,1
Wulfmer	BDF	55,6
	WOR	15,3
Wulfmer of Eaton	BDF	21,1;6;9. 45,1. 55,13
	CAM	42,1
Wulfric	SFK	8,46. 39,16. 46,1
Wulfsi	WOR	26,5
Wulfstan	BKM	26,4
Wulfward	BKM	42,1
Wulfward White	MDX	8,5. 10,1-2
Wulfwin	CAM	29,1-3;5;7-10
	SFK	35,1
Young Al(f)ward	BKM	14,21
Young Alnoth	BKM	4,29
Young Edward	BKM	14,22-23
Young Leofwin	BDF	24,18. 25,14. 48,1
Young Wulfward	BKM	5,5
thane, royal: *see also*	BRK	65
	BKM	57L
	DBY	17
	DEV	52
	DOR	56
	ESS	25,1
	GLS	78
	HAM	69
	HUN	29
	LIN	68
	NTH	60
	NTT	30
	SOM	47
	STS	17
	SRY	36
	WAR	44L
	WIL	67
	YKS	29
Thief: *see*		
Aelfeva	DEV	24,22
Edlufu (fem.)	DEV	25,1
Thief: *see also* Alware Pet		
Thorbert: *see* Goding	CAM	26,38
Thunder: *see* Walter	DOR	*55,16;42;44*
Tilley: *see* Alstan	DEV	*46,1-2*
Tilly: *see* Robert	DOR	*47,4;10*
Tilly: *see also* of Tilly		
Tinel: *see* Thurstan	KEN	5,196

	NTH	EH5
	WOR	14,2
Brictsi	KEN	D25. 5,8;21;26
	SRY	19,32
Edric	SOM	*5,39*
Edward	BKM	12,7-8. 14,22-23;38;45
	LIN	S8. 2,34. 56,1
Edwy	HEF	2,58. 10,10-11;21;24;47-49;54-55;70; 73
Godwin	BKM	12,12
	CAM	14,1;*6*;80. 18,3. 35,2
Leofric	LIN	63,1. CK,61
Leofwin	BDF	12,1. 24,18. 25,14. 48,1. E2
	DBY	6,29. 16,1
	ESS	38,4. 42,4
	HRT	13,1
	SHR	4,1,23
	SFK	16,*4*;30
Richard	WOR	25,1
Swein	DBY	8,1;3-6
	NTT	11,10
Ulfr	LIN	51,7
Wulfmer	SSX	10,54
Wulfnoth	KEN	*2,31*
Wulfric	NTT	S5
Wulfsi	NTT	10,3;16;35
Wulfward	BKM	5,5. 17,31
Wulfwin	CHS	9,4
	HUN	D17
Wulfwin of Weston	HUN	D10 (cf 25,1)
Wulfnoth	KEN	*2,31*
Wulfwy	HEF	29,1

CONCORDANCE OF SYSTEMS OF REFERENCE TO THE TWO VOLUMES OF DOMESDAY BOOK

This concordance serves two main purposes. Firstly, to enable readers of the Phillimore Edition of Domesday Book, who are consulting the extensive literature on Domesday, to narrow down the folio references usually quoted to the corresponding Phillimore reference quoted in this Index. It will also enable those readers to follow up any related entries which the Index reveals.

Secondly, it will enable those readers who are using this Index as a guide to their researches in the folios of the Farley or Facsimile Editions, or who are using the Victoria County History translations, to trace references in the Index and to find other folios in which related references may be found.

I. The various systems

The manuscript of the larger volume (here referred to as DB) is divided into numbered chapters, and the chapters into sections, usually marked by large initials and red ink. Farley did not number the sections and later historians, using his edition, have referred to the text of DB by folio numbers, which cannot be closer than an entire page or column. Moreover, several different ways of referring to the same column have been devised. In 1816 Ellis used three separate systems in his indices: (i) on pages i–cvii, 435-518, 537-570; (ii) on pages 1–144; (iii) on pages 145–433 and 519–535. Other systems have since come into use, notably that used by Vinogradoff, here followed. The present edition numbers the sections, the normal practicable form of close reference; but since all discussion of DB for two hundred years has been obliged to refer to folio or column, a comparative table will help to locate references given. The five columns below give Vinogradoff's notation, Ellis's three systems, and that used by Weldon Finn and others. Maitland, Stenton, Darby and others have usually followed Ellis (i).

Vinogradoff	Ellis (i)	Ellis (ii)	Ellis (iii)	Finn
152a	152	152a	152	152ai
152b	152	152a	152.2	152a2
152c	152b	152b	152b	152bi
152d	152b	152b	152b2	152b2

The manuscript of Little Domesday Book (here referred to as LDB) has one column per page but is again divided into numbered chapters and the chapters into sections, usually distinguished by paragraph-marks. Modern users of LDB have referred to its text by folio number, e.g. 152(a) 15 Section III, p. 00.

II. Key to the relation between Vinogradoff's notation of the folios and columns of the MS text of DB and the numbered chapters and sections of the Phillimore edition

KENT (KEN)

1a	D1	- D10
b	D11	- D24
c	D25	- M10
d	M11	- M24
2a	C1	- R1
b	P1	- Landholders
c	1,1	- 1,3
d	1,3	- 1,4
3a	2,1	- 2,7
b	2,7	- 2,11
c	2,12	- 2,16
d	2,16	- 2,22
4a	2,22	- 2,27
b	2,28	- 2,35
c	2,36	- 2,43
d	3,1	- 3,7
5a	3,7	- 3,15
b	3,16	- 3,23
c	4,1	- 4,9
d	4,10	- 4,16
6a	5,1	- 5,8
b	5,9	- 5,18
c	5,18	- 5,25
d	5,25	- 5,34
7a	5,34	- 5,43
b	5,43	- 5,51
c	5,52	- 5,59
d	5,59	- 5,70
8a	5,70	- 5,78
b	5,79	- 5,88
c	5,88	- 5,95
d	5,95	- 5,104
9a	5,104	- 5,115
b	5,115	- 5,124
c	5,124	- 5,128
d	5,129	- 5,138
10a	5,139	- 5,146
b	5,147	- 5,156
c	5,157	- 5,166
d	5,167	- 5,178
11a	5,178	- 5,192
b	5,192	- 5,203
c	5,204	- 5,217
d	5,218	- 6,1
12a	7,1	- 7,8
b	7,8	- 7,17

c	7,18	- 7,23
d	7,23	- 8,1
13a	9,1	- 9,12
b	9,12	- 9,23
c	9,24	- 9,35
d	9,36	- 9,48
14a	9,48	- 10,2
b	11,1	- 12,4
c	13,1	
d	blank	
15a-d	blank	

SUSSEX (SSX)

16a	Landholders	
b	1,1	- 2,1e
c	2,1f	- 2,8
d	2,8	- 3,4
17a	3,4	- 4,1
b	5,1	- 6,1
c	6,1	- 7,2
d	8,1	- 8a,1
18a	9,1	- 9,6
b	9,7	- 9,14
c	9,14	- 9,19
d	9,20	- 9,35
19a	9,35	- 9,55
b	9,56	- 9,74
c	9,75	- 9,91
d	9,91	- 9,109
20a	9,109	- 9,123
b	9,123	- 9,131
c	10,1	- 10,4
d	10,4	- 10,18
21a	10,19	- 10,28
b	10,29	- 10,38
c	10,39	- 10,51
d	10,52	- 10,65
22a	10,65	- 10,80
b	10,80	- 10,93
c	10,93	- 10,105
d	10,106	- 10,118
23a	11,1	- 11,5
b	11,6	- 11,12
c	11,13	- 11,21
d	11,21	- 11,30
24a	11,30	- 11,38
b	11,38	- 11,49

c	11,49	- 11,60
d	11,61	- 11,71
25a	11,71	- 11,81
b	11,82	- 11,92
c	11,93	- 11,105
d	11,106	- 11, 116
26a	12,1	- 12,4
b	12,4	- 12,9
c	12,9	- 12,18
d	12,18	- 12,29
27a	12,29	- 12,37
b	12,37	- 12,44
c	12,44	- 12,53
d	12,54	- 12,56
28a	13,1	- 13,9
b	13,9	- 13,17
c	13,18	- 13,28
d	13,28	- 13,38
29a	13,38	- 13,46
b	13,46	- 13,57
c	14,1	- 14,2
d	blank	

SURREY (SRY)

30a	Landholders	- 1,2
b	1,2	- 1,7
c	1,8	- 1,13
d	1,13	- 2,3
31a	2,3	- 4,1
b	4,1	- 5,3
c	5,3	- 5,11
d	5,11	- 5,22
32a	5,22	- 5,30
b	6,1	- 7,1
c	7,1	- 8,11
d	8,12	- 8,22
33a,b	8,23	- 8,27
c,d	blank	
34a	8,28	- 14,1. 8,22
b	14,1	- 18,1
c	18,2	- 19,4
d	19,4	- 19,15
35a	19,15	- 19,24
b	19,24	- 19,34
c	19,35	- 19,43
d	19,44	- 21,3
36a	21,3	- 22,4. 23,1
b	24,1	- 27,3. 22,5
c	28,1	- 32,2
d	33,1	- 36,10

HAMPSHIRE (HAM)

37a-c	blank	
d	Landholders	
38a	1,1	- 1,8
b	1,8	- 1,16
c	1,17	- 1,21
d	1,22	- 1,28
39a	1,28	- 1,37
b	1,37	- 1,45
c	1,45	- 1W7
d	1,W7	- 1,W20
40a	1,W20	- 2,5
b	2,5	- 2,10
c	2,11	- 2,17
d	2,17	- 2,25
41a	3,1	- 3,5
b	3,5	- 3,8
c	3,8	- 3,14
d	3,14	- 3,24
42ab	4,1. 6,13	- 6,15
cd	6,16	- 6,17
43a	3,24	- 3,27. 5,1-6,5
b	6,5	- 6,12. 7,1
c	8,1	- 13,1
d	13,1	- 15,2
44a	15,2	- 16,7
b	17,1	- 18,3
c	19,1	- 21,5
d	21,6	- 23,3
45a	23,4	- 23,15
b	23,15	- 23,23
c	23,23	- 23,35
d	23,35	- 23,46
46a	23,46	- 23,55
b	23,56	- 23,67
c	23,68	- 28,2
d	28,3	- 29,6
47a	29,6	- 29,16
b	30,1	- 34,1
c	35,1	- 35,9
d	36,1	- 39,5
48a	40,1	- 43,6
b	44,1	- 45,5
c	45,6	- 50,2
d	50,2	- 55,2
49a	55,2	- 60,2
b	61,1	- 67,1
c	68,1	- 68,11
d	69,1	- 69,11
50a	69,12	- 69,22
b	69,23	- 69,33

76a,b	1,31	
c,d	blank	
77a	2,6	- 3,9
b	3,9	- 5,2
c	6,1	- 8,6
d	9,1	- 11,5
78a	11,6	- 12,1
b	12,2	- 13,1
c	13,2	- 18,2
d	19,1	- 19,14
79a	20,1	- 25,1
b	26,1	- 26,21
c	26,22	- 26,40
d	26,41	- 26,61
80a	26,61	- 27,6
b	27,6	- 29,1
c	30,1	- 33,4
d	33,4	- 34,13
81a,b	42,1	
c,d	36,4	- 36,11
82a	34,13	- 36,3. 37,1-7
b	37,8	- 40,7
c	40,8	- 41,5. 43,1- 47,4
d	47,5	- 49,6
83a	49,7	- 50,4. 52,1-2
b	52,2	- 54,14. 51,1
c	55,1	- 55,17
d	55,18	- 55,36
84a	55,37	- 56,9
b	56,10	- 56,32
c	56,32	- 56,55
d	56,56	- 57,8
85a	57,9	- 58,3
b-d	blank	

SOMERSET (SOM)

86a	Landholders	
b	1,1	- 1,5
c	1,6	- 1,10
d	1,11	- 1,20
87a	1,20	- 1,28
b	1,28	- 1,35
c	2,1	- 2,10
d	2,11	- 5,5
88a	5,6	- 5,18
b	5,18	- 5,32
c	5,33	- 5,43
d	5,43	- 5,55
89a	5,56	- 5,70
b	6,1	- 6,8

c	6,9	- 6,17
d	6,18	- 7,15
90a	8,1	- 8,10
b	8,11	- 8,20
c	8,20	- 8,26
d	8,27	- 8,36
91a	8,37	- 10,1
b	10,2	- 16,2
c	16,3	- 17,6
d	17,7	- 19,9
92a	19,10	- 19,24. 19.25
b	19,24	- 19,39
c	19,39	- 19,54. 19,70
d	19,54	- 19,69
93a	19,71	- 20,3
b	21,1	- 21,17
c	21,18	- 21,35
d	21,36	- 21,54
94a	21,54	- 21,75
b	21,76	- 21,94
c	21,95	- 22,13
d	22,13	- 22,28
95a	23,1	- 24,15
b	24,16	- 24,29
c	24,29	- 25,7
d	25,7	- 25,20
96a	25,21	- 25,37
b	25,38	- 25,53
c	25,54	- 27,1
d	27,2	- 31,5
97a	32,1	- 35,2
b	35,3	- 35,18
c	35,19	- 36,7
d	36,7	- 37,5
98a	37,6	- 39,3
b	40,1	- 44,3
c	45,1-2	- 46,1-16
d	46,17	- 47,7
99a	47,7	- 47,23
b	47,24	- 47,25. 45,3-18
c,d	blank	

DEVON (DEV)

100a	C	- Landholders
b	1,1	- 1,11
c	1,11	- 1,23
d	1,23	- 1,35
101a	1,35	- 1,47
b	1,48	- 1,62
c	1,62	- 1,72
d	2,1	- 2,13

102a	2,14	- 3,4
b	3,5	- 3,20
c	3,21	- 3,37
d	3,38	- 3,59
103a	3,59	- 3,76
b	3,77	- 3,94
c	3,95	- 5,5
d	5,5	- 6,4
104a	6,4	- 9,1
b	9,2	- 13a,3
c	14,1	- 15,14
d	15,15	- 15,31
105a	15,32	- 15,44
b	15,44	- 15,58
c	15,59	- 15,74
d	15,75	- 16,7
106a	16,8	- 16,22
b	16,23	- 16,38
c	16,39	- 16,56
d	16,56	- 16,73
107a	16,74	- 16,88
b	16,89	- 16,104
c	16,105	- 16,120
d	16,120	- 16,135
108a	16,136	- 16,149
b	16,150	- 16,166
c	16,167	- 17,5
d	17,5	- 17,17
109a	17,18	- 17,34
b	17,35	- 17,53
c	17,53	- 17,70
d	17,71	- 17,89
110a	17,89	- 17,105
b	17,105	- 19,12
c	19,13	- 19,28
d	19,29	- 19,44
111a	19,44	- 20,14
b	20,14	- 21,11
c	21,12	- 23,2
d	23,2	- 23,15
112a	23,16	- 24,2
b	24,3	- 24,18
c	24,19	- 25,3
d	25,3	- 25,20
113a	25,21	- 28,4
b	28,4	- 29,2
c	29,2	- 31,4
d	32,1	- 34,1
114a	34,2	- 34,17
b	34,18	- 34,32
c	34,33	- 34,49
d	34,49	- 35,5

115a	35,5	- 35,19
b	35,20	- 36,5
c	36,6	- 36,21
d	36,22	- 39,3
116a	39,4	- 39,17
b	39,18	- 41,2
c	42,1	- 42,14
d	42,15	- 43,3
117a	43,3	- 47,5
b	47,5	- 48,8
c	48,8	- 51,2
d	51,2	- 51,16
118a	52,1	- 52,19
b	52,20	- 52,36
c	52,37	- 52,53
d	blank	
119a-d	blank	

CORNWALL (CON)

120a	Landholders	- 1,3
b	1,4	- 1,14
c	1,14	- 2,6
d	2,7	- 2,15. 4,1-6
121a	4,7	- 4,22
b	4,22	- 4,29. 3,1-8
c	3,4	- 3,7. 5,1,1-7
d	5,1,8,	- 5,1,22
122a	5,2,1	- 5,2,18
b	5,2,19	- 5,3,4
c	5,3,5	- 5,3,21
d	5,3,21	- 5,4,10
123a	5,4,11	- 5,4,18. 5,5,1-8
b	5,5,8	- 5,6,2. 5,4,19-20
c	5,6,2	- 5,6,6. 5,6,8- 5,7,8
d	5,7,9	- 5,8,10. 5,6,7
124a	5,9,1	- 5,12,3
b	5,13,1	- 5,14,4
c	5,14,5	- 5,21,1
d	5,21,1	- 5,24,12
125a	5,24,13	- 5,25,5
b	5,25,5	- 7,1
c,d	blank	

MIDDLESEX (MDX)

126a-c	blank	
d	Landholders	
127a	1,1	- 2,2
b	2,3	- 3,4
c	3,4	- 3,12
d	3,13	- 3,19

128a	3,20	- 3,29	141a	36,2	- 36,11
b	3,29	- 4,5	b	36,11	- 36,19
c	4,5	- 4,10	c	39,19	- 37,9
d	4,10	- 6,1	d	37,10	- 37,19
129a	7,1	- 7,7	142a	37,19	- 41,1
b	7,8	- 8.5	b	41,1	- 42,11
c	8,6	- 9,6	c	42,11	- 42,15
d	9,6	- 10,2	d	42a,1	- 44,1
130a	10,2	- 12,1			
b	12,1	- 15,2			
c	15,2	- 20,1			
d	20,1	- 25,3			

131a-d blank

HERTFORDSHIRE (HRT)

BUCKINGHAMSHIRE (BKM)

132a	B1	- B11	143a	B1	- B13
b	Landholders	- 1,2	b	Landholders	- 1,1
c	1,3	- 1,7	c	1,2	- 1,7
d	1,7	- 1,11	d	2,1	- 3a,1
133a	1,11	- 1,18	144a	3a,2	- 4,5
b	1,18	- 3,1	b	4,5	- 4,15
c	4,1	- 4,8	c	4,16	- 4,26
d	4,8	- 4,17	d	4,27	- 4,35
134a	4,17	- 4,25	145a	4,36	- 4,43
b	5,1	- 5,10	b	5,1	- 5,10
c	5,10	- 5,18	c	5,10	- 5,19
d	5,18	- 6,1	d	5,20	- 8,2
135a	7,1	- 8,3	146a	8,3	- 12,5
b	9,1	- 9,10	b	12,6	- 12,18
c	9,10	- 10,6	c	12,19	- 12,31
d	10,6	- 10,13	d	12,31	- 13,2
136a	10,14	- 10,20	147a	13,3	- 14,9
b	11,1	- 13,5	b	14,9	- 14,20
c	14,1	- 15,5	c	14,20	- 14,30
d	15,5	- 16,1	d	14,30	- 14,39
137a	16,1	- 16,11	148a	14,40	- 14,49
b	16,12	- 17,8	b	15,1	- 16,10
c	17,8	- 18,1	c	17,1	- 17,10
d	19,1	- 20,7	d	17,11	- 17,22
138a	20,7	- 22,1	149a	17,22	- 17,31
b	22,1	- 24,1	b	18,1	- 19,3
c	24,2	- 26,1	c	19,4	- 21,4
d	26,1	- 28,7	d	21,4	- 23,3
139a	28,8	- 31,6	150a	23,3	- 23,14
b	31,6	- 33,1	b	23,14	- 23,28
c	33,1	- 33,8	c	23,28	- 25,2
d	33,9	- 33,17	d	25,3	- 26,11
140a	33,17	- 34,5	151a	26,11	- 29,3
b	34,6	- 34,13	b	29,4	- 35,3
c	34,13	- 34,21	c	36,1	- 40,1
d	34,22	- 36,1	d	40,1	- 43,2
			152a	43,2	- 43,11
			b	43,11	- 47,1
			c	47,1	- 52,1
			d	52,2	- 53,10

178a	28,1	- X3
b-d	blank	

HEREFORDSHIRE (HEF)

179a	C1	- C15
b	A1	- Landholders
c	1,1	- 1,4
d	1,5	- 1,8
180a	1,8	- 1,10c
b	1,11	- 1,32
c	1,33	- 1,41
d	1.42	- 1,48
181a	1,49	- 1,61
b	1,61	- 1,75
c	2,1	- 2,11
d	2,12	- 2,21
182a	2,21	- 2,31
b	2,31	- 2,42
c	2,43	- 2,56
d	2,57	- 6,11
183a	7,1	- 7,9
b	8,1	- 8,8
c	8,9	- 9,10
d	9,10	- 9,19
184a	10,1	- 10,15
b	10,16	- 10,30
c	10,31	- 10,44
d	10,45	- 10,57
185a	10,57	- 10,70
a	10,71	- 13,2
c	14,1	- 15,3
d	15,4	- 17,2
186a	18,1	- 19,8
b	19,8	- 21,6
c	21,7	- 23,6
d	24,1	- 25,2
187a	25,3	- 29,1
b	29,1	- 29,20
c	30,1	- 36,3
d	blank	
188a-d	blank	

CAMBRIDGESHIRE (CAM)

189a	B1	- B14
b	Landholders	- 1,1
c	1,1	- 1,6
d	1,6	- 1,13
190a	1,14	- 1,23
b	2,1	- 3,3
c	3,3	- 5,2
d	5,3	- 5,11

191a	5,11	- 5,22
b	5,22	- 5,32
c	5,33	- 5,42
d	5,43	- 5,50
192a	5,50	- 5,58
b	5,58	- 6,3
c	7,1	- 7,8
d	7,8	- 9,2
193a	9,3	- 11,6
b	12,1	- 13,5
c	13,6	- 13,12
d	14,1	- 14,9
194a	14,9	- 14,19
b	14,19	- 14,27
c	14,28	- 14,38
d	14,39	- 14,48
195a	14,49	- 14,57
b	14,57	- 14,64
c	14,64	- 14,72
d	14,72	- 14,82
196a	15,1	- 17,1
b	17,2	- 18,3
c	18,3	- 19,3
d	19,4	- 21,5
197a	21,5	- 22,5
b	22,6	- 23,2
c	23,2	- 25,5
d	25,5	- 26,5
198a	26,6	- 26,17
b	26,17	- 26,24
c	26,24	- 26,33
d	26,34	- 26,42
199a	26,42	- 26,49
b	26,49	- 28,2
c	28,2	- 29,7
d	29,8	- 31,1
200a	31,1	- 31,7
b	32,1	- 32,8
c	32,8	- 32,16
d	32,17	- 32,23
201a	32,23	- 32,31
b	32,31	- 32,36
c	32,37	- 32,44
d	33,1	- 38,1
202a	38,1	- 40,1
b	41,1	- 41,12
c	41,13	- 44,2
d	blank	

HUNTINGDONSHIRE (HUN)

203a	B1	- B14
b	B15	- B21. Landholders

c	1,1	- 1,10
d	2,1	- 2,9
204a	3,1	- 5,2
b	6,1	- 6,7
c	6,7	- 6,16
d	6,16	- 6,26
205a	6,26	- 7,8
b	8,1	- 9,4
c	10,1	- 13,4
d	13,4	- 18,1
206a	19,1	- 19,11
b	19,12	- 19,23
c	19,23	- 19,32
d	20,1	- 20,7
207a	20,7	- 23,1
b	24,1	- 28,1
c	29,1	- 29,6
d	blank	
208a	D1	- D10
b	D11	- D26
c	D26	- D29
d	blank	

BEDFORDSHIRE (BDF)

209a	B	- Landholders
b	1,1	- 1,2b
c	1,3	- 2,3
d	2,3	- 3,3
210a	3,3	- 3,12
b	3,13	- 4,6
c	4,7	- 7,1
d	8,1	- 8,9
211a	9,1	- 14,1
b	15,1	- 16,2
c	16,2	- 16,9
d	17,1	- 18,1
212a	18,2	- 20,1
b	20,1	- 21,8
c	21,9	- 22,2
d	22,2	- 23,10
213a	23,10	- 23,18
b	23,18	- 23,27
c	23,27	- 23,40
d	23,40	- 23,52
214a	23,52	- 24,6
b	24,6	- 24,17
c	24,17	- 24,27
d	24,27	- 25,6
215a	25,6	- 25,14
b	25,14	- 30,1
c	30,1	- 32,5
d	32,6	- 32,16

216a	33,1	- 37,1
b	38,1	- 42,1
c	43,1	- 47,2
d	47,3	- 50,1
217a	51,1	- 53,4
b	53,4	- 53,14
c	53,15	- 53,28
d	53,29	- 54,3
218a	54,4	- 55,11
b	55,12	- 56,9
c	57,1	- 57,7
d	57,7	- 57,21

NORTHAMPTONSHIRE (NTH)

219a	B1	- B38
b	Landholders	- 1,3
c	1,4	- 1,13a
d	1,13a	- 1,20
220a	1,21	- 1,32
b	2,1	- 3,1
c	4,1	- 4,11
d	4,12	- 4,27
221a	4,28	- 5.3
b	5,4	- 6,10c
c	6,10c	- 6a,6
d	6a,7	- 6a,22
222a	6a,23	- 6a,34
b	7,1	- 9,6
c	9,6	- 12,4
d	13,1	- 17,5
223a	18,1	- 18,15
b	18,15	- 18,34
c	18,34	- 18,53
d	18,54	- 18,71
224a	18,72	- 18,89
b	18,90	- 19,1. 20,1- 21,6
ab	19,2	- 19,3
c	23,1	- 23,15. 24,1
d	23,16	- 23,19. 22,1-9
225a	25,1	- 26,9
b	26,9	- 30,9
c	30,10	- 34,1
d	35,1	- 35,7
226a	35,8	- 35,26
b	35,22	- 38,1
c	39,1	- 39,17
d	39,18	- 41,5
227a	41,6	- 43,5
b	43,5	- 45,5
c	45,5	- 47,2
d	48,1	- 48,17

228a	49,1	- 55,6
b	56,1	- 56,20a
c	56,20a	- 56,31
d	56,32	- 56,46
229a	56,46	- 56,64
b	56,65	- 60,5
c,d	blank	

LEICESTERSHIRE (LEC)

230a	C1	- C18
b	Landholders	- 1,3
c	1,3	- 1,7
d	1,7	- 3,1
231a	3,2	- 4,1
b	5,1	- 8,5
c	9,1	- 10,7
d	10,8	- 12,2
232a	13,1	- 13,15
b	13,16	- 13,29
c	13,30	- 13,46
d	13,47	- 13,63
233a	13,63	- 13,74
b	14,1	- 14,17
c	14,18	- 14,34
d	15,1	- 15,13
234a	15,14	- 16,9
b	17,1	- 17,20
c	17,21	- 18,2
d	18,2	- 19,14
235a	19,15	- 23,2
b	23,2	- 26,1
c	27,1	- 29,3
d	29,4	- 31,1
236a	32,1	- 39,2
b	40,1	- 40,19
c	40,19	- 40,37
d	40,38	- 42,10
237a	43,1	- 43,11
b	44,1	- 44,13
c,d	blank	

WARWICKSHIRE (WAR)

238a	B1	- Landholders
b	1,1	- 1,9
c	2,1	- 3,4
d	4,1	- 6,9
239a	6,10	- 10,1
b	11,1	- 13,1
c	14,1	- 15,6
d	16,1	- 16,14

240a	16,15	- 16,26
b	16,27	- 16,42
c	16,42	- 16,57
d	16,58	- 17,6
241a	17,7	- 17,22
b	17,23	- 17,44
c	17,45	- 17,59
d	17,60	- 17,70
242a	18,1	- 18,14
b	18,14	- 21,1
c	22,1	- 22,17
d	22,17	- 24,2
243a	25,1	- 28,5
b	28,6	- 29,1
c	29,2	- 31,7
d	31,7	- 36,2
244a	37,1	- 39,1
b	39,2	- 43,2
c	44,1	- 44,14. 45,1
d	44,15	- 44,16
245a-d	blank	

STAFFORDSHIRE (STS)

246a	B1	- Landholders
b	1,1	- 1,13
c	1,14	- 1,28
d	1,29	- 1,64
247a	2,1	- 2,16
b	2,16	- 2,22
c	3,1	- 5,2
d	6,1	- 7,18
248a	8,1	- 8,12
b	8,13	- 8,30
c	8,30	- 10,10
d	11,1	- 11,16
249a	11,17	- 11,33
b	11,34	- 11,49
c	11,50	- 11,65
d	11,66	- 12,14
250a	12,15	- 12,28
b	12,29	- 12,31
c	13,1	- 16,1
d	17,1	- 17,21. 16,2-3
251a-d	blank	

SHROPSHIRE (SHR)

252a	C1	- Landholders
b	1,1	- 3a,1
c	3b,1	- 3c,7
d	3c,8	- 3e,2

280a (Nottingham)
  b B1   - B16
  c S1   - S6

NOTTINGHAMSHIRE (NTT)

280a B1   - B20
  b (Derby)
  c S1   - S6
  d Landholders (also for RUT)
281a 1,1   - 1,13
  b 1,14   - 1,31
  c 1,32   - 1,50
  d 1,51   - 1,66
282a,b blank
  c 2,1   - 3,4
  d 4,1   - 4,8
283a 5,1   - 5,6
  b 5,7   - 5,19
  c blank
  d 6,1   - 6,11
284a 6,11   - 6,15
  b 7,1   - 8,2
  c 9,1   - 9,15. 9,21
  d 9,15   - 9,20. 9,22-28
285a 9,29   - 9,40
  b 9,40   - 9,53
  c 9,54   - 9,65
  d 9,66   - 9,76
286a 9,76   - 9,80. 9,82-93
  b 9,94   - 9,106. 9,81
  c 9,107   - 9,118
  d 9,118   - 9,127
287a 9,128   - 9,132
  b 10,1   - 10,15
  c 10,15   - 10,28
  d 10,29   - 10,46
288a 10,46   - 10,60
  b 10,61   - 10,66
  c 11,1   - 11,12. 11,13
  d 11,12   - 11,25
289a 11,26   - 11,33
  b 12,1   - 12,19
  c 12,19   - 13,11
  d 13,11   - 14,8
290a 15,1   - 15,10
  b 16,1   - 16,12
  c 17,1   - 17,12
  d 17,13   - 17,18
291a 18,1   - 19,1
  b 20,1   - 20,8
  c 21,1   - 23,2
  d 24,1   - 26,1

292a 27,1   - 29,2
  b blank
  c 30,1   - 30,13
  d 30,14   - 30,31
293a 30,31   - 30,46
  b 30,46   - 30,56

RUTLAND (RUT)

280d Landholders (with NTT)
293c R1   - 12
  d R12   - 20
294a R21
  b-d blank
295a-296d blank

YORKSHIRE (YKS)

297a-d blank
298a C1a   - C10
  b C11   - C28
  c C28   - C37
  d C38   - Landholders
299a 1Y1   - 1Y3
  b 1Y3   - 1Y7
  c 1Y8   - 1Y13
  d 1Y14   - 1Y18
300a 1Y18   - 1N20
  b 1N21   - 1N61
  c 1N62   - 1N94
  d 1N95   - 1N132
301a 1N133   - 1E44
  b 1E45   - 1W28
  c 1W29   - 1W72
  d 1W73   - 1L6
302a 1L7   - 1L8
  b 2A1   - 2A4
  c 2B1   - 2B5
  d 2B6   - 2B14
303a 2B15   - 2N7
  b 2N8   - 2N25
  c 2N26   - 2W5
  d 2W6   - 2W13
304a 2E1   - 2E14
  b 2E15   - 2E41
  c 3Y1   - 3Y7
  d 3Y7   - 3Y18
305a 4N1   - 4E2
  b 5N1   - 5N12
  c 5N13   - 5N27
  d 5N28   - 5N48

c	31E1	- 31W3
d	31W4	- 31N8
333a	31N8	- 31N10
b-d	blank	

334a-335d blank

(336a-372d Lincolnshire)

373a	CN1	- CE15
b	CE15	- CE27
c	CE28	- CE33. CW1-4
d	CW5	- CW24
374a	CW25	- CW39
b	CE34	- CE52. CW40-42
c,d	blank	

(375a-37d Lincolnshire)

379a	SN,Y	- SW,Sk. SW,BA1-3
b	SW,BA4	- SW,BA13. SW,Sf1-34
c	SW,Sf35	- Sf37. SW,O. SW,St. SW, Ag1-8
d	SW,Ag9	- SW,Ag16. SW,M. SW, An. SW,Bu1-5
380a	SW,Bu6	- SW,Bu49
b	SW,H1	- SW,Cr5
c	SN,L1	- SN,D4
d	SN,D5	- SN,D21. SN,Ma. SN, B1-6
381a	SN,B7	- SN,B27. SN,Bi. SN,A
b	SN,CtA1	- SN,CtA45
c	SE,He1	- SE,He11. SE,Wel. SE, C. SE,How. SE,Wei1-14
d	SE,Wei5	- SE,Wei7. SE,Sn. SE, Dr. SE,Wa. SE,P. SE, Hu1-6
382a	SE,Hu7	- SE,Hu8. SE,Tu. SE, Bt. SE,Sc. SE,Ac
b	SE,Th1	- SE,Th14. SE,So. SE, Mid. SE,No. SE,Hol-26
c,d	blank	

LINCOLNSHIRE (LIN)

336a	C1	- C11
b	C12	- C21
c	C21	- C33
d	S1	- S16
337a	T1	- T5
b	Landholders	
c	1,1	- 1,7
d	1,8	- 1,15
338a	1,16	- 1,31
b	1,32	- 1,39
c	1,40	- 1,66
d	1,67	- 1,87

339a	1,88	- 1,105
b	1,105	- 1,106
c	2,1	- 2,11
d	2,12	- 2,22
340a	2,23	- 2,35
b	2,35	- 2,42
c	3,1	- 3,11
d	3,12	- 3,26
341a	3,27	- 3,28. 3,30-36
b	3,37	- 3,48. 3,29
c	3,48	- 3,56
d	blank	
342a	4,1	- 4,5. 4,7-11
b	4,11	- 4,25. 4,6
c	4,26	- 4,39
d	4,40	- 4,51
343a	4,51	- 4,63
b	4,63	- 4,75
c	4,75	- 4,81
d	5,1	- 6,1
344a	7,1	- 7,13
b	7,14	- 7,26
c	7,27	- 7,39
d	7,39	- 7,52
345a	7,52	- 7,59
b	blank	
c	8,1	- 8,8
d	8,8	- 8,18
346a	8,18	- 8,32
b	8,33	- 9,2
c	10,1	- 10,4
d	11,1	- 11,9
347a	12,1	- 12,11
b	12,11	- 12,24
c	12,24	- 12,38
d	12,38	- 12,48
348a	12,49	- 12,58
b	12,59	- 12,71
c	12,71	- 12,84
d	12,85	- 12,97
349a	13,1	- 13,9
b	13,9	- 13,21
c	13,22	- 13,33
d	13,34	- 13,45
350a	14,1	- 14,13
b	14,13	- 14,25
c	14,26	- 14,38
d	14,39	- 14,52
351a	14,52	- 14,64
b	14,65	- 14,79
c	14,79	- 14,92
d	14,93	- 15,2

III. Key to the relation between the folio notation of the MS. Text of LDB and the Numbered Chapters and Sections of the Present Edition. See section I, above.

ESSEX (ESS)

1a	Landholders	
b	1,1	- 1,2
2a	1,2	- 1,3
b	1,3	- 1,4
3a	1,4	- 1,8
b	1,9	- 1,11
4a	1,12	- 1,14
b	1,15	- 1,19
5a	1,19	- 1,24
b	1,24	- 1,25
6a	1,25	- 1,27
b	1,27	
7a	1,28	- 1,29
b	1,29	- 1,31
8a	2,1	- 2,6
b	2,6	- 2,9
9a	Landholders	
b	3,1	- 3,5
10a	3,6	- 3,9
b	3,9	- 3,13
11a	3,13	- 4,2
b	4,3	- 4,9
12a	4,9	- 4,15
b	4,16	- 5,3
13a	5,3	- 5,8
b 5,8	- 5,12	
14a	5,12	- 6,5
b	6,6	- 6,9
15a	6,9	- 6,15
b	7,1	- 8,1
16a	8,1	- 8,8
b	8,8	- 8,11
17a	Landholders	
b	9,1	- 9,7
18a	9,7	- 9,12
b	9,13	- 10,1
19a	10,2	- 10,5
b	10,5	- 11,3
20a	11,3	- 11,8
b	12,1	- 14,2
21a	14,2	- 14,7
b	14,7	- 15,2
22a	15,2	- 17,2
b	18,1	- 18,5
23a	18,5	- 18,11
b	18,11	- 18,19
24a	18,20	- 18,25
b	18,25	- 18,34
25a	18,34	- 18,38

b	18,39	- 18,45
26a	18,45	- 20,2
b	20,2	- 20,7
27a	20,7	- 20,13
b	20,13	- 20,19
28a	20,19	- 20,23
b	20,24	- 20,27
29a	20,28	- 20,34
b	20,34	- 20,37
30a	20,37	- 20,42
b	20,43	- 20,46
31a	20,46	- 20,52
b	20,52	- 20,56
32a	20,56	- 20,62
b	20,63	- 20,67
33a	20,67	- 20,71
b	20,71	- 20,75
34a	20,75	- 20,79
b	20,79	- 20,80
35a	21,1	- 21,6
b	21,6	- 21,12
36a	22,1	- 22,5
b	22,6	- 22,9
37a	22,10	- 22,13
b	22,13	- 22,18
38a	22,19	- 22,24
b	23,1	- 23,3
39a	23,3	- 23,8
b	23,8	- 23,16
40a	23,16	- 23,28
b	23,28	- 23,34
41a	23,34	- 23,40
b	23,40	- 23,43
42a	24,1	- 24,5
b	24,5	- 24,10
43a	24,10	- 24,16
b	24,17	- 24,20
44a	24,20	- 24,24
b	24,24	- 24,28
45a	24,28	- 24,33
b	24,33	- 24,42
46a	24,42	- 24,46
b	24,46	- 24,53
47a	24,53	- 24,57
b	24,57	- 24,61
48a	24,61	- 24,66
b	24,66	- 24,67
49a	25,1	- 25,4
b	25,4	- 25,10
50a	25,10	- 25,15
b	25,15	- 25,19

107a	B3p	- B6
b	B6	- B7
108a	blank	
b	blank	

NORFOLK (NFK)

109a	Landholders	
b	1,1	- 1,2
110a	1,2	- 1,6
b	1,6	- 1,11
111a	1,11	- 1,16
b	1,16	- 1,19
112a	1,19	- 1,26
b	1,26	- 1,32
113a	1,32	- 1,41
b	1,41	- 1,48
114a	1,48	- 1,52
b	1,52	- 1,57
115a	1,57	
b	1,57	- 1,59
116a	1,59	- 1,61
b	1,61	
117a	1,61	
b	1,61	- 1,64
118a	1,65	- 1,67
b	1,67	- 1,70
119a	1,70	
b	1,71	
120a	1,71	- 1,76
b	1,76	- 1,78
121a	1,78	- 1,82
b	1,82	- 1,86
122a	1,87	- 1,89
b	1,89	- 1,94
123a	1,94	- 1,99
b	1,99	- 1,106
124a	1,106	- 1,116
b	1,116	- 1,122
125a	1,122	- 1,128
b	1,128	- 1,132
126a	1,132	- 1,136
b	1,136	- 1,139
127a	1,139	- 1,143
b	1,143	- 1,146
128a	1,146	- 1,150
b	1,150	- 1,152
129a	1,152	- 1,159
b	1,159	- 1,169
130a	1,169	- 1,176
b	1,176	- 1,182
131a	1,182	- 1,185
b	1,185	- 1,188
132a	1,189	- 1,192
b	1,192	- 1,194
133a	1,194	- 1,196

b	1,196	- 1,198
134a	1,198	- 1,201
b	1,201	- 1,203
135a	1,203	- 1,206
b	1,206	- 1,209
136a	1,209	- 1,210
b	1,210	- 1,212
137a	1,212	- 1,214
b	1,215	- 1,216
138a	1,216	- 1,218
b	1,218	- 1,221
139a	1,221	- 1,226
b	1,226	- 1,228
140a	1,228	- 1,231
b	1,231	- 1,236
141a	1,237	- 1,239
b	1,239	- 1,241
142a	2,1	- 2,4
b	2,4	
143a	2,5	- 2,8
b	2,8	- 3,1
144a	3,1	- 4,2
b	4,2	- 4,9
145a	4,9	- 4,11
b	4,11	- 4,17
146a	4,17	- 4,22
b	4,22	- 4,27
147a	4,28	- 4,31
b	4,31	- 4,34
148a	4,35	- 4,39
b	4,39	- 4,41
149a	4,41	- 4,45
b	4,45	- 4,50
150a	4,50	- 4,53
b	4,53	- 4,56
151a	4,56	- 5,2
b	5.2	- 5,6
152a	5,6	- 6,3
b	6,3	- 6,6
153a	6,6	- 6,7
b	7,1	- 7,3
154a	7,3	- 7,8
b	7,8	- 7,13
155a	7,13	- 7,16
b	7,16	- 7,18
156a	7,18	- 7,21
b	blank	
157a	8,1	- 8,2
b	8,3	- 8,7
158a	8,7	- 8,8
b	8,8	- 8,11
159a	8,11	- 8,13
b	8,14	- 8,17
160a	8,17	- 8,21
b	8,21	- 8,25
161a	8,25	- 8,29

b	17,18	- 17,24		b	29,1	- 29,5
218a	17,24	- 17,31		246a	29,5	- 29,8
b	17,32	- 17,38		b	29,8	- 29,11
219a	17,38	- 17,43		247a	30,1	- 30,4
b	17,44	- 17,52		b	30,4	- 31,1
220a	17,52	- 17,55		248a	31,2	- 31,5
b	17,56	- 17,62		b	31,5	- 31,6
221a	17,62	- 17,65		249a	31,6	- 31,10
b	18,1	- 19,2		b	31,10	- 31,15
222a	19,3	- 19,9		250a	31,15	- 31,17
b	19,9	- 19,11		b	31,17	- 31,22
223a	19,11	- 19,15		251a	31,22	- 31,28
b	19,16	- 19,21		b	31,28	- 31,33
224a	19,21	- 19,25		252a	31,34	- 31,37
b	19,26	- 19,32		b	31,38	- 31,41
225a	19,32	- 19,36		253a	31,41	- 31,44
b	19,36	- 20,1		b	31,44	- 31,45
226a	20,1	- 20,6		254a	32,1	- 32,3
b	20,6	- 20,8		b	32,3	- 32,7
227a	20,8	- 20,10		255a	32,7	- 33,2
b	20,10	- 20,14		b	33,2	- 33,6
228a	20,14	- 20,19		256a	34,1	- 34,3
b	20,19	- 20,24		b	34,3	- 34,6
229a	20,24	- 20,29		257a	34,6	- 34,9
b	20,29	- 20,34		b	34,9	- 34,15
230a	20,35	- 21,2		258a	34,15	- 34,19
b	21,2	- 21,5		b	34,20	- 35,3
231a	21,5	- 21,8		259a	35,3	- 35,8
b	21,8	- 21,13		b	35,8	- 35,13
232a	21,13	- 21,16		260a	35,13	- 35,18
b	21,17	- 21,21		b	35,18	- 36,5
233a	21,22	- 21,25		261a	36,5	- 36,7
b	21,25	- 21,28		b	37,1	- 37,3
234a	21,28	- 21,32		262a	38,1	- 39,1
b	21,32	- 21,37		b	39,1	- 40,1
235a	22,1	- 22,6		263a	41,1	- 43,2
b	22,6	- 22,13		b	43,2	- 45,1
236a	22,13	- 22,21		264a	46,1	- 47,6
b	22,21	- 22,23		b	47,6	- 48,3
237a	23,1	- 23,4		265a	48,3	- 48,8
b	23,4	- 23,8		b	49,1	- 49,5
238a	23,8	- 23,12		266a	49,5	- 49,9
b	23,12	- 23,16		b	50,1	- 50,5
239a	23,16	- 23,18		267a	50,6	- 50,10
b	24,1	- 24,5		b	50,10	- 51,3
240a	24,5	- 24,7		268a	51,3	- 51,8
b	24,7	- 25,1		b	51,8	- 52,3
241a	25,2	- 25,7		269a	52,3	- 54,1
b	25,7	- 25,12		b	54,1	- 56,2
242a	25,12	- 25,17		270a	56,3	- 57,3
b	25,17	- 25,25		b	58,1	- 59,1
243a	25,25	- 26,1		271a	59,1	- 61,1
b	26,1	- 26,3		b	61,1	- 62,2
244a	26,3	- 26,5		272a	62,2	- 64,4
b	26,5	- 27,2		b	64,5	- 65,7
245a	27,2	- 28,2		273a	65,8	- 65,16

SUFFOLK (SFK)

328a	6,301	- 6,304		356a	13,3	- 13,7
b	6,305	- 6,308		b	14,1	- 14,3
329a	6,308	- 6,311		357a	14,3	- 14,7
b	6,311	- 6,317		b	14,8	- 14,12
330a	6,317	- 6,319		358a	14,12	- 14,16
b	7,1	- 7,3		b	14,16	- 14,20
331a	7,3	- 7,6		359a	14,21	- 14,24
b	7,6	- 7,10		b	14,24	- 14,28
332a	7,10	- 7,15		360a	14,28	- 14,36
b	7,15			b	14,36	- 14,42
333a	7,16	- 7,20		361a	14,42	- 14,47
b	7,20	- 7,26		b	14,48	- 14,50
334a	7,26	- 7,33		362a	14,50	- 14,53
b	7,33	- 7,37		b	14,53	- 14,59
335a	7,37	- 7,42		363a	14,59	- 14,64
b	7,42	- 7,49		b	14,64	- 14,68
336a	7,49	- 7,56		364a	14,69	- 14,72
b	7,56	- 7,58		b	14,72	- 14,75
337a	7,58	- 7,61		365a	14,75	- 14,77
b	7,61	- 7,65		b	14,78	- 14,81
338a	7,65	- 7,68		366a	14,81	- 14,85
b	7,68	- 7,72		b	14,85	- 14,90
339a	7,72	- 7,75		367a	14,90	- 14,95
b	7,76	- 7,79		b	14,96	- 14,101
340a	7,79	- 7,85		368a	14,102	- 14,106
b	7,85	- 7,92		b	14,106	- 14,110
341a	7,92	- 7,98		369a	14,111	- 14,115
b	7,98	- 7,105		b	14,115	- 14,120
342a	7,105	- 7,111		370a	14,120	- 14,128
b	7,111	- 7,119		b	14,129	- 14,138
343a	7,119	- 7,122		371a	14,138	- 14,153
b	7,122	- 7,133		b	14,154	- 14,166
344a	7,133	- 7,138		372a	14,167. Landholders	
b	7,138	- 7,143		b	15,1	- 15,4
345a	7,143	- 7,148		373a	15,5	- 16,3
b	7,149	- 7,151		b	16,4	- 16,10
346a	8,1	- 8,6		374a	16,10	- 16,14
b	8,6	- 8,9		b	16,14	- 16,17
347a	8,9	- 8,14		375a	16,17	- 16,20
b	8,14	- 8,23		b	16,21	- 16,25
348a	8,23	- 8,32		376a	16,25	- 16,27
b	8,32	- 8,35		b	16,28	- 16,31
349a	8,35	- 8,42		377a	16,32	- 16,35
b	8,42	- 8,46		b	16,36	- 16,40
350a	8,46	- 8,49		378a	16,40	- 16,45
b	8,49	- 8,55		b	16,45	- 17,1
351a	8,55	- 8,56		379a	18,1	- 18,5
b	8,56	- 8,59		b	18,6	- 19,10
352a	8,59	- 8,66		380a	19,11	- 19,16
b	8,66	- 8,78		b	19,16	- 19,18
353a	8,78	- 9,1		381a	19,18	- 20,1
b	9,1	- 9,3		b	21,1	- 21,5
354a	9,3	- 11,2		382a	21,5	- 21,11
b	11,2	- 12,1		b	21,11	- 21,16
355a	12,1	- 12,6		383a	21,16	- 21,25
b	12,6	- 13,3		b	21,25	- 21,29